Announcing the Feast

The Entrance Song in the Mass of the Roman Rite

Jason J. McFarland, PhD

Foreword by Paul Turner

A PUEBLO BOOK

Liturgical Press   Collegeville, Minnesota
www.litpress.org

A Pueblo Book published by Liturgical Press

Cover design by David Manahan, OSB. Photo provided by Michael Jensen.

1   2   3   4   5   6   7   8

Library of Congress Cataloging-in-Publication Data

McFarland, Jason J.
   Announcing the feast : the entrance song in the Mass of the Roman rite /
Jason J. McFarland.
       p.   cm.
   "A Pueblo book."
   Includes bibliographical references (p.   ) and index.
   ISBN 978-0-8146-6261-8 — ISBN 978-0-8146-6262-5 (e-book)
   1. Introits (Music)—History and criticism.   I. Title.

ML3088.M34 2012
782.32'35—dc23   2011040895

"Carefully researched, clearly articulated and insightfully argued, *Announcing the Feast* will stand as a major resource for all involved in the study of liturgical music for years to come. A multidisciplinary *tour de force*. The careful reader will come away with presuppositions challenged, new ideas carefully nuanced and presented and a wealth to bring to the question of 'what is next' for the continuing task of implementing the reformed liturgy."

—Msgr. Kevin W. Irwin
Dean of the School of Theology and Religious Studies
The Catholic University of America, Washington, DC

"In these pages, we find a sure and sophisticated knowledge of the past, but also an understanding of the present and a sense of the future to which we are moving. McFarland's knowledge of the chant tradition is here for all to see, but so too is his sense of what is pastorally required at this time. This book is very welcome at this time, showing as it does how scholarship can be at the service of an experience of worship which is both traditional and contemporary, ever ancient and ever new. That was the vision of the Second Vatican Council, and it is the vision from which this book is born."

— ✠ Mark Coleridge
Archbishop of Canberra

"Jason McFarland assists all those who are responsible for the liturgical life of the Church to address the question, 'What shall we sing at the start of Mass?' and to answer it in a way that is faithful to the Council's call for authentic liturgical renewal."

— ✠ Allen Vigneron
Archbishop of Detroit

"This is a very important book for two straightforward reasons: it represents the best tradition of liturgical scholarship in shedding light on the complexity of the origins and development of the entrance song of the Mass; it does so at a time when the implementation of the new English translation of *The Roman Missal* naturally strengthens our desire to revisit the basic elements of the liturgy and to evaluate our experience in the light of tradition. This highly accessible study raises crucial questions for all who have a love and concern for the liturgy in general and liturgical music in particular."

—Msgr. Andrew R. Wadsworth
Executive Director, International Commission on
English in the Liturgy

This is an important book by a promising young scholar on a timely topic. It gives solid historical and theological information on the development of the entrance song or chant, with wise guidance on what this means for the Church's liturgical practice today."

—Fr. Anthony Ruff, OSB
Associate Professor of Theology, St. John's School of Theology·Seminary
Moderator of the popular liturgical blog *Pray Tell*

"*Announcing the Feast* is an important book for both liturgical scholars and pastoral musicians. McFarland's meticulous scholarship offers a history of the entrance song using a method that takes seriously the context of every worship event. This book will inspire those who read it to take another look at how their musical choices 'announce the feast.'"

—Judith M. Kubicki
Associate Professor of Liturgy
Fordham University
President, North American Academy of Liturgy

For my family

Contents

Illustrations

MUSICAL EXAMPLES

Example 1   Twelfth-century manuscript excerpt of the introit *Nos autem gloriari* for the Holy Thursday Evening Mass of the Lord's Supper

Example 2   Sixteenth-century manuscript excerpt of the introit *Nos autem gloriari* for the Holy Thursday Evening Mass of the Lord's Supper

Example 3   The introit *Nos autem gloriari* for the Holy Thursday Evening Mass of the Lord's Supper in the post-conciliar *Graduale Romanum*

Example 4   The introit *Nos autem gloriari* for the Holy Thursday Evening Mass of the Lord's Supper in the *Graduale Simplex, editio typica altera*

Example 5   Vernacular chant adaptation of the text and melody of the *Graduale Simplex* introit *Nos autem gloriari* for the Holy Thursday Evening Mass of the Lord's Supper from *By Flowing Waters* (Paul Ford, 1999)

Example 6   Metrical strophic hymn setting of a vernacular translation of the introit *Nos autem gloriari* for the Holy Thursday Evening Mass of the Lord's Supper from *Hymn Introits for the Liturgical Year* (Christoph Tietze, 2005)

Example 7   Metrical refrain hymn setting of a vernacular translation of the introit *Nos autem gloriari* for the Holy Thursday Evening Mass of the Lord's Supper (WAREHAM / Anthony Corvaia, 2002)

FIGURES

TABLES

Foreword

"I start with the readings." Ask the person who picks the music for Sunday Mass at your place of worship this question: "How do you choose the opening hymn?" And that's how the answer will likely begin.

Most of the people preparing music for Catholic worshiping communities have grown familiar with the Lectionary for Mass. They especially study the day's gospel, as well as the psalm if the cantor will sing it. They pray over the other readings to get a sense of the day's liturgy. They remain in tune with the season of the year or the feast to be celebrated. The Lectionary usually inspires the choice of the music.

The readings may be explained in the homily, according to the General Instruction of the Roman Missal (GIRM) 55 and 65. However, people like to match music with the readings as well. In Italy, the 1983 Missal contained a complete set of new collects for Sundays based on the readings of the day. The idea prompted others to make the ahistorical objection that the presidential prayers of the Missal usually have little in common with the Liturgy of the Word.

Whether it was the newness of the three-year cycle of readings or the richness of its treasures, the Lectionary became the womb out of which the music and prayer of Sunday worship were born.

The GIRM never saw it that way.

For example, the GIRM says, "The pastoral effectiveness of a celebration will be greatly increased if the texts of the readings, the prayers, and the liturgical chants correspond as aptly as possible to the needs, the preparation, and the culture of the participants" (352). When describing the Masses for Various Needs and Occasions, it speaks of "the rather broad possibilities of choice among the readings and orations" (369), and when addressing Funeral Masses, it suggests arranging and choosing "orations, readings, and the Universal Prayer" (385).

In planning a celebration, therefore, the GIRM treats elements such as the readings, the music, and the presidential prayers as equals. It never says, "Start with the readings."

The third edition of *The Roman Missal* is drawing attention to parts of the Mass that have hitherto lain in the shadow of the Lectionary, specifically the orations and antiphons. These elements enjoy a lively history of their own, having been assigned to certain days on the liturgical calendar for historical and theological reasons that do not always abut the choices made for the Lectionary.

Regarding the entrance antiphon, the post–Vatican II *Missale Romanum* has proffered one for each day of the liturgical year, but GIRM 48 has always allowed four choices for the entrance chant: the antiphon from the Missal or the *Graduale Romanum* (in that case with its psalm); the antiphon and psalm from the *Graduale Simplex*; a chant from another collection of psalms and antiphons; or "another liturgical chant that is suited to the sacred action, the day, or the time of year, similarly approved by the Conference of Bishops or the Diocesan Bishop." Most places of worship have ignored option one, the antiphon found in the Missal, and chosen option four—"another liturgical chant." Planners of the liturgy usually start with the readings before selecting from option four, and profitably so, but the GIRM never suggested that criterion.

The entrance antiphons used to give a name to the entire celebration. *Gaudete* is the first word of the entrance antiphon for the Third Sunday of Advent; *Laetare*, the first word for the Fourth Sunday of Lent. The entrance antiphon for a Funeral Mass begins with the word *Requiem*. By contrast, antiphons have often gone unnoticed in the postconciliar church, awaiting rediscovery.

With a revised translation of the antiphons, it is time to review them. We need studies of the history of these antiphons and the decisions that led to their appearance on certain days of the calendar.

If you want to know more about antiphons, let Jason McFarland be your guide. He has written a very readable background to their role in the Roman Rite. As a case study, he analyzes one of the most significant entrance antiphons of the liturgical year, the one that opens the Paschal Triduum: *Nos autem*.

If you have been choosing your opening hymn based on criteria such as repertoire, length of procession, season of the year, feast day—or the readings of the day—you have been overlooking the most obvious place to begin: the entrance antiphon.

Paul Turner

Acknowledgments

TEXTS

Excerpts from *Code of Canon Law: Latin-English Edition* © 1983, The Canon Law Society of America. Used by permission.

Psalm 67 from *A New Metrical Psalter* © 1986, The Church Hymnal Corporation. All rights reserved. Used by permission.

Psalm 67 from *The Revised Grail Psalms* © 2010, Conception Abbey / The Grail, admin. by GIA Publications, Inc., www.giamusic.com. All rights reserved. Used by permission.

English translation of Psalm 116 from *Lectionary for Mass for Use in the Dioceses of the United States of America* © 1998, 1997, 1970, Confraternity of Christian Doctrine, Washington, DC. All rights reserved. Used by permission.

English translation of *Nos autem gloriari* ("Come Let Us Glory") © 2002, Anthony Corvaia. All rights reserved. Used by permission.

Excerpts from the introduction to and English translation of *The Simple Gradual: An English Translation of the Antiphons and Responsories of the* Graduale Simplex *for Use in English-Speaking Countries* © 1968, International Commission on English in the Liturgy Corporation (ICEL); excerpts from the English translation of *The Liturgy of the Hours* © 1974, ICEL; excerpts from the English translation of *Documents on the Liturgy, 1963–1979: Conciliar, Papal, and Curial Texts* © 1982, ICEL; excerpts from "The Translation of the *Missale Romanum*: Questions and Issues Related to the Translation of Antiphons" © 2004,

MANUSCRIPT IMAGES

MUSIC

An Introduction to the Book and Its Method

Throughout the history of Christianity, many different types of music have accompanied the entrance of the presider and ministers during celebrations of the Eucharist. This great variety is the result of a number of factors: the social contexts in which Christianity developed and continues to develop (Palestinian Judaism, Hellenic culture, Roman culture, and today nearly every culture on the globe); the development of diverse musical styles; the liturgical sphere of influence of a particular rite (Rome, Antioch, Jerusalem, and so forth); the arrangement of church buildings and the processional routes therein; the type, availability, and use of musical instruments; and the degree to and manner in which the assembled faithful participated in the liturgy. Insofar as this variety has helped to adapt the liturgy to the needs of worshiping communities and faithfully passed on the Christian tradition, it is among the many praiseworthy developments in Christian worship since the beginning. The goal of this book is to discover within this variety a coherent theology of the entrance song of the Mass of the Roman Rite. In a broad sense, the questions are: how does the entrance song function within the Roman Rite and what is its purpose? More specifically, what is or should be expressed theologically by means of the text and melody of any particular entrance song?

One limitation of this book and the study of liturgy in general is that it is impossible to determine to what degree the theology put forward by a particular introit or other form of the entrance song might or might not have been integrated into the spiritual lives of members of particular Christian communities at any given period in the history of the church.[1] Nevertheless, it is possible to discern an

1. This limitation is inherent in the quest for meaning in a text. It is nearly impossible to access the "deep structure" and "ontological force" of a text in terms

overarching theology of the entrance song in Roman Catholic worship and specifically in present-day Roman Catholic worship in the United States. It is the delineation and interpretation of this theology that is the overarching goal and guiding question of this book.

What, then, is the entrance song? It is the first ritual song of the celebration of the Mass, which for most of the history of the Roman Rite has been the introit.

> **Introit** (from Latin *Introitus*). The first in the series of Gregorian chants that make up the proper of the Mass. It consists of an antiphon, a psalm verse or verses, and the doxology. The psalm verse(s) and doxology are sung to a simple formula. Both this simple formula and the more complex antiphon melody are in one of the ecclesiastical modes.[2] The choir sings the chant, as its name suggests, during the entrance of the celebrant and ministers at the beginning of the Mass.[3]

It is important to recognize, however, that the introit, which came into use in the Roman Rite sometime between the late fifth and late seventh centuries, does not encompass the entirety of the entrance song tradition. There are certain historical precursors to the introit, for example, such as the ancient pagan and Jewish practices of singing at the start of common ritual meals, or short sung acclamations from the assembly during the entrance of the presider at Mass in the fourth century. And, while one can certainly give examples of entrance

---

of systematic study (here "text" has the broadest possible meaning and includes much more than the written word—one might use the term "artifacts"), even if it is possible to access its "residue of meaning" or "surface structure." See Joyce Ann Zimmerman, *Liturgy and Hermeneutics* (Collegeville, MN: Liturgical Press, 1999), 17–18.

2. See *The New Grove Dictionary of Music and Musicians* (hereafter *New Grove*), s.v. "Introit (i)" (by Ruth Steiner). These modes are not exactly the same as the ancient Greek modes, and the creation of early ecclesiastical chant took place before any systematic practice of composing within the eight church modes had developed. The earliest ecclesiastical chants, therefore, often do not reflect perfectly the characteristics of any one mode. Only later chants fit the modes precisely. For more on the history and function of the ecclesiastical modes, see *Grove Music Online* (hereafter *Grove Online*), s.v. "Mode" (by Harold S. Powers et al.), http://www.oxfordmusiconline.com/subscriber/article/grove/music/43718 (accessed July 1, 2008).

3. See *The New Grove Dictionary of Music and Musicians*, 2nd ed. (hereafter *New Grove*, 2nd ed.), s.v. "Introit (i)" (by James W. McKinnon).

songs during present-day celebrations of the Mass, rarely are these songs the proper text and melody of the introit.

In practice, the entrance song's enactment never has been nor is it now uniform among all worshiping communities.[4] This assertion would be supported by a survey of any handful of parishes. Furthermore, while in the West most families of liturgical rites adopted something similar to the introit of the Roman Rite,[5] in the East the entrance of the ministers has taken a different form since at least the sixth century.[6]

Liturgical history reveals that the music of the liturgy has taken many forms. The presence of some type of music at the entrance procession of the Mass—in contrast to the introit in particular—dates to as early as the fourth century, when the celebration of the ritual moved into basilica buildings and incorporated elements of imperial ceremonial. Asserting these early origins can be only tentative, however, given the lack of direct historical evidence. What is certain is that in the Roman liturgy the use of a specific musical form known as the introit came to be common practice by at least the end of the

4. To be sure, there were periods during which a normative form of enactment prevailed: the introit as defined above in the Middle Ages, the recitation of the introit text by the priest after the prayers at the foot of the altar from 1570 until 1970, and today, the use of an entrance hymn. Methodologically speaking, however, one must recognize that there were in practice innumerable local variations in terms of the way in which the normative forms were enacted, even if these variations were often minute. The size and resources of a particular congregation would be two of the most prominent factors that influenced enactment, and one should not underestimate the influence of cultural context on performance practice.

5. The Burgundian *antiphona ad prelegendum*, Ambrosian *ingressa*, and Mozarabic *officium*, for example. See *New Grove*, 2nd ed., s.v. "Introit (i)." For more information on non-Roman liturgical rites in general, see Cyrille Vogel, *Medieval Liturgy: An Introduction to the Sources* (Washington, DC: Pastoral Press, 1986), passim; and Eric Palazzo, *A History of Liturgical Books from the Beginning to the Thirteenth Century*, trans. Madelein Beaumont (Collegeville, MN: Liturgical Press, 1998), passim.

6. As James McKinnon explains, "It was not until the late 5th or early 6th century that an entrance chant, the *Trisagion* [Ἅγιος ὁ Θεός, Ἅγιος ἰσχυρός, Ἅγιος ἀθάνατος, ἐλέησον ἡμᾶς], was introduced at Constantinople. In subsequent centuries the *Trisagion* came to be preceded by a set of three Ordinary antiphons, and was itself replaced on feasts of the Saviour by the antiphon *Hosoi eis Christon*, and on feasts of the Holy Cross by *Ton stauron*, but Constantinople never adopted the Roman practice of a Proper chant that varied with each date in the calendar." *New Grove*, 2nd ed., s.v. "Introit (i)."

seventh century. In the centuries after its introduction to the Mass, the classic form of the introit dis-integrated in terms of actual ritual practice in most places.[7]

Because of the sparseness of the historical record, it is impossible to assert a universal use of the introit in the Roman Rite. After its introduction, however, it is likely the introit continued to be sung at Mass in a majority of major liturgical centers, given the number of manuscripts and printed books that have survived to the present day. The important point is that the antiquity and universality of the integral performance of the introit at Mass should not be idealized or overstated. It is to be expected that once the liturgy began to be celebrated outside the introit's original liturgical and cultural context—the urban liturgy of Rome in the early Middle Ages—significant variations, adaptations, and deviations from the original form would take place.

In the reformed liturgy promulgated after the Second Vatican Council (1962–65) the introit remains the officially preferred musical form for the entrance song, even though several other forms are also permissible. For a number of reasons, however, including the transition to the vernacular, a lack of vernacular settings of the introit, and a concern for active participation by the assembly, most worshiping communities have replaced the introit with other musical forms, melodies, and texts since Vatican II.

Most histories of the introit have been written from a musicological perspective.[8] In recent years, a handful of authors have attempted

---

7. Certain communities truncated the introit very early on to include only one psalm verse, for example. In the late Middle Ages, the preparation and prayers of the presider came to dominate the beginning of the Mass. Organ versets or improvisation often replaced part or all of the introit, furthermore, beginning around the fifteenth century.

8. See, for example, David Hiley, *Western Plainchant: A Handbook* (Oxford: Clarendon Press, 1993). A musicologist, Hiley's focus is primarily the melodic characteristics of introit chants. He draws upon Josef Jungmann, *The Mass of the Roman Rite: Its Origins and Development*, trans. F. A. Brunner (New York: Benzinger Bros., 1951; repr., Allen, TX: Christian Classics, 1986; and Andrew Hughes, *Medieval Manuscripts for Mass and Office: A Guide to Their Organization and Terminology* (1982; repr., Toronto: University of Toronto Press, 1995). *Dictionnaire d'archéologie chrétienne et de liturgie*, s.v. "Introit" (by Henri Leclercq). This article must be taken as authoritative for its time, but there has been substantial research on the introit since the year of its publication. The most authoritative contributions are *New Grove*, s.v. "Introit"; *New Grove*, 2nd ed., s.v. "Introit"; *Grove Online*, s.v. "Introit"; and *Die Musik in Geschichte und Gegenwart*, s.v. "Introitus."

more comprehensive studies, though the focus tends to be the introductory rites of the Mass in general rather than the entrance song in particular.[9] While such work is foundational, this book offers a new perspective on the subject. Certainly, one's approach to history and theology matters, and a central assertion here is that the study of the entrance song, and indeed liturgy in general, is best served by a contextual method.

WHY A BOOK ON THE ENTRANCE SONG?

A study of the entrance song is especially pertinent for Roman Catholic liturgical studies today because of the promulgation of the new General Instruction of the Roman Missal (GIRM) and *Missale Romanum, editio typica tertia* (2002), and because there is a movement, though still nascent, to restore the important theological

---

9. See, for example: David Farr, "Newly-composed Eucharistic Entrance Antiphons, with Commentary," (PhD diss., Graduate Theological Union, 1986). Farr's 1,201-page study presents a good historical sketch of the introit, but its focus is quite broad. For example, he includes three chapters on psalmody and a consideration of all pre- and post-Reformation Western liturgical traditions. Mark R. Francis, "Uncluttering the Eucharistic Vestibule: The Entrance Rites through Time," *Liturgical Ministry 3* (1994): 1–12; and "Well Begun Is Half Done: The New Introductory Rites in the Revised Sacramentary," in *Liturgy for the New Millennium: A Commentary on the Revised Sacramentary*, ed. Mark R. Francis and Keith F. Pecklers (Collegeville, MN: Liturgical Press, 2000), 65–76. Both of Francis's studies focus on the introductory rites in general and not specifically upon the entrance song. Marc-Daniel Kirby, "The Proper Chants of the Paschal Triduum: A Study in Liturgical Theology" (STL thesis, The Catholic University of America, 1996). Kirby's concern is limited to a particular part of the liturgical year, but his detailed analysis of the Triduum chants is an important theological and methodological contribution. James W. McKinnon, *The Advent Project: The Later-Seventh-Century Creation of the Roman Mass Proper* (Berkeley: University of California Press, 2000). Joseph P. Metzinger, "The Liturgical Function of the Entrance Song: An Examination of Introits and Introit Tropes of the Manuscript Piacenza, Archivio Capitolare, 65" (DMA diss., The Catholic University of America, 1993). Metzinger's historical work, in contrast to his manuscript work, which focuses on introit chants, focuses on the introductory rites in general. Christoph Tietze, *Hymn Introits for the Liturgical Year: The Origin and Early Development of the Latin Texts* (Chicago: Liturgy Training Publications, 2005). *The New Catholic Encyclopedia*, s.v. "Introit" (by F. A. Brunner and Michel Huglo). *The New Catholic Encyclopedia*, 2nd ed. (hereafter *NCE* and *NCE*, 2nd ed., respectively), s.v. "Introit" (by F. A. Brunner and eds.).

"residue of meaning"[10] of the introit to the celebration of the Eucharist by encouraging its more frequent use.[11] Without a doubt, in most local parishes this meaning has long been untapped. Most important, the Missal has just been retranslated, and thus there is a renewed and broad interest in the Missal and its texts, of which the entrance antiphon is one.

From the outset, it is important to assert that any attempt to regulate the entrance song too strictly or to restore an exclusive use of the introit would be misguided. An unmediated return to the introit of the Middle Ages is not possible, as the context in which it developed is no longer today's context, and because other musical forms have taken root in its place. Indeed, there needs to be room for local liturgical, pastoral, musical, and theological creativity[12] in the Mass if it is to remain meaningful and effective in the lives of worshiping communities,[13] and the entrance song is a good and even traditional place for such creativity. There is a parallel, to be sure, between present-day alternatives to the introit—particularly vernacular liturgical songs—and the medieval practice of adding tropes and improvised

10. Zimmerman, *Liturgy and Hermeneutics*, 17. She states, "A text endures in time, and therefore it enjoys a certain autonomy, something that is not true for fleeting human discourse. A text embodies a residue of meaning originating in the discourse but surpassing it. The task of hermeneutics is to uncover this residue of meaning. . . . Rituals are rule-governed; they are executed according to a written or unwritten set of rules. This is the fixed meaning enabling the ritual to be repeated—so the encoded meaning is recoverable. With respect to liturgical texts, the residue of meaning recoverable by its fixation remains constant throughout liturgical tradition, even though the specific ceremonial that concretely shapes it changes from time to time" (ibid.).

11. See chapter 3 for examples of new collections of musical settings of the proper chants of the Mass.

12. Here "creativity" refers to creativity within the bounds of tradition and cultural context, which encompasses liturgical law, sound doctrine, appropriate pastoral sensitivity, and so forth. It pertains to how the universal liturgy is effectively expressed in particular contexts. It is not the same thing as improvisation. Gregorian chant is the creative product of a particular culture (Frankish), for example.

13. See Vatican Council II, Constitution on the Liturgy *Sacrosanctum Concilium* (1963) 37–40, and the Congregation for Divine Worship and the Discipline of the Sacraments, Instruction *Varietates Legitimae* (1994) 40. In this study, "local" has a broad meaning and refers to a variety of nonuniversal spheres of liturgical enactment: particular parish communities, dioceses, regions, Rites, nations, language groups, and so forth.

harmonies to the introit chants. The pervasiveness throughout history of musical creativity couched in a fidelity to tradition offers a model for present-day practice. It is worthwhile, therefore, to examine the entrance song tradition, not to argue for or against specific musical forms or genres, but to plumb the depths of the tradition for a solution to a contemporary pastoral problem. Namely, what should Roman Catholics sing at the beginning of the Mass?

The traditional axiom *lex orandi, lex credendi*[14] grounds this study, which presupposes a liturgical-theological stance that takes for granted the importance of the enacted liturgy as the primary source of liturgical theology,[15] and from which liturgical history and tradition have something important to offer to the study and enactment of liturgy today. It also highlights the value of music as an important locus for liturgical theology. The axiom values the contexts of a ritual's constitutive parts and of a rite as a single, cohesive ritual structure. This recognition of the importance of context is crucial to understanding the entrance song's historical development and theology, since a rite only exists in context, and the primary—in other words, the most immanent or most accessible through experience, even if not the most easily systematically interpreted—context is the enacted liturgy, which in turn is the primary source of the church's liturgical theology.

Another important consideration pertains to whether or not liturgical scholars have been asking the right questions about the entrance song. It is true, at least, that some questions concerning it have not yet been pursued adequately. This situation may exist because scholars presuppose the insignificance of the entrance song and the other processional chants of the Mass in comparison to other elements, such as the Eucharistic Prayer, or because scholars do not consider the study of liturgical music to be integral to the discipline of liturgical studies. It might also be true that many liturgical scholars perceive themselves to lack the skills necessary to study the

---

14. This axiom loosely translates as "what we pray is what we believe," or as stated by Prosper of Aquitaine (ca. 390–ca. 455), "legem credendi lex statuat supplicandi," or "the rule of belief is established by the rule of prayer." See his *Capitula coelestini* 8, in *Patrologia Latina* 51, p. 210.

15. This theological stance is in contrast to, for example, liturgical-theological reflection that focuses solely upon the texts found in liturgical books. In addition, while it is difficult to find fault with Prosper's axiom, one must admit that "prayer" (worship) and "belief" (doctrine) interact on many levels; one cannot be said to be a precursor to the other.

musical component of the liturgy.[16] In the past, the entrance song was usually explored from manuscript-based musicological and historical perspectives, rather than from a theological one. For this reason, an approach rooted in contextual theology is helpful, as it opens this inquiry to a wider variety of sources. A contextual theological framework provides a lens for focusing beyond musicological or manuscript concerns to the broader context of Christian ritual practice and its significance.

There are several specific problems, then, that were the motivation for this book and that it will in some way address:

- Much work still needs to be done in terms of gaining a more complete knowledge about the history, development, and theology of the entrance song. Such work needs to be contextual, needs to take the music of the liturgy seriously, and needs to move beyond exclusively musicological or manuscript-based concerns.

16. A similar problem occurs among musicologists, who sometimes do not take into account the insights of liturgical studies. As Christian Troelsgård says, "comparative liturgy and chant studies are intimately related. If we describe liturgy as a 'language' of religious expression and communication that go beyond the spoken word, chant is one of the non-verbal dimensions that accompanies the liturgical texts." Troelsgård, "Methodological Problems in Comparative Studies of Liturgical Chant," in *Comparative Liturgy Fifty Years after Anton Baumstark (1872–1948)*, ed. Robert F. Taft and Gabriele Winkler (Rome: Pontifical Oriental Institute, 2001), 981. Troelsgård's article "is . . . an invitation for collaboration between chant scholars and historians of liturgy, an invitation to work out a new and more detailed picture of . . . history" (ibid., 992). Peter Jeffery argues strongly for the interaction of musicological, liturgical, and ritual studies throughout his *Re-Envisioning Past Musical Cultures: Ethnomusicology in the Study of Gregorian Chant* (Chicago: University of Chicago Press, 1992). In a recent article Jeffery assesses what he sees as an excessively rationalistic, antiarchaeological, and antiritual bias in liturgical studies in the first half of the twentieth century. "It was because the reformers of Jungmann's generation could not 'read' the non-semantic languages of ritual . . . ritual objects and spaces, imagery and music . . . that they produced a liturgy so top-heavy with verbiage. . . . The dreaded 'archaeological' side of liturgy [has its] own forms of historical continuity, which (properly understood) can lead us reliably through gaps in the textual evidence." "The Meanings and Functions of *Kyrie Eleison*," in *The Place of Christ in Liturgical Prayer: Trinity, Christology, and Liturgical Theology*, ed. Bryan D. Spinks (Collegeville, MN: Liturgical Press, 2008), 143.

- Not making any use of the texts and chants of the introit tradition in liturgical celebrations today deprives Roman Catholics of their substantial theological riches.

- There is debate today as to the most appropriate musical form (antiphon/psalm, responsorial psalm, strophic hymn, refrain hymn, and so forth) to accompany the liturgical processions of the celebration of the Eucharist.[17]

- The implications of the additions and changes to the GIRM (USA)[18] have not yet been fully explored—especially the regulation of the entrance song suggested in nos. 46–48.

- It is unclear what the most appropriate or contextually conscious means by which to encourage and effect a reappropriation of the introit tradition's theological treasures in the day-to-day celebration of the Eucharist in the United States might be. Creative fidelity to tradition, which has many historical precedents, could be the basis for a solution to this problem.

MUSIC IN LITURGICAL THEOLOGY

In liturgical theology today, music and the other arts employed in the enactment of Christian worship need to play an important role. Any liturgical theology that systematically ignores the music of the liturgy is by definition incomplete. Music, especially singing, is an "integral" part of the liturgy (SC 112,[19] GIRM 39–41). As Kevin Irwin states, liturgical music is not only a "complementary element of the experience of liturgy" and a "complementary source" for liturgical theology that is intrinsic to liturgical celebration, but it is also "required for the integrity of the act of worship."[20] Like all elements of

17. See, for example, Kevin W. Irwin, *Context and Text: Method in Liturgical Theology* (Collegeville, MN: Liturgical Press, 1994), 236–38; and Anthony Ruff, *Sacred Music and Liturgical Reform: Treasures and Transformations* (Chicago: Liturgy Training Publications, 2007), 102–4, 563–602.

18. GIRM (USA) refers to the U.S. adaptation of the 2002 *Institutio Generalis Missalis Romani*. Hereafter, all references to the GIRM refer specifically to the GIRM (USA).

19. Vatican Council II, Constitution on the Sacred Liturgy *Sacrosanctum Concilium* (1963).

20. K. Irwin, *Context and Text*, 219.

liturgical celebration, the enacted music of the liturgy is "a complexus of sign-events,"[21] and through it, worshiping communities "express their existence before God."[22]

Music aids the full, conscious, and active participation of the assembly, and many ritual texts are most fully expressed when sung. Irwin reminds us that music supports and enhances how the primary elements of liturgy—namely, Word, euchology, and symbol—"are expressed and experienced in the act of liturgy."[23] Music is "intrinsically connected" to these primary elements in that it "is normatively the medium through which Word and euchology are communicated,"[24] and because, as Judith Kubicki and others have shown,[25] music functions symbolically in liturgical celebrations.

Specifically, this intrinsic and normative function of liturgical music means, methodologically, an emphasis on *lex agendi*—the enacted rites as a theological source—above all else when the goal is to gain access to the theology of the musical elements of the liturgy. This is true, first, because, as Irwin says, "theologizing from the *lex agendi* recognizes that the way the *lex orandi* is experienced depends to a large degree on the way the arts facilitate, enhance, or hinder *how* Scripture, symbols, and euchology are heard, understood, and appreciated in the act of liturgy."[26] Ritual music's function, generally speaking, then, is to facilitate the assembly's appropriation of Word, symbol, and euchology. Specifically, this function facilitates the appropriation of the meaning of particular liturgical readings, prayer texts, feasts, and so forth. It not only facilitates this appropriation, however, but also shapes it. Thus, it is crucial to understand how ritual music "shapes" in order to determine whether or not specific music is ritually appropriate for any given assembly in its particular context.[27] Focusing on the enacted rites opens the musical *lex*

21. Jan Michael Joncas, "Hymnum tuae gloriae canimus: Toward an Analysis of the Vocal Expression of the Eucharistic Prayer in the Roman Rite; Tradition, Principles, Method" (SLD diss., Pontifical Liturgical Institute, 1991), 378.

22. Mary E. McGann, *Exploring Music as Worship and Theology* (Collegeville, MN: Liturgical Press, 2002), 7.

23. K. Irwin, *Context and Text*, 219, 221.

24. Ibid., 219.

25. Judith M. Kubicki, *Liturgical Music as Ritual Symbol: A Case Study of Jacques Berthier's Taizé* (Louvain: Peeters, 1999), passim.

26. K. Irwin, *Context and Text*, 229.

27. For example, does a specific type or piece of ritual music facilitate the appropriation of the theology of a specific rite? To be sure, the determination of

agendi to critique, assessment, and revision.[28] This openness allows worshiping communities to maintain musical quality and effectiveness, and it helps them to understand how to judge quality in liturgical music.[29]

During the emergence of liturgical theology as a serious component of academic theological study in the wake of the twentieth-century liturgical renewal,[30] there have been an unprecedented number of explicit explorations into the theology of the liturgy.[31] Still, while there have been many contributors to the discipline of liturgical theology, the number concerned simultaneously with the study of the *musical component* of the liturgical experience and with *methodology* are few. Of late, however, there has been substantial work focusing on the means by which one can interpret the theology of liturgical music from a variety of perspectives.[32] These scholars

---

how ritual music functions and of how to judge its ritual appropriateness is a complex task, the details of which have yet to be worked out fully in the field of liturgical studies. Liturgical scholars would need to appropriate findings in the fields of cognitive neuroscience, aesthetics, acoustics, aural hermeneutics, and systematic musicology, to name a few, in order to reach a better understanding of how ritual music "works." See Jerry Tabor, ed., *Otto Laske: Navigating New Musical Horizons* (Westport, CT, and London: Greenwood Press, 1999), for one example of a methodological move in the right direction.

28. K. Irwin, *Context and Text*, 229.

29. Ibid.

30. Teresa Berger observes that "in the last half-century, the liturgy has (re-) emerged as a distinctive source for theological reflection. Theologians from a broad spectrum of ecclesial commitments now claim that liturgical practices are a fundamental site for understanding, interpreting, and configuring the Christian faith." Teresa Berger, "The Challenge of Gender for Liturgical Tradition," *Worship* 82:3 (May 2008): 243.

31. See, for example, the works of Mary Collins, I. H. Dalmais, Peter E. Fink, Albert Houssiau, Kevin W. Irwin, Aidan Kavanagh, Margaret Mary Kelleher, Edward J. Kilmartin, Gerard Lukken, Salvatore Marsili, David N. Power, Alexander Schmemann, Cypriano Vagaggini, Geoffrey Wainwright, and Joyce Ann Zimmerman. For descriptions of the work of some of the central figures in the discipline, see Kevin W. Irwin, *Liturgical Theology: A Primer* (Collegeville, MN: Liturgical Press, 1990), and his extensive bibliography in *Context and Text*, 352–88. See also Catherine Vincie, *Celebrating the Divine Mystery: A Primer in Liturgical Theology* (Collegeville, MN: Liturgical Press, 2008); and Dwight W. Vogel, ed., *Primary Sources of Liturgical Theology: A Reader* (Collegeville, MN: Liturgical Press, 2000).

32. See Joncas, "Hymnum tuae gloriae canimus"; Kubicki, *Liturgical Music as Ritual Symbol*; Mary E. McGann, *Exploring Music as Worship and Theology* and *A Precious Fountain: Music in the Worship of an African American Catholic*

work to answer the question of *how* one reflects theologically upon liturgical music, or better, how one *gains access to* its theological meaning.

METHODOLOGY

Organization

This book has two parts. The first is a contextual study of the entrance song focusing on two areas of inquiry: the development of the entrance song throughout history, and an exploration of the theology and ritual use of the entrance song grounded in liturgical law and ecclesiastical documents.[33] The second, which is grounded in the insights of the first, begins with a delineation of several models of the entrance song. Together these models serve jointly as a new lens through which to view the history and theology of the entrance song. The last section is a contextual theological analysis of the entrance song, focusing on the entrance song of the Holy Thursday Evening Mass of the Lord's Supper.

Community (Collegeville, MN: Liturgical Press, 2004); Mark David Parsons, "'With Sighs Too Deep for Words': Liturgical Song as Metaphor (PhD diss., Graduate Theological Union, 2003); William T. Flynn, "Paris, Bibliothèque de L'Arsenal, MS 1169: The Hermeneutics of Eleventh-Century Burgundian Tropes, and Their Implications for Liturgical Theology" (PhD diss., Duke University, 1992); Willem Marie Speelman, *The Generation of Meaning in Liturgical Songs: A Semiotic Analysis of Five Liturgical Songs as Syncretic Discourses* (Kampen, The Netherlands: Kok Pharos, 1995); and K. Irwin, *Context and Text*. Zimmerman, in *Liturgy and Hermeneutics*, 87–88, elaborates on the nature of K. Irwin's book: "He seeks to relate liturgy and theology by paying close attention to the relationship of various aspects of liturgy. The subtitle of this volume [*Method in Liturgical Theology*] is misleading; Irwin's is more a theoretical framework than a work in method as such and is groundbreaking in this regard." To be sure, the number of relevant studies multiplies significantly when one removes the explicitly methodological component. There have been many recent theological studies on the music of the liturgy. For the most important works in this regard, see the bibliography. See also Mark David Parsons, "Text, Tone, and Context: A Methodological Prolegomenon for a Theology of Liturgical Song," *Worship* 79:1 (January 2005): 54–69. Parsons provides a review and synthesis of recent efforts at "Christian music theology."

33. Liturgical theologians have long recognized the foundational nature of liturgical law or "competent authority" in the interpretation of liturgical "texts." Zimmerman, *Liturgy and Hermeneutics*, 11–14.

Foundations of a Contextual Method

Since the postmodern turn to the subject[34] in Western philosophical discourse, most theologians have taken for granted that, as Stephen Bevans notes, "the contextualization of theology—the attempt to understand faith in terms of a particular context—is really a theological imperative."[35] A contextual theology recognizes a dialectical, or more accurately, analogical relationship between present human experience and the Christian tradition—between context and meaning.[36] It recognizes that theology and all human discourse must be "unabashedly subjective" in that reality is mediated by meaning—a meaning given in the context of a particular culture and historical period, interpreted from within one's particular horizon and way of thinking.[37] Thus, "we can only speak about a theology that makes sense at a certain place and in a certain time."[38]

Contextual theology is nothing new. Every theologian throughout history wrote within his or her particular context.[39] The difference

34. See Zimmerman, *Liturgy and Hermeneutics*, 43.

35. Stephen B. Bevans, *Models of Contextual Theology* (Maryknoll, NY: Orbis Books, 1992), 1. There has been a parallel movement in Christology over the past half century, evidenced by the increasing emphasis on Christology "from below" in contrast to Christology "from above." See William P. Loewe, *The College Student's Introduction to Christology* (Collegeville, MN: Liturgical Press, 1996), passim.

36. Bevans, *Models of Contextual Theology*, 11.

37. See Bernard Lonergan, *Method in Theology* (1973; repr., Toronto: University of Toronto Press, 1996), 28, 76–77, 238.

38. Bevans, *Models of Contextual Theology*, 2. See also the concept of "World Church" in Karl Rahner, "Towards a Fundamental Theological Interpretation of Vatican II," *Theological Studies* 40 (1979): 716–27. The contextual situation becomes increasingly complex as time goes on. A theologian today must not only recognize his or her own cultural context but also the fact that one is continually assailed by other cultural contexts, which can result in a kind of overlap of cultural matrices. In this age of the "World Church," theological discourse must attempt to negotiate this ever-more complex and instantaneous interaction between cultures. See also Lonergan, *Method in Theology*, xi. The fact that the way in which theology is articulated must differ from context to context in no way denies the existence of universally relevant truth, ideas, and principles.

39. See Bevans, *Models of Contextual Theology*, 3–4. D. J. Hall makes the point well: "Contextualization . . . is the sine qua non of all genuine theological thought, and always has been." Hall, *Thinking the Faith: Christian Theology in a North American Context* (Minneapolis: Augsburg Press, 1989), 21. The effects of the unavoidably contextual nature of human discourse are easily seen in the influence of certain philosophies and movements on the aesthetics and principles of the Second Vatican Council (for example, minimalism and social justice), though one

today is the self-conscious recognition of this context and the realization that a truly objective and universal theological discourse is impossible.[40] This new systematic articulation of this theological reality has
led to new methodological approaches to the theological enterprise.

There are several underlying assertions to a consciously contextual
theology: Christianity is incarnational, reality is sacramental, and
revelation is contextual. In other words, if salvation is God's personal
self-offering to human beings (as both individuals and communities),
revelation must take place in a humanly comprehensible and therefore contextual manner.[41]

For the theologian today, this new stance has some practical implications. First, a theologian must in some way limit his or her field
of inquiry. This principle acknowledges the interdisciplinary nature
of modern scholarship, which by its very nature and breadth does not
allow any one person to have the expertise to paint an exhaustive or
comprehensive picture of a given topic. It recognizes the methodological difficulties in attempting comprehensive histories and universal

---

would not want to deny that the council also adapted, advanced, and shaped such
philosophies and movements. The current retreat from the idea of postmodernism
in the neotraditionalist movement in the Western church—even though such a
retreat is actually undeniably postmodern because it requires recognition of that
from which it turns away—is similarly reflective of today's general trend toward
cultural conservatism, though there is not yet enough historical distance to accurately delineate a motivating philosophy as such.

40. The use of the term "theological discourse" rather than "theology" allows
for the fact that some contextual theological methods recognize a universal Christian revelation. The meaningful and effective articulation of this revelation in a
particular place and time, however, is the methodological problem.

41. Bevans, *Models of Contextual Theology*, 7–10. To clarify, he goes on: "Incarnation is a process of becoming particular, and in and through the particular, the
divinity could become visible [in Jesus of Nazareth] and in some way . . . become
graspable and intelligible. It follows quite naturally that if that message is to continue to touch people through our agency, we have to continue the incarnation
process. . . . Christianity, if it is to be faithful to its deepest roots and most basic
insight, must continue God's incarnation in Jesus by becoming contextual. . . .
The ordinary things of life are so transparent of God's presence, one can speak
of culture and events in history—of contexts—as truly sacramental, and so re-
velatory" (ibid., 8–9). Irwin emphasizes similar points in terms of a "theology of
creation" and "sacramentality." He says that "it is here and now that, because of
Christ, our lives are supremely human and profoundly divine at the same time."
Liturgy, and the Christian life in general, "presume a sacramental world view."
K. Irwin, "A Sacramental World—Sacramentality as the Primary Language of
Sacraments," *Worship* 76:3 (May 2002): 197, 199.

theologies[42] and aims to shed a clearer, more accurate, and more specific light on a narrow field of study by focusing on a particular idea or question. Specificity and focus are necessary given the great and increasing speed at which knowledge expands today. A welcome result is that the interdisciplinary nature of academic pursuit requires deliberate collaboration among specialists in various fields of study.[43] Second, this new stance also implies there must be a critical edge in theological reflection, one that approaches reality with suspicion or a "dialectical imagination."[44] In other words, it articulates the self-evident fact that the theological articulation of Christian revelation can be distorted by human motives and systemic cultural problems.

The Contextual Method of This Study

This book is motivated by questions, and as Joyce Ann Zimmerman has said, "different questions, different method."[45] Therefore, the questions we hope to answer have shaped the structure of the book, rather than any particular methodology,[46] which is the point of contextual theological "method" in the first place. Indeed, if the book succeeds, it will have been an application of the theoretical framework suggested by Kevin Irwin in his crucial work *Context and Text*.

This theoretical framework, because it is open to all types of sources, can address the wide variety of sources cited in this book: musicological, historical, paleographical, legal, theological, linguistic, pastoral, and so on. Because it is open to all sorts of data, it is by necessity open to all sorts of means of interpretation.

Why, then, do the contextual studies of this book (Part One) focus on the history of the entrance song and its place in ecclesiastical documents? In truth, any number of other windows into the theology and enactment of the entrance song could have been chosen.[47] But one

---

42. Zimmerman emphasizes that "the plurality of methods suggests that in spite of our propensity to search for *the* meaning of a text, at best the process of interpretation produces only a viable meaning." Zimmerman, *Liturgy and Hermeneutics*, 47.

43. Lonergan, *Method in Theology*, 125–48.

44. Bevans, *Models of Contextual Theology*, 17.

45. Zimmerman, *Liturgy and Hermeneutics*, 47.

46. As Zimmerman notes, "Rarely can an interpreter commit herself or himself to a single method and use only that method. . . . We must have a dialogue of interpretations if we are to understand liturgy as a divine/human encounter." Zimmerman, *Liturgy and Hermeneutics*, 80–81.

47. Liturgical translation and ritual studies, for example.

must choose in order to keep the task manageable; other questions and windows must be left for another time or to another author.[48] It is not by chance that the contextual "method" as applied here is fairly systematic. When the contextual studies of Part One are put in dialogue with one another, they provide a glimpse of the "deep structure" of the entrance song and produce new insights into its theology and enactment, the result of which is Part Two.

This introduction concludes with figure 1 (below), which illustrates the structure and flow of the project as a whole. This diagram has both shaped and been shaped by the process of researching and writing this book—it is both a guide and a reflection.

Figure 1. Application of the contextual method.

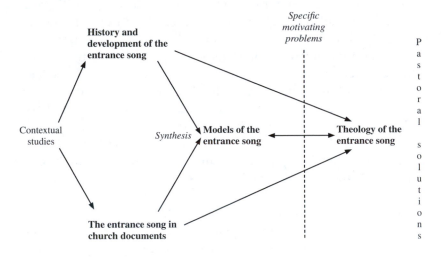

48. Zimmerman recognizes that "a hermeneut chooses a method because it promises to deliver an answer to a particular set of questions. This necessarily implies that the interpreter must let go of other questions, or address them in another interpretive moment." Zimmerman, *Liturgy and Hermeneutics*, 20.

PART ONE

Contextual Studies
of the Entrance Song

CHAPTER ONE

The Entrance Song in Its Historical Context

INTRODUCTION

In the historical study of Christian liturgy, a clear statement of limits is important. It is even more important when the goal is to consider such a broad span of time—for the purpose of this chapter, from the time of the first Christians until the time when the insights of the liturgical movement[1] began to be taken up in official church documents. Because of the span of time under consideration, it is not possible to present a comprehensive history of the entrance song for all eras, in all geographical regions, and within all ritual traditions. Instead, the goal is to frame a historical picture of the evolution, form, and function of the entrance song in the Roman Rite,[2] particularly in light of liturgical tradition and liturgical sources.

The focus here on a particular musical form (the introit) does not deny the historical significance of other musical forms or traditions. Indeed, a great variety of forms has been part of the liturgical

---

1. For a brief history of the liturgical movement, see *New Dictionary of Sacramental Worship*, s.v. "Liturgical Movement, The (1830–1969)" (by Virgil C. Funk).

2. For more on the importance of frames in historical writing, see Philip Weller, "Frames and Images: Locating Music in Cultural Histories of the Middle Ages," *Journal of the American Musicological Society* 50:1 (Spring 1997): 17–54.

tradition in the West, and today there is a variety of songs that accompany the entrance procession in the Mass of the Roman Rite. At the same time, however, one must recognize that entrance chants came to be the typical way—but certainly not the only way—to begin celebrations of the Eucharist in the West from very early on. In the Roman Rite, this chant was the introit, and thus it has a prominence within the tradition and a privileged status. And, for the past half millennium, the introit has been part of the normative form of celebrating the Mass of the Roman Rite.

The present study recognizes a dialectical or dialogical relationship between official sources and actual practice, in which actual practice is evaluated in terms of a normative form. Here the dialectic is between "normative" and "nonnormative" ritual-musical forms, not necessarily between "high quality" and "low quality," which indicate degrees of effective ritual enactment.

For centuries people cited an excerpt from the sixth-century *Liber Pontificalis* of Pope Celestine I (422–32) as proof that this pope introduced the introit into the Roman liturgy:

[Hic multa constituta fecit,] et constituit ut psalmi David CL	[He issued many decrees,] and he decreed that the 150 psalms of David
ante sacrificium psalli [antephanatim ex omnibus], quod ante non fiebat, nisi tantum epistula beati Pauli recitabatur et sanctum evangelium, (et sic missae celebrabantur).	should be sung before the sacrifice [antiphonally from all]; this used not to be done, but only the epistle of the blessed Paul was recited and the holy gospel, (and in this way Masses were celebrated).[3]

3. This redaction of the text is taken from Joseph Dyer, "The Introit and Communion Psalmody of Old Roman Chant," in *Chant and Its Peripheries: Essays in Honour of Terence Bailey*, ed. Bryan Gillingham and Paul Merkley (Ottawa: Institute of Medieval Music, 1998), 110–12. Dyer notes that "the two passages enclosed within square brackets occur only in the second edition of the *Liber Pontificalis* (ca. 550); the phrase in parenthesis occurs in the first edition (ca. 530), but not in every manuscript of this recension" (ibid., 112). Dyer relies upon the classic edition of the *Liber Pontificalis*, ed. Louis Duchesne (Paris: Boccard, 1955–57), 1:172–87. J. A. Lamb also notes that the "antephanatim ex omnibus" is likely "a gloss whose antiquity is suspect." Lamb, *Psalms in Christian Worship* (London: Faith Press, 1962), 87. See also *Dictionnaire d'archéologie chrétienne et de liturgie* (hereafter DACL), s.v. "Introit."

This interpretation originates in the interpretation of the passage by Amalar of Metz (ca. 775–ca. 850).[4] *Introitus* for Amalar had a broad meaning.[5] Walahfrid Strabo (ca. 808–49) also interpreted the passage as referring to the introit.[6] More recently, however, a number of scholars have convincingly discredited this view and instead see the passage from the *Liber Pontificalis* as referring to the gradual (responsorial psalm).[7] Indeed, both Jungmann (1949) and Lamb (1962) already view with suspicion the idea that the *Liber Pontificalis* refers to the introit.[8] One can still find scholarly works of relatively recent provenance, nevertheless, that either disagree with these scholars or are unaware of this development in historical understanding.[9] While the argument against the *Liber Pontificalis* as a record of the introduction of the introit into the Roman Rite is quite convincing, scholars have not settled the matter beyond a shadow of a doubt and, for lack of historical evidence, probably never will.

Another debated passage is from Augustine of Hippo's *Liber retractationem* II, 27: "Meanwhile a certain Hilary . . . attacked the custom which had begun then in Carthage . . . of singing [*dicerentur*] at the altar hymns from the Book of Psalms both before the oblation [*ante oblationem*] and while what had been offered was distributed to the people."[10] It is possible the first reference to singing a psalm refers to

---

4. See his ninth-century *Liber officialis* 3.5.2, ed. I. M. Hanssens, *Amalarii episcopi opera liturgica omnia* (Rome 1948).

5. He states, "Officium quod vocatur introitus missae habet initium a prima antiphona, quae dicitur introitus, et finitur in oratione quae dicitur a sacerdote ante lectionem." Ibid., 3.5.1.

6. See Alice Harting-Correa, ed. and trans., *Walahfried Strabo's Libellus de exordiis et incrementis quarundam in observationibus ecclesiasticis rerum: A Translation and Liturgical Commentary* (Leiden: Brill Academic, 1996), 128–33.

7. See Peter Jeffrey, "The Introduction of Psalmody into the Roman Mass by Pope Celestine I (422–432): Reinterpreting a Passage in the *Liber Pontificalis*," *Archiv für Liturgiewissenschaft* 26:2 (1984); and *New Grove*, 2nd ed., s.v. "Introit."

8. See Jungmann, *Mass of the Roman Rite*, 1:322; and Lamb, *Psalms in Christian Worship*, 86.

9. See, for example, John F. Baldovin, "Kyrie Eleison and the Entrance Rite of the Roman Eucharist," *Worship* 60 (July 1986): 340; Peter G. Cobb, "The Liturgy of the Word in the Early Church," in *The Study of Liturgy*, ed. Cheslyn Jones et al., rev. ed. (London: SPCK / New York: Oxford University Press, 1992), 221; and *Encyclopedia of Early Christianity*, s.v. "Music" (by Everett Ferguson).

10. See *Corpus Scriptorum Ecclesiasticorum Latinorum* 36, 144. Trans., James W. McKinnon, "The Fourth-Century Origin of the Gradual," *Early Music History* 7 (1987): 103.

an entrance psalm or an offertory psalm, but experts generally agree that the passage describes the gradual and communion.[11]

It would be an understatement to say with Joseph Dyer that "the date at which singing during the entry of the clergy was introduced to the Roman Mass is difficult to determine."[12] Indeed, the purpose of this chapter is not to discover the precise origins of the introit. The extant historical record is simply insufficient for the task. To assert a precise origin for the introit would be to harmonize sparse, sporadic, divergent, and geographically/culturally specific evidence, and thus be highly problematic, methodologically speaking.[13] Doing so could result in a false or unfounded historical picture of early Christian practice. While a uniform way of beginning the celebration of the Eucharist did develop in Rome after Constantine, one must be careful not to project this uniformity of practice back to prior centuries or to assume complete uniformity of practice in the West after the fourth century. Any historical reconstruction of early Christianity must take into consideration the late emergence of liturgical orthopraxis, the pluralistic character of the earliest faith communities, and possible literary suppression of heteropraxis.

FOUNDATIONAL CONTEXTS

There is no compelling evidence for a deliberate program of music composition for the worship of the earliest Christian communities. How the earliest followers of the risen Christ employed music is an

---

11. See McKinnon, "Fourth-Century Origin of the Gradual," 103.

12. Dyer, "Introit and Communion Psalmody," 110.

13. Paul Bradshaw has summarized well the care one must take when researching the early history of the liturgy: "First, we no longer generalize on the basis of very limited evidence. . . . Secondly, we no longer assume a high degree of continuity from one century to another. . . . [Third,] we do not always assume that what [the extant sources] claim to be the case is necessarily a simple and reliable statement of fact." Bradshaw, "The Changing Face of Early Liturgy," *Music and Liturgy* 33:1–2 (2007): 23–24. For more on this issue, stated in terms of archaeology, see Graydon F. Snyder, *Ante-Pacem: Archaeological Evidence of Church Life Before Constantine* (Macon, GA: Mercer University Press, 2003), 15; and, in terms of liturgical chant, see Christian Troelsgård, "Methodological Problems in Comparative Studies of Liturgical Chant," in *Comparative Liturgy Fifty Years after Anton Baumstark (1872–1948)*, ed. Robert F. Taft and Gabriele Winkler (Rome: Pontifical Oriental Institute, 2001), 981–84.

intriguing question. Could these proto-Christians, who, as pagans or Jews, were ritual beings and part of a ritual culture, escape the ancient musical traditions of their day: the ancient uses and significance of music associated with the pagan cults and with Jewish worship in the temple, synagogue, and home? It is difficult even to speak of a specifically Christian culture prior to what Graydon Snyder calls the new cult's "cultural break with Judaism."[14] Before this time—roughly the late first century and early second century—Christianity, though in many ways unique, was simply one of several movements within Judaism and one of many new religious movements in the Roman Empire.[15]

The Origins of Christian Culture and Music

The foundations of Christian worship music[16] lay within a first- and early second-century cultural matrix that was simultaneously Greek, Jewish, and Roman.[17] Because of its dominance in the Near East and in the Roman Empire, Greek music theory and philosophical

14. Snyder, *Ante-Pacem*, 1.

15. It is only in the late second century, with the cultural break with Judaism in the recent past, that we find evidence of a distinctively Christian culture. This cultural break was brought about through the eventual self-identification of Christians as a religious group in their own right, rather than as a sect within Judaism. The key here is that Christianity became distinct as a visible culture. Snyder notes, "This is not to say there was no Christian culture prior to 180 C.E. It is only to say that the nascent Christian culture either was not yet distinguishable from society in general, or the first Christians lacked sufficient self-identity to establish for itself symbols, language, art and architecture. From the beginning there had to have been social practices peculiar to the life of the first Christians." Ibid., 2. On the surge of new religious movements and the success of Christianity during the first centuries AD, see Donald F. Logan, *A History of the Church in the Middle Ages* (New York: Routledge, 2002), 3–12; and Rodney Stark, *The Rise of Christianity* (San Francisco: Harper San Francisco, 1997), passim.

16. According to Jan Michael Joncas, "describing primitive Christian worship music practices is quite difficult due to the scarcity of sources. No surviving musical artifacts, visual representations, or acoustic environments unassailably dated to the first century of the Christian movement survive. Only the twenty-seven documents that make up the New Testament and a handful of other 'subapostolic' writings (e.g., the *Didache*, the *First Letter of Clement to Rome*, the *Letter of Barnabas*) allow us to reconstruct in some way the liturgical life of the first generation of Christians." Joncas, "Liturgy and Music," in *Handbook for Liturgical Studies*, vol. 2, *Fundamental Liturgy* (Collegeville, MN: Liturgical Press, 1998), 287.

17. Ibid., 284.

understandings of music necessarily underpinned any music of the early Christians, even if not on a self-conscious level.[18] The typical Greek sense of musical propriety regarding music used in religious rites was also influential—for example, a general preference for vocal music over instrumental music.[19] The music of first-century imperial Roman culture also influenced the music of the first Christians, but as a counterpoint. Early Christians were concerned that what they sang be intelligible. In this characteristic, their music differed—probably deliberately—from pagan Roman music, which utilized archaic texts that had become incomprehensible.[20]

The music of the Jews in Palestine was also significant. All three traditional categories of Jewish music (Temple, synagogue, and home) had varying degrees of influence on early Christian music.[21] At the

---

18. See, for example, Philo, *Noah as Planter* 2.126; Plato, *Republic* 399E and *Laws* 669E; Plutarch, *On Music* 26–27, 33, 41; and Porphyry, *De abstinentia* 2.34.

19. See Herbert M. Schueller, *The Idea of Music: An Introduction to Musical Aesthetics in Antiquity and the Middle Ages* (Kalamazoo, MI: Medieval Institute Publications, 1988), passim; and *Encyclopedia of Early Christianity*, s.v. "Music."

20. Joncas, "Liturgy and Music," 285.

21. For a contextual study of the music of the Temple and of synagogues in the first century, see Edward Foley, *Foundations of Christian Music: The Music of Pre-Constantinian Christianity* (1992; rev. ed., Collegeville, MN: Liturgical Press, 1996), 25–50. See also Joncas, "Liturgy and Music," 287. Over recent years, the prevailing opinion as to the type and degree of influence Jewish worship had upon early Christianity has changed. See *Grove Online*, s.v. "Christian Church, Music of the Early" (by James W. McKinnon), http://www.grovemusic.com/ (accessed February 10, 2005). A survey of scholarship over the past century shows a gradual trend away from studies that ignore the Jewish roots of Christianity and toward a historical viewpoint that increasingly emphasizes the Jewish origins of Christian ritual practices. Today, scholarship tends to take the link between first-century Jewish practices and those of the early Christians as an a priori fact, while at the same time recognizing that a direct evolutionary relationship can only be asserted with serious qualifications. For example, a more careful analysis of the evidence has revealed, as the majority of liturgical scholars agree, that the earliest Christian forms of worship actually predate the development of what we today think of as Jewish worship. See, for example, Joan E. Taylor, *Christians and Holy Places: The Myth of Jewish-Christian Origins* (Oxford: Clarendon, 1993), passim; and Bradshaw, "Changing Face of Early Liturgy," 25–26. Charles Perrot reminds us, however, that "we cannot forget the phenomenon of re-Judaisation which quickly took place, even in Helleno-Christian communities (thus Col. 2:16-18, 23). Sometimes the allegedly Jewish origin of this or that Christian practice is merely a secondary historical phenomenon." Perrot, "Worship in the Primitive Church," *Concilium* 162 (1983): 3.

temple, a group of hereditary musical professionals or Levites performed the music, but in the synagogues the entire assembly would have taken part in spontaneous or unprogrammed singing under the leadership of the *sheliach tsibbur*, or emissary of the people. This congregational participation implies a simple form of music that was easy to sing. At times, the assembly would have heard the reader cantillate excerpts from the Hebrew sacred texts.[22]

The music of the typical Jewish home, particularly singing at meals, also must have influenced early Christian practice.[23] It is true,

22. Bradshaw recognizes among scholars a "growing consensus that in the first century there was no such thing as the Sabbath synagogue liturgy, in the sense that we can speak of it in later centuries. There were certainly regular synagogue assemblies on the Sabbath, which might last for hours, but they were for the primary purpose of reading and studying the Law and the Prophets rather than for liturgy in the sense that we might understand that expression. . . . They were classes rather than services. Hence the notion of psalms being sung or formal prayers being offered are anachronisms. It was only after the Temple had been destroyed that synagogues assumed the role of centres for worship and many of the former practices of the Temple liturgy were transferred to this context. The only possible synagogal influence on the origins of Christian worship, then, would have been the practice of reading publicly important texts." Bradshaw, *Changing Face of Early Liturgy*, 25. See also Daniel K. Falk, "Jewish Prayer Literature and the Jerusalem Church in Acts," in *The Book of Acts in Its Palestinian Setting*, ed. Richard Bauckham (Grand Rapids, MI: Wm. B. Eerdmans, 1995), 267–301; and Heather McKay, *Sabbath and Synagogue: The Question of Sabbath Worship in Ancient Jerusalem* (Leiden: E. J. Brill, 1994), passim. In larger buildings, however, public reading suggests that the readers cantillated/chanted the texts.

23. Fassler and Jeffery tentatively assert that "the earliest Christian musical tradition developed from a variety of sources, [including] the Jewish and Pagan customs of singing at gatherings around a meal. . . . Held in private homes during the first two centuries, such meals typically included Scripture reading, religious instruction, prayer, and singing. We find examples in the literature of Qumran, the *Letter of Aristeas* 175–215, and especially Philo's *The Contemplative Life*." Margot Fassler and Peter Jeffery, "Christian Liturgical Music from the Bible to the Renaissance," in *Sacred Sound and Social Change: Liturgical Music in Jewish and Christian Experience* (Notre Dame, IN: University of Notre Dame Press, 1992), 84–85. See also G. Vermes, *The Dead Sea Scrolls in English*, rev. complete edition (London: Penguin Books, 2004), 32, 83–84. Foley offers some useful insight into this issue: "Early Christian practice reflects patterns which are as meticulously different from, as they are broadly grounded on, Jewish tradition. There is, for example, much continuity in terms of texts, musical forms, and styles of 'musical' leadership and melodic building blocks — especially between Jewish synagogue, home rituals and emerging Christian cult. Many of the texts that were part of the lyrical horizon of early Christian worship (like the Infancy Canticles)

nevertheless, that evidence about such an influence is sparse.[24] This is not to say there were exact parallels in either the pagan or Jewish tradition; the assertion that the music of the Jewish home was influential on early Christian liturgy only recognizes that the practice of singing at meals was so prevalent in the cultural context of the first Christians that it is more likely than not to have influenced the development of their own musical practices. In any case, the logogenic (or "word-born") style of music in the Jewish tradition was particularly influential in early Christian music.[25] In addition, the Davidic psalms and Greek melodies probably also influenced Christian singing.[26] Finally, it is important to remember that pagan and Jewish festivals and holy days influenced the development of many of the earliest Christian feasts.[27]

Early Christian Singing

> Christian assemblies have at all times and in all places read the scriptures, prayed, and sung. The Christian liturgy was born in singing, and it has never ceased to sing. Singing must be regarded as one of the fundamental constituents of Christian worship.
> —Joseph Gelineau[28]

---

were borrowed from Judaism, the practice of publicly cantillating readings is distinctively Jewish, and even the priority of vocal music to the exclusion of instruments was a synagogal innovation. Yet, the tonal landscape of early Christianity cannot be understood simply in terms of continuity with Jewish synagogal or domestic worship. Texts were borrowed and adapted, the nature of public reading was redefined in terms of gospel and epistle, and the traditional patterns of Jewish chants—already under the influence of Hellenism—were increasingly influenced by the musical traditions of Gentile believers." Foley, *Foundations of Christian Music*, 67–68.

24. Joncas, "Liturgy and Music," 287. There is some evidence of early antiphonal Jewish religious singing. See Philo, *Contemplative Life* 80, 83–87.

25. Joncas, "Liturgy and Music," 287.

26. *Encyclopedia of Early Christianity*, s.v. "Music."

27. Fassler and Jeffery, "Christian Liturgical Music," 85.

28. Joseph Gelineau, "Music and Singing in the Liturgy," in *The Study of Liturgy*, ed. Cheslyn Jones et al. (New York: Oxford University Press, 1992), 494. See this article for a useful if somewhat dated history of the development of Christian liturgical music. When worship is framed in terms of Gelineau's three broad categories (Scripture reading, praying, and singing), it becomes clearer how integral music was to the early Christian liturgical experience.

A modest meal should sound with psalms, and if you have a good memory and a pleasant voice, you should take upon yourself the singer's office.

—St. Cyprian of Carthage[29]

Patristic and early Christian liturgical sources, from what limited evidence is available, show that during primitive eucharistic gatherings, the most common types of music were spontaneous responses or short acclamations.[30] These were performed either by an

---

29. Cyprian, *Ad Donatum* 16. The original Latin text reads, "Sonet psalmos convivium sobrium; et ut tibi tenax memoria est, vox canora, aggredere hoc munus ex more." Quasten notes that "in this way Christianity wholly retained the customs of antiquity, which made use of solo singing at meals." J. Quasten, *Music in Pagan and Christian Antiquity*, trans. Boniface Ramsey (Washington, DC: National Association of Pastoral Musicians, 1983), 131–32. In this context "psalm" is a generic term that does not refer specifically to the Hebrew psalms. For more on Cyprian—as well as Clement and Origen—and music, see Paul F. Bradshaw, *Eucharistic Origins* (New York: Oxford University Press, 2004), 106–14.

30. Justin Martyr's *First Apology* (ca. AD 150) is an important piece of historical evidence regarding the entrance song, but only indirectly. In the *Apology*'s two descriptions of mid-second-century celebrations of the Eucharist (paras. 65–66, 67), there is no account of an entrance song or of any introductory rites other than the assembling or gathering of the participants at the start of the liturgy, which in essence is a type of primitive and spontaneous introductory ritual movement. See Bradshaw, *Eucharistic Origins*, 47–77. One cannot necessarily take Justin's account at face value, however. Bradshaw emphasizes that "the idea that there was a single church in Rome at this period seems to be anachronistic: instead, there appears to have been a somewhat loose collection of Christian communities distinguished from one another by significant ethnic—and probably also liturgical—differences" (ibid., 63–64). See also A. Hamman, "Valeur et signification des renseignements liturgiques de Justin," *Studia Patristica* 13 (1975): 364–74; and Peter Lampe, *From Paul to Valentinus: Christians at Rome in the First Two Centuries* (Minneapolis and London: Fortress Press, 2003), 9–22. Christian singing, both inside and outside the eucharistic liturgy, receives a fair amount of attention in other writings of the church fathers. For specific patristic examples, see *Encyclopedia of Early Christianity*, s.v. "Music"; Quasten, *Music and Worship in Pagan and Christian Antiquity*, 89, 131; and *Grove Online*, s.v. "Christian Church, Music of the Early." Such references, however interesting and enlightening in terms of patristic thinking about music, reveal nothing of an entrance song and have received substantial treatment by a number of other authors. See, for example, Schueller, *Idea of Music*; James W. McKinnon, "The Meaning of the Patristic Polemic against Musical Instruments," *Current Musicology* 1 (1985): 69–82; McKinnon, *Music in Early Christian Literature* (Cambridge, UK: Cambridge University Press, 1987); and Quentin Faulkner, *Wiser than Despair: The Evolution of Ideas in*

individual or by a group moved to acclaim popular phrases.[31] Thus, the earliest Christian singing was in a sense responsorial in that these spontaneous acclamations were individual or communal responses to the liturgical celebration.[32] Congregational responses would have been perhaps a single word, such as "Alleluia" or "Amen," or a verse such as "His mercy endures forever"—something akin to improvisatory antiphons.[33] Individual responses could have been the same or as complex as an improvised hymn of praise. One imagines that primitive Christian worship music was interactive and participatory, ecstatic and joyous.[34]

While music was certainly a part of Christian worship from the beginning, specific historical evidence of such music is scarce. One sure trait of the earliest Christian music, however, is that it was pre-

---

the Relationship of Music and the Christian Church (Westport, CT, and London: Greenwood Press, 1996).

31. *Grove Online*, s.v. "Christian Church, Music of the Early." See also Foley, *Foundations of Christian Music*, 81–82; and Augustine, *De civitate Dei* 22:8. In a description of his entrance into the church on Easter morning in AD 426, Augustine recalls that he was greeted by shouts from the people: "Procedimus ad populum, plena erat ecclesia, peronabat vocibus gaudiorum: Deo gratias, deo laudes! Nemine tacente hinc atque inde clamantium. Salutaui populum, et rursus eadem feruentiore voce clamabant. Facto tandem silentio scripturarum divinarum sunt lecta sollemnia." It is possible these shouts were spontaneous musical ejaculations, though the evidence as it stands cannot prove and does not necessarily suggest such a hypothesis.

32. *Encyclopedia of Early Christianity*, s.v. "Music." See also Foley, *Foundations of Christian Music*, 61–63; Tertullian, *De oratione* 27, in *Patrologia Latina* 1:1194, and in *Corpus Christianorum Latinorum* 1:273; John Chrysostom, *Homily* 36 *in 1 Cor. 14:33*, in *Patrologia Graeca* 61:315; *Constitutiones apostolicae* 2.57.6, in *Sources Chrétiennes* 320, 329, 336; *Testamentum Domini* 2.11.22, ed. Grant Sperry-White (Cambridge, UK: Grove Books Ltd., 1991); and Pliny the Younger, *Epistula* 10.96, in *Complete Letters*, trans. P. G. Walsh (New York: Oxford University Press, 2009).

33. On a related note, Everett Ferguson records that "one report attributed the introduction of antiphonal singing to Ignatius of Antioch (Socrates, *H.E.* 6.8), but other testimony placed its introduction in Antioch at the middle of the fourth century (Theodoret, *H.E.* 2.19)." *Encyclopedia of Early Christianity*, s.v. "Eucharist" (by Everett Ferguson). See also Victor Saxer, *Vie liturgique et quotidienne Carthage vers le milièu du IIIe siècle* (Vatican City: Pontificio Istituto di Archeologia Cristiana, 1969), 220.

34. See Klaus-Peter Jörns, "Proclamation und Akklamation: Die antiphonische Grundordnung des frühchristlichen Gottesdienstes nac der Johannesoffenbarun," in *Liturgie und Dichtung*, vol. 1 (St. Ottilien: EOS Verlag, 1983), passim.

dominantly vocal and monodic.[35] We hear of "psalms, hymns, and spiritual canticles" in the New Testament (Eph 5:18). These are not distinct musical genres or forms but a variety of musical forms in use in the first century—a broad range of music that was characteristically text-centered, often popular, probably similar in structure to the Davidic psalms and Old Testament canticles, but usually explicitly christological and newly composed.

A desire to define themselves over and against the Jewish tradition meant that early Christians tended to avoid the direct incorporation of the Davidic psalms into their worship.[36] It is not until around AD 200 that there is explicit evidence of the use of these psalms in Christian liturgy, and only in the early third century does the Christian reappropriation of these psalms as a core set of musical texts begin.[37] Later in the third century, as Edward Foley notes, "patterns for their usage develop and clarify."[38]

Musical expression was ever present in and central to religion and culture in the Mediterranean region in the first century. The term "worship music" in this early Christian context does not refer to what would be called music or songs today, but rather what Foley calls "the aural aspect of that cult"[39]—except perhaps for newly composed

---

35. *Encyclopedia of Early Christianity*, s.v. "Music." Quasten states that "the primitive Church rejected all heterophony and polyphony." Quasten, *Music in Pagan and Christian Antiquity*, 66–67. See also ibid., 72.

36. *Grove Online*, s.v. "Christian Church, Music of the Early." See also Fassler and Jeffery, "Christian Liturgical Music," 85–86; Foley, *Foundations of Christian Music*, 59; and Joncas, "Liturgy and Music," 289. "Worship" here can refer to a variety of practices, not only the celebration of the Eucharist.

37. See the apocryphal *Acts of Paul*, ed. Wilhelm Schubart and Carl Schmidt (Hamburg: J. J. Augustin, 1936), 50–51.

38. Foley, *Foundations of Christian Music*, 74. See, for example, Clement of Alexandria, *Stromata* 7.7.49, in *Ante-Nicene Fathers*, vol. 2., ed. Alexander Roberts, James Donaldson, and A. Cleveland Coxe, trans. William Wilson (Buffalo, NY: Christian Literature Publishing Co., 1885); *Apostolic Tradition* 25, in *The Apostolic Tradition: A Commentary*, ed. Paul F. Bradshaw, Maxwell Johnson, L. Edward Phillips, and Harold W. Attridge (Minneapolis: Augsburg Fortress Press, 2002); *Didascalia Apostolorum* 6.5, in *The Didascalia Apostolorum: An English Version with Introduction and Annotation*, ed. Alistair Stewart-Sykes (Turnhout: Brepols, 2009); and Tertullian, *On the Flesh of Christ* 20.3, in *Patrologia Latina* 2:786, and *On the Soul* 9, in *Patrologia Latina* 2:660.

39. Foley, *Foundations of Christian Music*, 84. It is worth noting that our contemporary Western society is a culture of seers—a visual culture. We believe what we see. The first Christians and their Roman and Jewish contemporaries,

popular hymns[40] and psalms. It was primarily simple, logogenic, and lacking musical form and preconceived melody—in other words, a variety of musical interjections within a stable yet flexible ritual structure. Indeed, there were no defined roles for musical specialists in early Christian communities—no cantors, psalmists, and so on.[41] From the beginning through the early Middle Ages, Christian singing was a collection of musically and geographically diverse oral traditions. As James McKinnon says, "variety might very well have been its single most constant quality."[42]

TERMINUS POST QUEM AND ANTE QUEM FOR THE ORIGIN OF A GREGORIAN PROPER CHANT TRADITION AT MASS

The Toleration and Adoption of Christianity in the Roman Empire

In the fourth century, a monumental and irreversible transition takes place in the history of the liturgy, which signals the beginnings of what would become a unified and specifically Roman Rite. The Edict of Toleration (AD 311), Emperor Constantine's conversion to Christianity (AD 312), the Edict of Milan (AD 313), and the Emperor Theodosius's declaration of Christianity as the official religion of the Roman Empire (AD 380)[43] were catalysts for this transition in that they thrust Christianity into the center of the public sphere as the *cultus publicus*. Larger crowds for the Sunday Eucharist and for other liturgical and paraliturgical gatherings required larger church buildings. In Rome, the standard liturgical space came to be the long, rectangular public building called a basilica. Imperial privileges for bishops meant that some of the ceremonial that surrounded Roman

---

however, "lived in a world where hearing was believing" (ibid., 5). Categories that we would employ today, "such as distinctions between [singing] and speech—are anachronistic frameworks that the ancients did not employ" (ibid.). See also ibid., 18–25; and Paul Achtemeier, "*Omne Verbum Sonat*: The New Testament and the Oral Environment of Late Western Antiquity," *Journal of Biblical Literature* 109:1 (Spring 1990):12

40. For the earliest extant physical evidence of a Christian song, see A. W. J. Holleman, "The Oxyrhynchus Papyrus 1786 and the Relationship between Ancient Greek and Early Christian Music," *Vigiliae Christianae* 26 (1972): 1–17.

41. Foley, *Foundations of Christian Music*, 84.

42. *Grove Online*, s.v. "Christian Church, Music of the Early."

43. Logan, *History of the Church in the Middle Ages*, 9.

dignitaries began to surround the episcopal role of the liturgical president as well.[44]

These fourth-century developments show forth a trend toward elaboration, formalization, and imperialization in Roman liturgy.[45] The elaboration of Christian ceremonial through the adoption of elements of the imperial Roman ritual, the new basilica setting of many liturgical celebrations, and the development of stational liturgy created an environment in which the development of a formal entrance ritual seems inevitable.[46] The shape of the building created, first, the potential for long processional routes[47] from the entrance or sacristy

44. Charles Pietri asserts that "court ritual inspired a whole symbolism of gesture." Pietri, "Liturgy, Culture and Society: The Example of Rome at the End of the Ancient World (Fourth–Fifth Centuries)," *Concilium 162* (1983): 44.

45. See Fassler and Jeffery, "Christian Liturgical Music," 87.

46. The Eucharist would also have been celebrated in other types of worship spaces. The most prominent spaces, however, were basilicas, and thus the basilica space was the most likely to have influenced the structure and content of the official liturgy. For the most substantial studies on early Christian worship spaces, see Richard Krautheimer, *Early Christian and Byzantine Architecture*, 4th ed. (New Haven, CT, and London: Yale University Press, 1986); Krautheimer, *Rome: Profile of a City, 312–1308* (1983; repr., Princeton, NJ: Princeton University Press, 2000); Krautheimer et al., *Corpus basilicarum Christianarum Romae: The Early Christian Basilicas of Rome (IV–IX Centuries)* (Vatican City: Pontificio Istituto di Archeologia Cristiana, 1937–1977); L. Michael White, *The Social Origins of Christian Architecture*, vol. 1: *Building God's House in the Roman World: Architectural Adaptation Among Pagans, Jews, and Christians* (repr. of 1990 edition, Baltimore: Johns Hopkins University Press), vol. 2: *Texts and Monuments for the Christian Domus Ecclesiae in Its Environment* (Valley Forge, PA: Trinity Press International, 1997); and *Encyclopedia of Early Christianity*, s.vv. "Architecture," "House Church" (by L. Michael White).

47. The earliest Christian worship spaces, in contrast, facilitated gathering more so than processing. At the outset, most of the earliest Christians would have gathered in spaces owned by adherents to the new religious movement. The house church at Dura-Europos is the most famous example. See Foley, *Foundations of Christian Music*, 71, for a diagram of the building. See also Snyder, *Ante-Pacem*, 5–21. It is important to exercise caution, however, when implying that the structure of a worship space directly correlates to the rites enacted therein. "In theory, Christian worship could take place in any room sheltered by walls and a roof, or even in the open air. The connection of liturgy with a special structure is due to historical developments in Early Christianity. In the course of time this structure acquired the status of a sacred place, but from the liturgical point of view it was nothing more than a monumental shell." Sibile De Blauuw, "Architecture and Liturgy in the Late Antique and the Middle Ages: Traditions and Trends in Modern Scholarship," *Archiv für Liturgiewissenschaft* 33 (1991): 31.

to the sanctuary, and, second, what McKinnon calls a "new acoustical environment," which would have required certain characteristics of music sung therein.[48]

The Psalmodic Movement and the Selective Singing of Psalms

Two other crucial developments occurred during this period, in terms of the eventual development of the proper chants of the Mass: the "psalmodic movement" and the selective singing of psalms. In the fourth century, an unprecedented wave of enthusiasm for the Davidic psalms swept across the church.[49] The useful point in this regard is

---

Similarly, Pietri warns, "We should not try to establish too close a connection between architecture and ritual. It is not possible to distinguish in the building of the Episcopal basilica the influence of clergy with a clear programme and that of the architects creating a synthesis out of diverse elements in which technical constraints were as important as the desire to use a grandiose imperial language for this monument. Nevertheless, such a building did mark out a new space for the liturgy. It made possible processions." Pietri, "Liturgy, Culture and Society," 38.

48. *Grove Online*, s.v. "Christian Church, Music of the Early." Pietri elaborates: "From the beginning of the fourth century, the liturgy had received a new setting in which to mount its rites and assemble its people in prayer. The building of this church [the Lateran Basilica] transformed the setting of the liturgy. It gave it a permanent establishment, capable of containing for the first time in Rome the people gathered round their bishop in a single collective act of prayer. The monumentalism of the liturgical setting changed the style of worship." Pietri, "Liturgy, Culture and Society," 38.

49. See James W. McKinnon, "Desert Monasticism and the Later Fourth-Century Psalmodic Movement," *Music & Letters* 75:4 (November 1994): 505–521. Jeffery argues that "the psalmodic movement was motivated not only by monastic practices, but by a monastic way of reading the psalms." Peter Jeffery, "Monastic Reading and the Emerging Roman Chant Repertory," in *Western Plainchant in the First Millennium: Studies in the Medieval Liturgy and Its Music*, ed. Sean Gallagher et al. (Burlington, VT: Ashgate, 2003), 59. "While the reading and singing of the psalms probably had a place in Christian worship from the beginning, the rise of monasticism in the fourth century provoked a renewed interest in psalm-singing, at first in the East, but spreading to the West by the 380s" (ibid., 82). For an effective critique of McKinnon's thesis in this article, see Joseph Dyer, "The Desert, the City and Psalmody in the Late Fourth Century," in *Western Plainchant in the First Millennium: Studies in the Medieval Liturgy and Its Music*, ed. Sean Gallagher et al. (Burlington, VT: Ashgate, 2003), 11–44. McKinnon locates the source of the enthusiasm for the psalms with the rise of desert monasticism in the later fourth century. Dyer disagrees and believes one must look to the urban communities of ascetics that existed at that time for the origins of the psalmodic movement.

that this movement occurred in the later fourth century and that this movement instigated the inclusion of new psalmodic elements in the liturgy. It is certain that by this time psalms, sung responsorially,[50] were already part of the Mass at the gradual and communion.[51] This enthusiasm also resulted in the frequent use of the psalms at vigil services.[52] These popular psalmodic vigils could have led to a type of "entrance" or "opening" song practice, which would have developed to connect the psalmodic vigil to the subsequent celebration of the Mass.[53]

Through this wave of enthusiasm, it is as if the singing of Davidic psalms found a place in the eucharistic liturgy at every possible point—first, at the gradual, then at the communion, and then perhaps at the entrance and offertory.[54] Indeed, transitional points during the liturgy like the entrance, offertory, and communion processions are perfectly suited to this phenomenon of psalmodic elaboration.[55] One

50. Jeffery, "Monastic Reading," 45. "Responsorially" means that the psalm verses were sung by a soloist, and after each verse the congregation responded with an antiphon or refrain. The person singing the gradual would more accurately be called a lector or a reader rather than a cantor. He was typically an adolescent boy rather than an adult professional singer. See James W. McKinnon, "Lector Chant vs. Schola Chant: A Question of Historical Plausibility," in *Labore fratres in unum*, ed. David Hiley (Hildesheim: Georg Olms Verlag, 1995), 201–11.

51. McKinnon, "Desert Monasticism," 519. The primitive gradual was a full-fledged reading rather than a psalm sung between readings. In support of this assertion, McKinnon states, "There is no ancient evidence, Jewish or Christian, that readings were customarily paired with complementary psalms." *Grove Online*, s.v. "Christian Church, Music of the Early." The primitive communion psalm probably predated the psalmodic movement and functioned more as a part of the Mass Ordinary than as a proper chant. The evidence suggests that Psalm 33:8 (*Gustate et videte*) was the psalm used at this point in the service from the earliest times. See *Grove Online*, s.v. "Christian Church, Music of the Early"; and McKinnon, "Desert Monasticism," 519.

52. McKinnon, "Desert Monasticism," 509. This use might predate the development of the gradual in the eucharistic liturgy (ibid.). See also Jeffery, "Monastic Reading," 45.

53. McKinnon, "Desert Monasticism," 513.

54. There are also examples of "ante-evangelio" and "post-evangelio" chants, which might have served as accompaniments to the procession with the gospel book to and from the ambo.

55. See Robert F. Taft, *Beyond East and West: Problems in Liturgical Understanding*, 2nd rev. enlarged ed. (Rome: Pontifical Oriental Institute, 1987), 168. According to Taft, the "action points" of the liturgy are the most likely candidates for ritual expansion (ibid.). And Baldovin notes that "the vacuum at the beginning

sees in the psalmodic movement the inspiration for and beginnings of the eventual development of the cycle of proper chants for the Mass. The development of the selective rather than continuous singing of the psalms in the embryonic cathedral Office, and later in the proper chants of the Mass, furthermore, reflects the conscious intervention and creativity of what would become in Rome the *schola cantorum*—a group of musical professionals capable of filling out the liturgical year with the vast corpus of liturgical chant that has come down to us.

The Incorporation of Litany and Acclamatory Forms in the West

The first clear evidence of the use of *Kyrie Eleison* as an acclamation in the liturgy is from the late fourth century in Jerusalem and Antioch.[56] In Rome its use became standard by the sixth century, perhaps the fifth.[57] Its adoption reveals a liturgical situation in which litany[58] and acclamatory forms, which are similar to the antiphonal form of the introit, were replacing other forms in the liturgy. Such forms are better matched to the circumstances of the fourth century (and later) than are earlier forms, such as forms involving silent prayer by the assembly. During this period large assemblies, large church buildings, and processions were becoming the norm.[59]

Liturgical Homogenization

There also began during the fourth century what Bradshaw calls a "liturgical homogenization" throughout the church.[60] Before this

---

of the Eucharistic liturgy was filled in by the addition of an entrance psalm." Baldovin, "Kyrie Eleison," 343. The tendency of ritual points of transition or ritual "vacuums" to be filled in with music is a phenomenon that has occurred in other religious traditions. See J. H. Kwabena Nketia, "Musical Interaction in Ritual Events," in *Music and the Experience of God*, ed. Mary Collins et al. (Edinburgh: T. & T. Clark, 1989), 111.

56. Baldovin, "Kyrie Eleison," 336. See also John Wilkinson, ed. and trans., *Egeria's Travels to the Holy Land: Newly Translated with Supporting Documents and Notes*, 3rd ed. (Warminster, England: Aris & Phillips, 1999), 143; and *Apostolic Constitutions* 8:6, 9.

57. See Baldovin, "Kyrie Eleison," 337.

58. As Baldovin says, "Litanies represent a developed form of [intercessory] prayer with acclamations or responses." Baldovin, "Kyrie Eleison," 336.

59. Ibid.

60. See Bradshaw, "Changing Face of Early Liturgy," 7–9; and Bradshaw, "The Homogenization of Christian Liturgy—Ancient and Modern," *Studia Liturgica* 26:1 (1996): 1–15.

time, variety had been the rule.[61] The reasons for this homogeniza-tion were many and complex, but primarily a concern for orthodoxy and orthopraxis.[62] The liturgical practices within larger cities and monasteries began to be taken up in less influential areas more so than before. Also, a degree of mutual influence occurred between these larger cities and monasteries. Roman processions at Mass, for example, including the entrance song, have ancestors in the East, as "all of the processional terminology—*antiphona, litania, Kyrie Eleison*—is taken from the Greek."[63] This trend toward incorporative

61. Bradshaw explains that there "tends to be *variety* between different groups and regions, and not *uniformity*; and that the large measure of agreement in liturgical practice that can be seen in late sources is more often the result of a conscious movement towards standardization that did not begin until the fourth century—and frequently only in the second half of that century—rather than the survival of an ancient way of doing things that all Christians shared from the beginning, although that is not to deny that there may well be at least some instances where the latter is the case." Bradshaw, "Homogenization of Christian Liturgy," 3. See also Bradshaw, *Eucharistic Origins*, 69–75.

62. See Bradshaw, "Homogenization of Christian Liturgy," 6–8. He cites a concern for orthodoxy in the face of heretical movements and the phenomenon of an increasingly mobile population, which resulted in extensive travel throughout the empire and the consequent exposure to different liturgical traditions. He states, "Any tendency to persist in what appeared to be idiosyncratic liturgical observance was likely to have been interpreted as a mark of heterodoxy" (ibid., 7). Another reason for the homogenization was an increasing openness to pagan ritual practices that came with Christianity's move into the center of the social and political sphere—"because the character of pagan religion was very similar throughout the Roman Empire, the nature of the Church's response [within the Empire] tended to be similar everywhere" (ibid., 8). See also Bradshaw, *Eucharistic Origins*, 139–57. It is possible that the development of Mass proper chants was related to a catechizing or didactic trend that began in the fourth century, which was contemporaneous with the expansion of the faith to a larger and generally less fervent and less well-informed population. See Bradshaw, *Eucharistic Origins*, 140–42.

63. Baldovin, "Kyrie Eleison," 343. This is not to assert an Eastern origin of Roman chant melodies or proper chant texts. According to Hucke, "None of the forms of Western chant can be traced back to Jewish liturgy or even to early Christian times. The forms of Western chant were developed in the West, even if they were sometimes stimulated from the Orient." Helmut Hucke, "Toward a New Historical View of Gregorian Chant," *Journal of the American Musicological Society* 33:3 (Autumn 1980): 439. While there have been many developments and new insights since 1980, for the most part Hucke's view still stands. See also Hucke, "Die Entwicklung des christlichen Kultgesangs zum Gregorianischen Gesang," *Römische Quartalschrift* XLVIII (1953): 152ff.

homogeneity continued through the eighth century. During these four centuries, many local chant traditions developed but then were eventually replaced, or at best absorbed, by the traditions of more influential places, especially those of Rome.[64] Early liturgical homogenization had to do with larger liturgical forms and structures, but during later centuries, the process involved specific prayer texts and chants, which eventually led to the hegemony of the Gregorian chant tradition in the West.

Early Christian Liturgical Language in the West

In Roman liturgical chant, we presume the use of the Latin language. Early Christians also sang in Greek and Syriac, however. Indeed, the language of the Roman Christians was Greek for some time.[65] Christians in the west of North Africa had spoken Latin from the earliest times,[66] but it was not until the third century that it became a lingua franca in the Roman West. Indeed, Clement of Rome and Justin Martyr wrote in Greek and quoted a Greek Bible in the mid-first and mid-second centuries, respectively.[67] By the end of the

64. Peter Jeffery explains that "between about the fourth and the eighth centuries A.D., each major city or region seems to have developed its own local repertory of texts and melodies, although some common material circulated widely (with variations), and a few texts were known almost everywhere. Gradually, internal and external pressures provoked movements toward uniformity, and the traditions of the more influential centers began to replace or merge with some of the weaker ones. . . . Most [chant traditions] did not develop music notation, and only some adopted the theory of the eight Byzantine modes. By about the eighth century [the other major chant traditions of the Latin West] had begun to lose ground to the more prestigious liturgy and chant associated with the city of Rome. The central importance of Rome increased as missionaries pressed the boundaries of the Latin world outward into the lands of the Anglo-Saxons, the Germans and the Scandinavians, the Balts and the West Slavs, and the Finns and the Magyars, establishing Roman-derived liturgies among each of these peoples. As in the East, the increasingly irresistible processes of standardization and centralization led to, and were furthered by, the emergence of written collections of chant texts, the rise of liturgical rule books, the invention of music notation, and the adoption/translation of Greek music theory and the Greek modal system." Jeffery, *Re-Envisioning Past Musical Cultures: Ethnomusicology in the Study of Gregorian Chant* (Chicago and London: University of Chicago Press, 1992), 6–7.

65. *Grove Online*, s.v. "Christian Church, Music of the Early."

66. Ibid.

67. G. G. Willis, *A History of Early Roman Liturgy to the Death of Pope Gregory the Great* (London: Henry Bradshaw Society, 1994), 20–21.

fourth century, however, Ambrose quoted an early form of the Latin Roman Canon in *De sacramentis*,[68] and by the late second century, some Christians in Rome were using a Latin Bible.[69] The transition to Latin as the primary liturgical language was gradual, but it was nearly complete by the late fourth century. It was probably finalized during the reign of Pope Damasus (366–84), who was involved in Jerome's efforts at the translation of the Bible into Latin.[70]

The Transition from Psalms as Readings to Psalms as Chant

In the mid-fifth century, a transition began that was critically important to the eventual development of the entrance song in the Roman Rite. During this period, the way of thinking about the psalms in relation to Christian life and worship changed. The result is that by the late sixth century the rendition of psalms in the liturgy had become chant, which Peter Jeffery notes is "a category quite separate from the liturgical readings."[71] This transition from psalms as readings to psalms as chant was not sudden but based in the increasing influence of monastic liturgical practices.[72] It was only during and

---

68. See Ambrose, *De sacramentis* 55, 57, in *Patrologia Latina* 16.417–62. Willis notes that "Some twenty years earlier the Eucharistic Prayer at Rome is cited in Greek by an African writer, Marius Victorinus, writing in Latin at Rome." Willis, *History of Early Roman Liturgy*, 21.

69. Willis, *History of Early Roman Liturgy*, 20–21.

70. Ibid., 22. Massey Shepherd explains that "Damasus had a major role in the foundation of the Latin liturgy in the Roman Church, which reached a decisive settlement, after two centuries of development, enrichment, and experiment, in the work of Pope Gregory the Great (590–604). This is not to say that there was no Latin rite in Rome before Damasus. Certainly there were congregations using a Latin liturgy for at least a century before his pontificate, if not as early as the second century. But the Latin rite of Rome, as it came to be shaped in the fifth and sixth centuries, cannot be traced prior to his time." Shepherd, "The Liturgical Reform of Damasus I," in *Kyriakon: Festschrift Johannes Quasten*, ed. Patrick Granfield and Josef A. Jungmann, vol. 2 (Aschendorff: Münster Westfalen, 1970): 847–48.

71. Jeffery, "Monastic Reading," 82.

72. Ibid., 53. Here, Jeffery suggests that "we must ask what the promoters and practitioners of psalmody in the fourth century and later thought its essential purposes were. Following their testimony across the centuries, we can observe changing approaches to the reading of texts that take us through a series of dichotomies: (1) An original tension between 'psalm as reading' and 'psalm as song' grew into an exegetical confrontation, as an early tradition of studying the psalms as allegorical 'history' conflicted with a monastic approach to the psalm

after this transition that one would expect to see the development of complex liturgical chants based upon the Davidic psalms.[73]

A Fixed Corpus of Presidential Prayers and the Addition of Thursdays in Lent to the Liturgical Year

It may be the case, as some scholars believe, that the presidential prayers at Mass—the *Collecta, Super oblata,* and *Post communionem*—function as conclusions to the entrance, offertory, and communion processions, respectively.[74] If so, then it is significant that the majority of liturgical scholars agree that in Rome the annual cycles of proper presidential prayers and readings at Mass did not become fixed until the middle of the seventh century.[75] Following this line of thought, it could be the case that the corpus of proper chants was not fixed until around the mid-seventh century either.

Furthermore, it is clear that the cycle of proper chants for Lent was fixed before the Thursdays of Lent became days for liturgical celebration and were thus assigned chants of their own.[76] Since Gregory II (715–31) added the Thursdays of Lent to the liturgical year,[77] it must be the case that the proper chants of the Mass were fixed in Rome sometime before Pope Gregory made this change. The development of a fixed corpus of presidential prayers and the addition of Thursdays to Lent are not interdependent, but together they suggest that

---

as an ethical 'mirror' reflecting the individual soul. (2) After centuries of pressure from the Christian intelligentsia, the old pedagogy based on Homer, Vergil and the literature of classical antiquity gave way to a new Christian curriculum, in which the Psalter was the first text used to teach beginning readers. (3) This led to a situation in which learning to read the psalms became an essential part of monastic and clerical formation, with the result that the Psalter was perceived as a model or training ground for individual prayer. Psalmody became an activity distinct from liturgical reading, and sermons no longer made reference to the psalm texts" (ibid.).

73. László Dobszy, "Concerning a Chronology for Chant," in *Western Plainchant in the First Millennium: Studies in the Medieval Liturgy and Its Music,* ed. Sean Gallagher et al. (Burlington, VT: Ashgate, 2003), 225. Complicated chants are not necessarily descendants of simpler chants, however, "for throughout history many things develop in the opposite direction." Jeffery, *Re-Envisioning Past Musical Cultures,* 114.

74. Cobb, "Liturgy of the Word," 224–25.

75. *Grove Online,* s.v. "Mass (I)," http://www.grovemusic.com/ (accessed February 10, 2005) (by James W. McKinnon).

76. Ibid.

77. Ibid.

the proper chant tradition of the Roman Rite, including the introit, became fixed at some point between the mid-seventh century and early eighth century.

A cautious interpretation of the evidence, admitting the possibility that the development of the presidential prayers and proper chants are not related, does not allow for such specificity, however. The development of the proper chants certainly began after the late fourth century, and the chants were part of the Roman Rite by at least the early eighth century. Nevertheless, one would not expect the proper chants to have developed until after the late sixth century, since the transition from psalms as readings to psalms as chant was not complete until then.[78]

78. James McKinnon hypothesized that the Roman Mass proper was created in one grand effort in the late seventh century by the Roman Schola Cantorum. See McKinnon, *Advent Project*, passim. His article "Festival, Text and Melody: Chronological Stages in the Life of Chant?" in *Chant and Its Peripheries: Essays in Honour of Terence Bailey*, ed. Bryan Gillingham and Paul Merkley (Ottawa: Institute of Medieval Music, 1998): 1–11, gives an earlier version of the hypothesis. Edward Foley has called the book "both an engaging narrative and an encyclopedic reference work." *Theological Studies* 63:1 (March 2002): 197–98. The book seems to be an effort to heed the call of Peter Jeffery to create imaginative hypotheses of the early history of chant made in his 1992 book *Re-Envisioning Past Musical Cultures*. Some notable chant scholars, including Ruth Steiner, find McKinnon's hypothesis fascinating but unconvincing. See, for example, Peter Jeffery's review in the *Journal of the American Musicological Society* 56:1 (Spring 2003): 169–79. Given the controversial nature of McKinnon's theory, we will leave it aside in this study. If there was a single grand effort to create the Roman Mass proper, the question remains as to whether it was more an effort of compilation (the gathering together and filling out of a preexisting chant corpus) or of creativity (the focused and calculated creation of the entire proper).

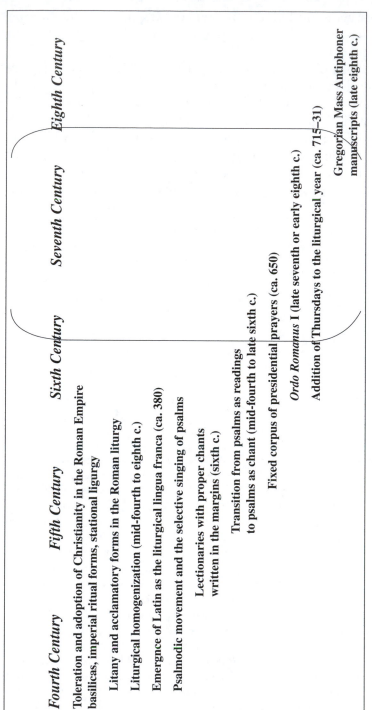

Figure 2. *Terminus post quem* and *ante quem* for the origin of a Gregorian proper chant tradition at Mass.

The Fully Developed Roman Rite Introit

Example 1. Twelfth-century manuscript excerpt of the introit *Nos autem gloriari* for the Holy Thursday Evening Mass of the Lord's Supper.[79]

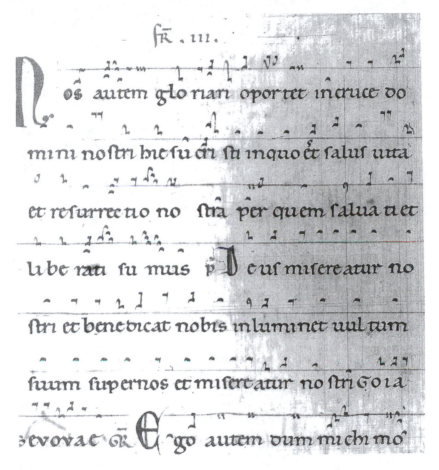

79. Rome Biblioteca Vaticana Rossiano 231. Twelfth-century Gradual from northern Italy. Dry-point staff with two colored lines. 148 fols. Dom Mocquereau Collection, Catholic University of America, Washington, DC. Used by permission.

Example 2. Sixteenth-century manuscript excerpt of the introit *Nos autem gloriari* for the Holy Thursday Evening Mass of the Lord's Supper.[80]

80. Perkins 4, folio 1, recto and verso, Gradual S.XVI © Ella Strong Denison Library, Scripps College. Used by permission.

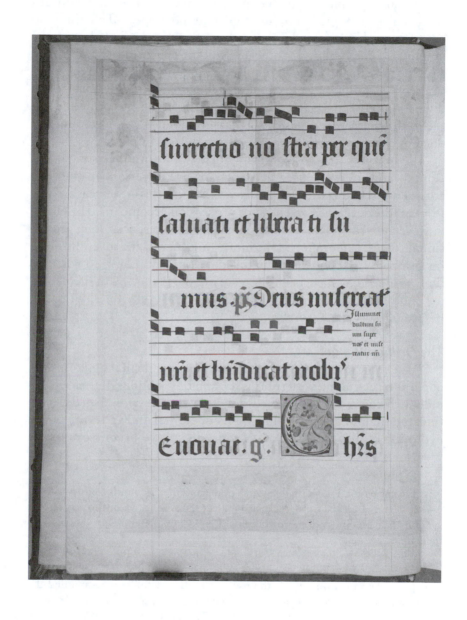

The introit chants of the Gregorian[81] and Old Roman traditions consist of a neumatic[82] antiphon sung and then repeated after a number of sung psalm verses. The number of verses depended upon the amount of time required for the entry of the clergy into the presbyterium or sanctuary. Once the required number of verses and the repetition of the antiphon were concluded, the doxology was sung—often divided into two parts (*Gloria Patri* and *Sicut erat*) by a repetition of the antiphon. A *versus ad repetendum* sometimes followed after the doxology and before the final repetition of the antiphon.

The introit is the most enduring form of the entrance song in the Roman liturgy. While its precise origins are uncertain—sometime between the late sixth and late seventh centuries—the reasons the Roman Rite developed an entrance procession accompanied by chant, however, are easy to understand.[83] Large worship spaces, long processional routes, elaboration of the liturgy in general, and an enthusiasm for psalmody all contributed to this development. Lamb conjectures that "psalms may have been sung during the gathering of the people . . . and perhaps the formal introit was at last only the final psalm before the service of worship."[84]

The *Ordines Romani*

The *Ordines Romani*[85] are liturgical documents that contain texts of certain rites along with rubrics for and descriptions of their enactment, which are often extremely detailed. At their core, they describe the stational and pontifical liturgies of Rome, and in terms of the evolution of liturgical books, they are primitive precursors to the

---

81. The earliest notated manuscripts date from the late ninth century.

82. "Neumatic" describes liturgical chant settings with two or three notes per syllable. Such chants are more complex than syllabic chants, but less so than melismatic chants.

83. Adrian Fortescue, *The Mass: A Study of the Roman Liturgy* (London: Longmans, Green & Co., 1937), 217. Fortescue conjectures that "it is perhaps safest to explain the introit merely as the psalm which inevitably accompanied the entering procession as soon as it was looked upon as a procession at all" (ibid.).

84. Lamb, *Psalms in Christian Worship*, 86. Lamb cautions, however, that while "it would seem that ceremonial considerations stimulated the development of the repertory . . . evidence for their origins and development is sparse" (ibid.).

85. For more on the *Ordines Romani*, see Michel Andrieu, *Les Ordines Romani du haut moyen âge*, vol. 2 (Louvain: Spicilegium Sacrum Lovaniense, 1948), XVII–XLIX; Palazzo, *History of Liturgical Books*, 175–85; and C. Vogel, *Medieval Liturgy*, 135–55.

Pontificale so-called.[86] All the extant manuscripts were copied in German and Frankish lands.[87]

The oldest description of the introit that has survived appears in Ordo I, the earliest version of which dates from the late seventh to early eighth century.[88] It is the only one of the *ordines* that in its earliest recension describes a purely Roman practice. It served as the starting point for many of the other *ordines*, several of which also describe the introit. While it is clear that the descriptions in the *Ordines Romani* reflect what is basically a common practice that had been transported north from Rome—antiphons sung with intervening psalm verses during the entrance procession at Mass—there do seem to be significant differences among them. It is especially the practice after the singing of the *Gloria Patri* that seems to vary in the different *ordines*.[89] The basic form, nevertheless, is clearly antiphon–psalm–doxology–antiphon, with exceptions for the number of psalm verses used, the repetition of the antiphon between psalm verses, the splitting of the doxology into two parts, and the inclusion of *versus ad repetendum*. The *versus ad repetendum*, perhaps a Frankish addition to the Roman practice,[90] were psalm verses sung after the end of the doxology but before the concluding antiphon.[91]

86. Palazzo, *History of Liturgical Books*, 178, 181, 195–99.

87. Tietze, *Hymn Introits*, 260.

88. Andrieu, *Ordines Romani*, 2:38–51. See also Palazzo, *A History of Liturgical Books*, 179; Tietze, *Hymn Introits*, 260–61; and Hiley, *Western Plainchant*, 496.

89. For example, Steiner notes that in Ordo I "the procedure after the singing of the Gloria Patri is not wholly clear: it describes the pontiff praying before the altar during the singing of the Gloria 'until the repetition of the *versus*.'" *New Grove*, s.v. "Introit (i)." See also Metzinger, "Liturgical Function of the Entrance Song," 13–14; and Willis, *History of the Early Roman Liturgy*, 72–77.

90. Tietze, *Hymn Introits*, 21. See also Hiley, *Western Plainchant*, 109. He states, "These *versus ad repetendum* appear in both the earliest Frankish sources and the Old Roman ones, also for the communion."

91. See Dyer, "Introit and Communion Psalmody," 110. Metzinger explains that "some MSS give a second introit verse, often specified as 'versus ad repetendum,' that is sung before the repetition of the antiphon. This is taken from the same psalm as the introit verse, often but not always, the next verse of the psalm. There are examples of this verse being chosen apparently because its text makes a good introduction to the repetition of the antiphon. The choice of the verse for the 'versus ad repetendum' varies considerably from MS to MS, suggesting that the use of a special verse for repetition is not an old practice." Metzinger, "Liturgical Function of the Entrance Song," 32–33. Steiner concurs, saying, "A number of manuscripts give supplementary verses, sometimes explicitly called *versus ad*

While the record preserved in the *Ordines Romani* does reflect some true regional variations in the structure of the introit at Mass, one must take into account the possibility that some of these variations are the result of more and less successful descriptions of a common practice, rather than accounts of significant differences.[92] *Ordo* IV, for example, is not a transcription of any particular liturgical celebration. Rather, as Vogel points out, it is "a deliberate adaptation of Ordo I to Frankish conditions. The author was trying to establish the Roman Rite in Gaul by means of a compromise with prevailing Frankish customs."[93] And he goes so far as to call Ordo XV—also a Frankish recension of Ordo I along with some other sources—a "work of propaganda."[94] Its purpose was to promote liturgical uniformity through the Romanization of the varied forms of the liturgy in use at the time in the Frankish lands. The author might never have even been to Rome.[95]

The *Ordines Romani* record much about the liturgy, but the concern here is with their descriptions of the introit. The table below, then, helps get to the point.[96] It outlines the structure of the introit in the relevant *ordines*. The paragraph numbers of the *ordines* are from Andrieu.

---

repetendum, for introits, and also for communions; but the sources frequently disagree as to the choice of the verse, and . . . they would not disagree if the practice were very old." *New Grove*, s.v. "Introit (i)."

92. Dyer suggests that "several of the ordines outline in greater or lesser detail how the introit and communion chants were sung, from which an idea of their complete form can be extrapolated." Dyer, "Introit and Communion Psalmody," 115. Tietze, on the other hand, considers Ordo XV a "highly gallicanized" version of Ordo I and says it bears "little resemblance" to the introit as described in Ordo I. Tietze, *Hymn Introits*, 21.

93. C. Vogel, *Medieval Liturgy*, 161.

94. Ibid., 153.

95. Ibid. See also Tietze, *Hymn Introits*, 21.

96. The design of this table is adapted from Dyer, "Introit and Communion Psalmody," 115–16. Others of the *Ordines Romani* also mention the introit, but they provide no significant details of its enactment.

Table 1. The Introit as Described in the *Ordines Romani.*[97]

Ordo I: (37, 40), 44, 50–52[97] (late 7th to early 8th c., Roman)	A	V1 [A? V2 A? V3 A? . . .] [A]	G	[A?]	S	[A?]	[VR?]	A
Ordo IV: 14–20[98] (late 8th c., Romano-Frankish)	[A]	[V1] [A? V2 A? V3 A? . . .] [A]	G	[A?]	S	[A]	VR	A
Ordo V: 14, 18, 21, 22 + **VI:** 22[99] (late 9th c., Romano-Germanic)	A	[V1] [A? V2 A? V3 A? . . .] [A]	G	[A?]	S	[A?]	[VR?]	[A]
Ordo XV: 13, 15[100] (late 8th c., Romano-Frankish)	A	V1 [A? V2 A? V3 A? . . .] [A]	G	[A?]	S	[A]	VR	[A]
Ordo XV: 122[101]	A	V1 [A? V2? A? V3? A? . . .] A	G	A	S	A	VR	A

97. A = antiphon, V1 = first psalm verse, V2/V3 = additional psalm verses, G = *Gloria Patri* (first half of the doxology), S = *Sicut erat* (second half of the doxology), VR = *versus ad repetendum*. Brackets indicate either elements that probably were part of the structure but are not mentioned in the text, or elements that might or might not have been part of the structure, depending upon one's reading of the text and understanding of the nature of the sources. The latter are distinguished with a question mark.

98. For the text, see Andrieu, *Ordines Romani*, 2:79–82. In vol. 1 Andrieu provides information on the manuscripts and editions of each of the *ordines*. In the remaining volumes he provides substantial background studies on each of them, which appear before his transcription of each text. See also Tietze, *Hymn Introits*, 260–63; and C. Vogel, *Medieval Liturgy*, 155–60.

99. For the text, see Andrieu, *Ordines Romani*, 2:159. See also Tietze, *Hymn Introits*, 263; and C. Vogel, *Medieval Liturgy*, 160–61.

100. For the text, see Andrieu, *Ordines Romani*, 2:211–213, 244. See also Tietze, *Hymn Introits*, 264; and C. Vogel, *Medieval Liturgy*, 161–62. Ordo VI is basically a poor synopsis of Ordo I. Its description of the introit is nearly identical to that of Ordo V, except that one finds in it a repetition of the antiphon after the doxology. See Vogel, *Medieval Liturgy*, 162; Tietze, *Hymn Introits*, 264; and especially Andrieu, *Ordines Romani*, 231–38.

101. For the text, see Andrieu, *Ordines Romani*, 3:97–98. See also Tietze, *Hymn Introits*, 264–66; and C. Vogel, *Medieval Liturgy*, 168.

102. For the text, see Andrieu, *Ordines Romani*, 3:120.

Ordo XVII: 18, 19, 25, 28[102] (late 8th c., Romano-Frankish)	A	V1 [A? V2? A? V3? A? . . .] [A]	G	[A?]	S	[A]	VR	A
Ordo XXXV: 1[103] (late 10th to early 11th c., Romano-Germanic)	A	V1 [A? V2 A? V3 A? . . .] [A]	G	[A?]	S	[A?]	[VR?]	[A]

The conclusions one derives from these manuscripts regarding the structure of the introit depends primarily upon one's view of the *ordines* as a whole. Do they represent a wide variety of substantial Frankish and German adaptations of the Roman practice, or do they represent what is basically a common practice that has been described more successfully in some of the *ordines* and less so in others?

In Ordo I, for example, what the text says for certain is that an antiphon is sung ("Et mox incipit prior scolae antiphonam ad introitum"[105]), presumably followed by psalm verses since earlier in the document the choir is asked who will sing the psalm ("Quis psallit?"[106]), and they answer that they will ("Ille et Ille"[107]). As the pope approaches the altar, the choir begins singing the *Gloria Patri* and then the *Sicut erat*, which are followed by a repetition of the antiphon.[108] The structure, then, is A–V1–V2–V3 . . . –GS–A.[109] But the text is not perfectly clear. Its description of the singing of the *Gloria*

103. For the text, see Andrieu, *Ordines Romani*, 3:178. See also Tietze, *Hymn Introits*, 266; and C. Vogel, *Medieval Liturgy*, 168–69.

104. For the text, see Andrieu, *Ordines Romani*, 4:73. See also Tietze, *Hymn Introits*, 267; and C. Vogel, *Medieval Liturgy*, 176.

105. Ordo I, no. 44.

106. Ibid., no. 37.

107. Ibid., no. 37.

108. Ibid., nos. 50–52.

109. This agrees with Tietze's analysis. See Tietze, *Hymn Introits*, 262. Based on his own analysis of the *Ordines Romani*, Peter Jeffery concludes that "the pope's entrance procession was marked by the Introit. The litany was sung upon arrival at the altar area, where the confession would be in a Roman basilica. The candles and other processional paraphernalia were put in their places. The pope intoned the Gloria, then greeted the people and said the collect." Peter Jeffery, "The Meanings and Functions of *Kyrie Eleison*," 192–93. He also suggests that "the general practice seems to have been that the Introit antiphon specifically accompanied the movements of the pope, whereas the litany or the *Kyrie* marked the arrival of the entire procession, though it was begun at the Pope's signal. As a

Patri and *Sicut erat* allows for the possibility that these two parts of the doxology were sung separately and that the antiphon was sung in between them, even though no such antiphon is mentioned in the text:[110] "Et respiciens ad priorem scolae annuit ei ut dicat *Gloriam*; et prior scolae inclinat se pontifici et inponit. Quartus vero scolae praecedit ante pontificem, ut ponat oratorium ante altare; et accedens pontifex orat super ipsum usque ad repetitionem versus [Ordo I, no. 50]. Nam diaconi surgunt quando dicit: *Sicut erat*, ut salutent altaris latera, prius duo et duo vicissim redeuntes ad pontificem. Et surgens pontifex osculat evangelia et altare et accedit ad sedem et stat versus ad orientem [Ordo I, no. 51]. Scola vero, finita antiphona, inponit *Kyrie eleison* [Ordo I, no. 52]." One might also interpret the text to describe a *versus ad repetendum* following the doxology.[111] Alternatively, then, the structure might have been: A–V1–V2–V3 . . . followed by either G–A–S–A–VR–A or GS–VR–A.[112] Such a structure might indeed make sense, given its similarity to the fuller description of the introit in Ordo XV (see table 1).

Finally, the question remains as to whether the antiphon was repeated after each verse of the psalm. Indeed, Jungmann, while not tending toward such a view, does admit it as a possibility.[113] And McKinnon, certainly one of the world's experts on the proper chants of the Mass, sees the repetition of the antiphon as a distinct

---

result the two do not always occur in a fixed order; the litany might precede the Introit, but if it did it was not restarted after the Introit" (ibid., 188).

110. See Dyer, "Introit and Communion Psalmody," 116.

111. See ibid. It is possible the text indicates that the psalm was repeated after the *Gloria Patri* and before the *Sicut erat*, but this is quite unlikely, since no such practice is found anywhere else in the *Ordines Romani* or in any other source. Tietze interprets *ad repetitionem versus* to refer to the antiphon sung after the entire doxology and not to any *versus ad repetendum*. One might question this interpretation, however, because the antiphon is mentioned again in no. 52. In addition, he takes *nam* (*Nam diaconi surgunt* . . .) to mean "meanwhile," and argues thereby that the *Gloria Patri* and *Sicut erat* had no intervening antiphon. Tietze, *Hymn Introits*, 262.

112. For the most part, this structure agrees with Dyer's analysis. See Dyer, "Introit and Communion Psalmody," 116.

113. He states, "Whether it was also repeated after each single verse of the psalm cannot be determined so far as the city of Rome itself is concerned." Jungmann, *Mass of the Roman Rite*, 1:323. See also ibid., 1:323n13. He also notes that in some Frankish MSS "we come upon [the] extension of the introit through the practice . . . of repeating the antiphon after each verse of the psalm" (ibid., 1:325).

possibility.[114] In truth, except for Ordo XV, the *Ordines Romani* never tell of the repetition of the antiphon after the psalm. While Ordo XV's account only explicitly indicates the singing of one psalm verse (other than the *versus ad repetendum* at the end), Dyer presumes more verses would have been sung if necessary to accompany the presider to the presbyterium.[115] If this is the case, the antiphon was almost certainly sung after each psalm verse because Ordo XV directs that the antiphon should be sung after the first verse. Perhaps the strongest argument for the repetition of the antiphon lies in the melodic and modal relationship of the antiphon to the psalm tones to which the verses and doxology were sung. The conclusion of the tone seems to lead back to the melody of the antiphon rather than to a repetition of the tone (see examples 1 and 2 above). Melodically, the antiphon's mode establishes which tone will be used for the psalm. The tone's conclusion, Huglo explains, "is chosen with the first notes of the antiphon in mind," and "the psalm tone used for the recitation of the psalm itself is often musically incomplete without the antiphon."[116]

The question as to whether the antiphon was repeated after the psalm verses is an important one, even if it cannot be definitively answered. If it is not repeated, the psalm is primary, with the antiphon sung only at the beginning and at the end of the introit. If it is repeated, the antiphon is primary, sung at the beginning of the introit, then repeated after each psalm verse and after both the *Gloria Patri*

114. James W. McKinnon, ed., *Antiquity and the Middle Ages: From Ancient Greece to the 15th Century* (Englewood Cliffs, NJ: Prentice Hall, 1991), 92. Here McKinnon takes the repetition of the antiphon as a matter of fact. He nuances this view later (2000), stating, "We do not know how often the antiphon was sung at this time, whether only at the beginning and end of the psalm, or also in some alternating pattern between the verses." McKinnon, *Advent Project*, 195.

115. Dyer states, "The schola cantorum prolonged the chant until all of the clergy and acolytes had entered the presbyterium and the pope gave the signal to conclude." Dyer, "Introit and Communion Psalmody," 115. He is referring here specifically to Ordo XV, although he assumes the same holds true for the accounts of the introit in the other *Ordines Romani*.

116. Ibid. See also *New Grove*, s.v. "Antiphon" (by Michel Huglo). This assertion assumes the melodies and psalm tones in the eighth and ninth centuries are the same as those to which we have access in the extant notated manuscripts. Such an assumption is justified, given the stability of the introit texts found in the earliest extant nonnotated manuscripts, which date from shortly after the time the earliest *Ordines Romani* were copied. As will be noted below, melodies were the vehicle for the accurate transmission of the texts.

and *Sicut erat*, and finally at the end after any *versus ad repetendum*. The difference between the two modes of performance expresses something about the relative theological and liturgical importance of the antiphon. The underlying question is this: Does Ordo XV describe an adapted and elaborated version of the original Roman practice, or is it simply the most successful description of the Roman introit that survives?

If one follows the more conservative mode of interpretation, two models of the introit emerge through the analysis of the *Ordines Romani*: first, the more basic, psalm-centered Roman introit as described in Ordo I and in the Romano-Germanic Ordos V(+VI) and XXXV, and, second, the more elaborate Romano-Frankish introit as described in Ordos IV, XV, and XVII, which certainly included *versus ad repetendum* in addition to either a single psalm verse followed by the antiphon or several psalm verses with a repetition of the antiphon after each.

While the *Ordines Romani* document the use of the introit at Mass, it is impossible to know for certain what the melodies of these introit chants were like. Such certainty comes only later with the advent of notated liturgical books. The story of the development and eventual eclipse of other chant traditions by Gregorian chant is a complex one, the details of which are outside the scope of this book. It must suffice to say with Margot Fassler and Peter Jeffery that "the medieval belief that the 'Gregorian' repertory was Roman assured its eventual hegemony over most of the other Western local traditions."[117]

---

117. Fassler and Jeffery, "Christian Liturgical Music," 93. In addition to Gregorian and Old Roman chant, the other dialects for which there is evidence include Gallican, Beneventan, and other southern Italian traditions, the traditions of the Italian north in Ravenna and Aquilea, and Mozarabic chant. Fassler and Jeffery explain that "only the local tradition of Milan, called Ambrosian chant because it was alleged to have been created by St. Ambrose, managed to survive into the twentieth century, despite some Romanization during the sixteenth century" (ibid., 94). There is also some evidence of a Celtic chant dialect. See *Grove Online*, s.v. "Plainchant" (by Kenneth Levy et al.), http://www.grovemusic.com/ (accessed February 10, 2005). For a study of the transmission of chant melodies, see Manuel Pedro Ferreira, "Music at Cluny: The Tradition of Gregorian Chant for the Proper of the Mass. Melodic Variants and Microtonal Nuances," 2 vols. (PhD diss., Princeton University, 1997). See also Sam Barrett, "Music and Writing: On the Compilation of Paris Bibliothèque National Lat 1154," *Early Music History* 16 (1997): 55–96; *Grove Online*, s.v. "Old Roman Chant" (by Helmut Hucke et al.), http://www.grovemusic.com/ (accessed February 10, 2005); Hucke, "Toward a New Historical View," passim; Peter Jeffery, "The Lost Chant Tradition

Even in the papal liturgy, Gregorian chant had completely replaced the ancient melodic tradition of Rome (Old Roman chant) by no later than the thirteenth century.[118] Thus, while there were at one time many regional chant dialects in the Latin West, eventually, as Fassler and Jeffery note, "the Gregorian chant tradition ultimately prevailed. Gregorian chant may have been a synthesis of Roman and northern (Gallican or Frankish) traditions, for the earliest surviving manuscripts (from the eighth to the tenth centuries) do not come from Rome but from farther north, mostly from within the Frankish Kingdom or Carolingian Empire. Thus they date from the period when a standardized liturgy of Roman origin (but one that included non-Roman elements) was being assembled and imposed on all the churches in the domain ruled by Charlemagne (c. 742–804)."[119] This Gregorian chant became and still remains the official chant of the Roman Church.

The Manuscript Tradition

Terminology

Texts of proper chants for the Mass first appear as supplementary material in books of liturgical readings—either lectionaries or psalters.[120] By at least the sixth century, lectionaries that contained proper chants—sometimes nothing more than notes in the margins—

------

of Early Christian Jerusalem: Some Possible Melodic Survivals in the Byzantine and Latin Chant Repertories," *Early Music History* 11 (1992): 151–90; McKinnon, *The Advent Project*, passim; Nino Pirrotta, "The Oral and Written Traditions of Music," in *Music and Culture in Italy from the Middle Ages to the Baroque: A Collection of Essays* (Cambridge, MA: Harvard University Press, 1984), 72–79; and Leo Treitler, *With Voice and Pen: Coming to Know Medieval Song and How It Was Made* (New York and Oxford: Oxford University Press, 2007). Richard Crocker, in contrast, prefers to leave such "prehistory" alone, regarding speculations about it as "romantic fantasy," and he advocates returning to a focus on the extant manuscripts. See his "Gregorian Studies in the Twenty-First Century," *Plainsong and Medieval Music* 4 (1995): 33–86; and then Treitler, *With Voice and Pen*, xi, for a counter argument.

118. Fassler and Jeffery, "Christian Liturgical Music," 94. See also Hucke, "Toward a New Historical View," 466. For a consideration of how religious orders such as the Cluniacs, Cistercians, and Carthusians influenced the development of liturgical chant, see *Grove Online*, s.v. "Plainchant."

119. Fassler and Jeffery, "Christian Liturgical Music," 93.

120. Jeffery, *Re-Envisioning Past Musical Cultures*, 63.

existed in the West.[121] At first, however, these chants were mostly graduals, tracts, and alleluias, rather than introits.[122] An Ambrosian fragment (ca. 700) is the earliest extant example of what one could call a gradual,[123] and the earliest extant collection of the Gregorian Mass proper dates from the late eighth century.[124] In the more fully developed manuscript tradition, which, as Jeffery says, is a "product of the move toward uniformity and standardization,"[125] one typically finds the introit in books called the *Graduale* or *Antiphonale Missarum*.[126] The definitive edition of the early Gregorian *Antiphonale Missarum* manuscripts is still Hesbert's *Antiphonale Missarum Sextuplex*.[127] In it he transcribes the contents of six manuscripts without musical notation, all of which date between the late eighth and early tenth centuries. They are of northern European provenance,[128] but their contents are Roman (Gregorian, not Old Roman),[129] with some variants that reflect local usage:

- The Gradual of Monza or *Modoetiensis* (8th c.)

- The Mass Antiphoner of Rheinau or *Rhenaugiensis* (8th–9th c.)

- The Mass Antiphoner of Mont-Blandin or *Blandiniensis* (8th–9th c.)

121. Ibid., 64. See Klaus Gamber, *Codices Liturgici Latini Antiquores*, 2nd ed., Spicilegii Friburgensis Subsidia 1 (Freiburg: Universitätsverlag, 1968), no. 250.

122. Jeffery, *Re-Envisioning Past Musical Cultures*, 63.

123. Jeffery describes it as "a double palimpsest fragment now at St. Gall." Ibid., 64.

124. Ibid. See Gamber, *Codices Liturgici Latini Antiquores*, no. 550.

125. Jeffery, *Re-Envisioning Past Musical Cultures*, 9.

126. The two terms refer to the same type of liturgical book.

127. René-Jean Hesbert, *Antiphonale Missarum Sextuplex, d'après les Graduel de Monza et les Antiphonaires de Rheinau, du Mont-Blandin, de Compiègne, de Corbie, et de Senlis* (1935; repr., Rome: Herder, 1967). For a list of prenotation graduals, see Peter Jeffery, "The Oldest Sources of the Graduale: A Preliminary Checklist of MS Copied before about 900 A.D.," *Journal of Musicology* 2:3 (Summer 1983): 316–21. Jeffery admits that this list is in need of "extensive revision, expansion, and improvement." Jeffery, *Re-Envisioning Past Musical Cultures*, 64, n. 26.

128. Hesbert, *Antiphonale Missarum Sextuplex*, IX, XII, XV, XIX, XXI, XXIII, XXV. See also *Grove Online*, s.v. "Plainchant."

129. Hesbert, *Antiphonale Missarum Sextuplex*, XXXI–XXXIV. See also Theodore Karp, *Aspects of Orality and Formularity in Gregorian Chant* (Evanston, IL: Northwestern University Press, 1998), 317.

- The Mass Antiphoner of Compiègne or *Compendiensis* (9th c.)

- The Mass Antiphoner of Corbie or *Corbiensis* (9th–10th c.)

- The Mass Antiphoner of Senlis or *Silvanectensis* (9th c.)

Table 2. The Introit *Nos autem gloriari* for the Holy Thursday Evening Mass of the Lord's Supper as Found in the *Antiphonale Missarum Sextuplex* Manuscripts.[130]

Rheinau	Mont-Blandin	Compiègne	Corbie	Senlis
FERIA V CENA DOMINI ANT. Nos autem gloria oportuit in cruce Domini nostri Ihesu Christi in quo & vita est & resurrectio nostra per quem salvati & liberati sumus. PSALM. Cantate Domino.	FERIA V QUOD EST CENA DOMINI ANT. Nobis autem gloriari oportet in cruce Domini. PSALM. Cantate Domino.	FERIA Vᵃ CAENE DOMINI ANT. Nos autem gloriari oportet. ut supra. PSALM. Cantate I.	FERIA V QUOD EST IN CAENA DOMINI CAP. LXXVII ANT. Nos autem gloriari oportet.	FERIA V QUE EST IN CENA DOMINI [ANT.] Nos autem gloriari oportet. PSALM. Cantate Domino.

The chant texts contained in these manuscripts and their respective liturgical assignments are nearly identical, and they represent the proper Mass chant tradition after it had developed into a stable and fixed corpus.[131]

---

130. Hesbert, *Antiphonale Missarum Sextuplex*, 93.

131. Levy notes that "in these late 8th- to early 10th-century sources the number of chant texts agrees closely with the contents of the 11th-century noted gradual from St. Gallen, Switzerland, *CH-SGs* 339." *Grove Online*, s.v. "Plainchant." The assignment of psalm verses to the antiphons is also quite stable, but it does sometimes vary from one manuscript to the next. See Hiley, *Western Plainchant*, 299. For example, the introit for the first Mass of St. John the Apostle is assigned a different psalm in Corbie than in the other manuscripts. See Hesbert, *Antipho-*

If the more conservative interpretation of the *Ordines Romani* above is correct, these manuscripts reflect some degree of regional variation, especially in terms of their use of *versus ad repetendum*. Rheinau and Corbie contain no *versus ad repetendum* at all, perhaps reflecting the introit practice as described in Ordos I, V(+VI), and XXXV. *Versus ad repetendum* are found throughout Compiègne and Senlis, on the other hand.[132] In this, these manuscripts are similar to Ordos IV, XV, and XVII and are clearly within the Romano-Frankish sphere of influence.[133] Mont-Blandin is a unique case. It does make

---

nale Missarum Sextuplex, no. 13. Note that the Monza manuscript contains only Lectionary chants, so it is not included in the table.

132. There are approximately 38 *versus ad repetendum* among the Compiègne introits—infrequent for some reason during the Easter season—and approximately 72 in Senlis.

133. For the texts of the *versus ad repetendum*, see Hesbert, *Antiphonale Missarum Sextuplex*, passim. Indeed, Compiègne and Senlis are located very near each other just a few miles north of Paris. Tietze asserts that the Compiègne and Senlis manuscripts are similar to Ordo XV in their use of only one psalm verse after the first time the antiphon is sung. He comes to this conclusion because the *versus ad repetendum* in these manuscripts are often the second verse of the psalm. This is usually the case, as he notes, in the Christmas season. It is also true on other days of the year, such as Easter Sunday. See Tietze, *Hymn Introits*, 22. It is often the case, however, that the *versus ad repetendum* are not the second verse of the psalm, but rather the verse of the psalm that is most relevant to the feast. For example, see Palm Sunday, where the first psalm verse is *Deus Deus meus* (Ps 21:2) and the *repet.* is *Diviserunt* (Ps 21:19); the Octave of Easter, where the introit is *Exultate Deo* (Ps 80:2) and the *repet.* is *Et cibavit illos* (Ps 80:17); the Ascension, where the introit is *Omnes gentes* (Ps 46:2) and the *repet.* is *Ascendit Deus* (Ps 46:6); Pentecost, where the introit is *Exsurgat Deus* (Ps 67:2) and the *repet.* is *Confirma hoc Deus* (Ps 67:29); and the Nativity of John the Baptist, where the introit is *Bonum est* (Ps 91:2) and the *repet.* is *Iustus et palma* (Ps 91:13). Interestingly, for the Christmas introit (*Cantate Domino*, Ps 97:1), the second verse of the psalm (*Notum fecit*), which is employed as the *repet.*, is also the verse most relevant to the feast. In other extant manuscripts, the text assignments vary greatly. The importance of the *versus ad repetendum* is a bit of a mystery, but if indeed the Romano-Frankish tradition eventually came to use only one psalm verse (the first) before the doxology, perhaps the *versus ad repetendum* was a means of retrieving the thematic connection between antiphon, psalm, and feast that had been lost. Also, it is not wholly clear whether the *versus ad repetendum* are verses that have not yet been sung, or if they are repetitions of psalm verses that had already been sung in the first part of the introit before the doxology. Tietze also interprets Ordos IV and XVII to allow for "one or more *versus ad repetendum*," but Compiègne, Senlis, and Mont-Blandin never indicate more than one. See Tietze, *Hymn Introits*, 263, 266; and Hesbert, *Antiphonale Missarum Sextuplex*, passim. On nonpsalmic *versus*

use of *versus ad repetendum*, but infrequently, and only on the more important days of the liturgical year.[134]

The earliest extant notated Gregorian *Antiphonale Missarum* manuscripts are from the late ninth century.[135] There also exist a handful of notated Old Roman Mass Antiphoner manuscripts. These date from a later period—the eleventh century and after—and contain texts and liturgical assignments nearly identical to those in the *Antiphonale Missarum Sextuplex* collection, with propers for certain local feasts and additions to the liturgical calendar comprising the primary differences between the Old Roman and Gregorian manuscripts.[136] The key difference between the two traditions is melodic

---

ad repetendum, see *New Grove*, s.v. "Introit." Steiner states here that sometimes the verses are chosen "so that their texts introduce the introit antiphon in its final repetition; in consequence they have a striking resemblance to introit tropes. The supplementary verse for a non-psalmodic introit is very often drawn from the same biblical passage as the introit antiphon," even when the first verse is from a psalm. *New Grove*, s.v. "Introit" (by Ruth Steiner).

134. Palm Sunday, Easter Sunday, the Octave of Easter, Ascension, Pentecost, and the Nativity of John the Baptist. See Hesbert, *Antiphonale Missarum Sextuplex*, nos. 73a, 80, 87, 102a, 106, and 119. When Compiègne, Senlis, and Mont-Blandin all employ *versus ad repetendum* on the same day, the texts assignments are nearly always identical. In a few instances, Mont-Blandin differs from the others, however. See, for example, Easter Sunday. Hesbert, *Antiphonal Missarum Sextuplex*, no. 80. In at least one instance, Compiègne and Senlis disagree. See, for example, the Third Sunday of Easter. Hesbert, *Antiphonale Missarum Sextuplex*, no. 89. Here the introit assignment is also different, which explains the different *versus ad repetendum*.

135. Hiley, *Western Plainchant*, 299. The earliest of the notated graduals appeared at the end of the ninth century in Brittany, Germany, and northern France, but later in other areas: England in the late tenth century, Aquitaine in the early eleventh century, and Italy sometime in the eleventh century. Manuscripts in which every chant is notated appear in the first part of the tenth century. Fassler and Jeffery, "Christian Liturgical Music," 90–91.

136. *New Grove*, 2nd ed., s.v. "Introit (i)" (by James W. McKinnon). He states, "Introits continued to be added to the repertory after the ninth century, largely to accommodate new sanctoral dates and votive Masses" (ibid.). The surviving Mass Antiphoner manuscripts of the Old Roman chant tradition are all quite late: Cologny-Genéve, Bibliotheca Bodmeriana, C 74 (Santa Cecilia in Trastevere, 1071); Vatican City, Biblioteca Apostolica Vaticana, Vat. Lat. 5319; and Vatican City, Biblioteca Apostolica Vaticana, Archivio di S. Pietro, F 22. Dyer, "Introit and Communion Psalmody," 119. Three more Old Roman manuscripts of lesser importance also survive. See John Boe, "Old Roman Votive-Mass Chants in Florence, Biblioteca Riccardiana, MSS 299 and 300, and Vatican City, Biblioteca

rather than textual.[137] There is no archetypal Mass Antiphoner. Liturgical books, as Huglo and Hiley note, are nearly always "composed of layers of material and the result of distinct traditions having been forged into a new usage."[138] It is also important to remember that such books are the result of local attempts to meet the practical needs of particular worshiping communities, so that their contents inevitably differ somewhat from place to place.

The purpose of the Mass Antiphoner was to collect in one book the proper texts to be sung at Mass. This means that, in addition to the introit, one would usually find the other processional chants with their psalm verses—the offertory and communion—along with the

---

Apostolica Vaticana, Archivio San Pietro F 11: A Source Study," in *Western Plainchant in the First Millennium: Studies in the Medieval Liturgy and Its Music*, ed. Sean Gallagher et al. (Burlington, VT: Ashgate, 2003), 216–318.

137. Thomas Connolly states, "The liturgy and texts of the two traditions are essentially the same. . . . The melodies to these texts differ, but not completely. There is, in most cases, a similarity of melodic contour between the Old Roman and Gregorian versions of the same text." Connolly, "Introits and Archetypes: Some Archaisms of the Old Roman Chant," *Journal of the American Musicological Society* 25 (1972): 158. He goes on to explain that "the Old Roman Introit Antiphons are more formulaic in style than the Gregorian. . . . The Gregorian Introit Antiphons have a general melodic resemblance to the Old Roman, even at points where the latter appear most formulaic. . . . These two facts taken together suggest that both [dialects] stem from a state of affairs that was at least as formulaic as the Old Roman. The evolution of dissimilar chant into a common type is highly improbable. The Old Roman Introit repertory, then, in so far as it has preserved more of this formulaic character, is surely close to this earlier state of affairs [and] the evolutionary development of Introit Antiphons seems to have been from formula to relaxation of formula. Since the Old Roman Introits are from comparatively late manuscripts and represent an apparently decayed formulaic style, it seems likely that at some earlier stage, Introits were sung in an even more formulaic way. It may, indeed, have been a completely formulaic style, akin to the recitation of the psalm tones" (ibid., 168–69). This hypothesis has since been challenged by Hucke in "Toward a New Historical View." It is possible that the more formulaic tradition reflects a later practice if it conforms more systematically to modal theory/categories. It might also be the case that, whatever dialect is earlier, the differences simply reflect cultural tastes—one typically tending toward elaboration (the Frankish) and the other toward formulism (the Roman). In short, the most one can say for certain is that the Old Roman melodies, when compared to the Gregorian, are "somehow related yet quite different." Fassler and Jeffery, "Christian Liturgical Music," 93.

138. *Grove Online*, s.v. "Gradual" (by Michel Huglo and David Hiley), http://www.grovemusic.com/ (accessed February 10, 2005).

gradual, the tract, and the alleluia and its verse. The contents of this type of liturgical book and what it was called were never codified, and often one or more of the chant genres was missing or collected in a separate book. Northern European manuscripts tend to be more comprehensive, while the church in Rome was more likely to subdivide the genres into smaller, separate collections. The *Cantatorium* often exists separately from the *Antiphonale Missarum* and contains the solo proper chants of the Mass (graduals, tracts, alleluias),[139] which are usually also included in the *Antiphonale Missarum* along with the choral chants (introits, offertories, communions).[140] Other relevant manuscript types included the *Responsoriale* (graduals) and *Antiphonarius* (introit and communion antiphons).[141]

From the late eight century on, the contents of the Roman Mass Antiphoner stayed remarkably stable.[142] All of the extant Mass Antiphoner manuscripts start with Advent. This is in contrast to many of the earliest Lectionary and Sacramentary manuscripts, which begin with the Nativity of the Lord,[143] and it suggests that the process of collecting antiphons into a book began later than the collecting of readings and presidential prayers. This later date of compilation does not necessarily imply anything about the antiquity of a stable corpus of Mass antiphons, however, because the compilation of antiphons into manuscripts took place only after the transition from oral to written transmission of chants had begun. A fully developed and stable corpus of proper chants for the Mass was probably in use before it was written down in manuscripts.

139. Fassler and Jeffery, "Christian Liturgical Music," 96.

140. See Jeffery, *Re-Envisioning Past Musical Cultures*, 67.

141. C. Vogel, *Medieval Liturgy*, 357. One of the major results of the research done by Antoine Chavasse is to have proven that the Mass Antiphoner and the Mass Lectionary evolved in tandem (ibid., 397n193). See also Chavasse, "Les plus anciens types du lectionnaire et de l'antiphonaire romains de la Messe," *Revue bénédictine* 62 (1952): 1–94; and Chavasse, "Cantatorium et antiphonale missarum: quelques procédédes de confection, dimanches après la Pentecôte graduels du sanctoral," *Ecclesia orans* 1 (1984): 15–55.

142. C. Vogel, *Medieval Liturgy*, 358. On the possibility of earlier manuscripts, see Kenneth Levy, "Charlemagne's Archetype of Gregorian Chant," *Journal of the American Musicological Society* 40:1 (Spring 1987): 1–30. He argues that the extant historical evidence suggests that there were indeed earlier manuscripts that simply did not survive to the present day. See also his longer and more recent work on the shift of ecclesiastical chant from oral to written transmission, *Gregorian Chant and the Carolingians* (Princeton, NJ: Princeton University Press, 1998).

143. C. Vogel, *Medieval Liturgy*, 358.

In the manuscripts that survive, there is a stable core repertoire of 145 introits in both the Gregorian and Old Roman traditions. There are six additional introits in the Gregorian tradition and four in the Old Roman. In the earliest extant Gregorian manuscripts that contain musical notation, the introit antiphon melodies are extremely stable from manuscript to manuscript, homogeneously neumatic and melodically complex in style, yet unique in that no two antiphons share the same melody. In fact, nearly every feast of the liturgical year has been assigned its own introit.[144] The chants preserved in the extant manuscripts, Jeffery notes, "are already completed works, not primitive or transitional collections drawn up during the period when the contents were still fluid."[145]

Mode and Performance

Modally, the introits are complex. Many do not fit neatly into the eight ecclesiastical modes.[146] Such modal ambiguity implies antiquity, as melodies that predated the imposition of the modal system and that were especially memorable—either because of their complex melodic lines or singular liturgical assignments—were more likely to have had their unusual characteristics preserved.[147]

In terms of performance, the introit is in its origins an antiphonal choral chant, which means the choir normally sang the antiphon, while a soloist or smaller group of singers sang the psalm verse(s) and *Gloria Patri*.[148] This practice is in contrast to responsorial chants like the gradual, in which a soloist sings the psalm verses in alternation

---

144. This is particularly the case in the Proper of Seasons, but much of the Proper of Saints also has unique introits. *New Grove*, 2nd ed., s.v. "Introit (i)."

145. Jeffery, *Re-Envisioning Past Musical Cultures*, 9.

146. Jeffery notes that in the extant manuscripts "we no longer have any melodies in a 'pure' state from the period before the adoption" of the modal system. Ibid.

147. According to Metzinger, "Editors of early manuscripts apparently encountered introit melodies that contained intervals impossible to notate within the modal system." Metzinger, "Liturgical Function of the Entrance Song," 36. Steiner argues that an introit antiphon "may be, in short, the antithesis of a textbook demonstration of the possibilities of its mode. This is not surprising, because it is likely that many introits were composed before the medieval system of the modes was fully worked out by the theorists." *New Grove*, s.v. "Trope (i), §3: Introit tropes" (by Ruth Steiner).

148. Or, if the antiphon was not repeated between the psalm verses, the choir, divided into two parts, would have sung the verses in alternation.

with a sung congregational response. Indeed, before the nineteenth century there was no tradition of singing the introit responsorially in the Roman Rite,[149] except perhaps for the *Gloria Patri*,[150] which the congregation could join in singing because the text did not vary. Jeffery observes that "it is by no means clear that every genre of Mass chant was originally sung by the congregation; the introit in particular may have been reserved to the choir from the beginning, if indeed its origin may be traced to a fourth-century adoption of imperial Roman ceremonial by Christian bishops."[151] From the outset, then, these chants were too complex for congregational singing.[152]

For centuries, the choir did not sing from the Mass Antiphoner during the liturgy but sang the chants from memory. Early manuscripts were too small for use by a group of singers. Books of chant that are clearly large enough for use by a choir during the liturgy do not appear until the fifteenth and sixteenth centuries. Prior to that time, Mass Antiphoner manuscripts were likely first created for the clergy to use during Masses without music and then, with the advent

149. Tietze, *Hymn Introits*, 21.

150. In fact, "the Carolingian reform had sought to have the *Gloria Patri* sung by the people." Jungmann, *Mass of the Roman Rite*, 1:325. See Charlemagne, *Admonitio generalis* 70, *Monumenta Germaniae Historica. Capitularia Regum Francorum*, vol. 1, Alfred Boretius, ed. (Hannover, 1883), 59.

151. Jeffery, *Re-Envisioning Past Musical Cultures*, 80. Jeffery does not put forward this fourth-century origin of the introit as a matter of fact, but merely as a reasonable hypothesis. Unfortunately, it is likely the case that insufficient evidence survives to put such a hypothesis to the test. He calls the question of the introit's origins "a good example of a very significant question that has never been investigated historically." And he continues, "The fact is that, for most of the chants of the Ordinary and Proper of the Mass, we do not know when or how they originated, what their original purpose or meaning was, and who originally sang them. Many other questions, such as the prevalence, personnel, and liturgical roles of choirs in the early church, are equally unexplored" (ibid., 80n57). Jeffery cites here Theodor Klauser, *A Short History of the Western Liturgy: An Account and Some Reflections*, 2nd ed., trans. John Halliburton (New York: Oxford University Press, 1979), 33–35. Klauser also suggests the fourth-century origin of the introit.

152. Peter Jeffery states, "It was the hegemony of a monastic approach to the psalms, and not some undocumentable mania for 'virtuosity,' that led to the medieval dominance of monastic and clerical choirs and the erosion of congregational singing." Jeffery, "Monastic Reading," 82. The dominance of the choral approach to the proper psalms originates in the fact that it was the monastic and cathedral clerics that guided the psalmodic movement in the urban centers of the Christian West.

of notation, as reference books for the choir master and singers.[153] The advent of liturgical choirs singing directly from a large book was the final step in the transition of liturgical chant from an oral to a written tradition.

Sources of the Antiphon Texts

Even though a detailed exploration of the theology and liturgical-musical function of Mass antiphons follows in chapter four, it is still useful to provide a basic definition of the antiphon here. In its essence, the antiphon in the Latin tradition is a monophonic prose text chant.[154] Its primary function is to introduce a psalm and to frame it, both textually and melodically, and in the case of the introit, to accompany the entrance procession. Through its text and melody, it sets the tone for the rest of the liturgical celebration.[155] Typically, the antiphon functions as a Christian or christological lens through which to interpret its accompanying psalm. Ritually, for many antiphons "it is hard to mistake the fact that the text selected had in view both the procession itself and the image of a higher reality from the day's celebration which the procession typified."[156]

Introit antiphon texts are usually specific to a particular day of the liturgical year. Antiphons for the most important feasts nearly always express a theme specific to the day, while others express a theme of the liturgical season.[157] The 145 chants of the core repertoire introit antiphons derive mainly from the Davidic psalms, but also from other

---

153. Jeffery, *Re-Envisioning Past Musical Cultures*, 67–68.

154. *New Grove*, s.v. "Antiphon."

155. Jungmann, *Mass of the Roman Rite*, 1:329. "This . . . was done often by selecting for the antiphon a psalm verse that seemed to fit the celebration. Thus for the Christmas midnight Mass Psalm 2 is sung at the introit, and verse 7 is chosen as the antiphon: *Dominus dixit ad me, Filius meus es tu*. Or in the introit of a *Confessor non pontifex*, Psalm 91, with the stress on verse 13 as antiphon: *Iustus ut palma florebit*" (ibid.).

156. Jungmann, *Mass of the Roman Rite*, 1:330. "Thus on Epiphany we read: *Ecce advenit dominator dominus*, and on the Wednesday of Pentecost week: *Deus dum egredereris*. And in Easter week, the crowd of newly baptized who have entered the Church are greeted on Saturday with: *Eduxit populum suum in exultatione, alleluia, et electos suos in laetitia*, and on Monday: *Introduxit vos Dominus in terram fluentem lac et mel*, and on Wednesday: *Venite benedicti Patris mei*" (ibid.).

157. Tietze, *Hymn Introits*, 23. Jungmann states, "There are days—like the Sunday after Pentecost—for which there is no special theme to which the introit antiphon might lead. Then the chant master takes up his psalter and chooses one

scriptural texts. Only one of the antiphons in this core repertoire is extrabiblical.[158] In contrast to the Office antiphon repertoire, the corpus of introit, offertory, and communion antiphons did not expand very much over time, and new antiphons were usually added only when new feasts were added to the calendar.[159]

Table 3. Core Repertoire Source Texts.[160]

	Psalmic	Biblical, nonpsalmic	Extrabiblical
In the entire core repertoire	101	43	1 (*Salus populi*)
In the Proper of Seasons	70	31	0
During Advent and Christmas	8	10	0
During Easter	11	10	0
During Lent	31	6	0

Nonpsalmic texts are more frequent on especially solemn days and seasons of the liturgical year. There is still debate among chant scholars as to whether psalmic[161] or nonpsalmic[162] introit antiphon

---

of the psalms that in some way expresses the relationship of the Christian community to God: trust, praise, petition." Jungmann, *Mass of the Roman Rite*, 1:330.

158. See *New Grove*, 2nd ed., s.v. "Introit (i)." Jungmann notes, however, that "here and there the Bible is sidestepped entirely. On certain saints' days there is a simple invitation to partake of the joy of the feast: *Gaudeamus omnes in Domini, diem festum celebrantes*. . . . One of the Masses of the Blessed Virgin begins with the happy greeting of the poet Sedulius: *Salve, sancta parens*." Jungmann, *Mass of the Roman Rite*, 1:329–30.

159. *New Grove*, s.v. "Antiphon."

160. See *New Grove*, 2nd ed., s.v. "Introit (i)." Here McKinnon states, "There is a 'core repertory' of 145 introits, that is, those chants that were both in use at Rome during the mid-8th century and adopted at that time by the Franks." This core repertoire is nearly equivalent to the corpus of chants found in Hesbert's *Antiphonal Missarum Sextuplex*. See also McKinnon, *Advent Project*, 207–8, 216–18.

161. This type of introit, in which both antiphon and verses were derived from the Psalms, was known as *regularis* in the Middle Ages. Jungmann, *Mass of the Roman Rite*, 1:329.

162. Introits with nonpsalmic antiphons were called *irregulares*. Jungmann, *Mass of the Roman Rite*, 1:329. "This irregularity is increased whenever the 'verse' is not taken from the psalms, as happens on the Feast of Our Lady of Sorrows" (ibid., 1:329n44).

texts are more ancient.[163] In any case, the nonpsalmic texts typically provided more specific references to the feast and more explicit christological allusions.[164]

How Source Texts Are Used

While nearly all antiphon texts find their ultimate source in Scripture, the proper chants of the Mass are not simply scriptural quotations.[165] Some are comprised of texts lifted directly from the Bible without alteration, but many of the antiphons represent what can more appropriately be called heavy linguistic borrowing.[166] The antiphon texts are interpretations and reappropriations of the biblical

163. Peter Wagner argues that the nonpsalmic antiphons are more ancient, because they are most typically found on the most important days of the church year. Antoine Chavasse, in contrast, argues for the greater antiquity of the psalmic antiphons. See P. Wagner, *Einführung in die gregorianischen Melodien: ein Handbuch der Choralwissenschaft*, I: *Ursprung und Entwicklung der liturgischen Gesangformen bis zum Ausgang des Mittelalters* (Leipzig, 1901): 54–63; and Chavasse, "Cantatorium et antiphonale missarum," passim. See also James W. McKinnon, "Antoine Chavasse and the Dating of Early Chant," *Plainsong and Medieval Music* 1 (1992): 123–47. McKinnon, given his view that the Mass proper was composed in one grand effort at the end of the seventh century, argues that the source of a particular antiphon text might have no chronological implications and "might simply indicate the greater care taken in selecting texts for dates of special significance." *New Grove*, 2nd ed., s.v. "Introit (i)." In *The Advent Project*, however, McKinnon admits that the numerically sequenced psalmic Lenten introits might be more ancient. McKinnon, *Advent Project*, 208–15.

164. Jungmann asserts, "It is understandable that feast days and festal seasons did much to break through this scheme of the *Introitus regularis* in order to give free vent to the expression of the mystery of the day. For the most part texts from the Scripture were used. Thus the introit antiphon for the third Christmas Mass proclaims, with the Prophet Isaias, the good news of the Nativity: *Puer natus est nobis et Filius datus est nobis*. And the antiphon for Whitsunday plays upon the pentecostal miracle with words from the Book of Wisdom: *Spiritus Domini replevit orbem terrarum*. A remarkable fact is this, that the text of the antiphon is frequently derived from the Epistle of the day: *Gaudete in Domini*; *Cum santificatus fuero*; *Viri Galilaei*; *De ventre matris meae*; *Nunc scio vere*." Jungmann, *Mass of the Roman Rite*, 1:329.

165. The biblical texts were not used in situ but were "singled out for a specific liturgical assignment." McKinnon, "Festival, Text and Melody," 5.

166. The presidential orations (*collectio, super oblata, post communionem*) of the Mass proper are also often full of Scripture, but more allusively so than the proper chants. See Bradshaw, "The Use of the Bible in Liturgy: Some Historical Perspectives," *Studia Liturgica* 22:1 (1992): 43.

tradition. They achieve a christological and liturgical recontextualization of Scripture and, as such, are an invaluable window into the church's ancient tradition of biblical interpretation.[167]

The introit antiphons make use of the biblical text in a variety of ways:[168]

- *Direct Quotation*, in which the antiphon text duplicates the biblical text exactly but is still contextualized by means of its interpretive interaction with its psalm verses and its broader liturgical context: "Mihi autem absit gloriari, nisi in cruce Domini nostri Iesu Christi, per quem mihi mundus crucifixus est, et ego mundo" (introit antiphon for the Memorial of St. John of the Cross, Gal 6:14).

- *Embellishment*, which involves the addition of one or two words to embellish or clarify who the addressee is in a biblical text that does not significantly change or enhance the meaning of the text: "Dixit Dominus Mariae Magdalenae: Vade ad fratres meos, et dic eis: Ascendo ad Patrem meum et Patrem vestrum, Deum meum et Deum vestrum" (introit antiphon for the Memorial of St. Mary Magdelene, John 20:17). *Dominus Mariae Magdalenae* is added to the text from John's gospel.

- *Enhancement*, in which more substantial nonbiblical phrases are added to the biblical text: "Nos autem gloriari oportet in cruce

---

167. Peter Finn argues that "the Latin texts of the antiphons in light of the numerous adaptations and their reliance on an earlier translation of the Scriptures seem to fall more naturally into the category of what *Liturgiam Authenticam* calls texts of 'ecclesiastical composition' that borrow from the Scriptures but often adapt the biblical texts and do not quote them literally." Peter Finn for the International Commission on English in the Liturgy (hereafter ICEL), "Translation of the *Missale Romanum, editio tertia*: Questions and Issues Related to the Translation of Antiphons" (unpublished study, Washington, DC, 2004), 2. Jungmann notes that "the other variable texts of the Mass, which are used for the individual formularies, are, apart from the readings, mainly intended for the chant (*introitus, graduale, offertorium, communion*). They thence exhibit in all cases a greater freedom, corresponding to their poetic character." Josef Jungmann, *The Place of Christ in Liturgical Prayer*, trans. A. Peeler (Collegeville, MN: Liturgical Press, 1989), 121.

168. These examples are from the current Roman Missal (2002/2008). For other descriptions of the techniques involved, see Metzinger, "Liturgical Function of the Entrance Song," 30–31; *DACL*, s.v. "Introit"; McKinnon, "Festival, Text and Melody," 6; McKinnon, *Advent Project*, 215–20; and *New Grove*, s.v. "Introit (i)."

Domini nostri Iesu Christi, in quo est salus, vita et resurrectio nostra, per quem salvati et liberati sumus" (introit antiphon for the Holy Thursday Evening Mass of the Lord's Supper, cf. Gal 6:14). Only the first part of this antiphon is clearly adapted from the Galatians text. The rest of the text seems to be extrabiblical, though certainly inspired by biblical themes. See chapter four for more on this antiphon.

- *Omission*, which means leaving out particular words, especially words that would hinder a reappropriation of the text: "Benedicta es tu, Virgo Maria, a Domino Deo excelso prae omnibus mulieribus super terram; quia nomen tuum ita magnificavit, ut non recedat laus tua de ore hominum" (introit antiphon for the Holy Name of Mary, cf. Jdt 13:18-19). *Quia hodie nomen tuum* is shortened to *Quia nomen tuum*.

- *Rearrangement*, in which parts of a biblical text are rearranged to better suit the occasion or to make the excerpted text more able to stand on its own outside its biblical context: "Misereris omnium, Domine, et nihil odisti eorum quae fecisti, dissimulans peccata hominum propter paenitentiam et parcens illis, quia tu es Dominus Deus noster" (introit antiphon for Ash Wednesday, Wis 11: 24-25, 27). In the biblical text the phrase beginning *et nihil* comes after the phrase beginning *dissimulas* (*dissimulans* in the antiphon).

- *Centonization*,[169] in which two or more intact biblical phrases from different books of the Bible or from different parts of the same book of the Bible are joined to create a new phrase with a new or more particular meaning: "Veniet Dominus et non tardabit, et illuminabit abscondita tenebrarum, et manifestabit se ad omnes gentes" (introit antiphon for Wednesday of the First Week of Advent, cf. Hab 2:3; 1 Cor 4:5). *Veniet . . . tardabit* is taken from Habakkuk and *et illuminabit . . . manifestabit* from 1 Corinthians. This antiphon is also an example of enhancement; *se ad omnes gentes* is not found in either biblical text.

---

169. Jeffery describes centonization as "the creation of a textual 'patchwork' or mosaic of quotations from and allusions to the Bible, Vergil, or some other pre-existing source." *Re-Envisioning Past Musical Cultures*, 91. One should not confuse this type of centonization with the other sense of the word in twentieth-century musicology: the *melodic* formulism of ecclesiastical chant.

- *Substitution*, which involves the replacement of one word of a biblical phrase with another to make the phrase more applicable to a particular feast or season: "Annuntiate de die in diem salutare Dei, annuntiate inter gentes gloriam eius" (Feast of St. Bartholomew, cf. Ps 95:2-3). *Dei* replaces the biblical word *eius*. The antiphon provided as an example of omission above also employs substitution. *Filia* is replaced by *Virgo Maria*.

- *Paraphrase*, where one or more biblical texts are the basis of a free adaptation that results in a new text: "In voluntate tua, Domine, universa sunt posita, et non est qui possit resistere voluntati tuae. Tu enim fecisti omnia, caelum et terram, et universa quae caeli ambitu continentur; Dominus universorum tu es" (introit antiphon for the Twenty-Seventh Sunday in Ordinary Time, cf. Esth 4:17 [13:9, 10-11]). The biblical text (below) has been substantially adjusted in the antiphon, perhaps to help it function as an antiphon within a Christian context, or simply to create a more aesthetically pleasing text that could be more easily sung: "Et dixit Domine Domine rex omnipotens in dicione enim tua cuncta sunt posita et non est qui possit tuae resistere voluntati si decreveris salvare Israhel / tu fecisti caelum et terram et quidquid caeli ambitu continentur / Dominus omnium es nec est qui resistat maiestati tuae."

A single antiphon can employ any number of these techniques. The result is, as McKinnon describes, "a suitable text, one of proper length and self-contained meaning that can stand apart from its scriptural context."[170] The source of a particular antiphon text is not always immediately obvious. Some antiphon texts may have grown out of quotations of Scripture found in early Christian sermons or writings.[171] Sometimes, McKinnon goes on to say, paraphrase has been employed to a degree that "it is no longer certain whether a text results from the conscious adaptation of a biblical passage or is an essentially new composition created by its author from his store of remembered biblical phraseology."[172] There were many translations of the Bible in circulation during the patristic period and early Middle Ages from which an antiphon text could have been adapted or

---

170. McKinnon, "Festival, Text and Melody," 6.
171. Jeffery, *Re-Envisioning Past Musical Cultures*, 63.
172. McKinnon, "Festival, Text and Melody," 8.

extracted.[173] Thus, the source of an antiphon text might be the Vulgate or some other "Old Latin" translation, and an antiphon text that seems to deviate from the Vulgate translation might be simply from another translation altogether rather than a conscious adaptation of the text. In Gregorian chant, the psalmic texts have two primary sources: the Roman Psalter for the antiphons and the Gallican Psalter for the psalm verses.[174] The Gallican Psalter replaced the Roman Psalter as the source of the introit psalm verses when the Roman chant began to be used in the Frankish lands.[175] Use of the Roman Psalter continued in many parts of Italy until Pope Pius V (1566–72) replaced it with the Gallican Psalter.[176] In terms of the antiphons based on the nonpsalmic biblical texts, newer antiphons are clearly grounded in the Vulgate, while antiphons for more ancient feasts reflect Old Latin translations.[177]

173. "Other possible sources," Metzinger says, "are the Latin translations of scripture made during the second and third centuries by a number of anonymous translators; these are collectively referred to as the 'Old Latin Bible.' Among these pre-Hieronymian translations are more than seventeen complete or partial Psalters, such as the Visigothic Psalter." Metzinger, "Liturgical Function of the Entrance Song," 30. See also ibid., 29; and *New Catholic Encyclopedia*, s.v. "Bible IV (Texts and Versions) 13 Latin Versions" (by B. M. Peebles). We know of these older translations, some as early as the second and third centuries, because we know Pope Damasus (366–84) employed Jerome "to begin the great work of revising the Old Latin texts of the Psalms and the New Testament in a more accurate and polished translation with a view to their liturgical use." Shepherd, "Liturgical Reform of Damasus I," 848.

174. Tietze, *Hymn Introits*, 23. He explains here that "the antiphons were musically more elaborate than the simple psalm tones, and thus the text could not be changed. The verses, however, sung in Rome to simple psalm tones, were more adaptable to the psalter that was in use in Gaul at the time. In a way, the cantors learning the cantus romanus took a shortcut; rather than relearning the whole book of Psalms and adopting the Roman psalter throughout, they applied the psalter that was already memorized, the Gallican psalter, to those parts of the compositions that were more adaptable" (ibid., 23–24). The Gallican Psalter is Jerome's (ca. 347–420) translation from Origen's *Hexapla*; it is the Psalter "iuxta septuaginta" in the Vulgate. The Vulgate's other version of the Psalter, "iuxta hebraicum," is also by Jerome. The "iuxta hebraicum" is directly from the Hebrew, quite different from the "iuxta septuaginta" and is rarely if ever used liturgically. See *Grove Online*, s.v. "Psalter, Liturgical" (by Joseph Dyer), http://www.oxfordmusiconline.com/ (accessed October 14, 2009).

175. Tietze, *Hymn Introits*, 23.

176. Ibid., 57. See also *Grove Online*, s.v. "Gradual."

177. Tietze, *Hymn Introits*, 24.

The tendency of some chant genres to contain highly altered scriptural texts more often than others tells us something about a genre's intended liturgical function. The gradual and alleluia were part of the Liturgy of the Word, for example, and thus it makes sense that these chant texts would remain closer to their biblical source texts. Introit antiphon texts, in contrast, are more likely to be textual adaptations, because one aspect of their liturgical function is to reflect the season or feast. Finally, it is important to acknowledge that some antiphon texts are consciously and deliberately not derived from the Scriptures. Such texts include the introit antiphon *Salus populi* (stational liturgy at the Basilica of Saints Cosmas and Damian) of the core repertoire, for example, as well as the introit antiphon *Salve, sancta*[178] *parens*. This latter antiphon derives from a work of the fifth-century poet Sedulius and is assigned to the votive Mass of the Blessed Virgin Mary.

THE ELABORATION OF THE NORMATIVE ENTRANCE SONG TRADITION

Later in the Middle Ages—roughly the ninth through eleventh centuries—Gregorian chant had become the liturgical-musical lingua franca throughout most of the West. Now that the chant was standardized and well established, new musical forms began to spring up as means of elaborating and embellishing it.[179] This expansion of the Gregorian repertoire, like the development and codification of Gregorian chant itself, flows from the Carolingian Renaissance and embodies the high point of musical creativity during these centuries.[180] Such forms were less prevalent in the city of Rome itself, however, which was characteristically resistant to change.

Introit Tropes

The introit trope is a genre of chants that functions solely to elaborate and extend the introit by adding music to the beginning of the antiphon or within the antiphon.[181] There are other types of liturgical

---

178. In some manuscripts, *santa*.
179. Fassler and Jeffery, "Christian Liturgical Music," 99.
180. Ibid., 102.
181. Ibid., 101; and *New Grove*, s.v. "Antiphon." See also Ellen Jane Reier, "The Introit Trope Repertory at Nevers: MSS Paris B.N. Lat. 9449 and Paris B.N. N.A. Lat. 1235," 3 vols. (PhD diss., University of California Berkeley, 1981) for an

tropes, but a great number were composed for the introit. One finds three types in the extant manuscripts: *meloform* (a melisma or melodic extension appended to the final cadence of an introit antiphon without additional text), *melogene* (additional text with no accompanying music which would have been sung to the introit antiphon melody with one note per syllable, also called a *prosula*), and *logogene* (new text with new music).[182] There is manuscript evidence for tropes beginning in the tenth century, though the practice probably began in the previous century.[183] The word *tropus* in the sources most often refers to the *logogene* type.[184] This and the *meloform* type were the ones

----

analysis of particular manuscripts. Liturgical and theological studies of tropes are few (most are musicological), but some of the most important include Ritva Jonsson, "The Liturgical Function of Tropes," in *Research on Tropes: Proceedings of a Symposium Organized by the Royal Academy of Literature, History and Antiquities and the Corpus Troporum, Stockholm, June 1–3, 1981*, ed. Gunilla Iversen (Stockholm: A. B. Dahlberg, 1983), 99–123; Niels K. Rasmussen, "Quelques réflexions sur la théologie des tropes," in ibid., 77–88; and Eugenio Costa, Jr., "Tropes et séquences dans le cadre de la vie liturgique au moyen âge (DTS diss., Institut Catholique de Paris, 1975).

182. McKinnon recounts that "the group of scholars at Stockholm University working on the Corpus Troporum project proposed that tropes added to the Gregorian repertory be divided into [these] three categories. . . . Logogene tropes are most commonly found with the introit and Gloria, but also with the offertory and communion; their texts frequently point up the theme of the feast day, to which the texts of the parent chants often bear a less tangible relationship, and the added verses generally respect the melodic style and tonality of the parent chant. Melogene tropes are most commonly found with the alleluias and offertory, frequently also with the Office responsory. . . . The texts of trope verses for introit, offertory and communion that have been edited in the series Corpus Troporum, from manuscripts mostly of the 10th to 12th centuries from all over Europe, already number many hundreds. Since the manuscript sources are highly variable in their selection of verses and in variant readings, musical editions have tended to concentrate on small groups of sources from particular areas." *Grove Online*, s.v. "Plainchant."

183. *New Grove*, s.v. "Antiphon." Hiley notes that "the earliest composition of introit tropes, if the testimony is trustworthy, is by Tuotilo of St Gall (known between 895 and 912), who is said by the St Gall chronicler Ekkehard IV (c. 990–1060) to have composed the introductory verses *Hodie cantandus est* in his youth. . . . It should nevertheless be noted that almost no introit tropes were known in both early 'western' and early 'eastern' sources, so that it is not possible to postulate a common basic layer on which later diverse collections were built." Hiley, *Western Plainchant*, 215–16.

184. *Grove Online*, s.v. "Plainchant."

most frequently used to embellish the introit.[185] As a rule, tropes were collected separately from the proper chants of the Mass in a book called the *Cantatorium*—which also contained gradual, tract, and alleluia chants—or in a separate book called a *Troper.*[186] Any standard melodic characteristics are difficult to discern, and one gathers there was not as much concern for precise preservation and transmission of the texts and melodies as there was for the antiphons.[187]

The appearance of tropes in the liturgy of the later Middle Ages reflects a general desire for local creativity within the stable ritual structure of the Mass.[188] They were most commonly composed for major feasts and served to lengthen the introit, and, through their didactic yet poetic texts, they make more explicit the theological meaning of the feast, the introit antiphon, and its psalm verse(s).[189] Tropes provided what Fassler and Jeffery call a "medieval exegetical interpretation" of the antiphon, psalm, and feast.[190] J. Michael Joncas observes that they "arose from a contemplative engagement with biblical and liturgical texts."[191] Like the *versus ad repetendum*, it is possible that some tropes clarified the theme or christological allusion that had once been created by the interplay of the antiphon and its second and subsequent verses, but that had been lost because only its first verse was used.[192]

185. Ibid.

186. An important exception is the MS *F-Pn* lat. 903, which contains the proper chants of the Mass along with their tropes. See *New Grove*, s.v. "Troper" (by Ruth Steiner).

187. Metzinger, "Liturgical Function of the Entrance Song," 42. See also Alejandro Planchart, "On the Nature of Transmission and Change in Trope Repertories," *Journal of the American Musicological Society* 41 (1988): 215–49.

188. Leo Treitler states, "'Local production for local use' is the way I characterized the written transmission of the early trope tradition in view of its variability." Treitler, *With Voice and Pen*, 429. Fassler and Jeffery assert that "it was also [by means of tropes] that specific regions customized their liturgical practices and preserved vestiges of the traditions displaced by the Gregorian repertory." Fassler and Jeffery, "Christian Liturgical Music," 102. Jan Michael Joncas notes that "the tropes were ephemeral; they responded to a particular location, era and culture." *"Ex Aetate Mediali Lux?* On the Use of Tropes for the *Cantus ad introitum,"* *Pray Tell Blog* (www.praytellblog.com), 3 January 2011, 14.

189. Hiley, *Western Plainchant*, 196–97, 220.

190. Fassler and Jeffery, "Christian Liturgical Music," 102.

191. Joncas, *"Ex Aetate Mediali Lux?,"* 14.

192. See, for example, the introit for Christmas Mass at night. The antiphon *Dominus dixit ad me: Filius meus es tu, ego hodie genui te* (Ps 2:7) has been tradi-

Like introit antiphons, tropes are texts of ecclesiastical composition. Though filled with biblical allusions, any single biblical source is usually difficult to determine.[193] William Flynn explains their function particularly well: "They were written in poetic and musical forms which were intended to interact with a formally authorized 'Gregorian' repertory in a way that would provide a type of prayed commentary on the liturgy directed towards the participants in three important ways: (1) inviting the participation of the worshippers, calling upon them to respond and give reasons for their response; (2) making connections between the present celebration and the relevant biblical story; and (3) offering an enriched web of scriptural allusions and combinations of symbol and imagery."[194] Of course, tropes could

---

tionally interpreted as words spoken by the Father about the Son. If only the first psalm verse traditionally associated with the antiphon is used (v. 1, "Why do the nations protest and the peoples grumble in vain?"), the christological interpretive interaction between the antiphon and psalm is lost. Verses 2 and 8 are the others traditionally sung with this antiphon, and they clarify the relationship between antiphon and psalm: "Kings on earth rise up and princes plot together against the Lord and his anointed"; "Only ask it of me, and I will make your inheritance the nations." Jungmann provides other examples: "The first verse, or, if the first verse served as antiphon, the one immediately following, often shows absolutely no connection with the *motif* for the day, whereas the idea is actually conveyed by the continuation of the psalms. Take the Wednesday in the Advent Ember week or the fourth Sunday of Advent; the psalm verse beginning *Caeli enarrant gloriam Dei* conveys no particular impression of Advent. But the psalm from which this verse is derived contains those phrases so often cited in this season with reference to Christ's coming like the orient sun: *Ipse tamquam sponsus procedens de thalamo suo* (Ps 18:6). In the third Mass of Christmas the introit verse is one that has certainly only a very general meaning: *Cantate Domino canticum novum*; but it is the beginning of Psalm 97 which serves as a Christmas psalm because of the words: *Notum fecit Dominus salutare suum* and *Viderunt omnes fines terrae salutare Dei nostri* (vv. 2f.). In the introit for Epiphany we find the verse: *Deus, iudicium tuum regi da*, from Psalm 71, but a fuller meaning is extracted from what follows, wherein the *reges Tharis* and others appear. On the Feast of Holy Bishops we read the introit verse: *Memento, Domine, David* (Ps 131); it is not till further in the psalm we find the connection with the theme of the day: *Sacerdotes tui induantur iustitiam* (v. 9; cf. v. 16)." Jungmann, *Mass of the Roman Rite*, 1:327–28.

193. Fassler and Jeffery, "Christian Liturgical Music," 99.

194. William T. Flynn, "Paris, Bibliothèque de l'Arsenal, MS 1169: The Hermeneutics of Eleventh-century Burgundian Tropes, and Their Implications for Liturgical Theology" (PhD diss., Duke University, 1992), 13. Ruth Steiner offers another description of their function: "The central preoccupation of tropes is

only achieve these things if those assembled were well versed in the Latin language. Indeed, tropes were mainly a feature of monastic liturgy, rather than a diocesan phenomenon, though one might expect they were also used in a few cathedrals with large groups of canons.[195]

Tropes are solo chants and are similar but not identical in melodic style to the antiphons.[196] Hundreds of them were written; there are 1,044 known tropes for the Christmas and Easter seasons alone.[197] The use of tropes with the introit continued through at least the twelfth century,[198] but in places particularly sensitive to the aesthetic of the liturgical reform of Pope Gregory VII (1073–85), especially among the Augustinians and Cistercians, the use of such embellishments declined after his reign.[199] By the time of the promulgation of the Missal of Pope Pius V in 1570, tropes had nearly if not completely fallen out of use. If a few monasteries still used them at that time, it is no surprise that none are found in Pius V's Missal, because its

---

always the text of the liturgical chant that is being introduced. The composer of the trope seems to have asked himself: 'By whom are these words spoken in the Bible? What is the context there? How do they apply here to the celebration of the day? What does the congregation need to be told about them to appreciate their full significance?' He seems to have seen his task as partly to explain and interpret the liturgical text, and partly to make it more dramatic by vividly calling up the biblical situations and characters with which it is connected." *New Grove*, s.v. "Trope (i), §3: Introit tropes."

195. Fassler and Jeffery state, "Considerable evidence suggests strongly that proper tropes were never as important in cathedral liturgies as they were among some Benedictines. The vast number of surviving manuscripts of tropes are indeed found in monastic rather than cathedral books." Fassler and Jeffery, "Christian Liturgical Music," 105–6.

196. Steiner explains, "The music of introit tropes invites comparison with that of the introits themselves. There are similarities, but also differences. . . . In general there seems to underlie the melodies of the tropes an interpretation of the medieval church modes that is comparable to the one expressed in the medieval treatises on the modes, and in the formulae displaying the qualities of the modes that are often a feature of the medieval chant tonaries. The restless, sometimes apparently purposeless, stepwise movement up and down the scale found in these formulae occurs rather often in tropes. An introit, on the other hand, may be (in terms of the notes of the scale that are actually used, and those that are selected for emphasis) almost unique, and embody an entirely individual melodic structure." *New Grove*, s.v. "Trope (i), §3: Introit tropes."

197. Hiley, *Western Plainchant*, 215–16.

198. Levy notes that "after the 12th century, the logogene type of trope rapidly fell out of use." *Grove Online*, s.v. "Plainchant." See also Hiley, *Western Plainchant*, 196.

199. Fassler and Jeffrey, "Christian Liturgical Music," 104–5.

form of celebration was based upon a parish/diocesan model and not a monastic or cathedral one.[200]

Harmonic Embellishment of Chant Melodies

It is very likely that harmonization has been part of the liturgical chant tradition from the beginning.[201] Indeed, Jeffery explains that "the study of musical cognition reveals that the tendency to harmonize spontaneously can easily be related to one of the ways that human beings recall melodies."[202] Harmonization was an important mnemonic device, then, during the period before the liturgical chants were written down. Improvised note-against-note harmonization, in which perfect intervals (*vox organalis*) were sung against the chant melody (*vox principalis*), namely *organum*, was certainly in use even before the turn of the first millennium.[203]

The twelfth and thirteenth centuries saw the advent of more complicated harmonic treatments of the antiphon melodies. Primarily a North Italian and Parisian phenomenon, these new forms (*organum purum, discant, discant clausulae, conductus*)—made possible by the contemporaneous invention in the West of exact rhythmic notation—consisted of countermelodies with more than one note for each note of the Gregorian melody.[204]

Polyphonic Settings of Proper Chants

From the thirteenth through sixteenth centuries, polyphonic choral introits that make use of the official proper chant texts and their

---

200. Jungmann's assertion, then, that "the Missal of Pius V eliminated all of these tropes as parasitic" certainly overstates the matter. Jungmann, *Mass of the Roman Rite*, 1:327.

201. That is, given the nature of human cognition and music making. See the *New Dictionary of Music*, s.v. "Improvisation" (by Bruno Nettle). Jeffery suggests that "in the Middle Ages [harmonic embellishments] may have been quite common, even a normal way of performing the chant." Jeffery, *Re-Envisioning Past Musical Cultures*, 115.

202. Jeffery, *Re-Envisioning Past Musical Cultures*, 116. See also Eric F. Clarke, "Generative Principles in Music Performance," in *Generative Processes in Music: The Psychology of Performance, Improvisation and Composition*, ed. John A. Sloboda (Oxford: Clarendon, 1988): 1–26.

203. Fassler and Jeffery, "Christian Liturgical Music," 103.

204. Ibid., 107–8. See also Robert F. Hayburn, *Papal Legislation on Sacred Music: 95 A.D. to 1977 A.D.* (Collegeville, MN: Liturgical Press, 1979): 17–23, on improvised harmonies and the use of adapted secular melodies in the Mass proper.

melodies are the primary point of interest in terms of the elaboration of the chant tradition.[205] Some fourteenth-century examples exist, but in the fifteenth century (see appendix A, example 13), particularly in northern Europe, such settings became more numerous.[206] After the sixteenth century, however, settings of the introit and other Mass propers became less common in the Roman Rite.[207] The Mass proper chant texts received little attention from serious composers after this time.

Isaac's *Choralis Constantinus* (see appendix A, example 14) was a set of polyphonic Mass propers for the whole liturgical year.[208] Isaac's

205. For example, plenary Masses, such as DuFay's *Missa Sancti Jacobi*; large collections of polyphonic Mass Proper cycles, including the Trent codices I-TRmp 88 (113v–220r) (14 cycles of proper chants with a few lacunae) and Heinrich Isaac's *Choralis Constantinus*; and often Requiem Masses, such as the musical setting by Johannes Ockeghem (d. 1497), which included the introit with the traditional chant functioning as a cantus firmus. See *New Grove*, 2nd ed., s.v. "Introit (ii)."

206. See *New Grove*, 2nd ed., s.v. "Introit (ii)." McKinnon notes that "during the 15th and 16th centuries German composers in particular created polyphonic settings of the Mass Proper that included introits. More common, perhaps, were transcriptions of the Gregorian introits into the vernacular by reformist congregations; there are German, English and Finnish examples of the practice, and most notably Czech examples produced by the Ultraquist party (see the splendidly illuminated manuscript *A-Wa 15502*)." *New Grove*, 2nd ed., s.v. "Introit (i)." For a summary of the musical Counter-Reformation, see *Grove Online*, s.v. "Polyphonic Mass to 1600" (by L. Lockwood and A. Kirkman), http://www.grovemusic.com/ (accessed February 10, 2005). Philip Cavanaugh suggests that "the sudden reappearance of Proper items c. 1425, after a century of largely secular musical activity, may be attributed to a new tide of religious feeling engendered by the reunification of the Church, successfully undertaken by the Council of Constance, 1414–18." Philip Cavanaugh, "Early Sixteenth-Century Cycles of Polyphonic Mass Propers, An Evolutionary Process or the Result of Liturgical Reforms?," *Acta Musicologica* 48:2 (July–December 1976): 153.

207. The Ordinary of the Mass, in contrast to the proper, continued to be set to music by nearly every influential composer from the fourteenth century through the decline of the patronage system in the nineteenth century. Even in the late nineteenth and early twentieth centuries the Ordinary was not completely ignored. It is worthwhile to note that in earlier periods, polyphony was more likely to be found in place of those monodic chants that had traditionally been sung by a soloist (alleluias, tracts, sequences) than in place of the choral chants like the introit. See *Grove Online*, s.v. "Mass."

208. On the *Choralis Constantinus*, see also *Grove Online*, s.v. "Polyphonic Mass to 1600." The *Grove* authors also note William Byrd's *Gradualia* as an important contribution to the corpus of Mass proper settings from this period. For a study of two other relevant collections, see Mack Clay Lindsey III, "Klosterneuburg,

collection, along with several others of the same period,[209] was at one time viewed as the culmination of a long process during which cycles of polyphonic Mass propers became more and more complete, gradually filling out the entire calendar. Philip Cavanaugh has shown such an evolutionary view of the process to be problematic, however.[210] Instead, differences between earlier collections[211] of polyphonic settings and Isaac's "complete" collection reflect the demands of efforts at liturgical reform.[212] The fifteenth and sixteenth centuries were a period of growing concern for a uniform celebration of the liturgy.[213] Indeed, several local efforts preceded the Council of Trent.[214] Prior to the Council of Trent, formularies for votive Masses had in practice come to replace the more ancient formularies of the Roman Rite.[215]

Chorherrenstift, Codices 69 and 70: Two Sixteenth-Century Choirbooks, Their Music, and Its Liturgical Use" (PhD diss., Indiana University, 1981).

209. For example, two choirbooks held at Annaberg (MSS 1126 and 1248) and four manuscripts at the University at Jena (MSS 30, 33, 35, Weimar A). See Cavanaugh, "Early Sixteenth-Century Cycles of Polyphonic Mass Propers," 151.

210. Ibid.

211. For example, Trent Codices 88 and 90.

212. As Cavanaugh states, "These collections cannot be viewed as the terminal stage of an evolutionary process leading to evermore complete polyphonic cycles but must be recognized as the answer to an immediate need stemming from a liturgical reform." Cavanaugh, "Early Sixteenth-Century Cycles of Polyphonic Mass Propers," 155.

213. Cavanaugh suggests that "perhaps the union with the Eastern Church, briefly accomplished by the Council of Florence (1438–1440), led reformers to strive for a liturgy that would better represent the ancient Roman Church and thus be more acceptable to the Greek Church." Ibid., 153.

214. Early figures central to these efforts at reform include the Bishop of Brixen Nicholas of Cusa and the Papal Master of Ceremonies John Burchard, who created a revised *Ordo Missae* in 1502. Cavanaugh points out that "from that time on the demands for a restored practice are frequently encountered and several individual dioceses undertook such reform for themselves. The German Reichstag at Speyer in 1526 clearly expressed the need for a reformed Mass book. A more determined effort was made by the provincial synod of Trier in 1549 which prescribed the Trier or other approved missals for all dioceses of the province. Similar enactments were in force in the provinces of Mainz. The concern over a uniform missal was shared also in Italy, Spain and Portugal." Ibid., 153–54.

215. Ibid., 152. According to Cavanaugh, "on Sundays throughout the year the Mass of the Holy Trinity was often sung and on Mondays the votive Mass of the Holy Spirit usually was celebrated. Fridays and Saturdays were reserved for the Mass of the Holy Cross and the Blessed Virgin, respectively. On Tuesdays the Mass of the Angels may have been celebrated and on Wednesdays that of a patron

Thus, it turns out that collections predating Isaac's, even if containing a smaller number of musical settings, were fairly complete.[216] These polyphonic settings comprise a vast creative effort and often achieve exquisitely beautiful ways of communicating the proper chant texts. To be sure, they reflect a concern to preserve and promote the ancient texts. At the same time, one should not overestimate their influence on actual liturgical practice. While they were certainly sung in the larger cathedrals, Fassler and Jeffery emphasize that "throughout the Middle Ages and the Renaissance, Gregorian chant . . . prevailed throughout Europe as the common repertory of liturgical music."[217]

THE DIS-INTEGRATION OF THE FORM AND FUNCTION OF THE INTROIT IN LITURGICAL PRAXIS

The introit of the early Middle Ages consisted of an antiphon text, derived from the church's textual tradition, which was sung with psalm verses during the entrance procession of the ministers at the beginning of the celebration of the Eucharist. Its open musical form made it an ideal accompaniment to a ritual unit like the entrance procession, that, from church to church—or even from celebration

---

saint; on Thursdays the Mass of the Holy Eucharist was usually sung. In actual practice this type of series may have been more limited due to an indiscriminate use of the *Requiem*, the *missa de beata Virgini* or other *missae favorabiliores*" (ibid.). See also Adolph Franz, *Die Messe im deutschen Mittelalter* (Freiburg, 1902), 151.

216. Cavanaugh, "Cycles of Polyphonic Mass Propers," 153. Note that another Trent Codex (no. 93) was discovered more recently and contains a body of polyphonic introit settings of a scope not matched until Isaac's *Choralis Constantinus* and the *Jena Choirbook*. See Brian Edward Power, "The Polyphonic Introits of 'Trento, archivio capitolare, MS 93': A Stylistic Analysis" (PhD diss., University of Toronto, 1999).

217. Fassler and Jeffery, "Christian Liturgical Music," 108. Treitler agrees, saying, "It is the music of the *Ars nova* that gets our attention, inevitably, because we can still perform it and hear it and study it. But that gives us a view of history that is in a way distorted, especially for this period of the late Middle Ages when written music was rather special and exceptional." Treitler, *With Voice and Pen*, 13. Pirrotta concurs: "The composers of the *Ars nova* were all monks, priests, canons, or church organists. . . . I have come to consider their activity as a private hobby, appreciated only by a few connoisseurs." Nino Pirrotta, "*Ars nova* and *Stile Novo*," in *Music and Culture in Italy from the Middle Ages to the Baroque: A Collection of Essays* (Cambridge, MA: Harvard University Press, 1984), 29.

to celebration in the same church—inevitably varied in length. If the procession was longer, more psalm verses were used; if shorter, fewer. The concluding doxology brought the entrance to a trinitarian climax that culminated in a reprise of the antiphon and the presider's greeting of the assembly. This pure form of the genre was inevitably short-lived, if ever there was such universal purity.

The Transition from Using a Variable Number of Verses to Using Only One

By no later than the middle of the ninth century, the typical musical form of the introit had likely changed in some places to make use of only one psalm verse—particularly in the churches in northern Europe where the Gregorian tradition took shape. This change eventually became universal and normative in the Roman Rite. There were several reasons for this change. To be sure, not every church building was a large Roman-style basilica. Some had different floor plans and different locations for the sacristy that were not as conducive to long entrance processions.[218] In many places, the celebration of the Liturgy of the Hours began to be normatively celebrated immediately before Mass, making a formal entrance procession redundant.[219] Also, the vesting of the priest came to take place in or around the sanctuary, in view of the assembly, again removing the need for an entrance procession.[220] Jungmann explains the situation well:

> Up till about 1000 [the entrance procession] continued to be a fully-developed ceremonial. . . . Not only in the Roman stational service but even in the Frankish Church, the entrance of the clergy had been a ceremony of capital importance, and in the descriptions and the allegorical explanations of Carolingian interpreters of the liturgy it

---

218. Metzinger, "Liturgical Function of the Entrance Song," 32. He states that "since the sacristy was situated near the chancel in this arrangement, the entrance procession has a shorter route from the side of the chancel barrier to the processional space in the middle of the schola; it no longer passed through the assembly." Ibid., 12. See also *New Grove*, s.v. "Introit (i)"; Michel Andrieu, *Les Ordines Romani du haut moyen âge*, 144–46; Cyrille Vogel, "Versus ad orientem: L'Observation dans les *Ordines romani du haut moyen âge*," *La Maison-Dieu* 70 (2e trimester, 1962): 71–99; and Thomas F. Mathews, "An Early Roman Chancel Arrangement and Its Liturgical Function," *Rivista di archeologia cristiana* 38 (1962): 71–95.

219. Jungmann, *Mass of the Roman Rite*, 1:269–70.

220. Ibid., 1:269.

assumed a formidable amount of space. But in the years that followed a change set in. . . . This change is easily explained by the medieval evolution of choir prayer and the development of the fixed regulation that the . . . Mass should each day immediately follow Terce or the other corresponding hour, for which the clergy were already assembled. An entrance procession was therefore superfluous. . . . The natural consequence of all this evolution was a change in the role of the introit; the introit would have to be sung, but not as an accompaniment to the few steps which as a rule were all that had to be taken to reach the altar. Instead of a processional, the introit became an introductory chant which in Rome already in the fourteenth century was not begun till the priest reached the altar steps.[221]

In most places and for centuries, then, the once open musical form became closed, severing the connection between the introit and the entrance procession. As has been noted already, the christological, festal, and seasonal allusions in an antiphon were also lost in cases when the verse to which the antiphon alludes is a verse other than the first.[222]

The Separation of the Choir's Liturgical Role from That of the Presider

At least by the mid-twelfth century, the liturgical function of the schola had begun to be separated from the liturgical function of the presider. Eventually, the presider was obliged to recite the chant texts, even when they were sung by the choir. In 1140 this was required for the introit, *Gloria, Credo, Sanctus*, and *Agnus Dei*, and then for all chant texts in the mid-thirteenth century.[223] Thereby the priest's actions became independent of the schola's singing, which, Jungmann says, was "no longer considered as a complementary part of the community celebration."[224] In addition, throughout the Middle

---

221. Ibid., 1:269–70. Jungmann also notes, however, that "in Romanesque structures the sacristy was not built near the entrance of the church but somewhere close to the choir. In these cases the entry called for in the ancient Mass regulations could be reinaugurated. Sometimes, in fact, it was consciously revived and given a greater development by marching the long way through the nave of the church . . . or at least a procession down the aisle on Sundays." Ibid., 1:270.

222. Lamb, *Psalms in Christian Worship*, 89.

223. See L. Fischer, *Bernhardi Cardinalis et Lateranensis Ecclesiae Prioris Ordo officiorum Ecclesiae Lateransis* (Munich, 1916), 80–85; and F. M. Guerrini, *Ordinarium iuxta ritum sacri Ordinis Fratrum Praedicatorum* (Rome, 1921), 235–44.

224. Jungmann, *Mass of the Roman Rite*, 1:106.

Ages, the preparation of the presider and other ministers at the start of Mass became increasingly lengthy and elaborate, and these accretions diminished the importance of the introit.[225] In the Pontifical of William Durandus (compiled ca. 1295), for example, while the schola is singing the introit, the ministers say Psalm 42 (*Iudica me Deus*) and the presider says a prayer of penitence. It seems the presider no longer makes any signals to the schola to indicate when they should begin singing the doxology of the introit.[226] This is in stark contrast to the record of the *Ordines Romani*, where, as is clear from the analysis above, the interaction of presider and schola is clearly present. Thus, the singing of the introit came to be of little consequence to what the presider was doing at the beginning of the Mass, and vice versa. By the time of the *Missale Romanum* of Pius V (1570), the quiet recitation of psalms and prayers by the presider and other ministers had become important parts of the introductory rites,[227] and the introit had ceased to function as the primary accompaniment to the entrance procession.[228] Indeed, the 1570 Missal does not even mention the singing of the introit by the schola, but instructs the presider: *incipit intelligibili voce*, "Introitum missae."[229] This elaborate struc-

---

225. This elaboration took place even though liturgical reform movements since the twelfth century had sought, and in some ways achieved, the simplification of the liturgy in the West. One notes, for example, the Cistercian reform of the twelfth century, the reform instigated by the papal Curia in the thirteenth century, and the reform of the Council of Trent itself. The spirit of the reform movements shifted, so that, by the time of the Council of Trent, the concern was less with the spiritual effectiveness of the liturgy and more with securing centralized Roman control and preventing haphazard change. For a general survey of changes in the Roman Rite, see *Grove Online*, s.v. "Mass, Liturgy and Chant" (by James W. McKinnon); and S. J. P. Van Dijk and J. Hazelden Walker, *The Origins of the Modern Roman Liturgy: The Liturgy of the Papal Court and the Franciscan Order in the Thirteenth Century* (Westminster, MD: Newman Press / London: Darton, Longman & Todd, 1960).

226. Michel Andrieu, *Le pontifical romain au moyen âge*, vol. 3, *Le Pontifical du Guillaume Durand* (Vatican City: 1940), 635–39.

227. See *Missale Romanum: Editio Princeps (1570)*, ed. Manlio Sodi and Achille Maria Triacca (Vatican City: Libreria Editrice Vaticana, 1998), 6, 9–11. See also Metzinger, "Liturgical Function of the Entrance Song," 21.

228. See *Missale Romanum: Editio Princeps (1570)*, 10–11. See also Metzinger, "Liturgical Function of the Entrance Song," 21; and Robert Cabié, *The Eucharist*, vol. 2 of *The Church at Prayer*, ed. A. G. Martimort (Collegeville, MN: Liturgical Press, 1986), 149–50.

229. *Missale Romanum: Editio Princeps (1570)*, 11.

ture of the introductory rites and the separation of the singing of the introit, the entrance procession, and the presider's preparation for Mass remained essentially the same in the Roman Missal until the twentieth-century liturgical reform.

Instrumental Introits

Examples of the substitution of instrumental compositions and especially organ playing for the introit—like those in the *Buxheimer Orgelbuch* (ca. 1470; see appendix B)[230]—abounded in the fifteenth century. In this type of substitution, John Caldwell explains, often "the instrumental introit replaces all or part of the sung liturgical introit of the Mass. Usually the plainchant of the antiphon was set in full as an organ piece, leaving the psalm verse and the doxology to be sung in plainchant."[231] After the fifteenth century, instrumental settings were less frequent, but still common. Frescobaldi, in his *Fiori musicali* of 1635 (see appendix B), replaced the introit with brief introductory toccatas.[232] Organists frequently juxtaposed their own improvisation with the singing of liturgical chant by the schola, but often organ versets or improvisation actually replaced portions of the liturgical text.[233]

In the seventeenth and eighteenth centuries, instrumental settings of the introit decreased in favor of ornate choral settings of the *Kyrie*, which entirely covered the introit said quietly by the presider.[234] Instrumental settings of the introit gained popularity again in the nineteenth and twentieth centuries in the form of organ accompaniments to Low Mass.[235] See, for example, Olivier Messiaen's *Messe de*

---

230. David Tunley notes that "the so-called organ mass was an extension of the age-old custom of responsorial singing in which priest and choir alternated in the chanting of plainsong. With the development of polyphony the choral response was often couched in elaborate versions of the plainsong. In the organ masses the instrument took over the role of the choir." Tunley, *François Couperin and 'the Perfection of Music'* (Burlington, VT: Ashgate Publishing, 2004), 52–53. The practice was regulated in the *Caeremoniale Parisiense* (1662).

231. *New Grove*, 2nd ed., s.v. "Introit (ii)" (by John Caldwell).

232. Ibid. See also John Caldwell, *English Keyboard Music before the Nineteenth Century* (Oxford: Blackwell, 1973/R).

233. *Grove Online*, s.v. "Organ Mass" (by E. Higginbottom), http://www.grovemusic.com/ (accessed February 10, 2005).

234. *New Grove*, 2nd ed., s.v. "Introit (ii)."

235. Ibid. "Liszt and Kodály provided short movements [for the introit]. The typical French 'organ mass' suites of Tournemire and others always begin with

la Pentecôte (1949–50; see appendix B). The art of organ playing as a replacement for the proper chants of the Mass was often improvisatory, and thus the extant manuscripts preserve only a small portion of the music actually played; published works do not necessarily reflect the music as it was actually played during the liturgy.[236] While some of the extant examples of the practice are exquisite works of art, their primary effect on the introit was to relegate its text to a sotto voce recitation by the celebrant, thus eliminating its function as an entrance chant and effectively censoring the official proper chant texts from the liturgical celebration.

THE BEGINNINGS OF THE REFORM AND RENEWAL OF THE ROMAN RITE ENTRANCE SONG

The Council of Trent

At the twenty-second session (17 September 1562) of the Council of Trent (1545–63), it was agreed that bishops should make every effort to "keep out of their churches the kind of music in which a base and suggestive element is introduced into the organ playing or singing."[237] A revised *Graduale Romanum* (Mass Antiphoner) was one of the most important results of the reform of liturgical music that followed the Council of Trent.[238] The success of Trent's liturgical and

---

an introductory movement for the entry of the ministers (ibid). See also Edward Higginbottom, "Organ Music and the Liturgy," in *The Cambridge Companion to the Organ*, ed. G. Webber and N. Thistlewaite (New York: Cambridge University Press, 1999), 130–47.

236. *Grove Online*, s.v. "Organ Mass."

237. "Ab ecclesiis vero musicas eas, ubi sive organo sive cantu lascivum aut impurum aliquid miscetur." Norman P. Tanner, ed., *Decrees of the Ecumenical Councils*, vol. 2 (London: Sheed & Ward / Washington, DC: Georgetown University Press, 1990), 737. See also *Grove Online*, s.v. "Plainchant."

238. Levy et al. recount that "on 31 May 1608 Paul V (pontificate 1605–21) granted G. B. Raimondi printing rights, and six musicians were commissioned as editors—Felice Anerio, Pietro Felini, Ruggiero Giovannelli, Curzio Mancini, Giovanni Maria Nanino and Francesco Soriano. By 1611 the membership had dwindled to two members, Anerio and Soriano, both of whom, like Guidetti, had been closely associated with Palestrina. When Raimondi died on 13 February 1614 publication was transferred to the Medici Press in Rome; the *Graduale . . . iuxta ritum sacrosanctae romanae ecclesiae cum cantu, Pauli V. pontificis maximi iussu reformato . . . ex typographica Medicaea* appeared in two volumes, in 1614 (the *Temporale*) and 1615 (the *Sanctorale*). The Anerio-Soriano Medicean edition

musical reforms can be overstated, however. No new liturgy was set forth immediately—the terms "Tridentine Mass" and "Tridentine Office" are misleading. The council's primary liturgical concerns were to standardize the Roman Rite throughout the West and to instigate the process of creating liturgical books that would enable this standardization.[239] Many goals of the council, including its musical reforms, Levy says, "were not realized, for despite the official imprimatur affixed to most chant books . . . a bewildering variety of chant melodies continued to flourish for another 300 years."[240]

Liturgical critics often disparage the introductory rites of the Mass of Pope Paul VI as unwieldy and lacking theological coherence.[241] It is also true, however, that this part of the Mass ritual was unwieldy in the 1570 *Missale Romanum*.[242] The 1570 Missal provided eleven options for the celebration of the Mass, though by the early twentieth century the most common forms were only four: the Pontifical Mass, the Solemn High Mass, High Mass, and Low Mass.[243] The Low Mass was the most frequently celebrated form in the majority of parishes, many of which would have lacked the resources required for the celebration of the more elaborate forms. It is the High Mass that is of most interest here because of its influence (along with *Ordo Romanus I*) on the reformed liturgy of Vatican II. In this form, the introit would have been sung by the choir while the priest said the prayers at the

---

of the gradual strongly reflected 16th- and 17th-century humanist interest in the relationship between text and melody. The liturgical texts were revised to 'improve' the quality and character of the Latin, cadential patterns were reshaped, certain stereotyped melodic figures were associated with certain words, melodic clichés were introduced to 'explain' words, melodies were made more tonal by the introduction of the B-flat, melismas were abbreviated, and accentual declamation was introduced to improve the intelligibility of the chanted text." *Grove Online*, s.v. "Plainchant."

239. Ibid.

240. Ibid. For more on the musical reform of the Council of Trent and particularly for examples of the abuses the council addressed, see Hayburn, *Papal Legislation on Sacred Music*, 25–31.

241. See, for example, Baldovin, "Kyrie Eleison"; M. Francis, "Uncluttering the Eucharistic Vestibule"; M. Francis, "Well Begun Is Half Done"; Ralph A. Keifer, "Our Cluttered Vestibule: The Unreformed Entrance Rite"; *Worship* 48:5 (1974): 270–77; Michael G. Witczak, "The Introductory Rites: Threshold of the Sacred, Entry into Community, or Pastoral Problem?" *Liturgical Ministry* 3 (Winter 1994): 22–27; Joyce Ann Zimmerman, "Liturgical Notes," in *Introductory Rites, Liturgical Ministry* 3 (Winter 1994): 35–36.

242. M. Francis, "Uncluttering the Eucharistic Vestibule," 2.

243. Ibid.

foot of the altar. After his prayers, the priest would silently repeat the introit antiphon text to himself.[244]

While the Tridentine introductory rites are for the most part an amalgamation of additions that had taken place over the preceding centuries, the form adopted at Trent was indeed the product of a liturgical reform and reflects a fairly consistent theology.[245] As such, it served to standardize the "fore-Mass" in the Roman Rite and even to simplify it. As a whole, the introductory rites were a ritualization of a liminal state, marking out the sacred from the daily and setting the tone for what was to follow.[246] For good or for ill, the shape of the rites also served to mirror the dominant theology and societal structure of the time. In these rites, Mark Francis states,

> God is transcendent, all powerful, and can only be invoked through the mediation of one who is specifically appointed and purified for this role: the priest. In order to enter into God's presence it is always necessary to acknowledge one's unworthiness. . . . It is through the good offices of the priest, who prays *for* the assembly that the unbloody sacrifice of the cross is re-presented and the grace of God bestowed on those present. For the faithful assisting at Mass, just being in the presence of God's awesome majesty is enough—there is no need to know or participate in the dangerous ways in which the priest is interceding for the assembly before God.[247]

Trent's concern that the spoken and sung texts of the liturgy be clearly intelligible reflected a more general concern for intelligibility in the culture of Europe during that time. Indeed, Fassler and Jeffery assert that the "concern for textual declamation and emotional expression ultimately brought Renaissance polyphony to an end, leading to the development of opera and the new Baroque style."[248] Though there were some significant exceptions, most of the best composers no longer concerned themselves with music for liturgical use. Renaissance polyphony continued to be performed in churches, however, and its principles of counterpoint were (and are still) central to the

---

244. Ibid., 4.

245. K. G. Fellerer, "Church Music and the Council of Trent," *Musical Quarterly* 39:4 (October 1953): 576–94; and M. Francis, "Uncluttering the Eucharistic Vestibule," 5.

246. See Francis, "Uncluttering the Eucharistic Vestibule," 4.

247. Ibid., 11–12.

248. Fassler and Jeffery, "Christian Liturgical Music," 114.

musical formation of composers, musicologists, and music theorists. Music in the so-called *stile antico*, which mimicked the Renaissance style, became popular in churches in the baroque period.[249]

Precursors to the Vatican II Reform of the *Graduale Romanum*

In the nineteenth[250] and early twentieth centuries, a chant revival began,[251] which encouraged the use of Gregorian chant, along with Renaissance polyphony, as the music best suited to the Roman Rite.[252] Dom Prosper Guéranger's (d. 1875) efforts at liturgical reform insti- gated the revision of the Mass Antiphoner,[253] and several important editions of chant books were published.[254] The intention to publish a Vatican edition of the major chant books was announced during a general congress in 1904 (4–9 April), and on 25 April of the same year the Vatican retained the right to publish the book by means of a *motu proprio*, in which Pius X required "that the restored melodies should

---

249. Ibid.

250. For more on the nineteenth century, see Hayburn, *Papal Legislation on Sacred Music*, 115–44, and on the Association of St. Cecelia in the U.S., 129–32.

251. It is at this time that we find the origins of groups like the Society of St. Cecelia (founded 1868). The enthusiasm for chant and for early liturgical forms in general was inspired in part by the rediscovery of many medieval manuscripts at this time. Dom Joseph Pothier (d. 1923) (a protégé of Dom Prosper Guéranger) and Dom André Mocquereau (d. 1930) were central figures in this regard. The abbey of Solesmes played a major role in early chant research, transcription, and publishing. See *Worship Music: A Concise Dictionary*, s.vv. "Cecilian Movement," "Mocquereau, André," "Solesmes."

252. Arnold and Harper note that "the trend towards antiquarianism, par- ticularly in the Cecilian movement (which although officially begun in the 1860s had much earlier roots), stressed the revival of older church music but did not provide incentives for composers to write new masses in a contemporary idiom. Furthermore, the decline of royal chapels after the French Revolution meant that few composers of significance had to compose church music as a major duty." The result is that "by the end of the 19th century settings were of two kinds: the 'concert mass' for soloists, full choir and orchestra, with virtually no attempt to provide suitable music for use in church, and the small-scale setting, often in a completely retrospective style and of little music ambition." *Grove Online*, s.v. "Mass 1600–2000" (by Arnold and Harper), http://www.grovemusic.com/ (ac- cessed February 10, 2005).

253. *Grove Online*, s.v. "Plainchant."

254. See ibid. and *Grove Online*, s.v. "Gradual" for histories of the publication of these books, the competition involved between publishers, and the philosophies that motivated the various publishers and composers.

conform to the ancient codices . . . and that the monks of Solesmes . . . be entrusted with the editing of the music."[255] The inspiration for this revision of the *Graduale Romanum* was, at least in part, Pius X's earlier *motu proprio* of 22 November 1903, *Tra le Sollecitudini* (TLS).

In 1908 the *Graduale Sacrosanctae Romanae Ecclesiae* was published, which remained the version of the Mass Antiphoner in force for the Roman Rite until the publication of the reformed *Graduale Romanum* in 1974.[256]

In the early twentieth century, there are rare examples of choral Mass settings by prominent composers that are deliberately suited for liturgical use, and, as Arnold and Harper note, "the revival of choral celebration of Holy Communion in the Anglican Church in the late 19th century marked the beginning of a steady stream of liturgical settings of Mass texts in English mostly for choir and organ."[257] On a smaller scale, serious composers in the Roman Catholic (in Latin) and Lutheran traditions also began to write similarly usable Mass settings.[258] Still, these settings are of little interest in terms of the historical development of the entrance song or introit, as most were *Missa brevis* settings and do not include any proper texts.

CONCLUSION

To be sure, the Vatican II liturgical reform—given official voice in the Constitution on the Sacred Liturgy (*Sacrosanctum Concilium*)—marks a turning point in the history of liturgical music. There came a paradigmatic shift in compositional style away from a focus on technique and artistic expression, and toward an approach in which the primary concern is pastorally effective liturgical enactment in

255. *Grove Online*, s.v. "Plainchant." Both of these requirements persist to the present day, though, of course, access to the early codices and the methods used to interpret them have since vastly improved.

256. Levy et al. caution that "although much labour and 'Romantic' scholarship went into the preparation of the Pothier, Vatican and Solesmes chant books, the latter cannot be considered critical editions in any sense, because they lack commentaries and do not specify the manuscript sources of each melody. Special collections, such as the Solesmes *Variae preces* (1896) and Carl Ott's *Offertoriale* (1935) provide some clues as to the sources. However, the modern chant books are by and large functional compilations." *Grove Online*, s.v. "Plainchant."

257. *Grove Online*, s.v. "Mass 1600–2000."

258. See ibid.

the typical parish community.[259] The shift to a pastoral focus and its concern for "full, conscious, and active participation" by not just the ministers and the choir but also the entire assembly is without question a laudable development. It has spurred the creation of a great variety of accessible music in a number of forms that enable congregational singing, drawing upon popular styles and more effectively enabling local (and often more culturally appropriate) music to find expression in the liturgy.[260]

It is true, nevertheless, that the pastoral requirements of the postconciliar liturgy meant that for the most part liturgical music would no longer be the cauldron for the highest forms of human musical-artistic expression that for centuries had been an integral part of the tradition.[261] It also meant that forms from previous centuries might no longer be usable in the liturgy. Is it true, as Arnold and Harper suggest, that "the tension between the liturgical purpose and creative treatment of the texts of the Mass . . . may have fractured permanently"?[262] "May" is the key word here. Certain major centers of musical and liturgical creativity are attempting solutions to this tension, and the rest of this study will offer some solutions to this apparent rupture.[263]

Prior to the modern liturgical movement and the liturgical reform of the Second Vatican Council, the "ultimate liturgical ideal" had come to be "the scrupulous observance of the Tridentine rubrics by the presiding priest and the dignified chanting of his prayers in Latin, while an expert choir, preferably with boy trebles, sang a chant Proper and an Ordinary by Palestrina or some contemporary."[264] As McKinnon notes, "This was all to change."[265]

---

259. Ibid. For another assessment of music and the liturgical reform, see Fassler and Jeffery, "Christian Liturgical Music," 122–23.

260. *Grove Online*, s.v. "Mass 1600–2000."

261. Ibid.

262. Ibid.

263. Perhaps this is a temporary fracture, resulting (necessarily) from a fundamental rethinking of liturgical participation after Vatican II. To be sure, Catholics of the Roman Rite are still learning how to celebrate within a multicultural and multilingual context, and today's culture experiences music in a dramatically different way than did past generations (as listeners rather than performers).

264. *Grove Online*, s.v. "Mass, Liturgy and Chant."

265. Ibid.

CHAPTER TWO

The Entrance Song of the Roman Rite in Recent and Contemporary Ecclesiastical Documents

The body of ecclesiastical norms regarding the celebration of the liturgy[1] is vast when one considers the entire worship tradition of the church over the past two millennia. Given this vast tradition, it is necessary to define which norms this chapter will consider. The focus here is the development, relevance, and implications of ecclesiastical norms regarding the Roman Rite entrance song in conciliar, episcopal, papal, and curial documents from the turn of the twentieth century up to the present day, with a focus on the liturgical reform of the Second Vatican Council.[2] A consideration of ecclesiastical norms concerning the entrance song is important, given that the goal of chapters three and four is to determine the most appropriate forms of the entrance song for present-day liturgical practice.

---

1. Such norms, "when properly understood and implemented, serve to ensure the beauty and prayerfulness of our worship of God and our celebration together as Christ's body. . . . The function of canon law is to provide harmony and unity in the external life of the Church as a reflection of its Spirit-guided inner unity." John Huels, *Liturgical Law: An Introduction* (Washington, DC: Pastoral Press, 1987), 1, 2.

2. For liturgical law and its regulation of the music of the liturgy, particularly for the periods prior to the twentieth century, see Robert F. Hayburn, *Papal Legislation on Sacred Music 95 A.D. to 1977 A.D.*; and Fiorenzo Romita, *Ius musicae liturgicae* (Turin: Marietti, 1936).

THE NATURE AND INTERPRETATION OF
LITURGICAL NORMS AFTER VATICAN COUNCIL II

Liturgy concerns the enactment of the church's rites by the community of the faithful. Since canon law governs the entirety of the church's activity,[3] the regulation of the church's liturgy[4] is part of canon law, even if the majority of liturgical norms are not contained in the *Codex Iuris Canonici*.[5] Specifically, as Frederick McManus says, liturgical norms "directly embrace the rule of celebration, affecting the actions (words, songs, ritual acts) and the circumstances or environment (churches and baptisteries, furnishings, vesture, and the like)."[6] Even though most liturgical law is not found in the Code,

---

3. Huels, *Liturgical Law: An Introduction*, 2.

4. That is, "the divine act of sanctification and the public, corporate human response. It is the public worship of God by the Church, Christ the Head and his members—done through signs, the deeds and words—that articulate communally the inward faith and worship and the divine gift of grace." Frederick R. McManus, "Liturgical Law," in *Handbook for Liturgical Studies*, ed. Anscar J. Chupungco, vol. 1, *Introduction to the Liturgy* (Collegeville, MN: Liturgical Press, 1997), 400.

5. "For the most part the Code does not define the rites which must be observed in celebrating liturgical actions." Canon Law Society of America, *New Commentary on the Code of Canon Law*, ed. John P. Beal, James A. Coriden, and Thomas J. Green (Mahwah, NJ: Paulist Press, 2000), canon 2. "There is another body of universal ecclesiastical law, even larger than the code, called liturgical law, consisting of norms too numerous and detailed to be included in the code. These laws are found chiefly in the liturgical books. Another important source of liturgical law since Vatican II is the particular laws on the liturgy enacted by Conferences of Bishops and diocesan bishops (c. 838). Although canon 2 speaks only of liturgical 'laws' (*leges*), the principle stated in this canon also applies to liturgical norms found in documents that are acts of executive rather than legislative power, such as directories or instructions published by a congregation of the Roman Curia on liturgical matters. All the liturgical books and rites contain an introduction, and some contain additional introductions to the various parts of the rites. These introductions . . . have some theological content, but they are largely juridical in nature. Within the rites themselves are found the rubrics . . . giving the precise directions for the proper execution of the rite. Both the rubrics and the juridical norms of the introductions are true ecclesiastical laws" (ibid., 50).

6. McManus, "Liturgical Law," in *Handbook for Liturgical Studies*, 400. Liturgical law is not the same as the closely related body of "sacramental law," which concerns such matters as matrimonial dispensations and requirements for ordination.

it is subject to the same principles of promulgation, interpretation, revocation, and dispensation.[7]

The nature of liturgical law in any era finds its source in the church's understanding of the nature of Christian liturgy. In the preconciliar period, the evidence in official documents is admittedly sparse, aside from that found in the official ritual books. There is, however, a definition of liturgy in Pope Pius XII's encyclical *Mediator Dei*[8] (30 November 1947), which was later elaborated in the instruction *De Musica Sacra* (DMS) (3 September 1958) from the Congregation of Rites:

"Sacra Liturgia integrum constituit publicum cultum mystici Iesu Christi Corporis, Capitis nempe membrorumque eius" (*Mediator Dei*). Propterea sunt "actiones liturgicae" illae actiones sacrae, quae, ex institutione Iesu Christi vel Ecclesiae eorumque nomine, secundum libros liturgicos a Sancta Sede approbatos, a personis ad hoc legitime deputatis peraguntur, ad debitum cultum Deo, Sanctis ac Beatis deferendum . . . ceterae actionis sacrae quae, sive in ecclesia sive extra, sacerdote quoque praesente vel praeeunte, peraguntur, "pia exercitia" appellantur.[9]

"The sacred liturgy comprises the whole public worship of the Mystical Body of Jesus Christ, that is, of the Head and of his members" (*Mediator Dei*). "Liturgical services" are therefore those sacred actions which have been instituted by Jesus Christ or the Church and are performed in their name by legitimately appointed persons according to liturgical books approved by the Holy See, in order to give due worship to God, the Saints, and the Blessed (cf. canon 1256). Other sacred acts performed inside or outside the church, even if performed by a priest or in his presence, are called "pious exercises." (DMS 1)[10]

---

7. *New Commentary on the Code of Canon Law*, 50.

8. "Often called the *Magna Charta* of the liturgical movement, this encyclical [*Mediator Dei*] was the first in the history of the Church to be devoted entirely to the liturgy. Although it was basically positive in tone, it contained various statements reflecting the apprehension and the spirit of unrest that the liturgical movement had initiated in various European countries. Nevertheless, the document did give the liturgical renewal decisive encouragement and a forward thrust." R. Kevin Seasoltz, *New Liturgy, New Laws* (Collegeville, MN: Liturgical Press, 1980), 7. See also *Mediator Dei, Acta Apostolicae Sedis* 39 (1947): 528–29.

9. *Acta Apostolicae Sedis* 50 (1958): 632.

10. Trans., *The Pope Speaks* 5:2 (1959).

This understanding is amplified and superseded by that of the Constitution on the Sacred Liturgy (*Sacrosanctum Concilium*; 4 December 1963) of the Second Vatican Council:

Merito igitur Liturgia habetur veluti Iesu Christi sacerdotalis muneris exercitatio, in qua per signa sensibilia significatur et modo singularis proprio efficitur sanctificatio hominis, et a mystico Iesu Christi Corpore, Capite nempe eiusque membris, integer cultus publicus exercetur.[11]	Rightly, then, the liturgy is considered as an exercise of the priestly office of Jesus Christ. In the liturgy, by means of signs perceptible to the senses, human sanctification is signified and brought about in ways proper to each of these signs; in the liturgy the whole public worship is performed by the Mystical Body of Jesus Christ, that is, by the Head and his members. (SC 7)[12]

This definition is in turn repeated and amplified by the *Codex Iuris Canonici* (1983):

Canon 834	
No. 1. Munus sanctificandi Ecclesia peculiari modo adimplet per sacram liturgiam, quae quidem habetur ut Iesu Christi muneris sacerdotalis exercitatio, in qua hominum sanctificatio per signa sensibilia significatur ac modo singulis proprio efficitur, atque a mystico Iesu Christi Corpore, Capite nempe et membris, integer cultus Dei publicus exercetur. No. 2. Huiusmodi cultur tunc habetur, cum deferetur nomine Ecclesiae a personis legitime deputatis et per actus ab ecclesiae auctoritate probatos.	No. 1. The Church fulfills its sanctifying function in a particular way through the sacred liturgy, which is an exercise of the priestly function of Jesus Christ. In the sacred liturgy the sanctification of humanity is signified through sensible signs and effected in a manner proper to each sign. In the sacred liturgy, the whole public worship of God is carried out by the Head and members of the mystical Body of Jesus Christ. No. 2. Such worship takes place when it is carried out in the name of the Church by persons legitimately designated and through acts approved by the authority of the Church.

---

11. *Acta Apostolicae Sedis* 56 (1964): 97–138; and *Sacrosanctum Oecumenicum Concilium Vaticanum II: Constitutiones, Decreta, Declarationes* (Vatican City: Polyglot Press, 1966), 3–69.

12. Trans., International Commission on English in the Liturgy, *Documents on the Liturgy 1963–1979: Conciliar, Papal, and Curial Texts* (Collegeville, MN: Liturgical Press, 1982), p. 6 (this source is hereafter referred to as DOL).

Canon 837

No. 1. Actiones liturgicae non sunt actiones privatae, sed celebrationes Ecclesiae ipsius, quae est «unitatis sacramentum», scilicet plebs sancta sub Episcopis adunata et ordinata; quare ad universum corpus Ecclesiae pertinent illudque manifestant et afficiunt; singula vero membra ipsius attingunt diverso modo, pro diversitate ordinum, munerum et actualis participationis.

No. 2. Actiones liturgicae quatenus suapte natura celebrationem communem secumferant, ubi id fieri potest, cum frequentia et actuosa participatione christifidelium celebrentur.

No. 1. Liturgical actions are not private actions but celebrations of the Church itself which is *the sacrament of unity*, that is, a holy people gathered and ordered under the bishops. Liturgical actions therefore belong to the whole body of the Church and manifest and affect it; they touch its individual members in different ways, however, according to the diversity of orders, functions, and actual participation.

No. 2. Inasmuch as liturgical actions by their nature entail common celebration, they are to be celebrated with the presence and active participation of the Christian faithful where possible.

Canon 839

No. 1. Aliis quoque mediis munus sanctificationis peragit Ecclesia, sive orationibus scilicet, quibus Deum deprecatur ut christifideles sanctificati sint in veritate, sive paenitentiae necnon caritatis operibus, quae quidem magnopere ad Regnum Christi in animis radicandum et roberandum adiuvant et ad mundi salutem conferunt.

No. 2. Curent locorum Ordinarii ut orationes necnon pia et sacra exercitia populi christiani normis Ecclesiae plene congruant.

No. 1. The Church carries out the function of sanctifying also by other means, both by prayers in which it asks God to sanctify the Christian faithful in truth, and by works of penance and charity which greatly help to root and strengthen the kingdom of Christ in souls and contribute to the salvation of the world.

No. 2. Local ordinaries are to take care that the prayers and pious and sacred exercises of the Christian people are fully in keeping with the norms of the Church.[13]

These documents provide insight into the church's self-understanding of the nature of the liturgy as expressed in official ecclesiastical documents during the immediately preconciliar, conciliar, and postconciliar periods, from which three complementary definitions of the nature of Christian liturgy emerge, respectively:

13. Trans., Canon Law Society of America, *Code of Canon Law: Latin-English Edition* (Washington, DC, 1983). Used by permission.

1. Liturgy, the cult due to God, the saints, and the blessed, is public worship by the Mystical Body of Christ according to the liturgical books approved by the Holy See. Instituted by Christ and the church—in essence, two parts of the same Body—and carried out in the name of Christ and the church, it is enacted by properly deputed persons.

2. Liturgy is the exercise of the priestly office of Jesus Christ by means of sensible signs, the sanctification by which is signified and effected in ways proper to each sign, which encompasses all public worship of God carried out by the Mystical Body of Christ—Head and members.

3. Liturgy is the exercise of the priestly office of Jesus Christ by means of sensible signs, the sanctification by which is signified and effected in ways proper to each sign, which encompasses all public worship of God carried out by the Mystical Body of Christ—Head and members—in the name of the church by properly deputed persons through acts approved by the authority of the church. It is distinct from other acts done according to the church's sanctifying function, such as extraliturgical prayer (which may be public or private), devotions, and works of penance and charity. It is by its nature public, and thus the participation of the faithful (with very few exceptions) is the norm.

These definitions reflect a common understanding of the nature of Christian liturgy. The emphasis on sensible signs in *Sacrosanctum Concilium* and the *Codex Iuris Canonici* recognizes the sacramental nature of human sanctification and thus relates the liturgy concretely and profoundly to the physical world. The Code incorporates the principle of *actuosa participatio* (SC 14) into its definition—a principle fundamental to the liturgical reform of the Second Vatican Council.[14]

14. On the meaning and significance of the conciliar principle of active participation, see Mary Collins, *Contemplative Participation: Sacrosanctum Concilium Twenty-Five Years Later* (Collegeville, MN: Liturgical Press, 1990); J. Lamberts, "Active Participation as the Gateway Towards an Ecclesial Liturgy," in *Omnes Circumadstantes: Contributions Towards a History of the Role of the People in the Liturgy*, ed. Charles Caspers and Marc Schneiders (Kampen: Uitgeversmaatschappij J. H. Kok, 1990), 234–61; J. Lamberts, ed., *La Participation Active: 100 ans après Pie X et 40 ans après Vatican II* (Louvain: Peeters, 2004); and Frederick R. McManus, *Liturgical Participation: An Ongoing Assessment* (Washington, DC: Pastoral Press, 1988).

The Code also distinguishes liturgy from other acts of sanctification (devotions and so forth), not to denigrate these other acts or to imply that the sanctification accomplished through them in Christ is separate from that accomplished by the liturgy, but to set the liturgy apart as a group of rites officially sanctioned and enacted in the name of the whole church.[15] Finally, in the 1983 Code, the source of these official rites, that is, where one can find the texts and rubrics of the liturgy, expands from "libros liturgicos a Sancta Sede approbatus" to "actus ab Ecclesiae auctoritate probatos." The texts of the liturgy are primarily found in the liturgical books approved by the Holy See, to be sure, but they are also found elsewhere, such as in books of approved experimental or *ad interim* texts or rites, proper texts for local saints and holy days, emendations to liturgical books issued by the Holy See, and other cultural adaptations to the rites that necessarily go beyond those provided for in the official liturgical books.[16]

Most important, liturgical law after the Second Vatican Council reflects a new style and a new spirit.[17] This *novus habitus mentis* is

---

15. See Peter C. Phan, *Directory on Popular Piety and the Liturgy: Principles and Guidelines; A Commentary* (Collegeville, MN: Liturgical Press, 2005), passim.

16. See *Sacrosanctum Concilium* 37–40.

17. McManus, "Liturgical Law," in *Handbook for Liturgical Studies*, 401. This new style and spirit is in contrast to what some perceive as the rubricism of the preconciliar interpretation of liturgical law. As McManus recounts, "Rubrics . . . have often been maligned, but more often criticized with good reason, as rigid and fussily concerned with external minutiae. Surely the rubrics of the past and the resulting ceremonial practice have shared the three ecclesial failings put down by the great council: triumphalism, clericalism, and legalism. Moreover, the conventional and contingent nature of most religious signs has often been overlooked as rubrics have been canonized and made sacrosanct. It has often been said that, prior to the liturgical revival, liturgy was defined as or equated with rubrics, the canonical norms that govern the celebration. There is or was a good deal of truth in that assertion about the mindset of the past." Frederick R. McManus, "The Church at Prayer: Going Beyond Rubrics to the Heart of the Church's Worship," *The Jurist* 53:2 (1993): 266. One must acknowledge, however, that there was certainly much more to preconciliar liturgy than rubrics and that the reformed liturgy is not immune to such a tendency. Indeed, rubricism or liturgical fundamentalism is an ever-present danger in the interpretation of liturgical law and the enactment of the liturgy. Such a perspective is an easy refuge from the complex hermeneutical skills necessary for good and useful interpretation of liturgical law, and it is effortless compared to the full and integral implementation of the postconciliar liturgical reform, with its labor-intensive need for catechesis and cultural adaptation. The problem arises when the proper execution of liturgical actions becomes an end in itself,

evident in the reformed postconciliar liturgical books and guided those responsible for the revision of the Code. "Contemporary liturgical law," McManus notes, "shares the pastoral approach of canonical revision in general, but often with a stronger base derived from the Conciliar liturgical renewal."[18] Indeed, this shift, he continues, "is amply confirmed by the way in which the revised liturgical books have been designed: the wealth of alternatives, the overall flexibility and openness to creativity, the choices allowed or encouraged among prayer texts and even more so among liturgical songs . . . the opportunities afforded to employ 'these or similar words,' and the very language of prescriptions or precepts."[19] Good liturgical law in the postconciliar period necessarily possesses several qualities that go beyond texts and rubrics.

- It brings out the relationship of the pastoral office and liturgical presidency.

- It promotes the public order and common good.

- It facilitates quality liturgical celebrations.

- It ensures the manifestation of the common Christian faith.

- It maintains the communion of churches.[20]

History demonstrates that liturgical law is constantly evolving. Just as the ideal of centralization and codification of a single and universal body of church law in many ways determined the ultimate structure of the 1917 *Codex Iuris Canonici*,[21] so too did the mind of the Second Vatican Council influence the form and content of the revised 1983 Code and the nature of postconciliar liturgical law. The fundamental goal of the council to renew the church and enable it to address the needs of a fundamentally changed culture meant that the Code and liturgical books could not simply be refined or

---

rather than a means to the sacramental manifestation of grace in the here and now. See Rembert G. Weakland, "Liturgy and Common Ground," *America* (20 February 1999).

18. McManus, "Liturgical Law," in *Handbook for Liturgical Studies*, 401.

19. Ibid., 401–2.

20. Ibid., 415–19.

21. See John A. Alesandro, "General Introduction," in *The Code of Canon Law: A Text and Commentary*, ed. James A. Coriden, Thomas J. Green, and Donald E. Heintschel (Mahwah, NJ: Paulist Press, 1985), 4.

reorganized in details, but that they had to be deeply and basically rewritten and reformed.[22] According to Pope Paul VI, "with changing conditions—for life [today] seems to evolve more rapidly—canon law must be prudently reformed; specifically, it must be accommodated to a new way of thinking proper to the Second Ecumenical Council of the Vatican, in which pastoral care and new needs of the people of God are met."[23]

The nature of liturgical law in the postconciliar era, as we have said, requires an explicitly new way of thinking. This means that the interpretation of liturgical norms must focus not only on the text and rubrics of the liturgical books but also on fundamentals of effective ritual enactment. The *nature of human cognition*, for example, is crucial in that the focus of the liturgy is the salvific divine-human encounter, which requires the liturgy to be communicable and intelligible. This means that the *pastoral dimension* of the liturgy is at least as important as any other dimension and, consequently, that the liturgy must be adapted to allow for active participation of the faithful so that it is effective in a *particular time and place*. This in turn implies that *quality, functionality,* and *beauty* are central to the effective enactment of the church's liturgy. Indeed, things like church buildings, vestments, vessels, and music, which are expressions of the rich heritage of the church, are products of particular cultures. All of this means that the celebration of the liturgy must move beyond any rubricism, legalism, or superficiality.[24] It is only then that Christians can discover the authentic meaning of liturgical law and take part in the theological riches of the liturgy.[25]

---

22. "Probably more than any of the twenty other ecumenical councils, Vatican II required a whole set of laws for its proper implementation. This was the direct result of John XXIII's decision to convoke a 'pastoral' council. The pastoral emphasis of the deliberations and decrees directly affected church discipline and ecclesial activity." Ibid., 5–7.

23. Paul VI, Address at the inauguration of the work of the Commission to reform the Code, *Communicationes* 1 (1969): 41.

24. McManus, "Church at Prayer," 269.

25. McManus, "Liturgical Law," in *Handbook for Liturgical Studies*, 411. For examples of well-executed postconciliar interpretation of liturgical law, see, for example, Ladislas Örsy, "The Interpreter and His Art," *The Jurist* 40 (1980): 27–56; John M. Huels, "The Interpretation of Liturgical Law," *Worship* 55 (May 1981): 218–37; John M. Huels, *One Table, Many Laws: Essays in Catholic Eucharistic Practice* (Collegeville, MN: Liturgical Press, 1986); John M. Huels, *Liturgy and Law: Liturgical Law in the System of Roman Catholic*

THE SOURCES OF LITURGICAL NORMS
AFTER VATICAN COUNCIL II

There are six major categories of liturgical norms in the post-conciliar period.[26] First are conciliar documents. When exploring the genuine meaning of liturgical law, it is vital to recognize the primacy of the documents of the Second Vatican Council, especially the Constitution on the Sacred Liturgy (*Sacrosanctum Concilium*). The Code and the postconciliar liturgical books and documents, McManus reminds us, are "always interpreted in the light of *Sacrosanctum Concilium* and not vice versa."[27] It is in essence a foundational document, rather than a document of extreme detail. It puts forth the fundamental principles of the reformed liturgy, drawing upon the entire liturgical tradition of the church and the ideals of the liturgical movement that had preceded the council, but leaves the specifics of implementation to the Holy See, episcopal conferences, and particular churches. As a document of an ecumenical council, whatever law it contains is universally binding for Catholics of the Roman Rite.

Second are officially promulgated liturgical books, and, for the purposes of this study, these books in their official English-language translations as prepared by the International Commission on En-

---

Canon Law (Montreal: Wilson & Lafleur, 2006); Thomas Richstatter, *Liturgical Law Today: New Style, New Spirit* (Chicago: Franciscan Herald Press, 1977); and Willibrod Slaa, "Liturgical Law: Existence, Exigency and Pastoral Dimension of Conciliar and Post Conciliar Liturgical Legislation" (JCD diss., Pontifical Urban University, 1983).

26. "Until the fourth century the Old and New Testaments, Apostolic traditions, real and apocryphal, custom, and synodal canons constituted the four main sources of ecclesiastical norms. During the course of the fourth century two other sources of authoritative norms emerged in the Christian Church: the writings of the Fathers of the Church and the letters of the bishops of Rome." Kenneth Pennington, "A Short History of Canon Law," http://faculty.cua.edu/pennington/Canon%20Law/ShortHistoryCanonLaw.htm.

27. McManus, "Church at Prayer," 275. "The canons are always to be understood in the light of the Vatican II Conciliar documents and their spirit, not vice versa. The same principle works for liturgical laws as well, for example, those found in the liturgical books or in post-Conciliar documents: these too are to be understood in the light of Vatican II's decisions, not vice versa." McManus, "Liturgical Law," in *Handbook for Liturgical Studies*, 411. For another description of the types and authority of ecclesiastical documents and their binding force, see Hayburn, *Papal Legislation*, 506–10, 513–19.

glish in the Liturgy (ICEL) and adapted by the United States Conference of Catholic Bishops (hereafter USCCB; formerly the National Conference of Catholic Bishops, hereafter NCCB). Each of these books contains an introduction (*praenotanda*) and rubrics that provide guidelines and instructions for the celebration of the liturgy. As John Huels explains, "the *praenotanda* include . . . major disciplinary rules affecting the preparation and celebration of the rites in question. Rubrics . . . usually are the more precise directions specifying what the minister or assembly is to say or do at a specific moment in the celebration. . . . The norms in these and the other liturgical books, whose revision was decreed by the Second Vatican Council and whose promulgation was authorized by the Apostolic See, are true ecclesiastical laws with the same binding force as the canons of the code."[28]

The third principal source of liturgical norms is Book IV of the Code, "De ecclesiae munere sanctificandi." Not all in Book IV is strictly speaking liturgical law—many of the canons pertain to sacramental matters that do not relate to the actual celebration of the rites, such as the construction of church buildings and cemeteries and rules about access to the sacraments.[29]

The fourth source of liturgical law is found in postconciliar legislation not wholly superseded by the 1983 Code and legislation issued after the Code's promulgation.[30] Depending on its purpose and context, such legislation can regulate the liturgy for the universal church or be restricted to a particular church. When intending to promulgate

---

28. Huels, *Liturgical Law: An Introduction*, 3.

29. Some other sections of the Code are also relevant, but less so. Book II speaks to the obligations and rights of the faithful—their right to the rites, the hierarchical structure of the church, and the nature of consecrated life. Book III contains a few relevant sections, especially those pertaining to preaching and the homily. Book V speaks of issues such as the purpose of ecclesiastical temporal goods and pious wills, while Book VI concerns legal infractions related to the sacraments and liturgy. Book VII is concerned with criminal and administrative procedures—in other words, the recourse available to help resolve disputes regarding worship.

30. Huels, *Liturgical Law: An Introduction*, 3. As Huels says, "Many post-Conciliar liturgical documents have been superseded by more recent legislation, and they cannot be viewed as true sources of law" (ibid., 3–4). Alesandro notes that "post-Conciliar interim legislation was an important source for the revision of the Code. Many of the canons incorporate verbatim, or at least substantially, the norms implementing various pastoral directives of the Council." Alesandro, "General Introduction," 5.

law, the pope (by means of an apostolic constitution or an apostolic letter *motu proprio*) can enact laws that are universally binding.[31] Documents such as instructions or papal encyclicals, in contrast, are not, strictly speaking, legal documents in their own right. Such documents fall into the categories of "general executory decrees"[32] and "instructions."[33] They expand upon and clarify already existing laws.[34] As Huels notes, "Both [general executory decrees and instructions] are binding, but a law, in a sense, is 'more binding.' . . . [They] are administrative rather than legal texts; they are means of implementing the law, expanding on how the law is to be observed, or clarifying its meaning. However, they are not supposed to contradict the law or create restrictions on rights, restrictions that are not found in the law itself. If perchance some regulation in any executory document is contrary to the law, that regulation lacks all force and should not be observed (canon 33, no. 1; canon 34, no. 2)."[35]

"Particular law" is the fifth category of liturgical law. It is issued by and for a particular diocese or country. Diocesan bishops and bishops' conferences have the right to enact such law.[36] However, as Huels explains, "often the regulations they issue are not true laws because they are not promulgated as such. They appear as guidelines or pastoral directives. This does not mean that their observance is optional, but it indicates that the authority who issued them does not wish them to have the same 'weight' that the law itself possesses."[37]

Custom, the sixth source of liturgical law,[38] is the "interpretation of liturgical law by the community."[39] It is the earliest source of ecclesiastical liturgical norms. Such law is comprised of the way the local worshiping community—that is, a particular parish, a particular region, or even a particular cultural group—acts, intending it to be binding for future liturgical praxis. Indeed, custom is not only a source of the law but also "the best interpreter of [the other sources of]

---

31. Huels, *Liturgical Law: An Introduction*, 9. He clarifies by saying, "The pope and ecumenical council are the only legislators for the universal church" (ibid.).

32. See canons 31–33.

33. See canon 34.

34. Huels, *Liturgical Law: An Introduction*, 9–10.

35. Ibid., 10.

36. See canons 29, 30, 835.1, 838.4.

37. Huels, *Liturgical Law: An Introduction*, 9.

38. See canons 23–28.

39. Huels, *Liturgical Law: An Introduction*, 9.

the law."[40] There are four categories of custom from the perspective of ecclesiastical norms: "iuxta legem,"[41] "praeter legem,"[42] "contra legem,"[43] and "factual."[44]

Finally, it is important to point out that not everything in a legislative document holds the force of law. One must read it with the usual rules of literary criticism in mind. According to Huels, "some statements that appear in texts of ecclesiastical law are not truly legal but are in fact theological in nature. Among these, some are divine-law statements from an ecumenical council or from Scripture or the natural law; others are statements of authentic teaching that are not divinely revealed dogma; a few others may be mere theological opinion subject to dispute and debate within the theological community."[45]

40. "Consuetudo est optima legum interpres" (canon 27). Huels states, "This maxim, adopted from Roman law, has long been an established principle of canonical interpretation. It demonstrates the great respect canon law has for the living practices of the community. It means that the best way to discover how a law is to be understood and implemented is to look to the ways the local Christian communities actually observe it." Huels, *Liturgical Law: An Introduction*, 23.

41. "In accord with the law"—the practice or custom at a particular church, or how the rubrics are interpreted in this place.

42. "Beyond the law" (see canons 26, 28)—a practice that has nothing to do with the current liturgical law, but which can become a law or norm in a particular place. In this case, for the custom to become law, the community must receive the custom as law willingly, and the custom must be reasonable. After a period of thirty years, the custom becomes law.

43. "Contrary to the law"—a practice that is contrary to what the law requires. The principle of "dissimulation" often comes into play here. A bishop, while knowing a custom to be contrary to liturgical law, might decide not to intervene in order to maintain peace and order.

44. Factual custom "is the actual practice of the worshipping community whether it be in accord with, beyond, or contrary to the law." Huels, *Liturgical Law: An Introduction*, 24. It is not law, but in most respects it functions as such since it is the accepted manner in which a community celebrates the liturgy. In other words, a factual custom is "a well-established practice accepted peacefully by the community" (ibid.).

45. Ibid., 11. See, for example, GIRM 16–26, which, for the most part, is a theological statement about the nature of the Mass. No. 39 of the same document on the importance of singing is another example of a nonlegislative statement contained in an otherwise legislative document. See also Örsy, "Interpreter and His Art"; and Örsy, "The Interpretation of Laws: New Variations on an Old Theme," *Studia Canonica* 17 (1983): 107–11.

ECCLESIASTICAL DOCUMENTS PERTAINING TO THE ENTRANCE SONG

The preconciliar, conciliar, and postconciliar documents[46] that follow contain general and specific norms that have governed the use and development of the text and music of the entrance song.[47]

Preconciliar Documents

Pope Pius X's *motu proprio Tra le Sollecitudini* (22 November 1903)[48] puts forward two basic general norms relevant to the entrance song. First, liturgical texts are to be in Latin (TLS 5, 7). Second,

---

46. For analyses of these documents and the reform of liturgical music during the time immediately following the council, see Lucien Deiss, *Spirit and Song of the New Liturgy* (1970; rev. ed., Cincinnati: World Library Publications, 1976); Joseph Gelineau, *Voices and Instruments in Christian Worship: Principles, Laws, Applications*, trans. Clifford Howell (Collegeville. MN: Liturgical Press, 1964); Helmut Hucke, "Musical Requirements of Liturgical Reform," *Concilium* 1 (1966): 45–74; Josef Jungmann, "Constitution on the Sacred Liturgy," in *Commentary on the Documents of Vatican II*, ed. Herbert Vorgrimler, vol. 1 (New York: Herder & Herder, 1967), 76–80; Frederick R. McManus, "Sacred Music in the Teaching of the Church," in *Crisis in Church Music?* (Washington, DC: Liturgical Conference, 1967), 14–26; Clement J. McNapsy, "The Sacral in Liturgical Music," in *Revival of the Liturgy*, ed. Frederick R. McManus (New York: Herder & Herder, 1963), 163–90; Anthony Milner, "The Instruction on Sacred Music," *Worship* 41 (1967): 322–33; Ernest Moneta Caglio, "Sacred Music," in *The Commentary on the Constitution and the Instruction on the Sacred Liturgy*, ed. Annibale Bugnini and Carlo Braga (New York: Benzinger Bros., 1965), 244–56; Rembert G. Weakland, "Music as Art in Liturgy," *Worship* 41 (January 1967): 5–15; and Rembert Weakland, "The 'Sacral' and Liturgical Renewal," *Worship* 49 (1975): 512–29. For a more recent exploration of the reform and renewal of church music in postconciliar ecclesiastical documents, see Weakland, *Themes of Renewal* (Beltsville, MD: Pastoral Press, 1995). For a summary of earlier legislation, see Hayburn, *Papal Legislation*, 1–15 (on the early popes) and 387–408 (on the effects of legislation on musical practice).

47. Note that in ecclesiastical documents the entrance song or introit is often considered together with the other processional chants of the Mass: the offertory and communion.

48. See also Hayburn, *Papal Legislation*, 219–31, 295–386; Jan Michael Joncas, *From Sacred Song to Ritual Music: Twentieth-Century Understandings of Roman Catholic Worship Music* (Collegeville, MN: Liturgical Press, 1997), 1–2, 3–5, 32–34, 51–52, 73–76, 100–101; and Judith M. Kubicki, "Tra le Sollecitudini (1903)," in *The Song of the Assembly: Pastoral Music in Practice*, ed. Bari Colombari and Michael R. Prendergast (Portland, OR: Pastoral Press, 2007), 1–3.

one is not to reorder, alter, or omit (either entirely or in part) those official liturgical texts that are to be sung (TLS 8–9). The document offers one exception in that it allows for a brief motet "to words approved by the Church" after the prescribed offertory chant (TLS 8).[49] Pope Pius XI's apostolic constitution *Divini Cultus Sanctitatem* (20 December 1928)[50] and Pope Pius XII's encyclical letter *Mediator Dei* (20 November 1947)[51] simply restate the norms of *Tra le Sollecitudini*.

The next document to discuss the entrance song in particular is Pius XII's encyclical letter *Musicae Sacrae Disciplina* (25 December 1955).[52] It recommends that the corpus of entrance chants (texts and melodies) be expanded to accommodate feasts new to the liturgical calendar and reiterates that all liturgical texts must be in Latin (MSD 44, 47).[53] Most important is its discussion of the substitution of the introit with another song for "serious reasons" by explicit permission of the Holy See. The extension of these exceptions to other places without such permission, however, is prohibited. In fact, even when the Holy See has allowed for an exception, it is better to employ the "easier and more frequently used" chants, rather than alternative texts or melodies (MSD 46).

Musicae Sacrae Disciplina recognizes that some exceptions are allowed, according to custom: "Where . . . some popular hymns are sung in the language of the people after the sacred words of the liturgy have been sung in Latin during the solemn Eucharistic sacrifice, local Ordinaries can allow this to be done 'if, in light of the circumstances of the locality and the people, they believe that [the custom] cannot prudently be removed'" (MSD III, 8).[54] Thus, even if exceptions are allowed in some circumstances, the introit found in the official liturgical books is always normative and preferable. Indeed, the concession concerning custom requires that the official texts be proclaimed during the liturgy in addition to any popular songs.

De Musica Sacra (3 September 1958),[55] an instruction from the Congregation of Rites, repeats the two exceptions of *Musicae Sacrae*

49. Trans., Vincent Yzermans, *All Things in Christ* (1952).

50. See also James Hansen, "Divini Cultus (1928)," in *Song of the Assembly*, 5–7; and Hayburn, *Papal Legislation*, 300.

51. See Genevieve Glen, "Mediator Dei (1947)," in *Song of the Assembly*, 9–11; and Hayburn, *Papal Legislation*, 307.

52. See Hayburn, *Papal Legislation*, 308.

53. Trans., *The Pope Speaks* 3:1 (1956).

54. This section of the letter quotes canon 5 of the 1917 *Codex Iuris Canonici*.

55. As an instruction, this document is a doctrinal explanation. It is not concerned with establishing new laws, but rather with making existing laws

Disciplina (DMS 13c, 14a).[56] It states that "in sung liturgical services no liturgical text translated verbatim into the vernacular may
be sung except by special permission" (DMS 13b, 14). Rather than
an expansion of the allowable use of vernacular liturgical texts by
"special permission," it is more likely that this statement is an effort
to discourage a practice that was taking place with at least some
frequency. It is forbidden, furthermore, to omit any sung liturgical
text unless the rubrics specifically allow for such an omission (DMS
21b). Even in cases of "reasonable cause,"[57] in which it is impossible
to sing the liturgical text according to the melodies given in the liturgical books, the texts must be chanted on a single note or on psalm
tones, or sung with organ accompaniment (DMS 21b).

In terms of official legislative ecclesiastical documents, *De Musica
Sacra* was of great importance regarding the renewal of the entrance
song in the Roman Rite. In essence, it restored the early form of the
introit. After a centuries-old tradition of using only one psalm verse
at the introit, *De Musica Sacra* stated that at the solemn Mass and the
Missa cantata, "if the priest and his ministers enter the church by a
rather long route, nothing forbids, after the chanting of the antiphon
of the Introit and its versicle, the chanting of many other verses of the
same psalm. In this case, the antiphon can be repeated after every one
or two verses, and when the priest has reached the altar, the psalm is
broken off, and if necessary, the *Gloria Patri* is sung and the antiphon
repeated" (DMS 27a).[58]

To be sure, the provision for more than one psalm verse takes
for granted that the introit will begin as the priest and his ministers
process to the altar, and not, as had been the case for centuries, once
the priest reached the foot of the altar.[59] *De Musica Sacra* couches

---

practically applicable. See also Hayburn, *Papal Legislation*, 398, 543; Joncas,
From Sacred Song to Ritual Music, 3, 17–20, 37–38, 76–81, 103–4; and Columba
Kelly, "De Musica Sacra et Sacra Liturgia (1958)," in *Song of the Assembly*, 13–15.

56. Trans., *The Pope Speaks* 5:2 (1959).

57. For example, if a parish lacks a choir and the assembly is unable to sing
the official chants on its own.

58. Trans., Hayburn, *Papal Legislation on Sacred Music*, 363.

59. Jungmann notes that "the rubric of the present-day Vatican Gradual
apparently takes the stand that the introit should again assume its rightful place
as the entrance song of the Mass, for it expressly orders that the introit be intoned
as the celebrant approaches the altar: 'When the priest starts toward the altar,
the cantors begin the introit.' There are liturgists who insist that the Vatican
Gradual introduced no change, that the introit is to be intoned only after the

this renewal or expansion of the introit form within a section titled "Participation of the faithful in the sung Mass," which seeks sung "active participation" in three degrees: (1) liturgical responses, (2) the Mass Ordinary, and (3) the proper chants of the Mass (DMS 25). Both looking to the past (allowing more than one psalm verse[60]) and looking to the future (recommending congregational participation in the entirety of the entrance song[61]), these requirements of *De Musica Sacra* are precursors to the congregational singing of the entrance song that stemmed from the liturgical movement and Vatican II liturgical reform.[62]

---

priest arrives at the foot of the altar. But actually the wording adopted is different from that in the older rubrics, substituting *accedente sacerdote ad altare* for the other reading, *cum . . . pervenerit ante infimum gradum altaris* (the rubric based on the Ceremonial of Bishops). The plain and obvious direction of the rubric is: Start the introit as soon as the celebrant appears in the sanctuary." Jungmann, *Mass of the Roman Rite*, 1:270n40.

60. *De Musica Sacra* provides no guidelines for the frequent instances when the introit antiphon is not taken from the psalms, or for those rarer cases in which the verses themselves are not taken from the psalms. The guidelines for the other proper chants of the offertory and communion antiphons, however, do address this issue, saying, respectively, "If the antiphon is not taken from a psalm, a psalm suitable to the solemnity may be chosen," and "If the antiphon is not taken from a psalm, one may choose a psalm fitting to the solemnity of the liturgical action." One should assume these guidelines also apply to the introit. Jungmann states, "In our time the tendency has been manifested more than once to restore the introit to a fuller form, at least on festive occasions, by substituting the original full psalm in place of its vestigial single verse. Thus at the coronation Mass of Pope Pius XI in 1922 the entire *Introitus* psalm was sung." Jungmann, *Mass of the Roman Rite*, 1:327.

61. Other than perhaps the *Gloria Patri*, no part of the introit had traditionally been sung by the congregation, only by the choir. "One must insist above all on this full participation in the [proper] chant in religious communities and in seminaries." *De Musica Sacra* 25c.

62. The prescriptions for the introit in the introduction to the 1974 *Graduale Romanum* (*Ordo Cantus Missae*) are as follows: "When the congregation has gathered and while the priest and ministers are going to the altar, the entrance antiphon begins. Its intonation may be shorter or longer as the circumstances warrant; better still, the whole assembly may begin the chant together. Thus the asterisk in the *Graduale* marking off the part to be intoned is to be regarded merely as a guide. When the choir has sung the antiphon, the cantor or cantors sing the verse, then the choir repeats the antiphon. The alternation between antiphon and versicles may go on as long as is necessary to accompany the entrance procession. The final repetition of the antiphon, however, may be preceded by the *Gloria Patri* and *Sicut erat*, sung as the one, final versicle. When the *Gloria Patri* and *Sicut*

In his short epistle *Iucunda Laudatio* (IL) to the director of the Pontifical Institute of Sacred Music (8 December 1961),[63] Pope John XXIII expresses his thanks to the institute, which Pius X had established during his pontificate. He emphasizes the importance of "the preservation of Latin as the language of Catholic worship" (IL), and notes that, while popular songs in the vernacular are sometimes permissible at less solemn liturgies, Latin should remain normative and retain its "regal scepter and . . . noble dominion" (IL). He implies a broader interpretation of norms concerning liturgical song in this letter, though, in that he praises missionaries who "have succeeded in preserving and adapting native music to Catholic rites" (IL).

The documents above provide some insight into the preconciliar discipline regarding liturgical music, though specific discussion of the entrance song is sparse. Furthermore, one should recognize that the norms they express might or might not reflect what was actually happening in parishes at the time. What is clear, however, is that prior to the Second Vatican Council, the official Latin texts and melodies for the introit were normative for the entrance song at Mass and that, at least in ecclesiastical legislation, the traditional form of the introit had been restored.

Conciliar and Postconciliar Documents

The Liturgy Constitution

Though there is nothing in *Sacrosanctum Concilium*[64] that deals specifically with the text and melody of the entrance song, the constitution puts forth several principles that influence its subsequent development:

---

erat have a special musical termination, this must be used with each of the other verses. If the *Gloria Patri* and the repetition of the antiphon would cause the chant to last too long, the *Gloria Patri* is omitted. When the procession is short, only one psalm verse is used or even the antiphon alone, without the verse." *Ordo Cantus Missae* no. 1, trans. ICEL, *Documents on the Liturgy 1963–1979: Conciliar, Papal, and Curial Texts* (Collegeville, MN: Liturgical Press, 1982), 1345.

63. *Acta Apostolicae Sedis* 53 (1961): 812. English-language summary, *The Pope Speaks* 7 (1961): 367–68. *Iucunda Laudatio* is an "apostolic epistle," which is "a less solemn papal letter, sometimes addressed to one person or a group in the Church but usually not to the universal Church." Seasoltz, *New Liturgy, New Laws*, 172.

64. See Joncas, *From Sacred Song to Ritual Music*, 4–5, 20–22, 38–39, 81–82, 104–5; and Nathan Mitchell, "Sacrosanctum Concilium (1963)," in *Song of the Assembly*, 17–20.

1. The active participation of the faithful in the liturgy (SC 14).

2. The permission for limited use of the vernacular in the liturgy (SC 54).

3. The pride of place of chant along with the admittance of all forms of liturgical music into the liturgy, including the people's own religious songs and traditional styles, that possess the required qualities (SC 112, 116, 118, 119).

4. The desire that the whole assembly be enabled to sing liturgical chant (SC 114).

In addition, *Sacrosanctum Concilium* encourages the composition of new music for the liturgy.[65] This music may utilize newly composed texts, though texts drawn from Scripture and the official liturgical books are preferred (SC 121). It is also in *Sacrosanctum Concilium* that one finds the mandate for what will become the *Graduale Simplex* and the revised *Graduale Romanum* (SC 114, 117).

The Postconciliar Gradual

The primary sources of the introit in the postconciliar liturgy, even though the *Missale Romanum*[66] also contains introit antiphon texts, are the *Graduale Romanum* and *Graduale Simplex*.[67] As official liturgical books, these two editions contain the official Latin texts and melodies for the processional chants of the Mass and are sources of

---

65. These new songs were not necessarily intended as replacements for the proper chants.

66. See Paul VI, Apostolic Constitution *Missale Romanum*, approving the new Roman Missal, 3 April 1969: *Acta Apostolicae Sedis* 61 (1969): 217–22; *Notitiae* 5 (1969): 142–46; DOL 202. Congregation for Divine Worship, Instruction *Constitutione Apostolica*, on the gradual carrying out of the Apostolic Constitution *Missale Romanum* (3 April 1969), 20 October 1969: *Acta Apostolicae Sedis* 61 (1969): 749–53; *Notitiae* 5 (1969): 418–23; DOL 209. For an account of the reform of the entrance song within the context of the preparation of the Missal of Paul VI, see Maurizio Barba, *La riforma Conciliare dell "ordo Missae": Il percorso storico-redazionale dei riti d'ingresso, di offertorio e di communione* (Rome: CLV Edizioni Liturgiche, 2002), 144–49. The conciliar schemas for its reform (nos. 16, 39, 44, 90) are also included in Barba's appendix.

67. See also Frederick R. McManus, "Gregorian Chant in Official Documents," in *Gregorian Chant in Pastoral Ministry Today* (Washington, DC: Center for Ward Method Studies, 1986), passim.

universal law governing the liturgy.[68] Their creation was no simple task, however, because the principles for the reform of liturgical music found in *Sacrosanctum Concilium* met immediately with opposition, and, as Annibale Bugnini recalls, "the problem of song was one of the most sensitive, important and troubling of the entire reform."[69] During the council, study group twenty-five was responsible for the implementation of *Sacrosanctum Concilium* 114 and 117—in other words, they were to prepare the postconciliar *editio typica* of the *Graduale Romanum*, to review and revise according to more recent scholarship the chant books produced during Pius X's reform, and to produce a book of less complicated chants that could be used in smaller parishes.[70] The monks of Solesmes, who had been intimately involved in the revision, compilation, and publication of books of chant for use in the Roman Rite for some time, collaborated with this study group.[71]

In order to fulfill the prescription of *Sacrosanctum Concilium* 117, a decree from the Congregation of Rites, *Sacrosancti Oecumenici Concilii* (3 September 1967),[72] authorized the publication of the *Grad-*

68. John Huels, general introduction to *The Liturgy Documents: A Parish Resource*, 3rd ed. (Chicago: Liturgy Training Publications, 1991), x.

69. Annibale Bugnini, *The Reform of the Liturgy* (1948–1975), trans. Matthew J. O'Connell (Collegeville, MN: Liturgical Press, 1990), 885. He states, "Two conceptions of the function of sacred song in the liturgy were now at work. One type of musician looked upon song primarily as an art form and an adornment of the celebration. Liturgists and pastors, on the other hand, as well as musicians more conscious of pastoral needs, saw song as having a structural role and serving to give better expression to the mystery being celebrated" (ibid.).

70. Ibid., 891.

71. Ibid.

72. Congregation of Rites (Consilium), Decree *Sacrosancti Oecumenici*, promulgating the *editio typica* of the *Graduale Simplex*, 3 September 1967: *Notitiae* 3 (1967): 311; DOL 532. See also Congregation of Rites, Introduction to the *Graduale Simplex*, 3 September 1967: Vatican Polyglot Press, 1967; *Notitiae* 3 (1967): 312–315; DOL 533. Consilium, Communication *Instantibus Pluribus* to the presidents of the national liturgical commissions, on norms for translation of the *Graduale Simplex*, 23 January 1968: *Notitiae* 4 (1968): 10; DOL 120. Congregation for Divine Worship, Decree *Cantus Faciliores*, promulgating the *editio typica altera* of the *Graduale Simplex*, 22 November 1974: *Notitiae* 11 (1975): 292; DOL 536. *Graduale Simplex, editio typica altera*, 22 November 1974: Vatican Polyglot Press, 1975; DOL 537.

uale Simplex.[73] Its purpose was to facilitate the use and appropriation of the chant tradition in smaller parish churches[74] that lacked the musical resources to sing the more complex chants in the *Graduale Romanum*, though it certainly found use in other contexts as well. Indeed, Bugnini states that "the book became the usual source for the Latin celebrations in the papal chapel. This is evidence that the need for such a book was not felt solely in 'smaller churches.'"[75] In light of its purpose, the book provides proper chants only for Sundays and major feasts[76] and seasonal chants for the remainder of the liturgical year. Both the proper and seasonal chants draw from the traditional Gregorian repertoire,[77] in accord with the mandate of *Sacrosanctum Concilium* 114 that the treasury of chant be preserved.

After the promulgation of the *editio typica* of the *Graduale Simplex*, ICEL published an English translation of its texts that Kevin Seasoltz notes "did not prove very successful."[78] The popular use of the *Graduale Simplex* (both Latin and English) was limited for many reasons, including the long-standing custom in many parishes and religious communities of singing hymns at Mass,[79] the general proliferation of other types of music by publishers, the inherent difficulty of adapting English texts to Latin melodies, and the perception that chant was too difficult or foreign for congregations to sing. For many, the musical aesthetic of the "new" way of celebrating the Mass did not leave room for traditional chant or English-language adaptations of

---

73. Seasoltz, *New Liturgy, New Laws*, 148. See also *Notitiae* 3 (1967): 311. ICEL recounts, "A substantial portion of the Latin text and musical settings had been experimented with at the daily Masses during the final period of the Second Vatican Council in 1965." ICEL, *The Simple Gradual: An English Translation of the Antiphons and Responsories of the Graduale Simplex for Use in English-Speaking Countries* (Washington, DC, 1968), "Introductory Information," 10.

74. The introduction to the *Graduale Simplex*, no. 1, states, "It is intended for those churches where the correct rendering of the more ornate melodies of the Roman Gradual is difficult." The text here is the same in both the *editio typica* and *editio typica altera*. See also *Sacrosanctum Concilium* 117; and *Musicam Sacram* 50b.

75. Bugnini, *The Reform of the Liturgy*, 121.

76. Seasoltz, *New Liturgy, New Laws*, 148.

77. The Solesmes monks used mainly simpler antiphons from the Divine Office.

78. Seasoltz, *New Liturgy, New Laws*, 148.

79. Ibid.

this chant. New vernacular musical settings of many varieties proved more successful than the *Graduale Simplex*.[80]

The *editio typica altera* of the *Graduale Simplex* was promulgated on 22 November 1974 to accommodate changes in the liturgical calendar, the neo-Vulgate translation of the Bible, and liturgical books published after 1967. This second amplified edition contained, in addition to the proper chants, the chants of the Ordinary of the Mass, the *Kyriale Simplex*,[81] and several appendices.[82] Regardless of the long-term success of the *Graduale Simplex* as a liturgical book—to be sure, it is rarely used today in parishes[83]—it did provide some important norms for the subsequent development of liturgical music:

1. Song is integral to Christian worship. The impetus for the book's creation was not only the thrust of *Sacrosanctum Concilium* 114 and 117 (preserving and encouraging the use of the Roman chant tradition), but also the principles that the normative enactment of the liturgy is to include singing and that many liturgical texts are best expressed through song.[84]

---

80. Ibid., 148–49.

81. Congregation of Rites (Consilium), Decree *Quum Constitutio*, promulgating the *editio typica* of the *Kyriale Simplex*, 14 December 1964: *Acta Apostolicae Sedis* 57 (1965): 407; DOL 529. Congregation of Rites (Consilium), *Kyriale Simplex*, 14 December 1964: Vatican Polyglot Press, 1965; DOL 530.

82. See *Notitiae* 11 (1975): 291.

83. In truth, as Bugnini says, it was "a final attempt to lend solemnity to the Latin liturgy and prevent a complete loss of the priceless patrimony of traditional Latin chant." Bugnini, *The Reform of the Liturgy*, 121. Its use did not persist, even though at first "the *Graduale Simplex* was very successful. Two printings were sold out in a short time. Many conferences asked permission to produce vernacular editions" (ibid.).

84. "The musical tradition of the universal Church is a treasure of inestimable value, greater even than that of any other art. The main reason for this preeminence is that, as sacred song closely bound to the text, it forms a necessary or integral part of the solemn liturgy. . . . Therefore sacred music will be the more holy the more closely it is joined to the liturgical rite." *Sacrosanctum Concilium* 112. "If the Eucharist is to be celebrated with greater artistic quality, that is with singing, and if the faithful are to participate in it, it is first necessary to have simpler melodies." Introduction to the *Graduale Simplex* 5. "Since these new texts have been selected solely for musical reasons, they are not to be used without musical notation" (ibid., 8).

2. Singing is one of the primary means of *actuosa participatio*.[85] Thus, it is critically important that all gathered for a particular liturgical celebration are enabled to sing.[86]

3. Artistic quality (both of the music itself and of its performance) is the ideal to strive for in all forms of liturgical music. The *Graduale Simplex* provides a model for future collections in the deliberate care that went into its creation. Its creation also emphasizes the fact that simpler music is often preferable to virtuosic music if it more readily enables quality performance.[87]

4. New collections of music for the celebration of the Eucharist are to be encouraged[88] to the degree they are in keeping with the nature of the rite and facilitate singing, active participa-

85. "To promote active participation, the people should be encouraged to take part by means of acclamations, responses, psalmody, antiphons, and songs." *Sacrosanctum Concilium* 30. "From a pastoral point of view [the creation of the *Graduale Simplex* means that] singing even in smaller groups now becomes possible." Introduction to the *Graduale Simplex* 4. "The congregation should sing the antiphon and the response to the psalms between the readings. At times the congregation's part may be taken by the *schola*. In view of their nature and the ease with which they may be sung, at least the responses to the psalms between the readings should be sung by the entire congregation" (ibid., 14b).

86. "The purpose of the *Simple Gradual* is to afford a greater opportunity for community participation in song—especially through congregational singing of brief refrains and responses to the longer verses sung by a cantor, *schola*, or choir." ICEL, Simple Gradual, "Introductory Information," 11.

87. See Introduction to the *Graduale Simplex* 5. "These simpler melodies cannot derive from the more ornate ones in the *Roman Gradual*. . . . Hence authentic melodies, suitable for the purpose, have been sought in the Gregorian chant, both from official editions and from manuscript sources of the Roman and other Latin rites. From this new selections of melodies, a new series of texts was also developed. Very rarely was a simple melody found which was set to one of the texts in the *Missal*. When agreement of text and melody could not be found, pieces were selected which have words similar or close in meaning to the texts of the *Roman Missal*" (ibid., 6–8).

88. "Other kinds of sacred music, especially polyphony, are by no means excluded from liturgical celebrations." *Sacrosanctum Concilium* 116. "The people's own religious songs are to be encouraged with care so that in sacred devotions as well as during services of the liturgy itself, in keeping with rubrical norms and requirements, the faithful may raise their voices in song" (ibid., 118). "In certain parts of the world . . . people have their own musical traditions and these play a great part in their religious and social life. Thus . . . due importance is to be attached to their music and a suitable place given to it, not only in forming their

tion, and quality musical performance. These new collections should include settings of both new texts and texts already part of the tradition, and they should, given the requirement of artistic quality, be prepared by skilled arrangers, composers, and editors.

5. Sung proper texts are integral to the celebration of the Eucharist, [89] as is the singing of psalms.[90] Newly composed proper texts should take up the theme or idea of the official text or follow the lead of the *Graduale Simplex* by reflecting the festal or seasonal theme or a theme from the readings of the day. Stable musical and textual traditions are essential for particular worshiping communities, even if what they are singing is not precisely the chant of the *Graduale Romanum*.

Most interesting among these foundations is the move toward new collections of sung texts for liturgical use.[91] Ecclesiastical norms prior to *Sacrosanctum Concilium* sought to limit the use of new

---

attitude toward religion, but also in adapting worship to their native genius" (ibid., 119).

89. "Not every Sunday has its own formulary in the Proper of Seasons. Each liturgical season has one or more formularies for use on all the Sundays of the season. Each feast of the Lord, however, has proper songs. The feasts which take the place of a Sunday have their own songs in the Proper of Saints. The Common of Saints is arranged as in the *Roman Missal*, but in such a way that only one formulary is provided for each order of saints. Several songs are given for each part of the Mass so that the one which best applies to the saint may be chosen." Introduction to the *Graduale Simplex* 11–13.

90. "For the entrance, offertory, and communion songs, the form to be used should consist of an antiphon repeated after the verses of the psalm." Ibid., 9. "The *Simple Gradual* is . . . an attempt to reintroduce the singing of the psalms in the eucharistic service. Instead of the proper antiphons of the *Roman Gradual* and *Missal* the *Simple Gradual* employs psalm verses with great variety and freedom of choice. It reestablishes the antiphon as a refrain and the response or alleluia as a true response. This development calls for a better orientation of the people toward psalms." ICEL, Simple Gradual, "Introductory Information," 10–11.

91. At first, "new collections" implied only the possibility of setting official proper chant texts to simpler melodies from within the tradition, in addition

musical settings and especially new texts, and when allowed, such music was, strictly speaking, not "liturgical."[92] The creation of the *Graduale Simplex* shows forth the flexibility and adaptability of the postconciliar liturgy according to the needs of particular worshiping communities,[93] and, in a sense, is a conservative response to the adaptations envisioned in *Sacrosanctum Concilium* 39–40,[94] *Musicam*

---

to using seasonal chants rather than the entire corpus of proper chants. Later, composers set the official proper texts to other (i.e., non-Gregorian) melodies. Texts other than those of the proper chants eventually came to be permitted at the entrance and communion, but, though it has come to be the practice in many places today, the intent was never to completely divorce such "new collections" from the official corpus of Latin proper chants. Indeed, these chants are the archetype or paradigm for "new collections."

92. Previous legislation allowed for the singing of devotional motets (*Tra le Sollecitudini* 8) or popular hymns (*Musicae Sacrae Disciplina* 47) at certain points during the liturgy. Polyphonic settings of the Mass Ordinary and proper sung by the choir or *schola* were also permitted.

93. As Bugnini states, "Its publication was certainly another step toward a new form of celebration. By making it easier to sing the proper parts of the Mass—singing often neglected in the past because of the difficulty of the chants in the *Graduale Romanum*—the new book helped to make the value of this chant understood." Bugnini, *The Reform of the Liturgy*, 121. In fact, it was imagined from the outset that vernacular editions of the *Graduale Simplex* would include significant adaptations. "The texts of antiphons, even those taken from the psalter, sometimes need modification: to achieve fully the meaning appropriate to a liturgical season or particular feast; to ensure the people's understanding of the text; to match the rhythmical and vocal requirements of chant in the vernacular. The types of chant in the *Graduale simplex* . . . may be adapted to the style of music and song typical of individual peoples. . . . Sometimes the texts of antiphons, of the psalm verse, or of the psalm itself as given in the *Graduale simplex* may create problems, with the result that a different choice of texts seems preferable: either because the text in the translation being used presents pastoral problems; or because it seems advisable to use collections of psalms and antiphons that may already be in use, familiar to many, and well accepted. In such cases the conference of bishops may choose other texts, but in a way consistent with the principles set forth in the Introduction of the *Graduale simplex*." *Instantibus Pluribus* 2b–3.

94. "It shall be for the competent, territorial ecclesiastical authority . . . to specify adaptations, especially in the case of . . . sacred music."

Sacram 9[95] and 32,[96] and *Liturgicae Instaurationes* 3c.[97] At the same time that it made clear the value of the church's chant tradition, it also made clear the importance of the active participation of the assembly by means of singing. Indeed, as Bugnini says, "the principle of songs in the vernacular would be extended to the entire Church in the reformed Roman Missal."[98] ICEL's original introduction to its translation of the *Graduale Simplex* clarifies the matter:

95. "The Church does not exclude any type of sacred music from liturgical services as long as the music matches the spirit of the service itself and the character of the individual parts and is not a hindrance to the required active participation of the people." Congregation of Rites, Instruction *Musicam Sacram*, on music in the liturgy, 5 March 1967: *Acta Apostolicae Sedis* 60 (1967): 300–320; *Notitiae* 3 (1967): 87–105; DOL 508.

96. Bugnini notes that "in some places there is the lawful practice, occasionally confirmed by indult, of substituting other songs for the entrance. . . . Discussion among the Fathers and experts [during the creation of *Musicam Sacram*] focused on individual points, with special attention to the most important. There was full discussion of no. 36 (no. 32 in the final text), which allowed the chants of the Mass to be replaced by other songs approved by the episcopal conferences. The instruction restricted itself to confirming the indults granted to certain countries for this purpose. . . . The paragraph was put to a vote and accepted. It would subsequently play a very important role, because the episcopal conferences would appeal to it as a basis for asking the same indult for their regions." Bugnini, *The Reform of the Liturgy*, 902–3.

97. The document states, "Congregational singing is to be fostered by every means possible, even by use of new types of music suited to the culture of the people and to the contemporary spirit." Congregation for Divine Worship, Instruction (third) *Liturgicae Instaurationes*, on the orderly carrying out of the Constitution on the Liturgy, 5 September 1970: *Acta Apostolicae Sedis* 62 (1970): 692–704; *Notitiae* 7 (1971): 10–26; DOL 52.

98. Bugnini, *The Reform of the Liturgy*, 903. On the extension of the use of the vernacular, see also *Sacrosanctum Concilium* 36, 54, 113; and Consilium, Letter *Dans sa récente allocution* of Cardinal G. Lercaro to presidents of the Conferences of Bishops and, for their information, to presidents of the national liturgical commissions, on issues regarding reform of the liturgy, 21 June 1967: *Notitiae* 3 (1967): 289–96; DOL 41, margin no. 486. On vernacular songs in the liturgy, see also: *Musicam Sacram* 32, 33, 36, 47, 53, 54, 59, 61. Consilium, Letter to the Italian Conference of Bishops, on liturgical music, 2 February 1968: *Notitiae* 4 (1968): 95–98, no. 1; DOL 512. Paul VI, Address to the 10th International Congress of Church Choirs, 6 April 1970: *Notitiae* 6 (1970): 154–57; DOL 518, margin no. 4223. Paul VI, Address to women religious taking part in the National Convention of the Associazione Italiana di Santa Cecilia, 15 April 1971: *Notitiae* 7 (1971): 241–43; DOL 519, margin no. 4225. Paul VI, Address at an audience for choir members, on the occasion of the tenth anniversary of the Consociatio

None of this means, however, that the alternative texts given in the new *Simple Gradual* need be used in their entirety on a particular occasion or that all parts of the proper must include psalm verses with antiphon or response. It is permissible to make only partial use of the *Simple Gradual*. For one thing, the *Simple Gradual* was not issued to supplant the *Roman Gradual*; it may be substituted for the latter in whole or in part.[99] Neither does the *Simple Gradual* preclude the development of further substitutes for the three processional chants—whether appropriate hymns or responsorial styles of song. On the contrary, the *Simple Gradual* enlarges the options and increases the flexibility of the sung parts of the eucharistic liturgy.[100]

Again, in order to fulfill the mandate of *Sacrosanctum Concilium* 114, the Sacred Congregation for Divine Worship promulgated the *Ordo Cantus Missae*[101] on 24 June 1972. This book indicated how the *Graduale Romanum* was to be accommodated to the reformed liturgy and provides the antiphon and psalm verse assignments for the entire liturgical year. The monks of Solesmes produced the revised edition of the *Graduale Romanum* in 1974 according to the provisions of *Sacrosanctum Concilium* and *Ordo Cantus Missae*.

It is clear that, while use of the *Graduale Simplex* is encouraged when its use would enhance the active participation of the faithful, the *Graduale Romanum* is still to be considered the normative source of the texts and melodies of the proper chants of the Mass. As such,

---

Internationalis Musicae Sacrae, 12 October 1973; DOL 522, margin no. 4236. Congregation for Divine Worship, Letter *Voluntati Obsequens* to bishops, accompanying the booklet *Iubilate Deo*, 14 April 1974: *Notitiae* 10 (1974): 123–26; DOL 523, margin no. 4239. Secretariat of State, Letter of Cardinal J. Villot to the Archbishop of Salzburg, on the occasion of the 6th International Congress of the CIMS (Salzburg, 26 August–2 September 1974), August 1974: *Notitiae* 10 (1974): 344–45; DOL 525, margin nos. 4244, 4255.

99. Introduction to the *Graduale Simplex* 203. "It is recommended that even in smaller churches, which use the *Simple Gradual*, certain pieces be sung from the *Roman Gradual*, especially those which are easier or which have been traditionally used by the people" (ibid.).

100. ICEL, Simple Gradual, "Introductory Information," 10.

101. Congregation for Divine Worship, Decree *Thesaurum Cantus Gregoriani*, promulgating the *editio typica* of the *Ordo Cantus Missae*, 24 June 1972: *Acta Apostolicae Sedis* 65 (1973): 274; *Notitiae* 8 (1972): 215; DOL 534. *Ordo Cantus Missae*, 24 June 1972: Vatican Polyglot Press, 1972; DOL 535. For a precursor to the *Ordo Cantus Missae*, see Congregation of Rites (Consilium), Decree *Edita Instructione*, promulgating *Cantus qui in Missali Romano Desiderantur*, 14 December 1964: *Acta Apostolicae Sedis* 57 (1965): 408.

it is a kind of archetype for the texts, melodies, and musical form for the entrance song at Mass. Its actual use, however, must be balanced with the other requirements of the postconciliar liturgy, such as the active participation of the faithful and the now nearly universal practice of celebrating the liturgy in the vernacular. Other sources, such as the Simple Gradual and even new collections of songs approved by the conferences of bishops, are also official sources for the entrance song, which to greater and lesser extents derive from the *Graduale Romanum* archetype. As the introduction to the *Graduale Simplex* states, "The *Roman Gradual* deserves the highest honor in the Church for its artistic and devotional quality, and its integrity and value should not be impaired. It is therefore hoped that it will be used in those churches which have a *schola cantorum* with the necessary technical training to sing the more elaborate melodies. Moreover, it is recommended that even in smaller churches, which use the *Simple Gradual*, certain pieces be sung from the *Roman Gradual*, especially those which are easier or which have been traditionally used by the people."[102]

While the primary reason for the production of the postconciliar *Graduale Romanum* was the preservation of the church's chant tradition[103] required by *Sacrosanctum Concilium*, those involved in its revision took great care to make it a usable liturgical book—even if it was primarily intended for use in communities with a particularly skilled *schola cantorum* or choir. Making the *Graduale Romanum* useful for the postconciliar liturgy required substantial revision of the preconciliar *Graduale*. These revisions were of six types:[104]

1. "Authentic Gregorian" chants for suppressed liturgical celebrations were reassigned to other days of the liturgical year so as to (a) retain important chants within the church's musical tradition, (b) provide chants for days new to the postconciliar Roman calendar, and (c) make some seasonal or generic chant assignments more "proper" or particular by replacing them with the orphaned chants.

---

102. Introduction to the *Graduale Simplex* 2–3. The text here is the same in both the *editio typica* and *editio typica altera*. Trans., ICEL.

103. *Ordo Cantus Missae*, I, paras. 2, 3.

104. See ibid.

2. Particularly important chants that had been lost to the Roman Rite were restored to liturgical use.

3. "Neo-Gregorian" (read "inauthentic") chants were replaced by true Gregorian chants wherever possible.

4. The authentic Gregorian repertoire was redistributed throughout the liturgical year to avoid excessive repetition, particularly in the commons.

5. The revised *Graduale Romanum* allows for the substitution of chants from the Proper of Seasons with other chants from the same season. This pastoral accommodation allows one to use the *Graduale Romanum* as a type of advanced *Graduale Simplex*.

6. The postconciliar *Graduale Romanum* often assigns a number of psalm verses to each antiphon, thus restoring the early medieval musical form of the introit described in chapter one. In all cases, it is permissible to use more than one psalm verse, even if additional verses are not provided. The introit can now vary in length to accompany the entrance procession.[105] The introit of the present *Graduale Romanum* is even more adaptable than its medieval ancestor in that (a) the congregation is encouraged to join in singing the antiphon if possible, (b) the *Gloria Patri / Sicut erat* may be omitted if it would make the entrance song longer than the entrance procession, and (c) the antiphon may be sung by itself for particularly short entrance processions.

Thus, the revision of the *Graduale Romanum* for use in the postconciliar liturgy was eminently pastoral, both functionally (to encourage congregational participation[106] and to intimately join the entrance chant to the entrance procession) and theologically (to put forth a richer and more feast-specific collection of texts).

---

105. See ibid., 1.

106. Note that significant congregational participation in the singing of the introit was a laudable innovation. From the earliest extant records of the Roman Rite introit, we know that these chants were sung by soloist and *schola*.

The Roman Missal

The *editio typica* (1970) of the *Missale Romanum* and its subsequent editions[107] contain few rubrics regarding the entrance song.[108] One finds the relevant directives concerning the entrance song in the various editions of the General Instruction of the Roman Missal.[109] The *Missale Romanum*, independent of the General Instruction, is important, however, as it contains entrance antiphon texts. Here we find the entrance antiphon texts in situ, and thus the *Missale Romanum* with its General Instruction is a primary source of liturgical law concerning the entrance song.

The antiphon texts of the *Missale Romanum* are not exactly the same as the antiphon texts in the *Graduale Romanum*.[110] The significance of this fact, however, is easily overstated since "the entrance and communion antiphons of the Missal were intended to be recited, not sung, and to inspire the creation of suitable songs in the vernacular."[111] In addition, as Peter Finn notes, the discrepancies between the two sources are not that numerous. For example, in the 2002 *Missale Romanum*, "of the twenty-seven Antiphons used on the Sundays of Advent and the Sundays and Feasts of the Christmas Season all but three are taken directly from the version of the Antiphons

107. An emended version of the *editio typica* was issued in 1971. The *editio typica secunda* was issued in 1975, and the *editio typica tertia* (the Latin edition currently in force) was issued in 2002 and emended in 2008.

108. "Populo congregato, sacerdos cum ministris ad altare accedit, dum cantus ad introitum peragitur." *Ordo Missae Cum Populo* 1. "Tunc sacerdos ascendit ad altare, illud veneratur osculo, et accedit ad missale in sinistro latera altaris collocato, et legit antiphonam ad introitum." *Ordo Missae Sine Populo* 4. This second rubric was omitted in the 2002 *Missale Romanum*.

109. First edition, 6 April 1969; second edition, 26 March 1970; third edition, 23 December 1972; fourth edition, 27 March 1975 (with an appendix of U.S. adaptations); fifth edition, 20 April 2000; fifth edition with corrections, 2002 (issued with the 2002 *Missale Romanum, editio typica tertia*); fifth edition with U.S. adaptations, 17 March 2003; fifth edition newly translated by ICEL for inclusion in the new English translation of the Missal, 2010.

110. It is worth nothing that differences between the *Graduale Romanum* and *Missale Romanum* are few in the entrance antiphons but much more numerous in the communion antiphons—primarily because of the addition of antiphons in the *Missale* that relate to the readings of the day. See Christoph Tietze, "Graduale or Missale: The Confusion Resolved," *Sacred Music* 133:4 (Winter 2006): 4–13; and A. Franquesa, "Antifonas del Introito y de la Comunion en las Misas sin Canto," *Notitiae* (1970): 213–21.

111. Bugnini, *The Reform of the Liturgy*, 891.

contained in the *Graduale Romanum*."[112] Indeed, the discrepancies mainly reflect two different stages of the reform of the liturgical books and perhaps a lack of editorial precision by the Holy See.

There are no musical settings in the *Missale Romanum* of the entrance antiphon texts, but as the current General Instruction implies, the processional chants are normatively sung (GIRM 46, 48). Thus, in order to facilitate the use of the proper chants, the editors of the 2002 *Missale* applied minor revisions to a few of the Latin antiphon texts to make them correspond to the chant texts found in the *Graduale Romanum*.[113]

Other Documents

Aside from *Sacrosanctum Concilium*, which is preeminent, postconciliar ecclesiastical documents regarding the liturgy fall into four categories in terms of legal authority. First are decrees, apostolic constitutions, *praenotanda* (introductions and general instructions) to the official liturgical books, and the liturgical books themselves (both the Latin and official vernacular editions). These sources contain universal laws, which, as such, have the same authority as the 1983 Code of Canon Law.[114] Second are papal apostolic letters, in which the pope can exercise his legislative authority, and third are instructions issued by the Roman curia. Instructions contain explanations of existing

112. Peter Finn for the International Commission on English in the Liturgy, "Translation of the *Missale Romanum, editio tertia*: Questions and Issues Related to the Translation of Antiphons" (unpublished study, Washington, DC, 2004), 2.

113. These revisions had to do with the addition of "alleluias" to certain Missal antiphons, which are integral to the chant melody, but which had been left out of previous editions of the postconciliar *Missale Romanum*. The entrance antiphon for Easter Sunday in the 1975 edition reads, "Resurrexi, et adhuc tecum sum: posuisti super me manum tuam: mirabilis facta est scientia tua, alleluia," while in the 2002 edition the intervening "alleluias" from the *Graduale Romanum* are added: "Resurrexi, et adhuc tecum sum, alleluia: posuisti super me manum tuam, alleluia: mirabilis facta est scientia tua, alleluia, alleluia." The editors did the same for the alternative entrance antiphon (*Surrexit Dominus vere*) and communion antiphon (*Pascha nostrum immolatus*) on Easter Sunday. These changes, though minute in light of the hundreds of antiphons in the *Missale*, emphasize the fact that the processional chants are normatively sung, that their texts are intimately connected with their melodies, and that in truth the Missal antiphons and Gradual antiphons should be the same. One can hope the Latin books are brought into synchronicity in the near future.

114. Huels, *Liturgy Documents*, 3rd. ed., xi.

laws or suggestions for making these laws practically applicable.[115] As Seasoltz explains, "Of their nature they are not strictly legislative; their application therefore allows for more flexibility than decrees."[116] Certain instructions, nevertheless, intend to implement changes to existing laws. Though, strictly speaking, such documents should have been issued as a decree or apostolic constitution, their intent to legislate makes them authoritative, unless they contradict law of higher authority. One must carefully study the text and its context in order to determine the intention of the legislator.[117]

The fourth category includes a variety of genres: letters, addresses, notes, and communications. While none of these are strictly legislative, each contains norms for the revision, translation, and composition of liturgical texts.[118] Fifth and finally are documents promulgated by episcopal conferences.[119] These documents fall into three categories: normative particular law,[120] such as Conference-specific adaptations to the GIRM; guidelines issued by the USCCB, such as Sing to the Lord;[121] and documents issued by the Bishops' Committee on Divine Worship (BCDW, formerly Bishops' Committee on the Liturgy). The GIRM is binding for all Roman Rite dioceses of the United States.[122] Documents from the Bishops' Committee on Divine Worship, on the other hand, are not liturgical law in the strict sense, but as Huels explains,[123] "This does not mean . . . that they are merely optional. They are the products of wide consultation among the American bishops and the liturgical experts who advise them, and their publication was approved by the Administrative Committee of

115. Seasoltz, *New Liturgy, New Laws*, 175.

116. Ibid.

117. Ibid., 176.

118. Ibid., 178–79.

119. See Bugnini, *The Reform of the Liturgy*, 891: "As the use of the vernacular in the liturgy was extended, the situation changed. . . . The principle role in choosing and adopting repertories of songs for celebrations in the vernacular had to be left to the episcopal conferences; a Roman group could only provide general criteria for passing judgment."

120. Such documents also require the approval of the Holy See.

121. USCCB, Sing to the Lord: Music in Divine Worship (14 November 2007). Sing to the Lord is an extensive revision of Music in Catholic Worship, 1972; the revised edition (1983) can be found in *Liturgy Documents*, 3rd ed., 277–92. Sing to the Lord supersedes this document as well as Liturgical Music Today (Bishops' Committee on the Liturgy, 1982), in *Liturgy Documents*, 3rd. ed., 297–310.

122. Huels, *Liturgy Documents*, 3rd ed., xi–xii.

123. Ibid., xii.

the NCCB [USCCB]. Many times their content is based directly on other documents that are legally binding."[124]

The most recent document from the BCDW, Sing to the Lord, holds more authority than previous U.S. documents on liturgical music because the whole body of Latin Rite bishops of the USCCB issued it as a formal statement. Sing to the Lord is a set of guidelines,[125] however, not particular law for the dioceses of the United States, since it was not submitted to the Holy See for approval. In many instances, nevertheless, the document quotes or is directly based on other legally binding documents and thus contains law even if the document itself is not strictly legislative. Furthermore, as Huels reminds us, "because the bishop is a true legislator for the liturgy in his diocese, any document . . . can become official policy within a diocese if the diocesan bishop so decrees."[126]

While an excessive concern with distinctions regarding canonical weight and sanctioned practices may be at variance with the nature and purpose of liturgical law,[127] it is possible to garner certain foundational norms from the conciliar and postconciliar documents, which have guided and continue to guide the development and enactment of the entrance song in the Mass of the Roman Rite.

FOUNDATIONAL NORMS
FOR THE POSTCONCILIAR ENTRANCE SONG

The Importance of Singing in the Liturgy

Sing to the Lord grounds itself in the importance of this particular norm. It states, "God has bestowed upon his people the gift of song. God dwells within each human person, in the place where music takes its source. Indeed, God, the giver of song, is present whenever his people sing his praises" (STTL 1). In a general sense, the third edition of the *Missale Romanum* (2002) emphasizes the importance of singing in the liturgy. It provides chants for nearly seventy more texts

---

124. Ibid.

125. See Sing to the Lord, introductory paragraph.

126. Huels, *Liturgy Documents*, 3rd ed., xii.

127. "The principle reasons or justifications for liturgical law do not prejudge the objective value and worth of specific laws, much less the desirable mean between greater and lesser firmness, between uniformity (an excess as opposed to unity) and a near total absence of law." McManus, "Liturgical Law," in *Handbook for Liturgical Studies*, 119.

than did the second edition (1975), and it has placed some music that was in the appendix of earlier editions within the body of the *Missale* itself. If, indeed, the purpose of liturgical music is "the glory of God and the sanctification of the faithful" (SC 112), then "the musical tradition of the universal Church is a treasure of inestimable value . . . [by means of which] a liturgical service takes on a nobler aspect" (SC 112, 113). This is especially true of liturgical song. Because it is "closely bound to the text, it forms a necessary or integral part of the solemn liturgy" (SC 112). It is with good reason, then, that "great importance should . . . be attached to the use of singing in the celebration of the Mass [and that] . . . every care should be taken that singing by the ministers and the people not be absent" (GIRM 40).

But what is it about singing that makes it "noble," of "inestimable value," and "integral" to liturgical celebration? First, "singing is the sign of the heart's joy" (GIRM 39) and a primary means by which such joy is expressed. This joy is the joy experienced of "God's love for us and of our love for him," and of our love for one another (STTL 2). Thus, while singing is never inappropriate, it should be part of the liturgy "especially on Sundays and holy days of obligation" (GIRM 40) and during other especially festive or solemn occasions (MS 7).[128]

Second, it adds "delight to prayer, fostering oneness of spirit" (SC 112), and thus it is a sign and means of unity among the gathered assembly. "As St. Ambrose exclaims, 'How close the bond of unity is when so many people join together in the one chorus. They are like the different strings of the harp that yet produces one melody. The harpist may often make mistakes while playing on just a few strings,

128. See also John Paul II, Apostolic Letter *Dies Domini*, 31 May 1998: *Acta Apostolicae Sedis* 90 (1998): 50. Trans., *The Liturgy Documents: A Parish Resource*, vol. 2 (Chicago: Liturgy Training Publications, 1999), 31: "In ways dictated by pastoral experience and local custom in keeping with liturgical norms, efforts must be made to ensure that the celebration has the festive character appropriate to the day commemorating the Lord's Resurrection. To this end, it is important to devote attention to the songs used by the assembly, since singing is a particularly apt way to express a joyful heart, accentuating the solemnity of the celebration and fostering the sense of a common faith and a shared love. Care must be taken to ensure the quality, both of the texts and of the melodies, so that what is proposed today as new and creative will conform to liturgical requirements and be worthy of the Church's tradition which, in the field of sacred music, boasts a priceless heritage."

but the artist who is the Holy Spirit never makes a mistake while playing on the hearts of a whole people'" (*Iubilate Deo*).[129]

Third, singing is a means of effectively expressing and experiencing the liturgical texts and "gives a more graceful expression to prayer" (MS 5). It enhances their audibility, helps keep the attention of the assembly during their proclamation, and makes them more memorable. Ideally, singing also shapes the faith and actions of those who participate in the liturgy: "The faithful . . . expressing their own faith in a harmonic and solemn way through song . . . will let their singing shape more and more each aspect of daily life" (*Mosso dal vivo desiderio* 15[130]).[131] Certainly, "charity, justice, and evangelization are . . . the normal consequences of liturgical celebration. Particularly inspired by sung participation, the body of the Word Incarnate goes forth to spread the Gospel with full force and compassion" (STTL 9).

Fourth, the fact that singing is integral to the liturgy implies something important about the type of music that is most appropriate to liturgical celebration: it must facilitate singing and be suited to the human voice. Liturgical chant offers a model in this regard. Chant was created within an aural culture and transmitted by memory from cantor to cantor and from cantor to choir. As such, it is music that instinctively fits the liturgical text and matches the requirements of the human voice. To be sure, "the Church does not exclude any type of sacred music from liturgical services" (MS 9), but for liturgical song, "singability" and the effective expression of liturgical texts are requisite characteristics.

Lastly, music helps to express "the shape of the rite" (STTL 68). Not only will liturgical song "be the more holy the more closely it is joined to the liturgical rite" (SC 112), but it is also true that certain texts are normatively sung because singing is a constituent element

129. Congregation for Divine Worship, preface to the Booklet *Iubilate Deo*, 11 April 1974: Vatican Polyglot Press, 1974; DOL 524, margin no. 4243. See also Ambrose, *Explanationes psalmorum* in Ps 1:9, *Patrologia Latina* 14, 925.

130. John Paul II, *Chirograph Mosso dal vivo desiderio*, celebrating the centenary of Pope St. Pius X's *motu proprio* on sacred music, *Tra le Sollecitudini*, 3 November 2003, *Pastoral Music* (February–March 2004): 9–23. A chirograph is a type of apostolic letter and carries the same legal authority. See also Mason, "The Pastoral Implications of John Paul II's Chirograph for the Centenary of the *Motu Proprio* 'Tra Le Sollecitudini' on Sacred Music," *Worship* 82:5 (September 2008): 386–413.

131. See also Sing to the Lord 5, which states, "Faith grows when it is well expressed in celebration."

of certain ritual elements of the liturgy. Acclamations, antiphons, and psalms are fully expressed only when sung, and processions are fully realized only when accompanied by song.

The Active Participation of the Faithful

It is a fundamental principle of the postconciliar liturgical reform that the full and active participation of the faithful is "the aim to be considered before all else" (SC 14). To be sure, liturgical song, including the entrance song,[132] is an important means by which to accomplish this active participation (SC 30). In fact, "singing is one of the primary ways that the assembly of the faithful participates actively in the Liturgy" (STTL 26). Active participation should be both "internal" and "external," and it is influenced by one's "role within the worship of the entire liturgical assembly" (STTL 10, 12, 13).[133] Note that the question is never "should the assembly sing?" but rather "what kind of music should the assembly sing?"

Pastoral considerations inevitably come into play when one considers how to best facilitate active participation. In terms of singing at the liturgy, there are two fundamental pastoral motives. First, the music must be within the ability of the gathered assembly.[134] This is determined not only in light of the actual musical skill of the members of a particular parish, but also in light of several other factors: Does the parish have a choir? If so, how skilled is the choir? How stable is the membership of the parish? What are the skill levels of the choir director, organist(s), cantor(s), and so forth? These factors taken together should determine "the choice of individual composi-

---

132. See *Musicam Sacram* 33 and *Ordo Cantus Missae* 1.

133. On the different roles in regard to liturgical singing, including those of the bishop, priest, deacon, assembly, choir, psalmist, cantor, organist, other instrumentalists, and music director, see Sing to the Lord 15–47 and GIRM 48, 103, 104. To be sure, "active participation" includes listening, contemplation, and meditation, as well as singing, processing, and praying aloud together. See, for example, James F. Caccamo, "The Listener as Musician: The Importance of Audience in the Moral Power of Music," in *God's Grandeur: The Arts and Imagination in Theology*, ed. David C. Robinson (Maryknoll, NY: Orbis Books, 2007), 59–79.

134. "So that the holy people may sing with one voice, the music must be within its members' capability." Sing to the Lord 27. "The choice of the style of music for a choir or congregation should be guided by the abilities of those who must do the singing. The Church does not exclude any type of sacred music from liturgical services as long as . . . [it] is not a hindrance to the required active participation of the people." *Musicam Sacram* 8.

tions for congregational participation" (STTL 70) and should also determine the balance between variety and stability in a parish's musical repertoire (STTL 27). It is for such pastoral reasons, for example, that it is permissible "to replace the text proper to a day with another text belonging to the same season" (*Ordo Cantus Missae*, DOL margin no. 4279).

The second fundamental motive is to ensure that the music program at a particular parish takes seriously the "legitimate requirements of adaptation and inculturation" (*Mosso dal vivo desiderio* 6). Indeed, "congregational singing is to be fostered by every means possible, even by new types of music suited to the culture of the people and to the contemporary spirit" (*Liturgicae Instaurationes* 3c).[135] Pastoral sensitivity to cultural context is particularly complex in the church in the United States because "cultural pluralism has been the common heritage of all Americans, and 'the Catholic community is rapidly re-encountering itself as an immigrant Church'" (STTL 57).[136] Cultural adaptation of this type is a complex process but would include, at the very least, music in the native language or bilingual music resources (STTL 57–58). "Culture" has not only to do with language and ethnicity, however. Other demographic factors, such as the median age of a parish community, must also be considered (STTL 70). Most basically, "the choice of individual compositions for congregational participation will often depend on those ways in which a particular group finds it best to join their hearts and minds to the liturgical action" (STTL 70).

Liturgical song is successful to the degree it matches the skill level and cultural requirements of the assembly and thus fosters active participation, because active participation is critically important from the perspective of faith formation. It is important to realize that "our participation in the Liturgy is challenging. Sometimes, our voices do not correspond to the convictions of our hearts. At other times, we are distracted or preoccupied by the cares of the world. But Christ always invites us to enter into song, to rise above our own preoccupations, and to give our entire selves to the hymn of his Paschal Sacrifice for the honor and glory of the Most Blessed Trinity" (STTL 14). To be sure, "a liturgical celebration can have no more solemn or pleasing feature than the whole assembly's expressing its faith and

---

135. "Consideration should . . . be given to the idiom of different languages and the culture of different peoples." GIRM 38.

136. Quoting USCCB, Welcoming the Stranger: Unity in Diversity (2001) 7.

devotion in song" (MS 16). It is by taking part in the liturgy again and again—with body, voice, mind, and heart—that one enters more deeply into the Christian mystery, for participating in the liturgy "is the primary and indispensable source from which the faithful are to derive the true Christian spirit" (SC 14).

Which Texts of the Mass Should Be Sung?

While singing is a normative part of liturgical celebration, not all liturgical texts are normatively sung. Texts "that are of greater importance and especially . . . those which are to be sung by the Priest or the Deacon or a reader, with the people replying, or by the Priest and people together" (GIRM 40) should be sung above all else.[137] Furthermore, if a text is set to music in the actual ritual book, here the *Missale Romanum*, it is particularly appropriate that it be sung at Mass.[138] In the 2002 *Missale Romanum*, for example, many prefaces for solemnities are set to music in situ and thus should be sung whenever possible. Strictly speaking, the *Graduale Romanum* is part of the *Missale Romanum*, as it is the source for the proper chants of the Mass. This fact implies that the entrance song and other chants in the *Graduale* are normatively sung, even if they are not the most important liturgical texts.[139]

It is permissible and desirable that sometimes the choir sing certain liturgical songs alone during the Mass, including the entrance song, depending upon the particular context of the celebration (STTL

137. "This includes dialogues such as . . . *The Lord be with you. And also with you*. . . . The dialogues of the Liturgy are fundamental because they 'are not simply outward signs of communal celebration but foster and bring about communion between priest and people.' By their nature, they are short and uncomplicated and easily invite active participation by the assembly. Every effort should therefore be made to introduce or strengthen as a normative practice the singing of the dialogues. . . . The acclamations of the Eucharistic Liturgy . . . arise from the whole gathered assembly as assents to God's Word and action. . . . They are appropriately sung at any Mass." Sing to the Lord 115a. See also *Musicam Sacram* 7.

138. See also Congregation for Divine Worship, Note *Passim Quaeritur*, on the music for inclusion in vernacular editions of the Roman Missal, May 1975: *Notitiae* 11 (1975): 129–32; nos. 2–3; DOL 538.

139. One must be guided by the principle of "progressive solemnity," however. If an entrance song is to be sung, therefore, the "dialogues and acclamations (Gospel Acclamation, *Sanctus*, Memorial Acclamation, Amen); litanies (*Kyrie, Agnus Dei*); [and] Responsorial Psalm" should also be sung. Sing to the Lord 116. See also *Passim Quaeritur* 2–3 and *Musicam Sacram* 29–31.

30; MS 16c),[140] but participation in the entrance song "on the part of the assembly is commended" (STTL 115b).[141] The assembly might participate by singing a hymn,[142] since "Church legislation today permits as an option the use of vernacular hymns at the Entrance," as long as they are "appropriate to the liturgical action" and "in conformity with Catholic teaching" (STTL 115d).[143]

The assembly and choir, or assembly and cantor, can also sing the entrance song together "in dialogue or alternation. . . . This approach often takes the form of a congregational refrain with verses sung by the choir" (STTL 29; see also STTL 37). Here, the proper antiphon and psalm of the entrance song should be used if circumstances permit. In light of liturgical history, it is the musical form most germane to the processions of the Mass of the Roman Rite.[144]

---

140. However, "the practice of assigning the singing of the entire Proper and Ordinary of the Mass to the choir alone without the rest of the congregation is not to be permitted." *Musicam Sacram* 16c.

141. "The assembly of the faithful should, as far as possible, have a part in singing the Proper of the Mass, especially by use of simple responses or other appropriate melodies." *Musicam Sacram* 33.

142. "Sometimes it is even quite appropriate to have other songs at the beginning, at the presentation of the gifts, and at the communion, as well as at the end of Mass. It is not enough for these songs to be 'eucharistic' in some way; they must be in keeping with the parts of the mass and with the feast or liturgical season." *Musicam Sacram* 36.

143. "At Mass, in addition to the *Gloria* and a small number of strophic hymns in the *Roman Missal* and *Graduale Romanum*, congregational hymns of a particular nation or group that have been judged appropriate by the competent authorities mentioned in the GIRM, nos. 48, 74, and 87, may be admitted to the Sacred Liturgy. . . . [T]hese popular hymns are fulfilling a properly liturgical role. . . . In accord with an uninterrupted history of nearly five centuries, nothing prevents the use of some congregational hymns coming from other Christian traditions." Sing to the Lord 115d.

144. See Sing to the Lord 117. This issue is debated today because, while hymns are germane to the Liturgy of the Hours, their use at the entrance, offertory, communion, and recession in the Eucharistic liturgy is not reflective of the ancient Roman Rite. Kevin Irwin favors the traditional antiphon/verse structure of the processional chants over the hymn form for the reasons mentioned above. Even further, Irwin points out that the substitution of hymns for the traditional antiphon/verses of the introit (and their theological themes) can delete a traditional and substantial body of Scripture put forth in the liturgy throughout the year. In his view, if hymns are to be used in spite of their stylistic inadequacy, they must be derived from the traditional introit texts. Indeed, hymns are only appropriate sources for liturgical theology "to the extent that their texts reflect the theology of

Without a doubt, responsorial or antiphonal singing is especially suitable for processions because such songs have an open musical form and thus a variable length that can accommodate the infinitely variable length of an entrance procession. Repeated antiphons also facilitate active participation because the gathered faithful can sing them from memory, in contrast to singing a hymn from a book, and thus engage more fully in the entrance procession.

The genre of a particular text has bearing on whether or not it should be sung (GIRM 40). Certain texts are "by their very nature"[145] intended for singing: psalms, acclamations, litanies, and antiphons (STTL 115b). Indeed, "it is above all necessary that those parts which of their nature call for singing are in fact sung and in the style and form demanded by the parts themselves" (MS 6). Sing to the Lord calls this the "ritual dimension of sacred music [which] refers to those ways in which [music] is 'connected with the liturgical action' so that it accords with the structure of the Liturgy and expresses the shape of the rite" (STTL 68). Because the entrance song accompanies the entrance procession, it must be processional music and facilitate the act of processing (STTL 115b).[146]

The entrance song falls into two categories in terms of genre: a constituent and primary element of the introductory rites, and one of the chants of the celebration of the Eucharist that accompanies a ritual action (GIRM 37). This means the music that accompanies the entrance of the ministers should facilitate the overall purpose of the

---

the entrance antiphons found in the *Graduale Romanum* or *Missale Romanum*." *Context and Text*, 236–38. See also Anthony Ruff, *Sacred Music and Liturgical Reform: Treasures and Transformations* (Chicago: Liturgy Training Publications, 2007), 102–4, 563–602. Ruff presents a generally positive evaluation of the use of strophic hymns in the Roman Rite Mass, especially as part of "a common heritage of many Western Christian traditions," but admits that its "form relates only with difficulty with ritual action" (ibid., 601). He cites the entrance procession as one of the "elements of the Eucharistic Liturgy most amenable to strophic forms" (ibid.).

145. See Congregation for Divine Worship, General Instruction of the Liturgy of the Hours, 2 February 1971; no. 282; DOL 426.

146. "The Entrance and Communion chant with their psalm verses serve to accompany the two most important processions of the Mass: the entrance procession, by which the Mass begins, and the Communion procession, by which the faithful approach the altar to receive Holy Communion." Sing to the Lord 115b. See also *Sacrosanctum Concilium* 112. "The tone of voice should correspond to the genre of the text itself, that is, depending on whether it is a reading, a prayer, a commentary, an acclamation, or a sung text; the tone should also be suited to the form of celebration and to the solemnity of the gathering." GIRM 38.

introductory rites, namely, "to ensure that the faithful, who come to-gether as one, establish communion and dispose themselves properly to listen to the word of God and to celebrate the Eucharist worthily" (GIRM 46). More specifically, the entrance song should "open the celebration, foster the unity of those who have been gathered, intro-duce their thoughts to the mystery of the liturgical time or festivity, and accompany the procession of the Priest and ministers" (GIRM 47).[147] It begins what is then concluded by the priest's greeting after the sign of the cross—namely, the manifestation of the "mystery of the Church gathered together," which is a prerequisite to authentic active participation in and celebration of the rest of the Mass (GIRM 50).[148]

Translating the Latin Proper Texts and Composing New Texts in the Vernacular

There are three principles put forth in the documents concerning the translation of the official Latin texts of the processional chants. First, conferences of bishops are the competent authority concerning adaptation in the liturgy (SC 22, 36, 39–40) and have the authority to promulgate vernacular translations (SC 36)[149] and alternative col-lections of songs, in accord with *Sacrosanctum Concilium* 37–40, which provides for the use of culturally appropriate musical forms. Second, translators are to strive for conformity with the original Latin text, but at the same time they are to ensure that, stylistically, the translation lends itself to being set to music (GIRM 392; MS 54).[150]

---

147. "Populo congregato, dum ingreditur sacerdos cum diacono et ministris, cantus ad introitum incipitur. Finis huius cantus est celebrationem aperire, unio-nem congregatorum fovere, eorumque mentem in mysterium temporis liturgici vel festivitatis introducere atque processionem sacerdotis ministrorumque comitari." *Institutio Generalis Missale Romanum* 47.

148. "When the Entrance chant is concluded, the Priest stands at the chair and, together with the whole gathering, signs himself with the Sign of the Cross. Then by means of the Greeting he signifies the presence of the Lord to the as-sembled community. By this greeting and the people's response, the mystery of the Church gathered together is made manifest." GIRM 50.

149. "The competent, territorial ecclesiastical authority . . . is empowered to decide whether and to what extent the vernacular is to be used." *Sacrosanctum Concilium* 36.

150. "It shall also be up to the Conferences of Bishops to prepare . . . a transla-tion of the other texts, so that, even though the character of each language is re-spected, the meaning of the original Latin text is fully and faithfully rendered. . . . It should be borne in mind that the primary purpose of the translation of the texts is not for meditation, but rather for their proclamation of singing during

Third, official vernacular translations are official liturgical texts and, as such, should not be altered in musical settings (LI 3).[151] Today, translation into the vernacular is guided by the norms set forth in the instruction *Liturgiam Authenticam*,[152] the fifth instruction on the proper implementation of *Sacrosanctum Concilium*. The instruction is not specifically concerned with music, however, which has its own unique requirements.[153]

The celebration of the liturgy in the vernacular has become a universal practice since the liturgical reform. Undeniably, "the use of the vernacular is the norm in most liturgical celebrations in the dioceses of the United States 'for the sake of a better comprehension of the mystery being celebrated'" (STTL 61).[154] Since at least 1968, the bishops' conferences have had "the power to allow use of the vernacular for all or some chants contained in the *Graduale Simplex* and to give approval to a text for such chants" (*Instantibus Pluribus* 1).

Translation of the official Latin liturgical texts—a crucial and indispensable task—is only one part of the adaptation of the liturgy

---

an actual celebration." GIRM 392. "Translators of texts to be set to music should take care to combine properly conformity to the Latin and adaptability to the music." *Musicam Sacram* 54.

151. "Under no consideration, not even the pretext of singing the Mass, may the official translations of its formularies be altered." *Liturgicae Instaurationes* 3.

152. Congregation for Divine Worship and the Discipline of the Sacraments, Instruction (fifth) *Liturgiam Authenticam*, on the orderly carrying out of the Constitution on the Liturgy, 7 May 2001.

153. Translation of the Latin texts into the vernacular is certainly a central and critical task given to the conferences of bishops. Many conferences of a particular language group have formed mixed commissions for the purpose of creating a common vernacular translation. In the United States and other English-speaking countries, ICEL plays a central role in this task. "The bodies of bishops concerned are to see to it that there is a single vernacular translation for a single language used in different regions." *Musicam Sacram* 58. See also the instruction from the Congregation for Divine Worship on the translation of liturgical text's *Comme le prévoit* (1969), which was superseded by *Liturgiam Authenticam* (2001), and the recent *Ratio Translationis* (2007) for the English language, also produced by the Congregation for Divine Worship. One should note that the 1973 ICEL translation of the proper antiphons of the Roman Missal did not take into account as a primary criterion of translation the "singability" of the antiphon texts. After all, the antiphon translations printed in the Missal were to be used only in the event there is no entrance song and the antiphon must be recited.

154. Quoting GIRM 12.

to particular churches and cultures, however (see SC 39).[155] After the completion of the translation of the official Latin texts, the bishops' conferences are to foster the expansion and improvement of this repertoire. It is not only the preservation of official Latin texts, then, that is important, but also the facilitation of the active participation of the assembly through music (see LI 3).[156]

Along with the new additions to the *Graduale Simplex* and post-conciliar *Graduale Romanum* from the Gregorian repertoire, the documents call for the composition of new texts and musical settings of the processional chants: "It is for the Conferences of Bishops to formulate the adaptations . . . and, once their decisions have been accorded the *recognitio* of the Apostolic See, to introduce them into the Missal itself. They are such as these: . . . the texts of the chants at the Entrance, at the Presentation of the Gifts, and at the Communion" (GIRM 390). Ecclesiastical norms, both in legislation and in the liturgical books themselves, allow for more flexibility for the processional chants of the Mass than for other elements of the proper, such as the presidential prayers.[157] This is not to say the ancient and official corpus of Latin introit texts are of no consequence, however. "Before the introduction of popular religious music into the vernacular as a substitute for the music traditional in the liturgy . . . there should be an effort in every nation to compile a collection of melodies with

---

155. "Within the limits set by the *editio typica* of the liturgical books, it shall be for the competent, territorial ecclesiastical authority . . . to specify adaptations, especially in the case of the administration of the sacraments, the sacramentals, processions, liturgical language, sacred music, and the arts. This, however, is to be done in accord with the fundamental norms laid down in this Constitution." *Sacrosanctum Concilium* 39.

156. "Congregational singing is to be fostered by every means possible, even by use of new types of music suited to the culture of the people and to the contemporary spirit." *Liturgicae Instaurationis* 3.

157. "It is up to conferences of bishops to prepare a collection of vernacular texts for the songs at the entrance, presentation of the gifts, and communion." Congregation for Divine Worship, Instruction *Constitutione Apostolica*, on the gradual carrying out of the Apostolic Constitution *Missale Romanum* (3 April 1969), 20 October 1969: *Acta Apostolicae Sedis* 61 (1969): 749–53; *Notitiae* 5 (1969): 418–23; no. 12; DOL 209. "In some places there is the lawful practice . . . of substituting other songs for the entrance, offertory, and communion chants in the *Graduale*. At the discretion of the competent territorial authority this practice may be kept, on condition that the songs substituted fit in with those parts of the Mass, the feast, or the liturgical season. The texts of such songs must also have the approval of the same territorial authority." *Musicam Sacram* 32.

vernacular texts, fully suited to the liturgical rites and having artistic worth" (*Le Sarei Grato* 3).[158] These new collections are to be "guided by the texts given in the new Roman Missal" (*Constitutione Apostolica* 12). Because the entrance song is a proper text, newly composed entrance texts should reflect the seasonal or festal character of their liturgical assignments, or even the theological theme[159] of the official text. In Ordinary Time, they should at least reflect the overarching paschal character of Sunday, and they might draw upon the other liturgical texts of the day.

If, then, new music for the entrance is to be fostered and approved by the conferences of bishops, given the *recognitio* of the Holy See and influenced by the official texts, who is to compose it? In 1964, Paul VI established the Consociatio Internationalis Musicae Sacrae.[160] While the task of CIMS was not explicitly the composition of new texts, one sees in its creation a recognition by the Holy See that it must actively engage musical and linguistic experts to assist in the reform and renewal of liturgical music.[161] Diocesan commissions[162] and especially bishops' conferences are to guide the creation of vernacular collections of songs. "Upon approval of such a collection, the conference of bishops will at the same time strongly encourage experts in the field to add to and improve this collection, guided by . . . the genius and idiom of each language" (*Constitutione Apostolica* 12). Proper texts for feasts specific to a diocese or religious order,

158. Consilium, Letter *Le Sarei Grato* to papal nuncios and apostolic delegates, on the course to follow in reform of the liturgy, 25 March 1964; DOL 79.

159. See chapter 4 for a discussion of the theology of the entrance song.

160. Paul VI, Epistle (autograph) *Nobile Subsidium*, establishing canonically the Consociatio Internationalis Musicae Sacrae, 22 November 1963: *Acta Apostolicae Sedis* 56 (1964): 231–34; DOL 500.

161. "The manifold objectives of these popes included the following: to create close ties between those dedicated to the art of sacred music and the Apostolic See; to put at the service of the Apostolic See an international institute that would keep it abreast of the needs of sacred music and also carry out the measures taken by the supreme authority of the Church in regard to sacred music; in a particular way, to provide missionaries with help for the solution of the difficult and important problem of music in mission lands and to coordinate efforts in this direction; finally, to promote publication of works on sacred music and studies of the Church's musical heritage." *Nobile Subsidium*, DOL 500, margin no. 4100.

162. "Each diocese should also, as far as possible, have two other commissions, one for music, the other for art." Paul VI, Motu Proprio *Sacram Liturgiam*, on putting into effect some prescriptions of the Constitution on the Liturgy, 25 January 1964: *Acta Apostolicae Sedis* 56 (1964): 139–44; DOL 20, margin no. 280.

including the processional chants of the Mass, should be composed by local experts.[163]

Official Sources of the Entrance Song in the Roman Rite

Official sources for settings of the entrance song are the *Graduale Romanum*, *Graduale Simplex*, and compilations approved by the conferences of bishops. GIRM 48 states:

> In the Dioceses of the United States of America, there are four options for the Entrance Chant: (1) the antiphon from the Missal or the antiphon with its Psalm from the *Graduale Romanum* as set to music there or in another setting; (2) the antiphon and Psalm of the *Graduale Simplex* for the liturgical time; (3) a chant from another collection of Psalms and antiphons, approved by the Conference of Bishops or the Diocesan Bishop, including Psalms arranged in responsorial or metrical forms; (4) another liturgical chant that is suited to the sacred action, the day or the time of the year, similarly approved by the Conference of Bishops or the Diocesan Bishop.
>
> If there is no singing at the Entrance, the antiphon given in the Missal is recited either by the faithful, or by some of them, or by a reader; otherwise, it is recited by the Priest himself, who may even adapt it as an introductory explanation.[164]

---

163. "The dioceses or religious institute most closely associated with offices and Masses common to several dioceses or religious institutes or to both dioceses and religious institutes should compose the texts and the others involved accept them." Congregation for Divine Worship, Letter *Novo Calendario Romano* to bishops and general superiors of religious, to speed up preparation of the particular calendars of dioceses and religious institutes, as well as of proper texts for the Roman Missal and Liturgy of the Hours, February 1974. *Notitiae* 10 (1974): 87–88; no. 3; DOL 482.

164. "Peragitur autem a schola et populo alternatim, vel simili modo a cantore et populo, vel totus a populo vel a schola sola. Adhiberi potest sive antiphona cum suo psalmo in Graduali romano vel in Graduali simplici exstans, sive alius cantus, actioni sacrae, diei vel temporis indoli congruus, cuius textus ad Conferentia Episcoporum sit approbatus. Si ad introitum non habetur cantus, antiphona in Missali proposita recitatur sive a fidelibus, sive ab aliquibus ex ipsis, sive a lectore, sin aliter ab ipso sacerdote, qui potest etiam in modum monitionis initialis eam aptare." *Institutio Generalis Missale Romanum* 48. In translation *without* the U.S. adaptations: "This chant is sung alternately by the choir and the people or similarly by a cantor and the people, or entirely by the people, or by the choir alone. It is possible to use the antiphon with its Psalm from the *Graduale Romanum* or the *Graduale Simplex*, or another chant that is suited to the sacred action, the day, or the time of the year, and whose text has been approved by the

In *Sing to the Lord* 144, the USCCB provides the following guidelines, which serve to clarify the General Instruction:

> The text and music for the Entrance song may be drawn from a number of sources.
>
> a. The singing of an antiphon and psalm during the entrance procession has been a long-standing tradition in the Roman Liturgy. Antiphons may be drawn from the official liturgical books—the *Graduale Romanum*, or the *Graduale Simplex*—or from other collections of antiphons and psalms.
>
> b. Other hymns and songs may also be sung at the Entrance, providing that they are in keeping with the purpose of the Entrance chant or song. The texts of antiphons, psalms, hymns, and songs for the liturgy must have been approved either by the United States Conference of Catholic Bishops or by the local diocesan bishop. (STTL 144)

The next chapter will be a consideration of these options and their implications for liturgical praxis.

CONCLUSION

The idea that the official text or "textual tradition" of the Roman Rite for the Church's liturgy is particularly significant in regard to the entrance song, since its official text is rarely sung in present-day liturgical celebrations. To be sure, a retrieval of an understanding of the proper chants as official liturgical texts in the *Missale Romanum*—as ancient as most other of the Latin texts therein—would be a positive development. Respect for the official texts should not lead to a rejection of vernacular collections of new songs for the Mass, however, but instead to a new synthesis of the ancient proper chant tradition and the present-day needs of local worshiping assemblies—a mutual enrichment in which the official texts are the foundation or seed for new compositions. A wholesale return to the medieval introit/psalm form is neither possible nor desirable; at the same time, composing new entrance songs that ignore the proper texts altogether is to "cheat the people."[165]

Conference of Bishops. If there is to be no singing at the Entrance, the antiphon given in the Missal is recited either by the faithful, or by some of them, or by a reader; otherwise, it is recited by the Priest himself, who may even adapt it as an introductory explanation" (ICEL, 2010).

165. In response to a query in regard to *Musicam Sacram* 33, the Congregation for Divine Worship emphasized the importance of using the official texts

The theological depth, antiquity, and ritual appropriateness of the official texts and antiphon/psalm form should also inspire conferences of bishops and composers to seek quality musical settings that can match the best qualities of the proper antiphons and psalms of the *Graduale Romanum* and *Graduale Simplex*. "To this end, it is important to devote attention to the songs used by the assembly. . . . Care must be taken to ensure the quality, both of the texts and of the melodies, so that what is proposed today as new and creative will conform to liturgical requirements and be worthy of the Church's tradition which, in the field of sacred music, boasts a priceless heritage" (*Dies Domini* 50). The concern for quality is not based on a generic or individual preference for a particular style of music, but on specific criteria, which should be employed by bishops' conferences, diocesan commissions, and parish music directors when selecting music for the liturgy. Sing to the Lord provides some clarity in this regard. One should ask: "Is this composition capable of meeting the structural and textual requirements set forth by the liturgical books for this particular rite?" (the "liturgical judgment," STTL 127); "Will this composition draw this particular people closer to the mystery of Christ, which is at the heart of this liturgical celebration?" (the "pastoral judgment," STTL 133); and "Is this composition technically, aesthetically, and expressively worthy?" (the "musical judgment," STTL 134).

---

of the liturgy rather than something else. But, given *Musicam Sacram* 32, an exception seems to apply to the processional chants of the Mass. "Query: Many have inquired whether the rule still applies that appears in the Instruction on sacred music and the liturgy, 3 September 1958, no. 33: 'In low Masses religious songs of the people may be sung by the congregation, without prejudice, however, to the principle that they be entirely consistent with the particular parts of the Mass.' Reply: That rule has been superseded. What must be sung is the Mass, its Ordinary and Proper, not 'something,' no matter how consistent, that is imposed on the Mass. Because the liturgical service is one, it has only one countenance, one motif, one voice, the voice of the Church. To continue to replace the texts of the Mass being celebrated with motets that are reverent and devout, yet out of keeping with the Mass of the day (for example, the *Lauda Sion* on a saint's feast) amounts to continuing an unacceptable ambiguity: it is to cheat the people. Liturgical song involves not mere melody, but words, text, thought, and the sentiments that the poetry and music contain. Thus texts must be those of the Mass, not others, and singing means singing the Mass not just singing during Mass." *Notitiae* 5 (1969): 406; DOL, p. 1299, R4. In any case, once collections of music are approved for liturgical use, even if they contain new texts in the vernacular, they become official texts of the Mass.

To be sure, the norms delineated throughout this chapter find strength in what McManus calls their "aim and reasonableness."[166] The nature of liturgical law is that it consists of "ordinances of reason" for the common good of the Christian community in official public worship.[167] The task ahead is to think of the norms not as a burden, but as a guide to understanding and enhancing the permissible forms of the entrance song and their effective ritual enactment. Sometimes this enactment will require accommodation and adaptation of the permissible forms, and the norms for such adaptation are present in the existing liturgical law. In sum, as McManus so wisely says, "a willingness to understand and observe the liturgical law as it is, along with all the post-Conciliar openness to change and creative growth, is a true sign of liturgical renewal."[168]

166. McManus, "Liturgical Law," in *Handbook for Liturgical Studies*, 415.
167. Ibid.
168. Ibid., 419.

PART TWO

Implications of the Contextual Studies for Worship and Theology

CHAPTER THREE

Models of the Entrance Song

[The entrance song is an] image of the choir of the prophets who announced the Messiah.

> —Amalarius of Metz, *Expositio Missae* (813–14)[1]

The idea of entrance has a truly decisive significance for the understanding of the eucharist. . . . [It is the] ascent and entry of the Church into the heavenly sanctuary.

> —Alexander Schmemann[2]

INTRODUCTION

Part one of this study has focused in detail upon, first, the historical origins and development of the entrance song in the Roman Rite and, second, the entrance song as revised and regulated by the liturgical reform of the Second Vatican Council.[3] The foundational goals have been, respectively, to paint a historical picture of the evolution and function of the entrance song in the Roman Rite through a careful

---

1. See Martin Gerbert, *Monumenta veteris Liturgiae Alemannicae*, vol. 2 (St. Blaise, 1779), 150; and Jungmann, *Mass of the Roman Rite*, 1:89, 90n74.

2. Alexander Schmemann, *The Eucharist: The Sacrament of the Kingdom* (Crestwood, NJ: St. Vladimir's Seminary Press, 1990), 50.

3. This focus on ecclesiastical norms and documents is not to deny the importance of many other aspects of the implementation of the liturgical renewal—first and foremost, the fervent work of local pastors, liturgists, musicians, and assemblies. History and ecclesiastical norms are but two windows of many into the function and development of the postconciliar entrance song.

analysis of the extant evidence, and to determine the functions and permissible forms of the entrance song in the postconciliar liturgy through an examination of the relevant ecclesiastical documents.

The purpose of the present chapter is to delineate several "models" of the Roman Rite entrance song. These models are grounded in the historical and legislative contextual studies of part one and function as lenses through which to view the liturgical enactment of the entrance song, past and present. The models of this chapter emerge from an early twenty-first-century perspective on the liturgy articulated in light of the principles and insights of the Vatican II liturgical renewal. While each model is only a generalization about a particular way of enacting the entrance song, taken together they help to define and offer possibilities for the ritual enactment of the entrance song in present-day local worshiping communities. Even more, the models offer a critical edge for the evaluation of such local enactment. The overarching question is, based on its historical and legislative contexts, What forms *may* the entrance song take today? and then, more specifically and subjectively, What form *should* it take?

Models as a means of theological reflection have been employed by a number of contemporary theologians[4]—most famously Avery

---

4. See, for example, Gerald A. Arbuckle, *Earthing the Gospel: An Inculturation Handbook for Pastoral Workers* (1990; repr., Eugene, OR: Wipf and Stock, 2002); Bevans, *Models of Contextual Theology* (Maryknoll, NY: Orbis Books, 1992); Stephen Bouma-Prediger, *The Greening of Theology: The Ecological Models of Rosemary Radford Ruether, Joseph Stiller, and Jürgen Moltmann* (New York: Oxford University Press, 1995); Steven Chase, *The Tree of Life: Models of Christian Prayer* (Ada, MI: Baker Academic, 2005); Raymond F. Collins, *Models for Theological Reflection* (Lanham, MD: University Press of America, 1984); George E. Demacopoulos, *Models of Spiritual Direction in the Early Church* (Notre Dame, IN: University of Notre Dame Press, 2006); Thomas J. Hastings, *Practical Theology and the One Body of Christ: Toward a Missional Ecumenical Model* (Grand Rapids, MI: Eerdmans, 2007); David J. Hesselgrave and Edward Rommen, *Contextualization: Meanings, Methods, and Models* (1989; repr., Pasadena, CA: William Cary Library, 2003); Julian Kunnie, *Models of Black Theology: Issues in Class, Culture, and Gender* (Philadelphia: Trinity Press International, 1994); Sally McFague, *Metaphoric Theology: Models of God in Religious Language* (Philadelphia: Fortress Press, 1982), and *Models of God: Theology for an Ecological, Nuclear Age* (Minneapolis: Augsburg Fortress Press, 1975); Christopher F. Mooney, *Theology and Scientific Knowledge: Changing Models of God's Presence in the World* (Notre Dame, IN: University of Notre Dame Press, 1996); John F. O'Grady, *Models of Jesus* (Garden City, NY: Doubleday, 1981), and *Models of Jesus Revisited* (Mahwah, NJ: Paulist Press, 1994); Thomas F. O'Meara, "Philosophical Models in Ecclesiology," *Theological Studies* 38:1 (March 1978): 3–21, and *Theology*

Dulles[5]—including a number of liturgical theologians,[6] as was pointed out in the introduction to this study. An approach that utilizes models allows for a methodologically sound means by which to generalize about entrance song practice, while being faithful to what in reality is a practice with innumerable variations.[7] A single model cannot fully describe the entrance song at any one historical moment, but it can reveal authentic characteristics of the entrance song in general. The fact that no one model is a complete description of reality requires the articulation of not just one model, but several.[8] In his

---

of Ministry (Mahwah, NJ: Paulist Press, 1999); Duncan Reid, *Energies of the Spirit: Trinitarian Models in Eastern Orthodox and Western Theology* (New York: Oxford University Press, 1997); Peter Schineller, "Christ and the Church: A Spectrum of Views," *Theological Studies* 37:4 (December 1976): 545–66; and David Tracy, *Blessed Rage for Order: The New Pluralism in Theology* (1975; repr. with new intr., Chicago: University of Chicago Press, 1996).

5. Avery Dulles, *Models of the Church* (New York: Doubleday, 1974). See also his *Models of Revelation* (New York: Doubleday, 1983). For information on the authors who influenced Dulles's concept of models, see Stephen P. Bevans, *Models of Contextual Theology* (Maryknoll, NY: Orbis Books, 1992), 23–24.

6. See, for example, Adrian Burdon, "'Till in Heaven'—Wesleyan Models for Liturgical Theology," *Worship* 71 (July 1997): 309–17; James Empereur, *Models of Liturgical Theology* (Bramcote, England: Grove Books, 1987); Maxwell E. Johnson, *Images of Baptism* (Chicago: Liturgy Training Publications, 2001); Kevin W. Irwin, *Models of the Eucharist* (Mahwah, NJ: Paulist Press, 2005); and Paul Turner, *Confirmation: The Baby in Solomon's Court*, rev. ed. (Chicago: Liturgy Training Publications, 2006).

7. These models function on an interpretive level above "functions" of the entrance song (e.g., gathering, processing, and so forth).

8. Ibid., 26. For example, "it is clear from the New Testament that the meaning of baptism was understood by means of several diverse, albeit complementary, images." M. Johnson, *Images of Baptism*, vi. "The images are many but the reality is one." World Council of Churches, *Baptism, Eucharist, Ministry* (1982), Baptism II, par. 2. As Johnson states, "These images provide for us models by which we might glimpse some of the manifold riches that baptism is and offers us. . . . However, because any one model is itself limited to features that fit the model and must suppress features that don't fit, none of these images should be taken individually in any kind of comprehensive way as the *only* way to envision baptism. . . . It is precisely because any given model does not present the whole picture of a particular phenomenon that a model can become a useful tool in illuminating significant aspects of the entire, in this case, baptismal process, which another model might necessarily suppress. Hence, like symbols themselves, models are most useful because they give rise to thought and invite further reflection." M. Johnson, *Images of Baptism*, ix–x. See also Turner, *Confirmation: The Baby in Solomon's Court*, xi–xii: "This book will present seven different models of Confirmation. They derive from

Models of the Eucharist, Kevin Irwin recognizes that, taken together, the models portray an "integral understanding" of the entrance song and should be understood "as mutually enriching and as presuming each other to be adequate," each with its own strengths and weaknesses, each relying on different "footing theologically, liturgically, and historically."[9] Bevans clarifies further by saying, "In terms of what Dulles names heuristic models, complex theological realities such as the church, God's grace, or human redemption [and, as the present study argues, the music of the liturgy] can be opened up to expression, reflection, and critique. These kinds of models suggest [and] disclose . . . a number of associations or possibilities. No one model is able to capture the Reality under consideration; each, however, can help a person enter into the Reality's mystery in a kind of supra-rational way."[10] Such models give an incomplete glimpse into reality but still authentically reveal it. Each provides a lens through which to view the world, the reality of which can only be articulated metaphorically. Their inadequacies require the articulation of not just one model but several, if one is to paint an adequate picture of the real world.[11]

Given the fourfold function of the entrance song,[12] as defined in ecclesiastical documents, to open the celebration, foster unity,[13] intro-

---

the liturgical books and pastoral practice of several churches. . . . It seems to me that each model influences the others, and this leakage causes inconsistencies within each form and for Confirmation as a whole. The purpose of this book is to explain the complexities of the word 'confirmation' by exploring the different forms of its celebration. In doing so, I hope to equip the reader to join in the critique and the conversation."

9. K. Irwin, *Models of the Eucharist,* 33–34.

10. Bevans, *Models of Contextual Theology,* 24.

11. Ibid., 26.

12. The term "entrance song" always refers to both the text and the music of the song, given that it is normatively sung. See GIRM 47 and chapter 2 of this study. In *New Dictionary of Sacramental Worship,* s.v. "Gestures, Liturgical," Robert Vereecke articulates a different but complementary set of functions for the entrance procession: "An entrance procession (a) expresses a particular attitude of celebration; (b) can symbolize a journey of the people; (c) expresses the relationship of the people who are gathering; and, (d) is functional in that it moves people and ministers to the place where the liturgical action will be."

13. See *New Dictionary of Sacramental Worship,* s.v. "Gathering Rites" (by Kenneth Hannon). He relates the introductory rites, including the entrance song, with the "establishment of identity."

duce the feast or season, and accompany the entrance procession,[14] it is likely that one model might emphasize one function more so than others. Because of this possibility, as Edward Foley says, "these different facets of an opening song need to be maintained in a dynamic tension, so that in the regular pattern of Eucharistic gatherings, each is properly respected."[15] This assertion implies three caveats to the enactment of the entrance song. First, no one model is perfectly adequate. Second, the choice of one model over another for a particular liturgical celebration must be contextually driven. Third, even if one model is the most appropriate in a particular context, one must take care to make sure none of the intrinsic functions of the entrance song is totally eclipsed by an exclusive use of one model.

The source of the models of the entrance song put forth in this chapter are derived directly but not verbatim from ecclesiastical documents[16]—in particular from the GIRM, which serves as the normative guide for the celebration of the liturgies of the *Missale Romanum* in the dioceses of the United States. Other important sources include the *Missale Romanum* itself, the historical data and conclusions of chapter one, the *Graduale Romanum*, the *Graduale Simplex*, and, because this study is concerned most immediately with liturgy in the United States, the USCCB document Sing to the Lord: Music in Divine Worship.[17]

14. For more on functional processions and other forms of liturgical movement, see *New Dictionary of Sacramental Worship*, s.v. "Gesture and Movement" (by Thomas A. Krosnicki).

15. Edward Foley, "The Structure of the Mass, Its Elements and Its Parts," in *A Commentary on the General Instruction of the Roman Missal: Developed under the Auspices of the Catholic Academy of Liturgy and Cosponsored by the Federation of Diocesan Liturgical Commissions*, ed. Edward Foley, Nathan D. Mitchell, Joanne M. Pierce (Collegeville, MN: Liturgical Press, 2007), 136.

16. All the models also have historical precedent, but the use of specific historical examples in this chapter creates methodological problems. One cannot assume that a particular model ever worked perfectly in a particular place and time, that one model was ever used exclusively, or that those participating in the liturgy found a particular model to be an effective means of performing the entrance song. These uncertainties make it very difficult to consider here architectural settings for worship, aesthetics, and so on.

17. In all instances, references are to the current editions of the liturgical books and documents. The other documents cited in chapter two are also important, but they do not explicitly put forth specific forms for the entrance song. Chapter four will take more direct account of the general principles delineated in chapter two.

As we have said, each of this chapter's models is equally per-missible, and one would choose a model in light of the practical circumstances of a particular worshiping assembly. But, all other things being equal and according to both historical precedent and ecclesiastical norms, the more a model conforms to the introit of the *Graduale Romanum* the better. This general preference does not imply a universal or unmediated return to the introit of the Middle Ages. On the one hand, it acknowledges that in certain contexts the use of an introit as the entrance song might be wholly inappropriate. On the other hand, it recognizes the importance of the introit antiphon texts to the liturgical tradition of the Roman Rite, in addition to the way that the introit (form, text, and melody), when utilized in its proper context, is especially successful at achieving the normative functions of the entrance song expressed in the GIRM.

We now move to the articulation of five models of the entrance song, which include (1) the proper antiphon and verses of the *Graduale Romanum*, (2) the proper or seasonal antiphon and verses of the *Graduale Simplex*, (3) alternative musical settings of the proper antiphon and verses of models one and two, (4) musical settings of texts other than the proper antiphons and verses, and (5) the spoken proper antiphon of the Roman Missal.

MODEL ONE: THE PROPER ANTIPHON AND VERSES OF THE *GRADUALE ROMANUM*

Proper antiphons from the liturgical books are to be esteemed and used especially because they are the very voice of God speaking to us in the Scriptures. The Christian faithful are to be led to an ever deeper appreciation of the psalms as the voice of Christ and the voice of his Church at prayer.

—STTL 117[18]

18. See also Second Vatican Council, Dogmatic Constitution *Dei Verbum* (1965) 21; and Paul VI, Apostolic Constitution *Laudis Canticum* (1970) 8.

Example 3. The introit *Nos autem gloriari* for the Holy Thursday Evening Mass of the Lord's Supper in the postconciliar *Graduale Romanum*.[19]

Sources, Texts, and Music

This model is nearly synonymous with the introit, which chapter one explored in detail. The U.S. adaptation of the GIRM provides for two variations on this model. The primary option within Model One is the Gregorian chant introit (antiphon, psalm verses, doxology[20]) as found in the *Graduale Romanum*. Many of the antiphons in

---

19. *Graduale Romanum* (Tournai, Belgium: Desclée & Co., 1974). Used by permission.

20. See *Ordo Cantus Missae* II:1.

the *Graduale Romanum* have only one accompanying psalm verse printed along with them, but liturgical history, tradition, and pastoral sense imply, however, that any number of psalm verses are to be used,[21] depending upon the length of the entrance procession. The antiphons for the more important feasts of the liturgical year have several assigned psalm verses. The employment of several verses is beneficial in two ways. It creates an "open" musical form, which allows for a variable musical length to match the infinitely variable length of the procession. In addition, sometimes the introit antiphon and psalm are intimately connected through the antiphon's typological or christological interpretation of one or more of its verses. For certain antiphons in the Gregorian corpus of introits, this interpretive connection between antiphon and psalm occurs in a verse other than the first. The openness of the form to more than one psalm verse restores the ancient connection. If the length of the entrance procession requires, the doxology may be omitted[22] and only one psalm verse used.[23] In these cases, tradition suggests that the psalm verse most closely connected to the feast or celebration be used. The antiphon may also be sung by itself if the procession is especially short.[24]

GIRM 48 also provides for the use of the entrance "antiphon from the Missal." While what is meant by this option is not entirely clear, it is likely the intent was to distinguish between the use of the Latin chant and its vernacular translation rather than to provide for the use of the antiphon alone as a normative option. It makes sense, in light of the clarification provided in Sing to the Lord 144, to assume that the intent of the GIRM is that the antiphon of the Roman Missal be sung with accompanying psalm verses and doxology except for especially short processions. Further, this option implies that not only the texts but also the *melodies* of the Gregorian chants might

21. The verses should be used consecutively, unless another tradition of use (or custom) can be gleaned from the sources. Where there is a question, the Antiphonal of the 1998 translation of the *Missale Romanum* by the International Commission on English in the Liturgy might be consulted. This Antiphonal provides verse assignments for every entrance and communion antiphon.

22. However, "when the *Gloria Patri* and *Sicut erat* have a special musical termination, this must be used with each of the other verses." *Ordo Cantus Missae* II:1.

23. Ibid.

24. Ibid.

be adapted in vernacular editions of the *Graduale Romanum*. This is a laudable goal in that many melodies are just as ancient and feast-specific as the texts they accompany, but such adaptation is notoriously difficult.[25]

Model One makes good sense, but its employment is complicated by some practical details. First, there is no official vernacular translation of the postconciliar *Graduale Romanum*. In theory, one would simply use the vernacular translation of the antiphons found in the current Roman Missal along with one of the translations of the psalms approved for liturgical use, following the psalm verse assignments in the *Graduale Romanum*.[26] Second, there are antiphons in the Roman Missal that are not found in the *Graduale Romanum* because the two liturgical books reflect different stages in the reform of the Roman Rite. Thus, on a handful of days in the postconciliar liturgical year, there is no proper chant to be found in the *Graduale Romanum*. Perhaps a revised *Graduale Romanum* from the Holy See will be forthcoming, which can then be translated and adapted by the conferences of bishops.

For the 2010 translation of the *Missale Romanum*, ICEL translated the antiphons with a careful eye to the "singability" of the texts.[27] Unfortunately, this careful work—the result of wide consultation—was set aside in the Holy See's final revision of the Missal translation. While this fact raises significant issues of ecclesiology and the nature of liturgical antiphons, all is not lost. The antiphon translation was replaced, where possible, by that of the *Revised Grail Psalms*, which sing well.[28]

25. See the introduction to ICEL's *Chants of the Roman Missal: Study Edition* (Collegeville, MN: Liturgical Press, 2011).

26. The Psalter of the current U.S. Lectionary for Mass (New American Bible) is not easily set to music; the translations were not done with the criterion of "singability" in mind. In the coming years, the U.S. might adopt the *Revised Grail Psalms: A Liturgical Psalter* (Chicago, IL: GIA Publications, 2011), which are easily sung.

27. ICEL formed a committee for the translation of the Missal antiphons, which met several times from 2005–6. The committee included a Scripture scholar, a musicologist, two Latinists, and a composer/pastor, all of whom are highly regarded in their fields.

28. See n. 26 above.

Performance

The entrance song, the other processional chants (offertory and communion), and the *Agnus Dei* are musical elements of the eucharistic liturgy that accompany other rites (GIRM 37b). When there is to be music at the entrance procession of the Mass, the GIRM provides basic directives as to how it should be sung. These options include being sung (1) alternately by the choir and the people,[29] (2) alternately by the cantor and the people,[30] (3) entirely by the people, and (4) by the choir alone.[31]

Given the complexity of the introit antiphon melodies, however, the use of the Latin chant from the *Graduale Romanum* would almost always require that the choir sing the entire entrance song on its own.[32] Even though it is true that from the earliest times the introit was the domain of the choir or *schola*,[33] in the liturgy of the postconciliar period the active participation of the assembly is a central concern that has served as a guide in the reform of the rites. In light of this concern, then, the GIRM takes the middle ground—its preferred performance practice is that the entrance song be sung by the

29. "An important ministerial role of the choir . . . is to sing various parts of the Mass in dialogue or alternation with the congregation. Some parts of the Mass that have the character of a litany, such as the *Kyrie* and the *Agnus Dei*, are clearly intended to be sung in this manner. Other Mass parts may also be sung in dialogue or alternation, especially the *Gloria*, the Creed, and the three processional songs: the Entrance, the Preparation of the Gifts, and Communion. This approach often takes the form of a congregational refrain with verses sung by the choir." Sing to the Lord 29.

30. "Especially when no choir is present, the cantor may sing in alternation or dialogue with the assembly. The cantor may . . . sing the verses of the psalm or song that accompany the Entrance, Preparation of the Gifts, and Communion." Ibid., 37.

31. "At times the choir performs its ministry by singing alone. Appropriate times where the choir might commonly sing alone include a prelude before Mass, the Entrance chant, the Preparation of the Gifts, during the Communion procession or after the reception of Communion, and the recessional." Ibid., 30.

32. "The assembly of the faithful should participate in singing the Proper of the Mass as much as possible, especially through simple responses and other suitable settings." Congregation of Rites, Instruction *Musicam Sacram* (1967) 33. "When the congregation does not sing an antiphon or hymn, proper chants from the *Graduale Romanum* might be sung by a choir. As an easier alternative, chants of the *Graduale Simplex* are recommended." Sing to the Lord 76.

33. In contrast to the responsorial psalm or *gradual*, in which the verses were traditionally sung by a soloist and the response by the assembly.

choir *and* the people, thus creating a hybrid choral/responsorial chant genre. For congregational participation of any kind within Model One, then, a vernacular *Graduale Romanum* is essential.[34]

Functional Strengths and Weaknesses

Model One's greatest strength is the particularity with which it leads the thoughts of the assembly "to the mystery of the liturgical season or festivity" (GIRM 47). Most of the introit antiphon texts in the *Graduale Romanum* are unique to one day of the liturgical year. The antiphon texts with their psalm verses not only announce the feast or engage the assembly in the theme of a liturgical season, but in doing so, they unite the worshiping assembly with prior generations of Christians in a tradition of scriptural interpretation. This model makes use of the ancient corpus of Gregorian chant antiphon texts that have been part of the Roman Rite since at least the late seventh century, along with the expanded antiphon repertoire of the *Missale Romanum*, which, though containing more repetitions of antiphons and oftentimes providing two options for a particular feast, still achieves a high degree of festal or seasonal specificity. This model is also ritually and functionally effective. The open musical form of the antiphon/psalm structure allows the length of the entrance song to match the length of the entrance procession. The original and most basic function of the introit is, after all, to accompany the entrance procession.

Another strength of this model, especially of the chants in the *Graduale Romanum*, is the text-centered nature of its melodies.[35] The

---

34. The GIRM implicitly requires the creation of such a liturgical book. The instruction prefers that the assembly take part in the entrance song, and the U.S. has adapted the text to list the antiphon of the Roman Missal before even the antiphon/psalm of the *Graduale Romanum* in its list of options. This (1) implies a preference for a vernacular translation of the introit text over the Latin original and (2) emphasizes the fact that the Roman Missal provides chant assignments not present in the *Graduale Romanum*. "The sequence of these four possible patterns [of performance] in the *IGMR2002* demonstrates the centrality of the assembly's voice in this musical ritual, since the possibility of the choir singing alone is given as the last option." Foley, et al., *Commentary on the General Instruction*, 136. "By its very nature song has . . . a communal dimension. Thus, it is no wonder that singing together in church expresses so well the sacramental presence of God to his people." Sing to the Lord 2.

35. "Gregorian chant draws its life from the sacred text it expresses." Sing to the Lord 78.

neumatic style of the introit antiphons and the simple recitation tones used to sing the psalm verses make the text clearly comprehensible in performance. As chapter one has shown, liturgical chant was born within a logogenic musical context that emphasized comprehensibility. For most worshiping assemblies, true comprehensibility would require the use of vernacular translations of the Latin texts. At the very least, when the original Latin chants are sung, translations in worship aids[36] and liturgical catechesis are essential and, indeed, implicitly required.[37]

The specificity of this model is also a weakness. Within one liturgical year a community would sing or hear dozens (and hundreds for those who attend sung daily Mass) of different entrance songs. In a parish in which stable, long-term membership is the norm, the assembly might become familiar with the texts and melodies in the span of a few years.[38] Parishes with less stable memberships, however, such as in university towns or political centers, would have difficulty establishing a common congregational repertoire of texts and music within Model One.[39]

36. "Whenever a choir sings in Latin, it is helpful to provide the congregation with a vernacular translation so that they are able to [understand] what the choir sings." Sing to the Lord 76. This principle can also be applied to Latin texts sung by the assembly. An earlier functional parallel was the use of bilingual "hand Missals" before the promulgation of the postconciliar vernacular liturgy.

37. "The use of the vernacular is the norm in most liturgical celebrations in the dioceses of the United States." Ibid., 61. "When the Latin language poses an obstacle to singers . . . it would be more prudent to employ a vernacular language in the Liturgy. In promoting the use of Latin in the Liturgy, pastors should always employ that form of participation which best matches the capabilities of each congregation." Ibid., 66. See also *Sacrosanctum Concilium* 54 and *Musicam Sacram* 47.

38. In certain large cathedrals or basilicas, or in communities with an especially advanced music program in the Western tradition, the choir might normatively sing the entire entrance song (the chant of the *Graduale Romanum*). Indeed, in places like this, virtuosic vernacular collections of entrance chants might also be useful.

39. "So that the holy people may sing with one voice, the music must be within its members' capability. Some congregations are able to learn more quickly and will desire more variety. Others will be more comfortable with a stable number of songs so that they can be at ease when they sing. Familiarity with a stable repertoire of liturgical songs rich in theological content can deepen the faith of the community through repetition and memorization." Sing to the Lord 27.

While it is true that active participation by the assembly pertains not only to singing but also to listening, another weakness of Model One is the fact that the Latin chants are generally too difficult for congregational singing. Even if the choir always sings the entirety of the introit, it is crucial that the assembly become familiar with the corpus of texts and melodies if Model One is to be successful. If the choir always sings the introit alone, the creation of a common congregational repertoire would be less of a concern in terms of the practical details of quality performance. But the permanent and exclusive adoption of this practice might inhibit the entrance song's function of fostering "the unity of those who have gathered" (GIRM 47), as singing together is a useful way to foster the assembly's sense of coming together as a community of believers at the start of the liturgy.[40] This is not to deny that the choir[41] is a part of the parish community[42] or that some degree of active participation occurs by the rest of the assembly even when the choir sings the entire entrance song.[43]

40. "Participation must also be external, so that internal participation can be expressed and reinforced by . . . singing. The quality of our participation in such sung praise comes less from our vocal ability than from the desire of our hearts to sing together of our love for God." Ibid., 13. "Singing is one of the primary ways that the assembly of the faithful participates actively in the Liturgy." Ibid., 26. For a broad study of the issue, see John Bell, *The Singing Thing: A Case for Congregational Song* (Chicago: GIA Publications, 2000).

41. "The choir must not minimize the musical participation of the faithful. The congregation commonly sings unison melodies, which are more suitable for generally unrehearsed community singing. This [unison singing] is the primary song of the Liturgy." Sing to the Lord 28.

42. "Choirs comprise persons drawn from the community." Sing to the Lord 28.

43. "Even when listening to the various prayers and readings of the Liturgy or to the singing of the choir, the assembly continues to participate actively as they 'unite themselves interiorly to what the ministers of choir sing, so that by listening to them they may raise their minds to God.'" Sing to the Lord 12, quoting *Musicam Sacram* 15.

MODEL TWO: THE PROPER
OR SEASONAL ANTIPHON AND VERSES
OF THE *GRADUALE SIMPLEX*

Example 4. The introit *Nos autem gloriari* for the Holy Thursday Evening Mass of the Lord's Supper in the *Graduale Simplex, editio typica altera.*[44]

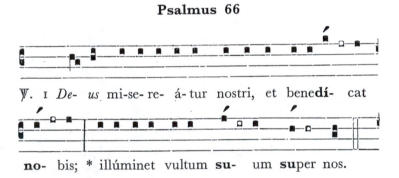

Antiphona ad introitum

N os autem * glo-ri- á-ri opór- tet in cruce

Dómi-ni nostri Ie-su Christi.

Psalmus 66

℣. 1 *De- us* mi-se- re- á-tur nostri, et benedí- cat

no- bis; * illúminet vultum su- um super nos.

Example 5. Vernacular chant adaptation of the text and melody of the *Graduale Simplex* introit *Nos autem gloriari* for the Holy Thursday Evening Mass of the Lord's Supper from *By Flowing Waters* (Paul Ford, 1999).[45]

44. *Graduale Simplex, editio typica altera* (Vatican City: Typis Polyglottis Vaticanis, 1975). Used by permission.

45. Paul Ford, *By Flowing Waters: Chant for the Liturgy; A Collection of Unaccompanied Song for Assemblies* (Collegeville, MN: Liturgical Press, 1999), 72–73. Used by permission. For vernacular adaptation of the *Graduale*, see the *Graduale Parvum*, László Dobszay with Guy Nicholls, Martin Baker, Bill East, and Laurence Hemming, eds. London: T. & T. Clark (Continuum), 2012.

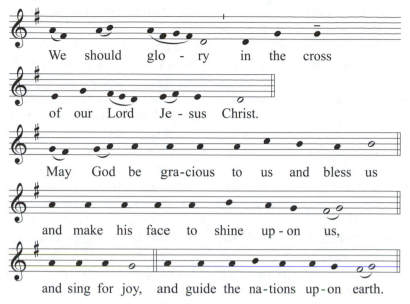

We should glo - ry in the cross

of our Lord Je - sus Christ.

May God be gra-cious to us and bless us

and make his face to shine up - on us,

and sing for joy, and guide the na-tions up - on earth.

This model is the most specific in terms of source, text, and melodic stability. The chants for Model Two are all found in the *Graduale Simplex*—basically a simplified *Graduale Romanum* that employs the principle of commons—and its official vernacular translation, the Simple Gradual. While being similar to Model One in nearly every way—musical form, text-centeredness of melodies, ritual functionality—Model Two overcomes most of Model One's weaknesses. First, it would take a particular assembly much less time to become familiar with its smaller repertoire of chants. Thus, *unionem congregatorum fovere* could be more easily achieved. Second, the simplicity of the antiphon melodies would mean that the choir would never need to sing the *Graduale Simplex* chants without the assembly. Third, this model provides seasonal chants for the entire liturgical year. This means that unlike Model One, which to be useful would require new musical settings and psalm verse assignments for those antiphons in the *Missale Romanum* that are not in the *Graduale Romanum*, the *Graduale Simplex* as a liturgical book for use at worship is usable "as is" and requires no supplementary material. In creating vernacular settings, the goal would be recognizable adaptations of the chant melodies of the *Graduale Simplex* that truly fit the nature of the vernacular language.

One of Model Two's greatest strengths is also its greatest weakness: its use of seasonal chants. The model mutes some of the festal specificity that is possible in Model One. Many introit antiphons traditionally associated with a particular day of the liturgical year are not provided in the *Graduale Simplex*, in favor of a smaller, more congregationally usable collection of chants. One should not overstate this problem, however. The *Graduale Simplex* retains the ancient tradition of chant assignments for the most important days of the liturgical year (with alternative, simpler chant melodies)[46] and can always be supplemented by the *Graduale Romanum*. Another weakness is that the simplified melodies separate some ancient texts from their ancient melodies, which they have been associated with for centuries.[47] It does maintain a particular text/melody relationship, however—in other words, one text, one melody.

Even though the original purpose of this collection of chants was to enable smaller parishes to participate in the church's Gregorian chant tradition, Model Two might also be a pastorally appropriate option for large communities that wish to maintain a high degree of congregational participation in the entrance song, while at the same time using Gregorian chant.

46. The simpler chant melodies were borrowed mainly from the Divine Office.
47. Compare examples 3 and 4.

MODEL THREE: ALTERNATIVE MUSICAL SETTINGS OF THE PROPER ANTIPHON AND VERSES

Example 6. Metrical strophic hymn setting of a vernacular translation of the introit *Nos autem gloriari* for the Holy Thursday Evening Mass of the Lord's Supper from *Hymn Introits for the Liturgical Year*.[48]

Meter: LM
Suggested Tune: Duguet

Antiphon:
    Then let us glory in the cross
    Of Jesus Christ, who sets us free;
    He rescues us and gives us life
    That we may sing eternally.

Verses:
    My God be merciful to us,
    Bless us, shine on us from above;
    Let all earth's people know your ways,
    All nations know your saving love.

    Let all the nations praise you, Lord,
    Let them praise you, be glad, and sing;
    You judge with equity all lands
    And rule the nations as their king.

    Let all the nations praise you, Lord,
    And may the earth yield its increase;
    Then God, our God, will bless our land
    And nations worship him in peace.

Doxology:
    Then praise the Father, praise the Son,
    And praise the Spirit equally,
    Who was before the light of day,
    Is now, and reigns eternally.

48. Reprinted from Christoph Tietze, *Hymn Introits for the Liturgical Year: The Origin and Early Development of the Latin Texts* (Chicago: Liturgy Training Publications, 2005), 161. Antiphon text (*Nos autem gloriari*) by Christoph Tietze, from *Introit Hymns for the Church Year* © 2005, World Library Publications, wlpmusic.com. All rights reserved. Used with permission. The translation of Psalm 67 [66] from Chris Webber, *A New Metrical Psalter* © 1986, The Church Hymnal Corporation. Used by permission. All rights reserved.

Example 7. Metrical refrain hymn setting of a vernacular translation of the introit *Nos autem gloriari* for the Holy Thursday Evening Mass of the Lord's Supper.[49]

Text: Introit for Holy Thursday; Psalm 66. Adapt. Anthony Corvaia. © 2002 Anthony Corvaia
Tune: WAREHAM, LM; William Knapp, 1698-1768

Example 8. Responsorial setting of a vernacular translation of the introit *Nos autem gloriari* for the Holy Thursday Evening Mass of the Lord's Supper from "Newly-composed Eucharistic Entrance Antiphons" (David Farr, 1986).[50]

PSALM 23   Tone X

      ANTIPHON

50. David Farr, "Newly-composed Eucharistic Entrance Antiphons, with Commentary" (PhD diss., Graduate Theological Union, Berkeley, 1986), 113. Used by permission.

Example 9. Responsorial setting of a vernacular translation of the introit *Nos autem gloriari* for the Holy Thursday Evening Mass of the Lord's Supper from *The Simple Gradual for Sundays and Holy Days* (Clifford Howell, 1969).[51]

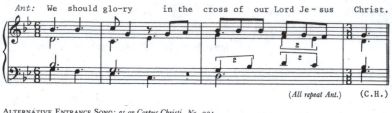

Psalm 66

1. *Semi-Choir:* O Gód, be grá¦cious and bléss us
   and let your fáce shed its¦ líght upón us.
   So will your wáys be knówn¦ upon éarth
   and all nátions learn your¦ sáving hélp.
   [*Gel: repeat C&D Bev: repeat A&D Mur: repeat*]
   Full Choir: Let the péoples práise¦ you, O Gód;
   let áll the¦ péoples práise you. *Ant.*

2. *Semi-Choir:* Let the nátions be glád¦ and exúlt
   for you rúle the¦ wórld with jústice.
   With fáirness you¦ rúle the péoples,
   you gúide the ná¦tions on éarth.
   [*as verse 1*]
   Full Choir: Let the péoples práise¦ you, O Gód;
   let áll the¦ péoples práise you. *Ant.*

3. *Semi-Choir:* The éarth has yíeld¦ed its frúit
   for Gód, our¦ Gód, has bléssed us.
   May Gód still gíve¦ us his bléssing
   till the énds of the¦ éarth revére him.
   [*as verse 1*]
   Full Choir: Let the péoples práise¦ you, O Gód;
   let áll the¦ péoples práise you. *Ant.*

There is no Doxology.

51. John Ainslie, ed. The Simple Gradual for Sundays and Holy Days (London, Dublin, and Melbourne: Geoffrey Chapman, 1969), 47.

Example 10. Responsorial setting of a vernacular translation of the introit *Nos autem gloriari* for the Holy Thursday Evening Mass of the Lord's Supper from *Psallite: Sacred Song for Liturgy and Life* (Collegeville Composers Group, 2008).[52]

Our glo - ry and pride   is the cross of Je - sus Christ;

re - deemed by him,   we have life, raised from the dead.

O God, be gracious   and   bless us
So will your ways be known up - on   earth

and let your face shed   its   light upon us.
and all nations learn your sav - ing   help.

Let the peoples   praise   you,   O   God;

let all the   peo - ples praise you.

Music and text from *Psallite,* Wilfrid Weitz, O.S.B., 1912–1991, adapt. by The Collegeville Composers Group
with the permission of Saint Andrew's Abbey of Valyermo,
© 2005, The Collegeville Composers Group. All rights reserved.
Published and administered by the Liturgical Press, Collegeville, MN 56321. Used with permission.

52. Collegeville Composers Group, *Psallite: Sacred Song for Liturgy and Life* (Collegeville, MN: Liturgical Press, 2008), 178. Used by permission.

Sources, Texts, and Music

What Model Three suggests is the use of new musical settings of the vernacular translation of the proper antiphons and psalm verses of the *Graduale Romanum* and/or *Graduale Simplex*.[53] Such musical settings can be in any musical style, as the examples above show, but, in contrast to vernacular settings in Models One and Two, are not concerned with maintaining melodic characteristics of particular Gregorian chants or with maintaining a "Gregorian style"—for example, using typical Gregorian intervals and modes. Several composers have completed such settings for the entire liturgical year.[54] Model Three encompasses two possibilities: metrical settings of the antiphon along with reciting tones for the psalm verses (see examples 8, 9, and 10) and metrical hymn settings of the antiphon and psalm verses (see examples 6 and 7). Last, it is within Model Three that choral settings of the proper antiphons and psalms find their place (see appendix A for several examples).

Performance

Vernacular settings are inherently more suited to congregational singing, except in those rare places where the entire congregation is familiar with Latin—for example, at some seminaries or gatherings of bishops, clergy, liturgical chant scholars, and so on. Given the variety of musical forms Model Three permits, performance of the entrance song could be entirely by the congregation, by the congregation in alternation with the cantor or choir, or by the choir alone. Model One, on the other hand, would generally not allow for a congregation-alone performance of the entrance song.

Functional Strengths and Weaknesses

Model Three is the only one of these five models that has the potential to achieve all four of the functions of the entrance song as articulated in the GIRM without qualification or limitation (see GIRM 47). Like Model One, it achieves a high degree of festal specificity. Its

---

53. "Composers seeking to create vernacular translations of the appointed [entrance and communion] antiphons and psalms may . . . draw from [the antiphons in the *Missale Romanum* and] the *Graduale Romanum*, either in their entirety or in shortened refrains for the congregation or choir." Sing to the Lord 77

54. In addition to the examples above, see Columba Kelly, *Entrance and Communion Antiphons for Sundays and Feasts* (Portland, OR: Oregon Catholic Press, 2008).

source texts can be the proper antiphons and psalms of the Roman Missal and *Graduale Romanum*. Like Model Two, it facilitates congregational singing and fosters a sense of unity among the gathered assembly. This is especially true of Model Three in that *any* musical style is permissible. For many Roman Rite Catholics throughout the world, the Gregorian musical style would be completely foreign, and their own native musical styles would more effectively foster a sense of unity and common musical heritage. Like Models One and Two, this model can be an effective means of opening the celebration and, if an open musical form is utilized, it can successfully adapt to the variable length of the entrance procession.

Model Three can also utilize the antiphons and psalm verses of the *Graduale Simplex*. The pastoral motivation here would be to create a smaller, seasonal, common repertoire of music for the entrance song in a particular worshiping community. Such a pastoral need could be met more effectively by Model Four below, however. The complexity of the Gregorian melodies of the *Graduale Romanum* are no longer a stumbling block, so there is no need to eclipse the festal specificity of the *Graduale Romanum* in order to facilitate congregational participation. Imitation of the Latin melodies is also no longer a concern, so Model Three can oftentimes achieve a more natural melodic contour and stress pattern for the vernacular language.

One weakness of this model is that it eclipses the melodic tradition of the Latin chants. The association of a particular melody with a particular text can help the assembly learn and become familiar with a large number of texts. The infinite melodic variability of Model Three diminishes the utility of melody as a mnemonic device.

MODEL FOUR: MUSICAL SETTINGS
OF TEXTS OTHER THAN THE PROPER ANTIPHONS
AND VERSES

Example 11. Metrical refrain hymn "Lift High the Cross" for use as the entrance song at the Holy Thursday Evening Mass of the Lord's Supper (CRUCIFER, Nicholson / Kitchin, Newbolt, 1916).[55]

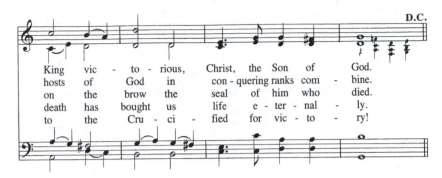

King vic - to - rious, Christ, the Son of God.
hosts of God in con - quering ranks com - bine.
on the brow the seal of him who died.
death has bought us life e - ter - nal - ly.
to the Cru - ci - fied for vic - to - ry!

Example 12. Metrical strophic hymn "In the Cross of Christ I Glory" for use as the entrance song at the Holy Thursday Evening Mass of the Lord's Supper (RATHBUN, Conkey / Browning, 1849).[56]

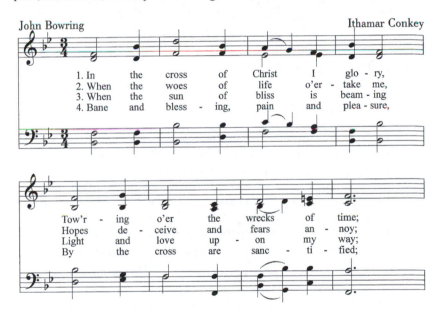

John Bowring   Ithamar Conkey

1. In the cross of Christ I glo - ry,
2. When the woes of life o'er - take me,
3. When the sun of bliss is beam - ing,
4. Bane and bless - ing, pain and plea - sure,

Tow'r - ing o'er the wrecks of time;
Hopes de - ceive and fears an - noy;
Light and love up - on my way;
By the cross are sanc - ti - fied;

56. Words: John Browning. Music: Ithamar Conkey, RATHBUN, 1849. Public domain.

All   the   light   of   sa - cred   sto - ry
Nev - er   shall   the   cross   for - sake me,
From   the   cross   the   ra - diance   stream - ing
Peace   is   there   that knows   no   mea - sure,

Gath - ers   round   its   head   sub - lime.
Lo!   it   glows   with peace   and   joy.
Adds   more   lus - ter   to   the   day.
Joys   that   thro' all   time   a   -   bide.

Sources, Texts, and Music

This Model is currently the one most often employed in parishes across the United States:

> In the years immediately following the liturgical reforms of the Second Vatican Council, especially because of the introduction of vernacular language, composers and publishers worked to provide a new repertoire of music for indigenous language(s). In subsequent decades, this effort has matured, and a body of worthy vernacular music continues to develop. . . . Today, as they continue to serve the Church at prayer, composers are encouraged to concentrate on craftsmanship and artistic excellence in all musical genres. (STTL 84)

> In accord with an uninterrupted history of nearly five centuries, nothing prevents the use of some congregational hymns coming from other Christian traditions, provided that their texts are in conformity with Catholic teaching and they are appropriate to the Catholic Liturgy. (STTL 115d)

Neither the GIRM nor Sing to the Lord requires that melodies be approved by the conference of bishops or diocesan bishop; only texts must be approved. The GIRM provides no specific criteria for the selection of such a "suitable song," other than that the song must be from an "approved" collection and perform the functions of the entrance song (GIRM 47). Sing to the Lord provides three "judgments" that help to answer the question, "Is this particular piece of music appropriate for this use in the particular Liturgy?" (STTL 126).

- Liturgical: "Is this composition capable of meeting the structural and textual requirements set forth by the liturgical books for this particular rite?" (STTL 127)

- Pastoral: "Does a musical composition promote the sanctification of the members of the liturgical assembly by drawing them closer to the holy mysteries being celebrated? Does it strengthen their formation in faith by opening their hearts to the mystery being celebrated on this occasion or in this season? Is it capable of expressing the faith that God has planted in their hearts and summoned them to celebrate?" (STTL 130)

- Musical: "Is this composition technically, aesthetically, and expressively worthy?" (STTL 134)

In the end, it is up to the local community to weigh the criteria and choose the most appropriate song.

The principle that texts and songs to be used in the liturgy need to meet with episcopal approval (see GIRM 48) is not new to ecclesiastical legislation.[57] Another recent articulation of the principle is found in *Liturgiam Authenticam* 108:[58]

> Sung texts and liturgical hymns have a particular importance and efficacy. Especially on Sunday, the "Day of the Lord," the singing of the faithful gathered for the celebration of Holy Mass, no less than the prayers, the readings and the homily, express in an authentic way the message of the Liturgy while fostering a sense of common

57. See Congregation for Divine Worship, Instruction *Constitutione Apostolica*, on the gradual carrying out of the Apostolic Constitution *Missale Romanum* (3 April 1969), 20 October 1969, no. 12; DOL 209; Congregation for Divine Worship, Instruction *Liturgiae Instaurationes* (1970) 3; and Congregation for Bishops, Directory *Ecclesiae Imago* (1973) 90d.

58. Fifth Instruction on the implementation of the Constitution on the Liturgy, on the vernacular translation of the liturgical books of the Roman Rite, Congregation for Divine Worship and the Discipline of the Sacraments, 28 March 2001. For a discussion and critique of *Liturgiam Authenticam* from a liturgical music perspective, see Bob Hurd, "Liturgiam Authenticam (2001)," in *Song of the Assembly*, 75–77.

faith and communion in charity. If they are used widely by the faithful, they should remain relatively fixed so that confusion among the
people may be avoided. Within five years from the publication of this
Instruction, the Conferences of Bishops, necessarily in collaboration
with the national and diocesan Commissions and with other experts,
shall provide for the publication of a directory or repertory of texts
intended for liturgical singing. This document shall be transmitted
for the necessary *recognitio* to the Congregation for Divine Worship
and the Discipline of the Sacraments.[59]

This directive follows the heading "De novis textibus liturgicis in
lingua vulgari conficiendis," so it does not intend that the proper
entrance antiphons and psalm verses, whether in the vernacular
or Latin, would be included in such a directory. Such texts are
already found in the official liturgical books. Because it is the text
that requires approval and not the musical setting, vernacular settings of the proper antiphons and psalms do not require episcopal
approbation.

This renewed call for bishops to guide the faithful in the selection
of vernacular liturgical songs follows logically upon principles put
forth in the fourth instruction on the implementation of the Constitution on the Sacred Liturgy (*Sacrosanctum Concilium*), *Varietates
Legitimae*, the focus of which was liturgical inculturation. It is the
responsibility of the episcopal conference to regulate the introduction
of elements to the liturgical celebration not found in the official liturgical books (see VL 31–32). Indeed, Model Four is in itself a type of
liturgical inculturation. In terms of melody, musical style, or musical
form, this instruction defines no intrinsic limits on the types of music
that can be used in the liturgy (see VL 40). Still, *Varietates Legitimae*
prefers Models One, Two, and Three because singing the official text

---

59. Trans., USCCB, 2001. "Cantus et hymni liturgici peculiaris momenti et
efficacitatis sunt. Praesertim dominica, 'die Domini', cantus populi fidelis ad
celebrationem sacrae Missae congregati, non minus quam orationibus, lectionibus
et homilia, ratione authentica nuntium afferant Liturgiae, dum sensum communis
fidei et communionis in caritate fovent. Si a populo fideli diffusius adhibentur, satis
sint stabiles, ita ut confusio in populo vitetur. Intra quinquennium ab aditione huius
Instructionis computandos, Conferentiae Episcoporum, necessarium operam con-
ferentibus Commissionibus nationalibus aut dioecesanis ad quas pertinet, aliisque
peritis, edendum curent directorium seu repertorium textuum cantui liturgico
destinatorum. Eiusmodi repertorium transmittatur, necesariae recognitionis causa,
ad Congregationem de Cultu Divino et Disciplina Sacramentorum."

is the ideal, and other songs should "grow organically from forms already existing" (VL 40, 46).[60]

It is clear in Sing to the Lord that when the document speaks of settings of texts not found in the liturgical books, it is referring mainly to strophic hymns.[61] Though other forms[62] are certainly permitted and encouraged,[63] the fact remains that hymns have in practice been the most common substitutes for the proper antiphons and psalms of the Mass. In many local worshiping communities, hymns have become the norm (and even custom) for the processions of the Mass.

60. The incorporation of new texts and musical forms into the liturgy should be seen on the whole as positive progress in the reform and renewal of the liturgy. Anscar Chupungco observes that "by and large modern liturgical renewal is conditioned by historical data, and the program of adaptation can be realized only in the light of historical development of liturgical forms. This means in effect that progress in the liturgy has to recognize the process of evolution, whereby original forms are elaborated and brought to fuller perfection in the course of history. Obviously not every detail of evolution has been felicitous or praiseworthy." Chupungco, "Greco-Roman Culture and Liturgical Adaptation." *Notitiae* 15 (1979): 202. See also *Sacrosanctum Concilium* 21 on removing accretions out of harmony with the liturgy.

61. "At Mass, in addition to the *Gloria* and a small number of strophic hymns in the *Roman Missal* and *Graduale Romanum* [none of these at the Entrance], congregational hymns of a particular nation or group that have been judged appropriate by the competent authorities mentioned in GIRM, nos. 48, 74, and 87, may be admitted to the Sacred Liturgy. Church legislation today permits as an option the use of vernacular hymns at the Entrance, Preparation of the Gifts, Communion, and Recessional." Sing to the Lord 115d.

62. Another form of Model Four is offered by Jan Michael Joncas in "*Ex Aetate Mediali Lux*? On the Use of Tropes for the *Cantus ad introitum*." *Pray Tell Blog* (www.praytellblog.com), 3 January 2011. Here he suggests singing a repeated phrase or mantra, like the popular Taizé chants (ibid., 6–7). While this form departs from the norms of the GIRM, it harkens to early Christian practice in which the primitive precursor to the entrance song might have been short acclamations of praise (see chapter 1).

63. "Sufficiency of artistic expression, however, is not the same as musical style, for 'the Church has not adopted any particular style of art as her own. She has admitted styles from every period, in keeping with the natural characteristics and conditions of peoples and the needs of the various rites.' Thus, in recent times, the Church has consistently recognized and freely welcomed the use of various styles of music as an aid to liturgical worship." Sing to the Lord 136. See also *Sacrosanctum Concilium* 123.

The repertoire is vast and includes hymns from both Roman Catholic and non-Catholic traditions.[64]

Performance

Advocates of the antiphon/psalm form typically cite its variable length as a characteristic that makes the form especially suitable for accompanying liturgical processions. This is indeed true. This advocacy, however, is often within the context of a critique of the use of hymns in the Roman Rite Mass.[65] Closed forms like the hymn cannot vary in length along with the infinitely variable length of liturgical processions. If one is to do justice to their integral poetic form, hymn texts should be performed in their entirety. Practically speaking, this often results in either the truncation of the poetic text or the arrest of the ritual progression of the introductory rites in order to complete the hymn, even if it is longer than the entrance procession.[66]

On the other hand, one can assert that the psalm is also a closed poetic form that should be sung in its entirety and that singing only a handful of verses violates this form. This is an important point that deserves further study and reflection. In the *Liturgy of the Hours* we note, for example, that psalms are generally chanted from beginning to end.

However, even though the psalms form the heart of the Office,[67] at the entrance and communion processions of the Mass, psalms are used in a different way. Here the antiphons are most important and, because they are sung in alternation with the verses,[68] comprise a larger part of the entrance song. One of the purposes of the verses is to amplify the antiphon's themes and to allow the assembly to meditate upon them. Furthermore, it is part of the ancient tradition

---

64. "In accord with an uninterrupted history of nearly five centuries, nothing prevents the use of some congregational hymns coming from other Christian traditions, provided that their texts are in conformity with Catholic teaching and they are appropriate to the Catholic liturgy." Sing to the Lord 115d.

65. See K. Irwin, *Context and Text*, 236–38.

66. A similar problem characterized the truncated introit form, which used only a single psalm verse, in that it might be too short to accompany the entire entrance procession.

67. "In the liturgy of the hours the Church in large measure prays through the magnificent songs that the Old Testament authors composed under the inspiration of the Holy Spirit." General Instruction of the Liturgy of the Hours 100; DOL 426.

68. See *Ordo Cantus Missae* II:1.

and still part of the current liturgical norms[69] that the verses of an entrance song need not begin with the first verse of a psalm and that verses can even be taken out of order or skipped altogether—a type of large-scale centonization. The acceptability and integrity of such use relies upon the ancient tradition of performance and of liturgy's use of Scripture more so than upon any study of poetic form. In terms of the strophic hymn, there is no such tradition of free rearrangement and/or elimination of verses.

This is not to deny, to be sure, that Scripture scholars today might rightly balk at such free adaptation of the psalms and their poetic structure. As David Power suggests, "Exegetically, some of this accommodated use causes embarrassment. . . . Christian congregations need to be careful not to reduce readings about Israel to Christian and sacramental symbolism."[70] He also reminds us, however, that "what needs to be remembered is that it is their quality as poetry which makes the psalms so adaptable. Their expression of emotion and their rich imagery fit quite a diversity of situations, as will be found indeed with poems that written in one set of circumstances readily fit into others."[71]

Functional Strengths and Weaknesses

The weakness of this model is twofold. First, when the song is a strophic metrical hymn, it has a closed musical form. There is no real solution to this problem, other than to play instrumental interludes between the verses to lengthen it or to select especially short or long hymn texts, depending on the details of a particular liturgical celebration. Second, Model Four has the capacity to eclipse completely the proper chant tradition of the Roman Rite in favor of new texts or texts from other traditions.

The strengths of this model, however, greatly outweigh its weaknesses. Good vernacular texts set to music are extremely memorable. Model Four would thus be very effective in creating a common repertoire and fostering a sense of unity among the assembly at the start of the Mass. Such songs can also effectively announce the feast or season. The means by which Model Four achieves this entrance song function is admittedly different from how it is achieved by the

---

69. See Introduction to the *Graduale Simplex* 15.

70. David N. Power, *"The Word of the Lord": Liturgy's Use of Scripture* (Maryknoll, NY: Orbis, 2001), 60, 62.

71. Ibid., 60.

antiphon/psalms of Models One, Two, and Three. Similar to tropes, sequences, and Latin liturgical hymns, newly composed vernacular songs add a fresh "didactic, theological, . . . and poetic"[72] perspective to the celebration of the liturgy.[73] Such songs, carefully chosen, can be effective sources of festal specificity and can provide fresh interpretations of the liturgical-theological tradition,[74] while at the same time providing opportunities for local creativity and inculturation within the fixed ritual structure of the Mass. Within this local creativity, vernacular entrance songs can be even more particular and specific than the proper antiphons and verses in that they can add elements of local interpretation and insight.[75]

A Variation on Model Four

A possible variation on Model Four is to combine it with Model One or Two. The entrance antiphon (from either the *Graduale Romanum* or the *Graduale Simplex*, or in a new vernacular setting) is sung by the choir before the entrance procession begins. After the antiphon, the procession begins in the usual way, accompanied by a hymn.[76] While this variation or hybrid model does retrieve the official entrance antiphon text, it is, strictly speaking, a deviation from liturgical norms, which provide several options but do not speak of a combination thereof. It is a compromise solution, because even

---

72. David Hiley, *Western Plainchant: A Handbook* (Oxford: Clarendon Press, 1993), 196.

73. "It is not enough that cultural elements [incorporated into the liturgy through inculturation] be free of error; they should also have the connaturality to be integrated with the liturgical mystery." Chupungco, "Greco-Roman Culture," 217.

74. This is especially so when hymns or other vernacular songs are written with a particular feast or seasonal theme in mind. Ideally, these songs might even be loosely based upon the proper antiphon texts.

75. Hymns can also function as liturgical "propers." "They allow an appropriate emphasis to be made according to the season or the occasion. They do this within the overall context which the creeds, like the fixed texts and the stable ritual scheme, continue to recall." Geoffrey Wainwright, *Doxology: The Praise of God in Worship, Doctrine and Life; A Systematic Theology* (New York: Oxford University Press, 1980), 215.

76. In fact, this hybrid model is the one most often experienced by the author in his experience as a member of the choir at the Basilica of the National Shrine of the Immaculate Conception, Washington, DC. There, this hybrid has been the norm since at least 1997 for Masses at which the choir is present. To be sure, however, the basilica is not the typical parish.

though it retrieves the text, it ignores the ritual function of the antiphon—that is, to accompany a procession.[77]

MODEL FIVE: THE SPOKEN PROPER ANTIPHON OF THE ROMAN MISSAL

Source and Text

The GIRM provides that the presider can recite the entrance antiphon of the Roman Missal if there is no singing during the entrance procession.[78] The antiphon texts in the Roman Missal are in place there primarily for this purpose,[79] even though the antiphon may be sung by itself when necessary.[80]

---

77. Jan Michael Joncas describes the motivation for this hybrid model well: "I believe that [this model] tries to preserve the heritage of the *antiphona ad introitum*, using the textual-musical unity as a prelude piece rather than a processional. The vernacular hymns serve as the true processional, even though as a "closed" form it is less suited to accompany the unpredictable time it will take the procession to move through the Eucharistic space. What I salute is the creativity of those promoting [this model]; they strike me as the good stewards lauded in the Gospel who bring forth from their storeroom 'things both new and old.'" Joncas, *"Ex Aetate Mediali Lux?"* 8.

78. "If there is no singing at the entrance, the antiphon in the Missal is recited either by the faithful, or by some of them, or by a lector; otherwise, it is recited by the priest himself, who may even adapt it as an introductory explanation." GIRM 48. "Only in the absence of song is the entrance antiphon used as a spoken or recited text. Since these antiphons are too abrupt for communal recitation, it is preferable when there is no singing that the priest, the deacon, or another minister adapt the antiphon and incorporate it in the introduction to the Mass of the day." USCCB, foreword to the Sacramentary (1985).

79. Paul VI explains that "the text of the *Graduale Romanum* has not been changed as far as the music is concerned. In the interest of their being more readily understood, however, the responsorial psalm . . . as well as the entrance and communion antiphons have been revised for use in Masses that are not sung." Paul VI, Apostolic Constitution *Missale Romanum*. Speaking of the work of Group 14, which was assembled during the Second Vatican Council to study forms of singing within the Mass, Bugnini relates that "the entrance and communion antiphons of the Missal were intended to be recited, not sung, and to inspire the creation of suitable songs in the vernacular." Annibale Bugnini, *The Reform of the Liturgy (1948–1975)*, trans. Matthew J. O'Connell (Collegeville, MN: Liturgical Press, 1990), 891.

80. "Vel etiam sola antiphona, nullo addito versu." *Ordo Cantus Missae* II:1.

Performance

In certain situations, it might be necessary or preferable that there be no music at the beginning of Mass and that the Roman Missal antiphon be recited.[81] Certainly, Masses said by the priest with only one other minister present are normally celebrated without music, and there are several other situations in which this model might be appropriate:

1. A Mass at which no cantor or organist or other musical leader can be present.[82] In this circumstance, silence at the entrance might be appropriate if the assembly has no shared musical repertoire or would be unable to sing without musical accompaniment or leadership from a cantor.

2. A Mass at which there are no music books or worship aids available.

3. A Mass at which there is no entrance procession (for example, in a worship space with no processional route or when the Liturgy of the Hours is combined with Mass).

No matter the circumstance, however, if those participating in the liturgy desire to sing, it is never inappropriate to begin in song,

---

81. *Musicam Sacram* 7 recognizes that in some circumstances there will be no singing at a liturgical celebration. Furthermore, "singing by the gathered assembly and ministers is important at all celebrations. Not every part that can be sung should necessarily be sung at every celebration." Sing to the Lord 115.

82. Jan Michael Joncas points out, but does not really recommend, the possibility of using instrumental music before Mass even when there is no sung entrance song. Joncas, *"Ex Aetate Mediali Lux?"* 3. (This is not the same as an instrumental prelude to Mass.) Such music is related to the instrumental introits shown in appendix B of this book. This practice must certainly occur in some places, but it is at odds with the liturgical norms, since "resources to [sing the entrance song] are clearly present" (ibid.). In such cases, it would be more appropriate to sing the opening dialogue between priest and people, without any preceding instrumental music, if for some reason it is pastorally prudent not to sing the entrance song (see ibid.). It is worth recounting an experience of the author at the Basilica of the National Shrine of the Immaculate Conception at a Mass to open the annual meeting of the United States Conference of Catholic Bishops. At this Mass, instrumental music functioned by itself as the processional music. During the procession of the bishops to the sanctuary, an ensemble played Aaron Copeland's *Fanfare for the Common Man*. A hymn followed for the rest of the procession. While not envisioned by the liturgical norms, it worked well in this unique circumstance.

for "singing is the sign of the heart's joy" (see Acts 2:46 and GIRM 39). Singing at the beginning of the liturgy might still be desirable, for example, for the purposes of opening the celebration, fostering unity, and announcing the feast, even if there can be no entrance procession, so that the liturgy might begin in a more joyous manner than could be achieved by a simple recitation of the Roman Missal antiphon. Indeed, music "make[s] the liturgical [texts] of the Christian community more alive and fervent so that everyone can praise and beseech the Triune God more powerfully, more intently and more effectively" (MSD 31; see STTL 5).

Functional Strengths and Weaknesses

Model Five is a model for exceptional circumstances. In terms of the functions intrinsic to the entrance song, it achieves only one: the introduction of the assembly's "thoughts to the mystery of the liturgical time or festivity" (GIRM 47). To be sure, then, a recited antiphon from the *Missale Romanum* is better than the omission of this part of the Mass entirely. It is important to remember, however, that "psalms are poems that are meant, whenever possible, to be sung" (STTL 15b; see GIRM 102). The proper antiphons facilitate this musical proclamation of the Psalter, and they are also inherently musical texts.

CONCLUSION

> The Church awaits an ever richer song of her entire gathered people. "The faith of countless believers has been nourished by melodies flowing from the hearts of other believers. In song, faith is experienced as vibrant joy, love, and confident expectation of the saving intervention of God."
>
> —Sing to the Lord 85[83]

Each of the five models serves to describe one way of enacting the entrance song at Mass. They generalize, of course, and cannot account for every possibility, which can only be thoughtfully and carefully dealt with in local parish communities. In a broad sense, the models show forth the need for the creation or compilation of a vernacular

---

83. Quoting Pope John Paul II, Letter to Artists (1999) 12.

Roman Gradual.[84] All the models taken together (with the exception of Model Five) would comprise this liturgical musical resource.[85] A truly usable collection of this sort would require the assignment of psalm verses to all the antiphons in the Roman Missal and the Missal's antiphons to be singable translations of the Latin.[86] Further, the proper chant tradition would be greatly enriched by quality songs of the type described by Model Four. The directory from the conference of bishops would help this "Vernacular Gradual" to become a reality—an invaluable liturgical resource, to be sure.

84. See Jo Hermans, "The Directory of Liturgical Songs in the Vernacular: Background and Liturgical Criteria" *Antiphon* 11:1 (2007): 64.

85. ICEL seems the most logical organization to create or compile such a resource. Given their governing statutes, however, a revised edition of the Latin *Graduale Romanum* would need to be promulgated first.

86. The translation of the sung texts of the Latin typical editions must be "understandable by participants, suitable for proclamation and singing . . . and the relationship between the text and the liturgical action" must be taken into account by the translators. *Varietates Legitimae* 53. This is the case in the 2010 translation of the Missal, even if using the translation of the ICEL antiphon committee would have been far better. The Missal uses the Revised Grail Psalms, as we have said. The 1998 Sacramentary provided verse assignments for all of the Missal antiphons. ICEL has now produced a much less comprehensive list of assignments for the 2010 Missal. See *Antiphonary: Excerpted from the Roman Missal*, ICEL, 2011.

CHAPTER FOUR

Toward a Theology of the Entrance Song at Eucharist

INTRODUCTION

Foundations for a Theology

The articulation of a theology rightly comes after the contextual studies of chapters one and two and the models of chapter three.[1] The goal of this chapter is to discover within these contexts and models an emerging theology of the entrance song at Mass. In a broad sense, how does the entrance song function within the Roman Rite, and what is its purpose? In a more specific sense, what does or should a text and melody of a particular entrance song express theologically? The historical and legislative contexts form the foundation for

---

1. Peter Jeffery says, "Theologically one might say that eternal truths become incarnated in historical texts. But from a historical perspective, liturgies develop in the opposite order: action is primary, then text, then theology. Human beings do not begin with timeless principles, then formulate texts, and finally add ceremonies. . . . Historically speaking, theology comes last. The systematizers and commentators and reformers appear on the scene after the actions and texts are already in place, once the need is beginning to be felt for interpretation or improvement." Jeffery, "The Meanings and Functions of *Kyrie Eleison*," in *The Place of Christ in Liturgical Prayer: Trinity, Christology, and Liturgical Theology*, ed. Bryan D. Spinks (Collegeville, MN: Liturgical Press, 2008): 141–42. See also Ronald Grimes, "Victor Turner's Definition, Theory and Sense of Ritual," in *Victor Turner and the Construction of Cultural Criticism: Between Literature and Anthropology*, ed. Kathleen M. Ashley (Bloomington: Indiana University Press, 1990), 141–42.

theological reflection, while the articulation of a theology must take place in dialogue with the models of the entrance song so as to be connected to actual liturgical praxis.[2]

Any theology of the entrance song that seeks to be relevant must in its formulation take into account practical issues or specific motivating problems regarding its ritual enactment in particular worshiping communities.[3] The problem from the perspective of this study is the question as to what Roman Catholics should sing at the beginning of Mass. This general problem encompasses a number of more specific problems:

- What are the most appropriate musical forms for the entrance song at Mass in view of the song's function?

- What kind of regulation of the entrance song would be most pastorally appropriate in light of the General Instruction of the Roman Missal 48, and what resources might facilitate a more integral enactment of the entrance song?

- How should the proper chant tradition of the *Graduale Romanum* and *Missale Romanum* in general, as well as the texts of particular introit antiphons and verses, influence the present-day entrance song in terms of musical form, text, enactment, and theology? In other words, is it possible to restore the important theological "residue of meaning"[4] of the introit to the celebration of the Mass of the Roman Rite?

2. Here, a consideration of "actual liturgical praxis" means a consideration of precisely defined models that are enacted in worshiping communities. The methodology of this study does not allow direct access to the communal and individual experience of the enacted liturgy. Participant-observer studies, reader-response criticism, and ethnography, for example, would be more able to directly access liturgical experience and systematically articulate its meaning, even though these methods also have limitations. See, for example, Mary McGann, *A Precious Fountain: Music in the Worship of an African American Catholic Community* (Collegeville, MN; Liturgical Press, 2004); and McGann, *Exploring Music as Worship and Theology* (Collegeville, MN: Liturgical Press, 2002). She states, "As yet . . . little has been done to develop methods for studying music within a community's worship performance, and for assessing how a community's musical performance affects the entire continuum of liturgical action, shaping and expressing an embodied theology. This essay addresses that challenge." *Exploring Music as Worship and Theology*, 10–11.

3. See Figure 1: Application of the Contextual Method; and McGann, *Exploring Music as Worship and Theology*, 10–11.

4. Joyce Ann Zimmerman, *Liturgy and Hermeneutics* (Collegeville, MN: Liturgical Press, 1999), 17. See also Joyce Anne Zimmerman, *Liturgy as Lan-*

Arguing for the importance of the theology of the introit tradition does not favor one particular model of the entrance song over another.[5] The point is that the introit antiphons and their accompanying verses comprise an ancient and official part of the liturgical tradition and, therefore, should influence present-day liturgical praxis. The readings and presidential prayers exert such influence; why not the antiphons? Likewise, a theology of the entrance song is not synonymous with a theology of the introit. For the broader entrance song tradition, past and present, encompasses a variety of musical forms and models. Nevertheless, the introit, if not encompassing the entire entrance song tradition, does form the heart of this tradition in the Roman Rite.

If the chants of the *Graduale* and *Missale* function together as an entrance song archetype, then not only should the general characteristics of the introit chants[6] be embodied in the entrance songs used at Mass today, but the theological themes and scriptural allusions of particular introit texts, and perhaps even particular introit melodies, should as well. How this theology is articulated in practice is left to the inexhaustible depths of human creativity, within the bounds of liturgical history and tradition, ecclesiastical law, ritual and pastoral effectiveness, and culture-specific judgments of quality.[7]

---

guage of Faith: A Liturgical Methodology in the Mode of Paul Ricouer's Textual Hermeneutics (Lanham / New York / London: University Press of America, 1988), 48–49; and Paul Ricoeur, *Interpretation Theory: Discourse and the Surplus of Meaning* (Fort Worth: Texas Christian University Press, 1976), 25–29.

5. Anscar Chupungco reminds us that "the Church's attitude towards culture is not governed by an a-priori principle in favor or against any particular cultural form." This also applies to musical forms, which develop within particular cultures. Chupungco, "Greco-Roman Culture and Liturgical Adaptation," *Notitiae* 15 (1979): 218.

6. These characteristics include musical form, relationship of text and music, festal/seasonal specificity, openness to elaboration and local creativity, appropriateness to the human voice, etc., and they enable the introit to function effectively as an entrance song. See Anthony Ruff, "The Music 'Specially Suited to the Roman Liturgy': On the One Hand . . . ," *Pastoral Music* 32:5 (June–July 2008): 15–16. The functions of the entrance song as articulated in current ecclesiastical legislation are likely based on the characteristics of the introit, rather than vice versa.

7. J. H. Kwabena Nketia offers some useful insights in regard to how different musical forms are appropriate for different cultural groups and should influence inculturated entrance song forms. He states, "People's approach to the nexus relationship between music and ritual is determined by their belief system, the forms of musical expression and communication they cultivate, the meanings they assign to specific sounds and movements and the modes of interaction they

Methodological Perspectives on the Theology of Liturgical Music

It is through the interaction of context and function that theological themes emerge, along with basic conclusions about pastoral solutions[8] to this book's motivating problems. There are many approaches to articulating a theology of liturgical music.[9] Mark David Parsons has delineated three such approaches that prevail among liturgical-musical theologians today. The first is a text-centered approach in which "the text has primary significance and music becomes . . . a channel through which a text is transmitted. . . . Music in worship can *assist* the communication event . . . but fundamentally the process is carried by the words associated with the music."[10] In this model "texted musical forms are primary," "musical expression is not integral to worship" (even if it is desirable), and "music enables a congregational response" by preparing the assembly to receive Word and sacrament and then acting as a vehicle through which they can voice their praise.[11] The second approach focuses on music qua music. The idea is "that music has theo-

---

establish in ritual and worship." Nketia, "Musical Interaction in Ritual Events," in *Music and the Experience of God* (Edinburgh: T. & T. Clark, 1989), 123.

8. See figure 1.

9. Significant works on the theology of music include, among others, Jeremy Begbie, *Theology, Music and Time* (Cambridge, UK: Cambridge University Press, 2000); Teresa Berger, *Theology in Hymns? A Study in the Relationship of Doxology and Theology According to* A Collection of Hymns for the Use of the People Called Methodists (*1780*), trans. Timothy E. Kimbrough (Nashville: Kingswood Books, 1995); Albert Blackwell, *The Sacred in Music* (Louisville, KY: Westminster / John Knox Press, 1999); Lucien Deiss, *Visions of Liturgy and Music for a New Century* (Collegeville, MN: Liturgical Press, 1996); Q. Faulkner, *Wiser Than Despair: The Evolution of Ideas in the Relationship of Music and the Christian Church* (Westport, CT: Greenwood Press, 1996); Kathleen Harmon, *The Mystery We Celebrate, the Song We Sing: A Theology of Liturgical Music* (Collegeville, MN: Liturgical Press, 2008); Erik Routley, *Words, Music and the Church* (Nashville, TN: Abingdon Press, 1968); Don E. Saliers, *Music and Theology* (Nashville, TN: Abingdon Press, 2007); Victoria Sirota, "An Exploration of Music as Theology," *The Arts in Religious and Theological Studies* 5 (Summer 1993): 24–28; Karen B. Westerfield Tucker, "Music as a Language of Faith," *Ecclesia Orans* 23 (2006): 81–98; Brian Wren, *Praying Twice: The Music and Words of Congregational Song* (Louisville, KY: Westminster / John Knox Press, 2000).

10. Mark David Parsons, "Text, Tone, and Context: A Methodological Prolegomenon for a Theology of Liturgical Song," *Worship* 79:1 (January 2005): 57.

11. Ibid., 58. See also Erik Routley, *Hymns Today and Tomorrow* (Nashville, TN: Abingdon Press, 1964), 18–21; and Routley, *The Divine Formula: A Book for Worshipers, Preachers and Musicians and All Who Celebrate the Mysteries* (Princeton, NJ: Prestige Publications, 1986), 117–28.

logical potential without words"[12] and can surpass the limitations of language. In this model "music itself has theological significance," "the text becomes secondary to music," and, therefore, "music is integral to worship."[13] The third approach focuses on liturgical music's function. It "ascribes theological significance to music primarily by virtue of its utility to Christian worship," which implies that "theological meaning in music is functional," the text identifies its function, and "music is integral" to worship because it functions to promote participation.[14]

As the models of the previous chapter demonstrate, varied approaches work best not in isolation but in conversation with one another.[15] Thus, each of the three approaches to the theology of liturgical music are adequate, as long as one does not assume any particular approach to be exhaustive or completely sufficient. Each approach offers different insights. As always, the choice of approach should not be determined by a personal or intellectual commitment to a particular method, but rather by determining which method is most appropriate in a specific context for a specific task.

The theology articulated in this chapter, then, utilizes aspects of each approach. First, our concerns are primarily *functional* in that our focus is the function and purpose of the entrance song at Mass and because our intention is to determine what kind of music best facilitates this function and purpose. From this perspective, as Parsons explains, "music realizes its theological potential through its contextualization in worship as a functional process."[16] Second, our concerns are also *textual*. Entrance song texts in general have a particular liturgical function. As Parsons explains, "In the practice of liturgy, the text is an 'explicit performative' that indicates how to read the ritual act of singing and understand the liturgical act being accomplished."[17] Thus, the genre of the entrance song text influences how it is set to music and how it is performed. The text also reveals something about the larger ritual categories of entrance procession and introductory rites of which it is a constituent part. And our concern is also with specific entrance song texts and what they express

12. Parsons, "Text, Tone, and Context," 59.

13. Ibid., 62–63.

14. Ibid., 67–68.

15. According to Parsons, "Liturgical song represents a mutuality between liturgical texts, musical experience, and ritual processes that establishes the fulfillment of God's Word by its incarnation in ordinary experience." Ibid., 69.

16. Parsons, "Text, Tone, and Context," 67.

17. Ibid., 67–68.

theologically in terms of feast-specific and seasonal themes. Third, one must affirm that music is integral to worship, because the entrance song is expressed through (and only through) music and can thereby fulfill its function and, finally, because music is the normative means by which the entrance song's text is expressed.

It is important to state that this chapter brackets an exploration of the theology of music as sound (music qua music) and the affective dimension of music. The methodology here employed does not grant access to this dimension. This bracketing is justified and does no harm—even though a study in this vein would be worthwhile— because the origins of liturgical chant melodies mainly had to do with the aural transmission of liturgical *texts*, and because we do not analyze any particular melodies or musical settings in terms of music theory, aesthetics, and so forth. As Peter Jeffery reminds us, "A chant melody records a reading of its text; the melody is the record of its maker's responses to the relationships among word order, syntax, and phrasing and to the ways these are related to the text's meaning. . . . In this process, melody plays a role similar to that of punctuation by clearly marking off syntactical units."[18]

Function, text, and facilitation, then, form the groundwork for a theology. This theology emerges through the interplay of *function* and *text*, and out of this theology emerge principles that *facilitate* solutions to our pastoral problems. *Function* encompasses many different aspects of the entrance song: how it opens, disposes, accompanies, unifies, announces, and appropriates within its liturgical context. *Text* involves a consideration of the content and context of the words of a particular entrance song. The text examined here will be the entrance antiphon and psalm verses of the Holy Thursday Evening Mass of the Lord's Supper (*Nos autem gloriari*). This particular text opens the Paschal Triduum[19] and is thus one of the most important entrance chants of the liturgical year. This text's context is vast: the origin and

---

18. Peter Jeffery, "Chant East and West: Toward a Renewal of the Tradition," in *Music and the Experience of God*, ed. Mary Collins, David N. Power, and Mellonee Burnim, *Concilium* 202 (Edinburgh: T. & T. Clark, 1989), 24. Thus the primary way in which the chant melodies are related to their texts is through syntax. The melodies do not as a rule reflect Latin accent patterns, nor do they often reflect the semantics of the text by word painting (see ibid.). See also Ritva Jonsson and Leo Treitler, "Medieval Music and Language: A Reconsideration of the Relationship," in *Music and Language*, Studies in the History of Music 1 (New York: Broude, 1983), 22.

19. See Congregation of Rites, Instruction *Ordo Hebdomadae Sanctae Instauratus*, 16 November 1955.

development of the Holy Thursday Mass and of the broader liturgical times of which it is a part, the manuscript tradition of the *Nos autem gloriari* introit and the textual sources of this antiphon, and the theological themes expressed in the text and their relationship to other texts within the immediate liturgical orbit (Holy Week, Triduum, Easter). The point of *facilitation* is that, out of a theology, one can sketch the boundaries of what the Roman Rite entrance song should be and then delineate criteria for choosing particular entrance songs for the Mass.

THE THEOLOGY OF THE ENTRANCE SONG: FUNCTION, TEXT, AND FACILITATION

The Theological Function of the Entrance Song in Its Ritual Context

The entrance song at Mass falls into two ritual categories. First, it is a constituent element of the introductory rites. Second, it is the music that accompanies the entrance procession of the Mass. This means that the entrance song should help to accomplish the overall purpose of the introductory rites and achieve the basic functions of a Roman Rite entrance song.

"*The entrance song opens the celebration of the Eucharist*" (GIRM 47). On a purely functional level, the entrance song brings order to the assembly by focusing everyone's attention toward the liturgy that has just begun. It is a kind of culmination of the gathering of the assembly that necessarily has taken place before Mass. When the entrance song begins, all the elements of the ritual come together—it actualizes a symbiosis of movement, music, text, and even architecture, because processional routes are in many ways determined by the floor plan of a church building. As the first ritual element of the Mass, the entrance song also sets the tone for the entire liturgical celebration and can determine the overall mood of the celebration (festive, somber, etc.).[20]

"*The entrance song, along with the other introductory rites, disposes the assembly to listen to the Word of God and to celebrate the Eucharist worthily*" (GIRM 46). In a less tangible but real manner, it is by means of the entrance song that the gathered community shifts from an everyday to a ritual mode of acting;[21] this is also true because the

---

20. See *New Dictionary of Sacramental Worship*, s.v. "Gestures, Liturgical."

21. See, for example, the USCCB document Built of Living Stones: "The Church marks time as holy by setting aside Sunday and by celebrating the liturgical year

people are gathered together as the church (the Body of Christ, the living temple) out of the everyday world and into the house of God.[22] Through the song and through the community's act of singing, God invites the assembly and those gathered to establish their identity as church, to recognize God's presence, and to invite one another to the eucharistic feast.

"The entrance song accompanies the entrance procession of the priest and ministers at the beginning of Mass" (GIRM 47).[23] Because the entrance song is liturgical music that accompanies ritual action and is thus "closely . . . joined to the liturgical rite" (SC 112), it must meet "the demands of the rite itself" (STTL 128). The entrance procession at Mass is truly a functional procession. One of its primary purposes is to move persons from one place to another. The entrance procession is also surrounded by layers of theological interpretation, of course, but it differs from certain other liturgical processions, such as processions with images of the Blessed Virgin Mary or processions

---

with its rhythm and seasons. It demonstrates God's reign over all *space* by dedicating buildings to house the Church and its worship. Each Sunday the baptized are challenged to reset from their daily labors, to contemplate the goodness of God, to make present the victory and triumph of Christ's death (SC, no. 6), to enter the joy of the Risen Lord, [and] to receive the life-giving breath of the Spirit." USCCB, Built of Living Stones: Art, Architecture, and Worship (Washington, DC: USCCB Publishing, 2000), no. 20.

22. Speaking of the entrance rite in general (and not about any song in particular), Schmemann says it is the "ascent and entry of the Church into the heavenly sanctuary." Alexander Schmemann, *The Eucharist: The Sacrament of the Kingdom* (Crestwood, NY: St. Vladimir's Seminary Press, 1988), 50. See also USCCB, Built of Living Stones 16–17. The entrance song possesses liminal qualities. It is a type of ritual threshold on the other side of which the assembly recognizes itself more fully as the church. Every enactment of the Mass is itself a liminal experience that occurs outside one's everyday life and that ideally works to transform the participant so that afterward one is conformed more fully to the Body of Christ. The celebration of the Eucharist reveals a permanent communal bond among the members of the Body of Christ, but is also a "momentary community" or *communitas* that is not the same as one's "community of work" or "neighborhood." See Ronald Grimes, "Emerging Ritual," in *Proceedings of the North American Academy of Liturgy*, Annual Meeting, Saint Louis, January 2–5, 1990 (Valparaiso, IN: North American Academy of Liturgy, 1990), 25.

23. For studies of liturgical processions in general, see, for example, Baldovin, "Kyrie Eleison and the Entrance Rite of the Roman Eucharist," *Worship* 60 (July 1986): 36; Herman Wegman, "Procedere und Prozession: eine Typologie," *Liturgisches Jahrbuch* 27 (1977): 28–39; and I. H. Dalmais, "Note sure la sociologie des processions," *La Maison-Dieu* 43 (1955): 37–43.

for a good harvest.[24] The focus of this other kind of procession is not on getting from one place to another; the focus is on giving witness to the community's faith and, indeed, on the act of processing itself.[25]

Getting the priest and ministers from the entrance or the sacristy of the church building to the sanctuary was the originating function of the entrance procession and introit during the era when the liturgy experienced a period of formalization, imperialization, and elaboration. The length of the introit varied in accord with the length of the procession, but from the late Middle Ages, the functional relationship between the length of the introit and the length of the entrance procession dis-integrated. This functional connection was restored, however, in the reform of the liturgy, so that today one can confidently assert that processional chants should accompany processional movement (STTL 115b).

"The entrance song establishes and intensifies the unity of the gathered assembly" (GIRM 46–47). In other words, as Baldovin states, the entrance song helps the assembly "to be and become more intensely the body of Christ."[26] The entrance song finds its origins not only in the ritual needs of an entrance procession but also in the desire of the assembly to joyfully acclaim and respond to the paschal mystery. In the Mass today, it accomplishes this unity in large part through the act of singing together. Through the entrance song, the community truly enters the celebration of the Eucharist,[27] affirming its identity as the community of the redeemed and as Christ's body,[28] while recognizing and welcoming the priest celebrant as a symbol of Christ the head.[29]

24. *New Dictionary of Sacramental Worship*, s.v. "Gesture and Movement in the Liturgy."

25. Ibid.

26. Baldovin, "Kyrie Eleison," 334. As Nketia says, "The significance of the music of a ritual occasion does not lie only in the symbolic interaction it generates, but also the means it provides for the affirmation of communal values and the renewal of the bonds and sentiments that bind a community or the devotees of a god." Nketia, "Musical Interaction in Ritual Events," 117.

27. See Lucien Deiss, *Visions of Liturgy and Music*, 121.

28. Jeremy Begbie notes that "the Holy Spirit opens our present (and us) to Christ's past and future, and, as in the case of music, this entails not the refusal of 'our' temporality, but its healing and re-formation." Begbie, *Theology, Music and Time*, 173. See also St. Augustine of Hippo, who states, "Let us recognize both our voice in his, and his voice in ours." Augustine, *Ennarationes in Psalmos* 85:1, trans. ICEL, 1974.

29. See Deiss, *Visions of Liturgy and Music for a New Century* (Collegeville, MN: Liturgical Press, 1996), 121.

Liturgical chant as a whole, as Robert Taft says, is "both proclamation and acclamation: proclamation of the *mirabilia Dei* culminating in
the Paschal Mystery of Christ and pointing to his return in glory, and
acclamation of Christ present to the Church in the *actio*."[30] The entrance
song also has a particular function in this regard in that *it announces
the feast or season through the appropriation of the Word of God and other
ancient liturgical-textual traditions to the assembly* (see GIRM 47). It
serves to announce and recall those things most basic to the Christian
world of meaning and to particularize the liturgical celebration to follow.

The official introit antiphons and verses are a good example of
this "announcing" and "appropriating" function of the entrance song
in that they convey not only specific themes but also specific texts.
The introit antiphon texts make use of scriptural (and sometimes
nonscriptural) texts in a variety of ways. They are, however, not proc-
lamations of long excerpts from the Scriptures, as in the Liturgy of
the Word. Neither are they simple scriptural allusions, which one
frequently finds in the presidential prayers of the Mass. Consider,
for example, the collect for 21 January, the memorial of St. Agnes,
Virgin and Martyr:

Almighty ever-living God,	Omnipotens sempiterne Deus,
who choose what is weak in the	qui infirma mundi eligis,
world to confound the strong,	ut fortia quaeque confundas,
mercifully grant,	concede propitius,
that we, who celebrate the heavenly	ut, qui beatae Agnetis martyris
birthday of your Martyr Saint Agnes,	tuae natalicia celebramus,
may follow her constancy in the	eius in fide constantiam
faith.	subsequamur.
Through our Lord . . .[31]	Per Dominum.[32]

Here, the first half of the collect alludes to 1 Corinthians 1:27, which
reads, "Rather, God chose what is foolish in the world to shame the
wise, and God chose what is weak in the world to shame the strong"

---

30. Robert Taft, "Toward a Theology of Christian Feast," in *Beyond East and
West* (Washington, DC: Pastoral Press, 1984), 7–9.

31. Excerpt from the English translation of *The Roman Missal* © 2010, ICEL.

32. This prayer is found in the 2002/2008, 1975, 1970, and 1962 editions of
the Missale Romanum. It is derived from the *Sacramentarium Veronese* and *Sacramentarium Gelasianum*. For more precise source details, see Cuthbert Johnson,
Sources of the Roman Missal (1975), Notitiae 32 (1996): 105.

(NRSV).[33] The collect does not directly quote the passage, and it surrounds the allusion with a substantial amount of other text.

Indeed, antiphons are a unique liturgical-textual genre. Their purpose is neither to proclaim nor to allude to the ancient Christian textual tradition, but to *appropriate* it. In so doing, antiphons reflect and pass on a tradition of textual interpretation. This occurs through the way a specific antiphon text employs the textual tradition and relates to and interacts with its verses to produce a particular Christian meaning, and then how the antiphon and verses together relate to and reveal something about a specific day of the liturgical year, thereby announcing "the mystery of the liturgical time or festivity" (GIRM 47).

There are three primary interpretive relationships, then: the interaction of an antiphon and the broader scriptural/textual tradition of the church, the interaction of an antiphon and its verses, and the interaction of the entrance song and a liturgical feast. This interaction is the essence of the Mass antiphon as a textual genre, and this relationship between Scripture and liturgical celebration is an integral characteristic of the Roman Rite.

Antiphons are not scriptural texts in the same way as the readings at Mass, even if both are what David Power calls "the oral and liturgical exchange of Christian communities."[34] Rather, as *Liturgiam Authenticam* 23 implies, they are "texts of ecclesicestical composition" ("textuum manu ecclesiastica compositorum"),[35] which draw on "centuries of ecclesial experience in transmitting the faith of the Church received from the Fathers" (LA 20). Unlike a Scripture reading, as Power says, "the genre of [which] will command to some extent the place that it is given" in the liturgy, it is the genre and liturgical function of the antiphon and entrance song that has over time *determined the text* and the way the text makes use of the scriptural, psalmic, and other early textual traditions of the church.[36] Antiphons were composed *for* the liturgy. The biblical readings, while inextricably

---

33. The text of the Vulgate reads, "sed quae stulta sunt mundi elegit Deus ut confundat sapientes et infirma mundi elegit Deus ut confundat fortia."

34. David N. Power, *"The Word of the Lord": Liturgy's Use of Scripture* (Maryknoll, NY: Orbis, 2001), 44.

35. See Peter Finn for the International Commission on English in the Liturgy, "The Translation of the *Missale Romanum, editio typica tertia*: Questions and Issues Related to the Translation of the Antiphons" (unpublished study, Washington, DC, 2004), 2.

36. D. Power, *"Word of the Lord,"* 45.

bound up with the liturgy, exist separately from it as a witness to salvation history.[37]

The Theology of the Entrance Song as Text: *Nos autem gloriari*

Table 4. Latin Text and English Translations of *Nos autem gloriari*.

Graduale Romanum (1974) *Graduale Simplex* (1975) Antiphon	The Sacramentary (1973)	*The Roman Missal* (2010)
Nos autem gloriari opportet in Cruce Domini nostri Iesu Christi; in quo est salus, vita et resurrectio nostra: per quem salvati, et liberati sumus.[38]	We should glory in the cross of our Lord Jesus Christ, for he is our salvation, our life and our resurrection; through him we are saved and made free.[39]	We should glory in the Cross of our Lord Jesus Christ, in whom is our salvation, life and resurrection, through whom we are saved and delivered.[40]
Psalm 66 (67)		
1. Deus misereatur nostri, et benedicat nobis: illuminet vultum super nos, et misereatur nostri.[41]	1. O God, be gracious and bless us and let your face shed its light upon us (and have mercy on us).	
2. Ut cognoscamus in terra viam tuam: in omnibus gentibus salutare tuum.	2. So will your ways be known upon earth, and all nations learn your salvation.	
3. Confiteantur tibi populi, Deus: confiteantur tibi populi omnes.	3. Let the peoples praise you, O God; let all the peoples praise you.	

37. Because the antiphons are often not simply quotations from Scripture, treating them as such is very problematic from the perspective of liturgical translation and the creation of vernacular editions of the liturgical books.

38. The *Graduale Simplex* antiphon ends after "Christi."

39. Trans., ICEL, 1973.

40. Trans., ICEL, 2010.

41. "Et misereatur nostri" is not found in the *Graduale Simplex*.

4. Laetentur et exsultent gentes, quoniam iudicas populos in aequitate, et gentes in terra dirigis.	4. Let the nations be glad and shout for joy, with uprightness you rule the peoples; with fairness you rule the peoples, you guide the nations on earth.
5. Confiteantur tibi populi, Deus, confiteantur tibi populi omnes.	5. Let the peoples praise you, O God; let all the peoples praise you.
6. Terra dedit fructum suum; benedicat nos Deus, Deus noster.	6. The earth has yielded its fruit for God, our God, has blessed us.
7. Benedicat nos Deus, et metuant eum omnes fines terrae.[42]	7. May God still give us his blessing that all the ends of the earth may revere him. [43]

A consideration of liturgical text *as text* is important because a particular text influences its musical setting and performance and, more important, expresses themes and ideas of a particular liturgical feast or season. In so doing, as Margaret Mary Kelleher notes, the text "plays a mediating role by providing certain imagery for God, oneself, and the Christian community."[44] Any entrance song rightly so-called must be able to function as such. In a reciprocal manner, however, a particular entrance song text reveals something about the function of *the* entrance song as it pertains to a particular liturgical celebration. In other words, *an* entrance song, when enacted, accomplishes the functions of *the* entrance song through its unique text and melody. As an example of a particular entrance song text, then, we turn to the introit of the Holy Thursday Evening Mass of the Lord's Supper.

The Origins of the Feast

According to Egeria's account, in Jerusalem by the late fourth century, Christians celebrated the Eucharist at 2:00 p.m. on the Thursday before Easter Sunday at the Martyrium (the basilica built over

---

42. The *Graduale Romanum* includes only the first three psalm verses.

43. Trans., *The Revised Grail Psalms: A Liturgical Psalter* © 2010 Conception Abbey / The Grail, administered by GIA Publications, Inc., 7404 S. Mason Ave., Chicago, IL 60638, USA, www.giamusic.com/rgp. All rights reserved. Used by permission.

44. Margaret Mary Kelleher, "Liturgy and the Christian Imagination," *Worship* 66:2 (March 1992): 148.

the place where the cross was discovered).[45] A second Eucharist took place immediately following the first (around 4:00 p.m.).[46] The location of this second celebration—the Post Crucem chapel next to Golgotha—must have been of some significance, but there is no indication in the extant sources as to how or why. Egeria's record indicates that "on this one day the Offering is made Behind the Cross, but on no other day in the whole year."[47] John Baldovin and George Gingras suggest that the Eucharist held at Post Crucem was simply to accommodate the overflow crowd that could not take part in the first Eucharist at the Martyrium.[48] If this was the case, then the location's significance might simply be that it was close to the Martyrium and thus a logical solution to a practical problem. Thomas Talley suggests, however, that this second Eucharist was celebrated at this particular time and place to accommodate Johannine Christians, who believed Jesus' death coincided with the traditional time of the slaying of the lambs for the temple feast.[49] Indeed, the Post Crucem liturgy was celebrated at this time just behind the place where tradition locates Jesus' death on the cross.

After the second Eucharist, the crowd was dismissed to go home and take their final meal before the Easter fast was to begin.[50] At 7:00 p.m., all gathered at the Eleona (the chapel on the Mount of Olives) to begin an all-night vigil of readings, hymns, and prayers.[51] There "they read the passages from the Gospel about what the Lord said to his disciples when he sat in the very cave which is in the church."[52] At midnight, the vigil moved to the Imbomon (the place of Jesus' ascension), then, at cockcrow, to "the place where the Lord prayed."[53]

---

45. *Egeria's Travels to the Holy Land: Newly Translated with Supporting Documents and Notes*, 3rd ed., ed. John Wilkinson (Warminster, UK: Aris & Phillips, 1999), 35.1.

46. Ibid., 35.2. See also John Baldovin, *Liturgy in Ancient Jerusalem* (Nottingham, England: Grove Books Limited, 1989), 40.

47. Wilkinson, ed., *Egeria's Travels*, 35.2.

48. See Baldovin, *Liturgy in Ancient Jerusalem*, 40, citing the George E. Gingras edition: *Egeria: Diary of a Pilgrimage*, Ancient Christian Writers: The Works of the Fathers in Translation 38 (New York: Newman Press, 1970), p. 236.

49. Thomas J. Talley, *The Origins of the Liturgical Year*, 2nd emend. ed. (Collegeville, MN: Liturgical Press, 1991), 45.

50. Wilkinson, ed., *Egeria's Travels*, 35.2.

51. Ibid., 35.3.

52. Ibid., 35.3–4.

53. Ibid., 36.1.

Here, Luke 22:41 was read.[54] Next, while it was still dark, they processed to Gethsemane where there was a reading about the Lord's arrest.[55] Then, on Good Friday morning, when day was breaking, they processed, singing, from Gethsemane into Jerusalem, ending at the atrium Before the Cross.[56] Though it took place on Good Friday, it was the gathering Before the Cross that marked the end of the vigil that had begun the night before. The central theme that emerges from Egeria's account of the liturgical celebrations on the Thursday before Easter, then, is the commemoration and celebration of the cross.

Baldovin argues that the first Eucharist at the Martyrium "seems to have commemorated the Last Supper of Jesus," while admitting that "Egeria . . . says nothing about a thematic character to this celebration."[57] His argument is strengthened by two slightly later (fifth century) lectionaries, both of which reflect liturgical practice in Jerusalem. The Armenian Lectionary provides readings that pertain to the institution of the Eucharist for this celebration, and the Georgian Lectionary provides for a foot-washing service at the afternoon Eucharist at the Martyrium.[58] In the Armenian source, the second Eucharist has moved from the chapel Post Crucem to the more spacious atrium Before the Cross,[59] likely to accommodate a larger assembly. It also provides for a third celebration of the Eucharist at Sion (the site of the Last Supper) later in the afternoon.[60]

The Armenian Lectionary is more specific than Egeria's account as to which readings were proclaimed where. During the first Eucharist at the Martyrium, Psalm 22 (23) (*Dominus reget me et nihil mihi deerit*) and 1 Corinthians 11:23-32 (a Eucharist institution narrative)

---

54. Ibid., 36.1 and p. 154n2.

55. Ibid., 36.2–3.

56. Ibid., 36.3–4.

57. Baldovin, *Liturgy in Ancient Jerusalem*, 40. See also Wilkinson, ed., *Egeria's Travels*, p. 153.

58. Baldovin, *Liturgy in Ancient Jerusalem*, 40. It also provides for a service for reconciling penitents. This source does not provide a second or third Eucharist on Thursday. See Michel Tarchnischvili, ed., *Le grand lectionnaire de l'Église de Jérusalem (Ve–VIIIe siècle)* (Louvain : Secréteriat du Corpus SCO, 1959–60).

59. Baldovin, *Liturgy in Ancient Jerusalem*, 40; and Talley, *Origins of the Liturgical Year*, 44.

60. Baldovin, *Liturgy in Ancient Jerusalem*, 40. See Athanase Renoux, *Le Codex arménien Jérusalem 121*, vol. 2, *Édition comparée du texte et de deux autres manuscrits*, *Patrologia Orientalis* 36.2:168 (Turnhout, 1969), 269; and Talley, *Origins of the Liturgical Year*, 38.

were read, along with Matthew's account of the institution of the Eucharist.[61] There were no readings at the second Eucharist, and at the third the readings were the same as at the first, with the exception that the gospel account of the institution is now taken from Mark.[62] Finally, this source clearly indicates that the reading at the Eleona was the Last Supper discourse from the Gospel of John (13:16–18:1).[63]

By the fifth century, then, it is clear that the commemoration of the Last Supper was integral to the liturgies of the Thursday before Easter.[64] Note, however, that only in the Armenian Lectionary does a celebration of the Eucharist take place at the site of the Last Supper—not in Egeria's account. This likely represents a later stage of liturgical development in Jerusalem.[65] Is it possible, then, that in the early centuries there was a gradual shift in which the remembrance of the institution of the Eucharist came to be more theologically discrete—less connected to the other aspects of the broader Easter celebration? Perhaps cross and table competed as the central theme of the Thursday before Easter from the beginning. Indeed, the eventual inclusion of Holy Thursday as part of the Triduum might reflect a gradual shift from a cross/resurrection–centered theology to one more Eucharist centered.

All of this information has been included here to make a single point: the liturgies of the Thursday before Easter, from very early on, focused not only upon the Eucharist and Last Supper but also upon the cross. In fact, the entire day—from the afternoon Eucharist at the place where the cross was discovered to the second Eucha-

---

61. Renoux, *Le Codex arménien Jérusalem* 121, vol. 2, no. 39. See also Wilkinson, ed., *Egeria's Travels*, 185; and Talley, *Origins of the Liturgical Year*, 45.

62. Talley, *Origins of the Liturgical Year*, 45.

63. Armenian Lectionary, no. 39.

64. In the Old Gelasian Sacramentary, the tripartite liturgical structure of Thursday of Holy Week is present: reconciliation of penitents, chrism Mass, and the evening Mass of the Lord's Supper. See Leo Cunibert Mohlberg, ed., *Liber Sacramentorum Romanae Aeclesiae Ordinis Anni Circuli (Cod. Vat. Reg. lat. 316 / Paris Bibl. Nat. 7193, 41/56) (Sacramentarium Gelasianum)* (Rome: Casa Editrice Herder, 1960), 55–64. See also Mario Righetti, *Manuale di Storia Liturgica*, vol. 2 (Milan: Editrice Àncora, 1969), 206; and Herman Wegman, *Christian Worship in East and West: A Study Guide to Liturgical History*, trans. Gordon W. Lathrop (Collegeville, MN: Liturgical Press, 1990), 80, 17–75.

65. Talley observes that "celebrations that commemorate events at the very place of their occurrence represent a secondary stratum in the hagiopolitan liturgical tradition." Talley, *Origins of the Liturgical Year*, 54.

rist that took place near Golgotha behind the cross—is imbued with the remembrance of the cross. It is clear from the vigil that follows, which concludes Before the Cross, and from the remaining services on Friday that the cross is the context that envelopes the entirety of the Triduum until the Easter resurrection.

As in Jerusalem, the liturgies of the Triduum in Rome were stational. The station for the Mass of the Lord's Supper was the Basilica of St. John on the Lateran hill, the cathedral of Rome. It is not clear exactly when this station came to be associated with this particular liturgy,[66] but likely from the start. Originally dedicated by Constantine as St. Savior in AD 324, the dedications to Sts. John the Baptist and John the Evangelist were added in the tenth and twelfth centuries, respectively. According to tradition, the basilica houses a piece of the table at which Jesus and his apostles celebrated the Last Supper. An ancient altar is also a fixture of the basilica—for centuries, only the bishop of Rome has been allowed to celebrate the Eucharist at it. Its possession of both artifacts makes the Lateran a logical location for the celebration of the Holy Thursday evening Mass, though it does not reflect in any explicit way the cross context so fundamental to Holy Thursday in Jerusalem.

The History of the Triduum and Its Restoration

The Paschal Triduum, which forms the immediate context for the Holy Thursday evening Mass, "shines forth as the high point of the entire liturgical year" (Universal Norms for the Liturgical Year and the Calendar 18).[67] In the postconciliar Roman Missal it begins with the Holy Thursday Evening Mass of the Lord's Supper and ends after Evening Prayer on Easter Sunday (UNLYC 19). Other liturgical celebrations that take place earlier in the day on Holy Thursday, namely, any reconciliation of penitents and the chrism Mass at which the oils and chrism are blessed by the bishop, fall outside the Triduum and

---

66. None of the manuscripts of the *Antiphonale Missarum Sextuplex* indicate the station for this Mass, though they do for other days. Many old Sacramentary manuscripts indicate that an evening Mass took place at St. John Lateran on Holy Thursday, however. See *Liber Sacramentorum Paduensis (Padova, Biblioteca Capitolare, Cod. D 47)*, eds. Alcestis Catella, Ferdinandus Dell'Oro, and Aldus Martini, Biblioteca "Ephemerides Liturgicae," Subsidia, Monumenta Italiae Liturgica III (Rome: CLV Edizioni Liturgiche, 2005), 237.

67. Trans., ICEL, 2010. See also *Sacrosanctum Concilium* 5, 106.

are part of Holy Week.[68] As Cyrille Vogel notes, the Triduum grew out of an earlier, more basic celebration of the resurrection on Easter Sunday, as a period of intense preparation: "The period preparing for Easter was gradually established by working back from the feast itself. The step-by-step formation of a full Lent can only be understood by working back from Easter through the Triduum, Holy Week and, ultimately, all the weeks of Lent and even pre-Lent."[69]

With the exception of the Easter Vigil, then, the Triduum is the most ancient liturgical form of preparation for Easter. Such a period is one of two "primitive constants of the annual liturgical cycle."[70] Vogel asserts that the earliest Triduum consisted of Good Friday, Holy Saturday, and Easter Sunday, and not Holy Thursday, Good Friday, and the Vigil of Easter on Saturday. Friday and Saturday were days of fasting since at least the beginning of the third century and culminated in the celebration of the Eucharist on Easter morning.[71] The distinction is not perfectly clear, however, since liturgical days begin the preceding evening at the vigil, thus including Holy Thursday evening.[72] This structure of the Triduum endured into at least the fifth century.[73] The period of preparation for Easter was extended by the fifth century to include Holy Week—the time between Palm Sunday and Holy Thursday evening.[74]

Lent, the prolonged period of preparation for Easter, was officially established in Rome by the late fourth century.[75] Between the fourth and seventh centuries, this preparatory period was extended from three weeks to seventy days,[76] ending on Holy Thursday evening, which began the Triduum. "In the seventh century," however, as Vogel notes, "the paschal Triduum as a distinct entity faded from view and

---

68. See GIRM 204a, 380; and Universal Norms for the Liturgical Year and the Calendar 16a, 31. See also Baldovin, *Liturgy in Ancient Jerusalem*, 40.

69. Cyrille Vogel, *Medieval Liturgy: An Introduction to the Sources* (Washington, DC: Pastoral Press, 1986), 309.

70. Ibid., 308.

71. Ibid., 309 and 385n85, citing Ambrose (*Epistula* 23), Augustine of Hippo (*Epistula* 55), and the *Apostolic Tradition*.

72. C. Vogel, *Medieval Liturgy*, 309.

73. Ibid. See also ibid., 385n86.

74. Ibid., 309.

75. Ibid.

76. Ibid., 310.

the fast days [of Lent] were henceforth calculated backwards from Easter Sunday, rather than from Holy Thursday as before."[77]

This subsumption of the Triduum into Lent persisted for centuries and was only universally and officially remedied for the Roman Rite under Pope Pius XII (1939–58). In 1951 he restored the celebration of the Easter Vigil for experimental use.[78] The experiment was such a success that the pope mandated the restoration of Holy Week and the other parts of the Triduum. This revised rite, the *Ordo Hebdomadae Sanctae Instauratus*, was promulgated in 1955 for first use in 1956.[79] In this liturgical book, the Triduum is once again clearly distinguished from Lent. Most important for our purposes, as Anthony Ward states, the decree of promulgation "laid down that the Mass *In Cena Domini* of Maundy Thursday was to be celebrated '*vespere, hora magis opportuna, non autem ante horam quintam post meridiem, nec post horam octavam*'(*Maxima redemptionis* 7). With this simple disposition, the *veritas temporum* of this celebration was restored and the scene set for a rediscovery of the spiritual and theological wealth of the celebration, with the habitual participation of the people."[80]

These restored rites for Holy Week and the Triduum were incorporated into the *Missale Romanum* (1962) and then further revised—their overall structure remaining intact—to accommodate the liturgical reforms of the Second Vatican Council (1962–65) as part of the postconciliar *editio typica* of the *Missale Romanum* (1970). The rites have been incorporated into the subsequent editions of the reformed *Missale Romanum* (1975, 2002) and remain the normative

---

77. Ibid.

78. Congregation of Rites, *De Solemni Vigilia Paschali Instauranda*, *Acta Apostolica Sedes* 43 (1951), 128–37. See also Robert F. Hayburn, *Papal Legislation on Sacred Music 95 A.D. to 1977 A.D.* (Collegeville, MN: Liturgical Press, 1979), 341.

79. Congregation of Rites, Decree *Maxima Redemptionis* (16 November 1955), *Acta Apostolica Sedes* 47 (1955), 838–47. "Additional decrees of clarification were issued on March 15, 1956 [*Acta Apostolica Sedes* 48 (1956), 153], and February 1, 1957 [*Acta Apostolica Sedes* 49 (1957), 91]." Hayburn, *Papal Legislation on Sacred Music*, 341.

80. Anthony Ward, "Euchology for the Mass 'In Cena Domini' of the 2000 *Missale Romanum*," *Notitiae* 45:11–12 (2008): 611–34. This article provides a brief but useful study of the sources of the collect, prayer over the offerings, and Eucharistic Prayer (preface and embolisms) of the Holy Thursday Evening Mass of the Lord's Supper found in the current *Missale Romanum*. It does not consider the introit.

form for celebrating Holy Week and the Triduum in the Roman Rite. On 16 January 1988, the Congregation for Divine Worship issued the circular letter *Paschalis Solemnitatis* on the preparation and celebration of the Easter liturgies. It is not a revision of the rites of Holy Week and the Triduum, but an exhortation for a more observant celebration of the rites currently in force, as well as a more overt explanation of the details of their theology and enactment.[81]

The Introit Nos autem gloriari

Before the late seventh or early eighth century, the Holy Thursday evening Mass in the Roman Rite had no introit because it began with the offertory.[82] The Mass was assigned texts for the introductory rites and Liturgy of the Word, and thus for the introit, by Gregory II (715–31) or perhaps Sergius I (687–701).[83] At this time, the introit

81. Compared to the detail contained in *Ordo Hebdomadae Sanctae Instauratus* or *Institutio Generalis Missalis Romani*.

82. Marc-Daniel Kirby, "Proper Chants of the Paschal Triduum: A Study in Liturgical Theology" (STL thesis, Catholic University of America, 1996), 99n35. See also Righetti, *Manuale di Storia Liturgica*, v. 2, 206. See, for example, A. Wilmart, "Le lectionnaire d'Alcuin," *Ephemerides Liturgicae* 51 (1937): 136–97. There are no readings assigned in the manuscript for the Holy Thursday evening Mass. The contents and arrangement of Alcuin's Lectionary date from the early seventh century and, aside from some minor details, reflect Roman practice. See C. Vogel, *Medieval Liturgy*, 340–42; and Gamber, *Codices liturgici latini antiquiores*, 1:438–39.

83. Kirby notes that these texts were assigned "for use in non-cathedral or monastic churches." Kirby, "Proper Chants of the Paschal Triduum," 99n35. This seems to imply that the texts were added for parish church use, and that in cathedrals and monasteries the liturgy continued to begin at the offertory, having been preceded by two other Masses (reconciliation of penitents and the chrism Mass). The tradition of using the account of the Last Supper in 1 Corinthians on Holy Thursday looks to have been maintained from the earliest times, as we know it was already listed in the Armenian Lectionary for use on Holy Thursday. The Comes of Würzburg (early seventh century, reflecting Roman usage) does not list any readings for the evening Mass but assigns the 1 Corinthians text to the chrism Mass. When the evening Mass was supplied with its own readings, the 1 Corinthians reading was one of them. The Epistolary of Würzburg assigns no gospel reading to Holy Thursday. In the Tridentine Lectionary, which is based on the late eighth-century Comes of Murbach (a Romano-Frankish Lectionary), this assignment is maintained, and the account of Jesus washing his disciples' feet (John 13:1-15) is also assigned. It is an abbreviation of the gospel reading traditionally assigned to Tuesday of Holy Week (John 13:1-32), which included the account of Judas's betrayal. The reading assignments for the evening Mass

Nos autem gloriari was borrowed from the antiphon's more ancient and likely original liturgical assignment—Tuesday of Holy Week,[84] where the antiphon is sung with Psalm 66 (*Deus misereatur nostri*).[85] The manuscripts of the *Antiphonale Missarum Sextuplex* (eighth and ninth centuries) reflect this change.[86] What one finds in these manuscripts represents a chant tradition that has already developed nearly complete melodic and textual stability, so that what one finds from manuscript to manuscript are minute differences in detail, not transformations of text or melody.[87] Any earlier layers of development have been lost to history. Consequently, paleographical interpretation and comparison of the chant in various manuscripts is not particularly revealing or useful for the purposes of this study, and the antiphon provides a stable text for theological reflection.

---

in the post–Vatican II Lectionary are Exodus 12:1-9, 11-14; 1 Corinthians 11:23-26; and John 13:1-15. See G. Morin, "Le plus ancien lectionnaire ou Comes de l'Eglise romaine," *Revue bénédictine* 27 (1910): 41–74; and A. Wilmart, "Le Comes de Murbach," *Revue bénédictine* 30 (1913): 25–69. Note that Morin's edition includes both the epistolary and the evangelary, even though these are really separate lists. See also C. Vogel, *Medieval Liturgy*, 349–55, especially 354–55; and Christoph Tietze, *Hymn Introits for the Liturgical Year: The Origin and Early Development of the Latin Texts* (Chicago: Liturgy Training Publications, 2003), 59–81, especially 69–70.

84. Hesbert writes, "L'introït, nous venons de le rappeler, est emprunté à la messe du Mardi." Hesbert, *Antiphonale Missarum Sextuplex*, LIX. See also Kirby, "Proper Chants of the Paschal Triduum," 95, 99.

85. See *Antiphonale Missarum Sextuplex*, 90–91; and Kirby, "Proper Chants of Paschal Triduum," 95.

86. See Kirby, "Proper Chants of the Paschal Triduum," 95, 97; and Hesbert, *Antiphonale Missarum Sextuplex*, 92–93. The manuscript from Monza, which only includes the Lectionary chants, does not reflect this change.

87. The minute differences in melodic detail are of interest to chant musicologists, however. To explore these variations, one would begin with the various notated Gradual manuscripts available in facsimile editions and might find that certain variants are typical of a particular region or sphere of liturgical influence. In such an exploration, it would be important for the novice chant researcher to recognize that the Office antiphon *Nos autem gloriari* is not the same as the Mass introit antiphon that begins like it. The text of the Office antiphon is shorter, and the melody is different. As one would expect, the Office antiphon melody is not unique (but the *Nos autem gloriari* introit antiphon is) and is comprised mainly of a theme that occurs frequently in mode seven (mixolydian) Office antiphons.

In four of the six *Antiphonale Missarum Sextuplex* manuscripts,[88] the psalm assigned to the antiphon is Psalm 95 (*Cantate Domino*) rather than Psalm 66, as on Tuesday of Holy Week. This assignment makes sense, given the psalm's ancient association with the mystery of the cross.[89] At some point in the Middle Ages, the assigned psalm was changed to Psalm 66 (*Deus misereatur nostri*). The reason for the change is not clear—perhaps to match the use on Tuesday of Holy Week. Both psalms are psalms of praise and relate to the antiphon through their mention of salvation (*salutare*).

While our focus here is the use of *Nos autem gloriari* on Holy Thursday, it is also employed on certain other days of the liturgical year, which comprise part of the context of the antiphon as a discrete liturgical chant. *Nos autem gloriari*, then, is not unique to Holy Thursday but to feasts of the cross. The assignments of the antiphon are fairly (but not exactly) consistent among the sources. Psalm verse assignments also differ from feast to feast and serve to make each introit distinct both textually and theologically.

88. Though it does for most other feasts, the Corbie manuscript includes no psalm verse assignment for *Nos autem gloriari* on Holy Thursday.

89. Kirby explains that "Psalm 95 is frequently used in connection with the mystery of the Cross, partly because of a reading of verse 10, found in the so-called Italic version: *Dicite in gentibus quia Dominus regnavit a ligno*. The last two words are, in fact, a Christian gloss. See the Alleluia verse for the Friday within the Octave of Easter, *Graduale Romanum*, 212, and the fourth strophe of the hymn *Vexilla Regis* [dicendo nationibus: regnavit a ligno Deus], sung at Vespers during Holy Week and on September 14." Kirby, "Proper Chants of the Paschal Triduum," 97n33. See also Bernard Capelle, "Regnavit a ligno," in *Travaux liturgiques de doctrine et d'histoire*, vol. 3 (Louvain: Abbaye du Mont César, 1967), 211–14.

Table 5. The Liturgical Uses of *Nos autem gloriari*.

Day of the Liturgical Year	Liturgical Book or Manuscript	Liturgical Function	Assigned Psalm (Vulgate numbering of *Psalmi iuxta LXX*)
Tuesday of Holy Week	*Rheinau Antiphonal*	Introit	66[90]
		Communio	Not provided.
	Mont-Blandin Antiphonal	Introit (begins *Nobis*)	66? (MS indicates *Deus me.*)[91]
		Communio	66? (MS indicates *Ut supra.*)[92]
	Compiègne Antiphonal	Introit (begins *Nobis*)	66
	Corbie Antiphonal	Introit	66
	Senlis Antiphonal	Introit	66
	Missale Romanum (1570)	Introit	66
	Graduale Romanum (1908)	Introit	66
	Missale Romanum (1962)	Introit	66
	Graduale Romanum (1974)[93]	Introit	66

90. The first two verses of this psalm constitute the text of another introit antiphon (its verses are the subsequent verses of the same psalm), which is employed in the *Graduale Romanum* (1908) and *Missale Romanum* (1962) for the Votive Mass *pro Fidei Propagatione*. It is also found in the *Missale Romanum* (2008), where it functions as the entrance antiphon for the Votive Mass for the Evangelization of Peoples.

91. The letters "me" are merely the beginning of a word, the rest of which cannot be deciphered from the manuscript. Hesbert suggests the full word might be "meus," which implies Psalm 21. This is possible, but its deviation from what seems an otherwise universal assignment of Psalm 66 would be puzzling. Perhaps the scribe merely misspelled "misereatur."

92. "Ut supra" in these manuscripts indicates that the psalm for the communion is the same as for the introit.

93. In the postconciliar editions of the *Missale Romanum*, the introit antiphon for Tuesday of Holy Week is *Ne tradideris me, Domine*.

Holy Thursday Evening Mass of the Lord's Supper	Rheinau Antiphonal	Introit	95
	Mont-Blandin Antiphonal	Introit (begins Nobis)	95
	Compiègne Antiphonal	Introit	95
	Corbie Antiphonal	Introit	Not provided.[94]
	Senlis Antiphonal	Introit	95
	Missale Romanum (1570)	Introit	66
	Graduale Romanum (1908)	Introit	66
	Missale Romanum (1962)	Introit	66
	Graduale Romanum (1974)	Introit	66
	Graduale Simplex (1975)[95]	Introit[96]	66
	Missale Romanum (1970/1975/2002)	Introit	N/A
Ignatius of Antioch (1 February)	Missale Romanum (1570)[97]	Introit (Mihi autem absit gloriari[98])	131 (Memento domine David)
	Graduale Romanum (1908)	Introit (Mihi autem absit gloriari)	131
	Missale Romanum (1962)	Introit (Mihi autem absit gloriari)	131

94. The lack of an assigned psalm verse might imply that the verse from Tuesday of Holy Week should be used (Psalm 66), but this would deviate from what seems to be an established tradition of using Psalm 95 in the other four manuscripts.

95. The occurrences of *Nos autem gloriari / Mihi autem absit gloriari* are fewer in the *Graduale Simplex* than in the *Graduale Romanum* (1974) not because the chant assignments are different between the two books, but because the *Graduale Simplex* only contains chants for the more important days of the liturgical year.

96. The text of the antiphon *Nos autem gloriari* is abbreviated in the *Graduale Simplex* (it ends after *Iesu Christi*) and is set to a simpler chant melody.

97. For St. Ignatius of Antioch, for St. Francis of Assisi, and for the Votive Mass of the Holy Cross, *Mihi autem absit gloriari* appeared in earlier manuscripts/editions of the Missal and Gradual but not in manuscripts as early as those collected in the *Antiphonal Missarum Sextuplex*.

98. The introit antiphon *Mihi autem absit gloriari*, while not the same antiphon as *Nos autem gloriari*, is related to it. Both are based in Galatians 6:14; in fact, *Mihi autem absit gloriari* is an exact quotation of this biblical verse. It is included

Finding (*Inventio*) of the Holy Cross (3 May)[99]	*Compiègne Antiphonal*	Introit (begins *Nobis*)	66
		Communio	66
	Missale Romanum (1570)	Introit	66
	Graduale Romanum (1908)	Introit	66
Exaltation of the Holy Cross (14 September)	*Corbie Antiphonal*	Introit	92 (*Dominus regnavit decore*)
		Communio	104 (*Annunciate inter gentes*)
	Senlis Antiphonal	Introit	92
		Communio	Not provided.
	Missale Romanum (1570)	Introit	66
	Graduale Romanum (1908)	Introit	66
	Missale Romanum (1962)	Introit	66
	Graduale Romanum (1974)	Introit	66
	Graduale Simplex (1975)	Introit	66
	Missale Romanum (1970/1975/2002)	Introit	N/A

in this table because in the *Graduale Romanum* (1974) it is replaced by *Nos autem gloriari* for the feasts of Ignatius of Antioch and Francis of Assisi, though in the postconciliar *Missale, Nos autem gloriari* has been replaced by other chants on these two feasts. Note also that *Mihi autem absit gloriari* is not the same as the introit and offertory antiphons that begin *Mihi autem nimis*. These two antiphons, which employ the same text but different melodies, were used for feasts of the apostles in the preconciliar *Missale* and *Graduale* and are included in the Common of Apostles in the 1974 *Graduale*. They are not found in the postconciliar *Missale Romanum*.

99. In 1955, because of the addition of St. Joseph the Worker to the universal calendar on 1 May, this feast was displaced by that of Sts. Philip and James and removed from the universal calendar.

Stigmata of Francis of Assisi (17 September)	Graduale Romanum (1908)	Introit (*Mihi autem absit gloriari*)	141(*Voce mea ad dominum*)[100]
	Missale Romanum (1962)	Introit (*Mihi autem absit gloriari*)	141
Francis of Assisi (4 October)	Missale Romanum (1570)	Introit (*Mihi autem absit gloriari*)	141
	Graduale Romanum (1908)	Introit (*Mihi autem absit gloriari*)	141
	Missale Romanum (1962)	Introit (*Mihi autem absit gloriari*)	141
	Graduale Romanum (1974)[101]	Introit (now *Nos autem gloriari*)	141
Ignatius of Antioch (17 October[102])	Graduale Romanum (1974)[103]	Introit (now *Nos autem gloriari*)	131
John of the Cross (14 December)	Missale Romanum (1970/1975/2002)	Introit (*Mihi autem absit gloriari*)[104]	N/A

100. Psalm 141 is the psalm traditionally believed to have been prayed by Francis immediately before his death.

101. In the postconciliar editions of the *Missale Romanum*, the introit antiphon for this feast is *Vir Dei Franciscus reliquit*.

102. The feast for Ignatius was moved to this date in the postconciliar liturgical calendar.

103. In the postconciliar editions of the *Missale Romanum*, the introit antiphon for this feast is *Christo confixus sum cruci*.

104. This feast was added to the universal calendar in 1738, where it was assigned to 24 November. In the 1908 Gradual, the introit antiphon is *Os iusti meditabitur* (which is still on 24 November). In the 1962 Missal, the introit antiphon is *In medio Ecclesiae* (taken from the Commons; the feast was still on 24 November). In the 1974 Gradual, the antiphon assigned is again *Os iusti meditabitur* and, as of 1969, the feast has been transferred to 14 December, the anniversary of his death—this has been made possible by the suppression of the octave the Immaculate Conception. In the postconciliar editions of the *Missale Romanum*, the antiphon is *Mihi autem absit gloriari*.

Votive Mass of the Holy Cross	*Missale Romanum* (1570)	Introit	66
	Graduale Romanum (1908)	Introit	66
	Missale Romanum (1962)	Introit	66
	Graduale Romanum (1974)	Introit	66
	Graduale Simplex (1975)	Introit	66
	Missale Romanum (1970/1975/2002)	Introit	N/A

This table shows forth a gradual move toward standardization in terms of the introit for feasts of the cross. From its original liturgical assignment of Tuesday of Holy Week, *Nos autem gloriari* is "borrowed" very early on for the Exaltation of the Cross,[105] Finding of the Cross, votive Mass of the Cross, and most importantly for this study, the Holy Thursday Evening Mass of the Lord's Supper. In some of the earliest manuscripts the antiphon serves as both the introit and the communion, but not on Holy Thursday. In addition, the feasts of Ignatius of Antioch,[106] the Stigmata of Francis of Assisi, and Francis of Assisi[107] were assigned the similar antiphon text *Mihi autem absit gloriari*, which directly quotes Galatians 6:14.[108] In the postconciliar

105. It is less likely that the original liturgical assignment was the Exaltation of the Cross, which is also an ancient commemoration. See Talley, *Origins of the Liturgical Year*, 47.

106. The commemoration of Ignatius of Antioch can be called a "feast of the cross" for several reasons. In his famous *Letter to the Smyrnaeans* (ca. 110), he argues against Docetism, emphasizing that Jesus truly suffered in the flesh (2:1) on the cross and that the Eucharist is indeed Christ's flesh (7:1). Further, the letter begins, "I glorify God, even Jesus Christ, who has given you such wisdom. For I have observed that you are perfected in an immoveable faith, as if you were *nailed to the cross* of our Lord Jesus Christ, both in the flesh and in the spirit" (1:1, my italics). There is also a tradition that sees Ignatius's journey to Rome for martyrdom, during which he wrote his seven letters to the Christian churches, as his own Way of the Cross.

107. Francis's association with the cross is strong, given his experience of the stigmata.

108. The appropriation of the scriptural tradition is much more complex in *Nos autem gloriari*, as will be shown later in this chapter.

Graduale Romanum, the antiphons for Ignatius and Francis were changed to *Nos autem gloriari.*

The early proliferation of the antiphon probably speaks to its popularity and success in communicating the necessary themes regarding the cross in relation to certain feasts. The reasons for the replacement of *Mihi autem absit gloriari* with *Nos autem gloriari* in the 1974 *Graduale Romanum* are not known, but one can guess the change was an attempt at simplifying the repertoire. Perhaps the collective *nos* was deemed preferable to the singular *mihi.*

From at least the mid-twentieth century, one can see a parallel trend toward simplification and specificity. The feast of the Finding of the Cross, which was likely seen as an unnecessary thematic duplication of the Exaltation of the Holy Cross,[109] was removed from the universal calendar in 1955. In the postconciliar calendar, the feast of the Stigmata of Francis of Assisi was removed, again to simplify the calendar and to avoid any duplication of the 4 October commemoration of Francis.[110] The trend toward specificity in terms of the proper chants of the Mass is especially clear in the postconciliar *Missale Romanum*, which reflects a more advanced stage of liturgical reform than do the postconciliar *Graduale Romanum* and *Graduale Simplex*. In the *Missale Romanum*, Tuesday of Holy Week, the feast of Francis of Assisi, and the feast of Ignatius of Antioch are assigned unique entrance antiphons other than *Nos autem gloriari*. As a result, *Nos autem gloriari* now appears only three times in the postconciliar Missal: Holy Thursday,[111] the Exaltation of the Cross, and the votive Mass of the Cross. It is also true that in the reformed Missal there is now only one occurrence of the related antiphon *Mihi autem absit gloriari*: for St. John of the Cross.

---

109. Though at that time in the Roman Church, the feasts commemorated two different occasions: the feast of the Exaltation of the Cross commemorated the retrieval of the cross from the Persians, and the feast of the Invention of the Cross commemorated the finding of the cross by St. Helen.

110. This feast was removed from the liturgical calendar by Pius V in his 1570 *Missale Romanum* as part of a general program of simplification, but it was later reintroduced by Urban VIII.

111. It is interesting that the *Graduale Simplex* provides a second option for the introit on Holy Thursday evening: *Sacerdos in aeternum* with Psalm 109 (*Dixit Dominus Domino meo*) from the Solemnity of the Most Holy Body and Blood of Christ. This antiphon emphasizes the institution of the ordained priesthood and thus moves away from the broader theme of *Nos autem gloriari.*

The Antiphon's Use of the Biblical Text

Table 6. Source Texts of the Antiphon *Nos autem gloriari*.

Antiphon	Nos autem gloriari oportet in cruce Domini nostri Iesu Christi, in quo est salus, vita et resurrectio nostra, per quem salvati et liberati sumus.	
	Latin Vulgate	**Douay-Rheims** (American Edition, 1899)[112]
Galatians 6:14	mihi autem absit gloriari nisi in cruce Domini nostri Iesu Christi per quem mihi mundus crucifixus est et ego mundo	But God forbid that I should glory, save in the cross of our Lord Jesus Christ; by whom the world is crucified to me, and I to the world.
John 11:25	dixit ei Iesus ego sum resurrectio et vita qui credit in me et si mortuus fuerit vivet	Jesus said to her: I am the resurrection and the life: he that believeth in me, although he be dead, shall live.
1 Corinthians 1:28-31	et ignobilia mundi et contemptibilia elegit Deus et quae non sunt ut ea quae sunt destrueret	And the base things of the world, and the things that are contemptible, hath God chosen, and things that are not, that he might bring to nought things that are:
	ut non glorietur omnis caro in conspectu eius	That no flesh should glory in his sight.
	ex ipso autem vos estis in Christo Iesu qui factus est sapientia nobis a Deo et iustitia et sanctificatio et redemptio	But of him are you in Christ Jesus, who of God is made unto us wisdom, and justice, and sanctification, and redemption:
	ut quemadmodum scriptum est qui gloriatur in Domino glorietur	That, as it is written: He that glorieth, may glory in the Lord.

112. The Douay-Rheims translation is employed here because it is the one that most closely matches the Latin Vulgate from which most of the antiphons are derived.

Psalm 7:2	Domine Deus meus in te speravi salvum me fac ex omnibus persequentibus me et libera me	O Lord my God, in thee have I put my trust: save me from all them that persecute me, and deliver me.
Psalm 70:2	in iustitia tua libera me et eripe me inclina ad me aurem tuam et salva me	Deliver me in thy justice, and rescue me. Incline thy ear unto me, and save me.
Psalm 107:7	ut liberentur dilecti tui salvum fac dextera tua et exaudi me	That thy beloved may be delivered. Save with thy right hand and hear me.
Daniel 3:88	quia eruit nos de inferno et salvos fecit de manu mortis et liberavit de medio ardentis flammae et de medio ignis eruit nos	For he hath delivered us from hell, and saved us out of the hand of death, and delivered us out of the midst of the burning flame, and saved us out of the midst of the fire.
4 Esdras 12:34	nam residuum populum meum liberabit cum misericordia, qui salvati sunt super fines meos, et iucundabit eos, quoadusque veniat finis, dies iudicii, de quo locutus sum tibi ab initio.	But in mercy he will set free the remnant of my people, those who have been saved throughout my borders, and he will make them joyful until the end comes, the day of judgment, of which I spoke to you at the beginning (NRSV).[113]
2 Timothy 4:18	liberabit me Dominus ab omni opere malo et salvum faciet in regnum suum caeleste cui gloria in saecula saeculorum amen	The Lord hath delivered me from every evil work: and will preserve me unto his heavenly kingdom, to whom be glory for ever and ever. Amen.

---

113. The New Revised Standard Version is used here because the verse is not found in the Douay-Rheims translation.

Deuteronomy	si postquam audieris haec	If after thou hast heard these
7:12-13	iudicia custodieris ea et fe-	judgments, thou keep and
	ceris custodiet et Dominus	do them, the Lord thy God
	Deus tuus tibi pactum et	will also keep his covenant to
	misericordiam quam iuravit	thee, and the mercy which he
	patribus tuis	swore to thy fathers:
	et diliget te ac multiplicabit	And he will love thee and
	benedicetque fructui ventris	multiply thee, and will bless
	tui et fructui terrae tuae fru-	the fruit of thy womb, and
	mento tuo atque vindemiae	the fruit of thy land, thy corn,
	oleo et armentis gregibus	and thy vintage, thy oil, and
	ovium tuarum super terram	thy herds, and the flocks of
	pro qua iuravit patribus tuis	thy sheep upon the land, for
	ut daret eam tibi	which he swore to thy fathers
		that he would give it thee.

Again, antiphons are more a reflection of a tradition of biblical interpretation than they are scriptural quotations. The textual sources of the antiphon also comprise part of its context. The primary text appropriated by the antiphon is Galatians 6:14.[114] Marc-Daniel Kirby asserts that the antiphon's list of benefits (*salus, vita, resurrectio*) "are to be compared with" the list found in Deuteronomy 7:12, which pertain to faithful observance of the Law.[115] But this comparison only applies by means of ex post facto theological interpretation of the antiphon. There is no evidence that the Deuteronomy text is one of the antiphon's sources.

In the *Rheinau* manuscript—one of the earliest of the *Antiphonale Missarum Sextuplex* manuscripts—the *Nos autem gloriari* antiphon does not contain the word "*salus,*" but only "*vita*" and "*resurrectio*". It is possible, then, that this form of the antiphon reflects an earlier stage of development and that the source text for this section of the antiphon is John 11:25, which speaks of *resurrectio et vita*. The equally early manuscript of *Mont-Blandin*, however, does contain the word *salus*, as do *Compiègne* and *Corbie*. The full text of the antiphon is not found in the *Senlis* manuscript. The *Rheinau* variation implies one of three things: that at some point early on the word *salus* was added to the antiphon, that *Rheinau* reflects a variant textual tradition for this antiphon, or that the scribe inadvertently left out the word *salus* when copying the manuscript. The latter is the most likely, especially

114. The postconciliar Missal provides the citation as "cf. Gal 6.14."
115. Kirby, "Proper Chants of the Paschal Triduum," 96.

since a variation in the text would also imply a variation in what by that time was almost certainly a common melodic tradition. It is also possible that John 11:25 was the inspiration for this part of the antiphon text in all the manuscripts, or that some Old Latin version of John 11:25 included the word *salus*. But all of these possibilities, however interesting and plausible, cannot be proven based on the extant evidence.

Kirby's argument that 1 Corinthians 1:28-31 was the inspiration for the second half of the antiphon (beginning *in quo est salus*) is more convincing. The list of benefits found in 1 Corinthians 1:30 (wisdom, justice, sanctification, redemption) could have been the inspiration for the list in the antiphon, and the appearance of *gloriari* in both the antiphon and the Scripture passage might indicate some relationship between the two texts.[116] Still, this connection is not self-evident. The final phrase, *salvati et liberati sumus*, could have been adapted from any number of biblical texts. Forms of the words *salvati* and *liberati* occur together in Scripture only sixteen times, and of these a smaller number are possible source texts (see Table 6 above). 2 Timothy 4:18 seems the most likely candidate, even though it is possible the words were so common to Christian parlance when the antiphon was composed as to require no direct textual source.

Nos autem gloriari employs several methods of textual adaptation typical of liturgical antiphons in order to express its cross-centered theme or theology.[117] The antiphon *substitutes* the singular *mihi* of Galatians 6:14 with the plural *nos*. It also *omits absit* and *nisi*. If 1 Corinthians is indeed a source text, then bits and pieces of it were incorporated into the antiphon through *centonization*. The antiphon could also be said to *substitute* the benefits listed in the 1 Corinthians text with other benefits. Finally, either *enhancement* (with the addition of the final phrase *salvati et liberati sumus*) or *centonization* and *paraphrase* (if the phrase has a biblical source) were employed.

Theological Themes and Ideas Expressed by the Chant in Context

The introit *Nos autem gloriari* functions in a multilayered liturgical context. First, the chant functions as the song that accompanies the entrance of the ministers. Second, it functions as the entrance song for the Holy Thursday Evening Mass of the Lord's Supper, at which "the

116. Ibid., 97.

117. See the discussion of the use of biblical texts in antiphons in chapter 1 and in Kirby, "Proper Chants of the Paschal Triduum," 96.

Church begins the Easter Triduum" (*Caeremoniale Episcoporum* 297), and which serves to commemorate "the institution of the Eucharist,[118] the institution of the priesthood, and Christ's command of brotherly love" (PS 45). Third, it functions as the first text of the great Easter Triduum, wherein "is celebrated the paschal mystery, that is, the passing of the Lord from this world to his Father. The Church, by the celebration of this mystery through liturgical signs and sacramentals, is united to Christ, her spouse, in intimate communion" (PS 38). Thus, the theological themes and connections are multivalent, depending not only on these layers of liturgical context but also upon the singers and/or hearers of the chant.[119] Some will hear the antiphon as talking about grace received (the fully initiated among the assembly), others grace restored (penitents who were reconciled to the church on Thursday morning), and others grace to come (the elect and those to be received into full communion at the Easter Vigil).[120]

The church throughout the liturgical year moves from mystery to mystery, but also within the one Great Mystery—that is, the mystery of the cross through which people are saved from death through Jesus' death and his rising in glory. As Philip Pfatteicher notes, "the mystery of the risen Christ is so radically different from all human expectations" that the entire Triduum and indeed the entire Easter season and liturgical year are required "liturgically to ponder it."[121] *Nos autem gloriari* both begins the Triduum and reaches forward to Easter Sunday,[122] telescoping the suffering of the cross, wherein is found *salus, vita et resurrectio nostra*, into the glory of the resurrection *per quem salvati et liberati sumus*. The introit is both a lens through which to view the Triduum and the climax of the previous Holy Week. It announces the joyous sense of relief that follows Lent—our fasting is over and our salvation finally at hand.

118. GIRM 3 states that "the Christian people are drawn on Thursday in Holy Week, which is the day of the Lord's Supper . . . to show particular devotion towards this wonderful Sacrament."

119. See Kirby, "Proper Chants of the Paschal Triduum," 100.

120. See ibid., 100–101.

121. Philip H. Pfatteicher, *Commentary on the Lutheran Book of Worship: Lutheran Liturgy in Its Ecumenical Context* (Minneapolis: Augsburg Fortress, 1990), 292.

122. Kirby notes that both *Nos autem gloriari* and the introit for Easter Sunday are in mode four, "subtly suggesting that the Cross and the Resurrection are two facets of a single mystery." Kirby, "Proper Chants of the Paschal Triduum," 99.

The ritual function of *Nos autem gloriari* is the same as any other introit—to accompany the entrance of the ministers, to open the celebration, and to unite the assembly through common song. The introit urges the assembly to action—to gather, to sing together, to worship. This particular introit is especially effective in this regard, however, with its use of the plural/collective *nos*. This word reflects and emphasizes the exceptionally communal nature of Holy Thursday: "According to the ancient tradition of the Church, all Masses without the participation of the people are on this day forbidden" (PS 47).[123]

Its particular theological function, however, is unique among introits. Rather than announcing the themes of the Holy Thursday Mass—Eucharist, priesthood, *mandatum* (PS 45)—it announces the entirety of the Triduum by inviting the assembly into, as Kirby says, "the wider context of a universal soteriology, and a confession of the benefits that ever flow from the glorious and glorifying Cross of Christ."[124] The sung antiphon connects the glorification of the assembly in Jesus' cross to their glorification in his resurrection, and its psalm verses express their praise and wonderment. The cross serves as a bridge between Lent and Easter—as both an instrument of death and the tree of life. The antiphon reflects this dichotomy, which is the great mystery of salvation. By means of the other liturgical texts of the Mass of the Lord's Supper, this overarching theology of the cross is tied to the institution of the Eucharist and the other themes particular to the day.[125] The connection between Jesus' death on the cross and the Lord's Supper is made in the collect:

> O God, who have called us to participate
> in this most sacred Supper,
> in which your Only Begotten Son,
> *when about to hand himself over to death,*
> entrusted to the Church a sacrifice new for all eternity,
> the banquet of his love,
> grant, we pray,
> that we may draw from so great a mystery,

---

123. The document also states that "hosts for the Communion of the faithful should be consecrated during that celebration [and] . . . the Eucharist [is to be] borne directly from the altar . . . at the moment of communion for the sick and infirm who must communicate at home, so that in this way they may be more closely united to the celebrating Church" (PS 48, 54).

124. Kirby, "Proper Chants of the Paschal Triduum," 101.

125. See also ibid., 99–100.

the fullness of charity and of life.
Through our Lord Jesus Christ, your Son,
who lives and reigns with you in the unity of the Holy Spirit,
one God, for ever and ever.[126]

But the connection is even more effectively made in the responsorial psalm (Psalm 116:12-13, 15-16bc, 17-18; 1 Cor 10:16), where the imagery of "blood" and "death" is clearly linked to the eucharistic "cup" and "sacrifice of thanksgiving":

R. Our blessing-cup is a communion with the Blood of Christ.

How shall I make a return to the LORD
   for all the good he has done for me?
The cup of salvation I will take up,
   and I will call upon the name of the LORD. R.

Precious in the eyes of the LORD
   is the death of his faithful ones.
I am your servant, the son of your handmaid;
   you have loosed my bonds. R.

To you will I offer sacrifice of thanksgiving,
   and I will call upon the name of the LORD.
My vows to the LORD I will pay
   in the presence of all his people. R.[127]

Thereby, the profound paradox of the Eucharist is revealed, with the joyous *koinonia* of the Mass firmly rooted in the bloody sacrifice of the cross.

Choosing an Entrance Song: The Principle of Facilitation[128]

The profound theology expressed in and through the use of the Holy Thursday entrance antiphon at Mass would certainly enhance any parish's liturgy, but again, we return to our deceptively simple

126. Excerpt from the English translation of *The Roman Missal* © 2010, ICEL. My emphasis.

127. The English translation of the Psalm Response from Lectionary for Mass © 1969, 1981, 1997, International Commission on English in the Liturgy Corporation. All rights reserved. The English translation of the Psalm verses from Lectionary for Mass for Use in the Dioceses of the United States © 1998, 1997, 1970, Confraternity of Christian Doctrine, Washington, DC. All rights reserved.

128. The term "enactment" might be preferable to "facilitation," but the latter has been retained because it fits better with the models delineated in Parson's article.

question: What exactly should Catholics sing at the beginning of the Mass? Chapter three included several models and examples, and now we put forth some specific criteria for selecting entrance songs for particular celebrations. These criteria—functional, aesthetic, pastoral, and traditional—are grounded in the liturgical, pastoral, and musical judgments of Sing to the Lord 127–36. As always, the effective application of these criteria must be contextually driven, and each criterion must always be applied in conversation with the other three.

1. Is the Song Functionally Appropriate?

Here, liturgical function pertains to both the ritual and theological functions of the entrance song, which are inseparable. Simply said, liturgical music should cohere in style and text with the purpose of the rite.[129]

- Is the song processional music? Music that is to accompany a procession should match fairly closely the speed at which the procession will be moving, and it should match a particular culture's idea of what type of music is appropriate for processions (see GIRM 47).

- Can the song's musical form be accommodated to fit the variable length of an entrance procession (see GIRM 47)?

- Does the music set the appropriate tone for the celebration? In other words, can it effectively open the celebration, and is it appropriately festive, solemn, and so forth (see GIRM 46–47)?

- Does the text announce the day's particular feast by drawing upon the textual tradition of the church (see GIRM 47)?

- Is the text (if it is an original text) or translation of the text (if it is the proper chant of the day) suitable for singing and sufficiently engaging so as to bear repetition (see LA 62)?

- Does the enactment of the song allow all gathered to actively participate in the manner proper to their liturgical role (see SC 28)? This implies both that the active participation of the assembly must be facilitated and that, when fitting, the cantor and choir should not hesitate to sing the entrance song on their

---

129. Kevin W. Irwin, *Context and Text: Method in Liturgical Theology* (Collegeville, MN: Liturgical Press, 1994), 237. See also ibid., 238–39 and 245 on "intrinsicality" and "genre."

own, which according to tradition and ecclesiastical norms is a function proper to their ministry. Mutual respect is always paramount in this regard, in order to avoid abuses of power or conflicts of interest between different liturgical ministries.

2. Is the Song Aesthetically Appropriate?

Aesthetic appropriateness and adequacy are to some degree contingent upon the cultural context of the group engaging in the ritual action,[130] and thus specific aesthetic principles and judgments are difficult to establish. Nevertheless, it is possible to suggest some general principles. Most basically, liturgical music must be of high quality, however "quality" is defined in a particular context.

- Does the song bring beauty to the liturgical celebration? "Beauty" implies a degree of musical (melodic, harmonic, rhythmic) complexity and memorability. Chapter two emphasized the importance of singing in the liturgy; beauty comprises part of the reason why singing is important (see SC 112, GIRM 39–40, STTL 1–2).

- Is the text of the song a quality text?[131] If it is an original text, does it draw "from Sacred Scripture or from the liturgical patrimony" (LA 61)? Do original texts reflect the literary and rhetorical genre of the Roman Rite introit as far as possible (LA 58)? Would the text, whether original or a translation of the Latin, meet the standards of high-caliber poetry? To be sure, the survival of antiphon texts for centuries speaks to their quality.

3. Is the Song Pastorally Appropriate?

This criterion is arguably the most important and most contextually determined. If a song is of high quality from a musical/textual perspective, and if it functions effectively as an entrance song, what

130. See ibid., 221, 250.

131. Quality is difficult to define, and its requirements, always culture-specific, can be reached in a variety of ways. As David Power reminds us, "Those texts survive best which have a rhetorical and poetic force. In their creative power, they both make connections with the past and are open to interpretations that point to the future that may arise out of the present that is being lived through." D. Power, *Word of the Lord*, 45.

good is it unless it successfully engages a particular assembly within a particular celebration of the Mass, thereby appropriating and passing on its theological themes? It is especially for pastoral reasons that the *lex agendi* must always be emphasized as methodologically important,[132] because it is through the actual performance of the liturgy that the theology of the entrance song is truly "communicated and created by and for the Church."[133]

- Does the song enable and promote the active participation of the assembly (SC 14)?[134] Without an actively participatory and engaged assembly, none of the ritual and theological functions of the entrance song can come to fruition in a particular celebration of the Mass. Active participation can mean a variety of things, and how it is achieved will vary depending upon the type of song (see SC 30). The assembly might sing the entire song, or it might be sung in dialogue with the cantor or choir. Though congregational singing is the norm (STTL 28–30), the choir might even sing the entire song. When the choir sings the entrance song, it is crucial that the assembly participates by active listening (MS 15). In such cases, one must ask if the song is in a style comprehensible to the assembly; if not, another song should be chosen, or time should be taken to make it familiar.

- Can the song be enacted effectively in a particular assembly? Liturgy is an event, not only a prescribed ritual spelled out in liturgical books,[135] and thus the entrance song is, among other things, a musical performance.[136] This implies both that pastors need to strive to ensure that their assemblies have the best musical leadership possible, and that directors of music make sure a song is not beyond the skills of the musicians and the rest of the assembly, while at the same time working constantly to improve these skills (see STTL 45, 120–21). The development of a parish-specific repertoire—related, of course, to the broader

132. See the introduction to this book and K. Irwin, *Context and Text*, 55, 219, 229, 233.

133. Margaret Mary Kelleher, "Liturgy: An Ecclesial Act of Meaning," *Worship* 59:6 (November 1985): 489. See also K. Irwin, *Context and Text*, 65, 230–31.

134. See also Parsons, "Text, Tone, and Context," 58, 68.

135. See Zimmerman, *Liturgy and Hermeneutics*, 19.

136. "Performance" here means "something accomplished or done," not an "artistic presentation" as at a concert or play.

diocesan, national, cultural, and universal repertoires—is crucial in this regard. Pastors themselves should aspire to a high level of musical competence.

• Does the song help to unite the assembly (GIRM 47)? This unitive quality of the entrance song relates of course to active participation and effective performance. Chapter two has shown that singing is one of the primary means of establishing unity among a liturgical assembly. The assembly, therefore, must be afforded the opportunity to participate in it and must be able to sing it naturally, even instinctively.

• Does the song dispose the assembly to listen to the Word of God and celebrate the Eucharist worthily (GIRM 46)? This is a rather amorphous requirement of the entrance song and one difficult to define for particular celebrations. Quality of text and music come into play again here, however, as does the source of an entrance song text. A song of high quality is more likely to engage the assembly and bring them to the prayerful and celebratory state of mind proper to the Mass. The corpus of ancient proper introits is one certain source of texts that can achieve this requirement. They are of high quality and often relate to the texts that will be proclaimed in the rest of the liturgy. Composers of new entrance song texts should take the ancient tradition as the paradigm, while at the same time working to find new ways to properly "dispose the assembly."

• All else being equal, the effective communication of the theology of an entrance song can be assumed to occur to the degree inculturation has been successfully achieved. Is, then, the song appropriate to its specific cultural context? If the song is newly composed, it should avoid textual imagery or musical styles that might be considered oppressive[137] within its specific context, while at the same time it should take the opportunity when it presents itself to challenge cultural characteristics that might be contrary to the Gospel (SC 37). Liturgical music both reflects and forms culture. This also means that, to be useful, theological

---

137. For example, certain words or phrases might be considered racist, sexist, etc.; minority groups might associate a particular musical style with groups or cultures that oppress them or discriminate against them.

reflection upon the music of the liturgy must always be stated in terms relevant to the context of the music under consideration.[138]

4. Is the Song Faithful to the Broad Tradition of the Roman Rite?: Creative Fidelity

> In larger churches where the resources permit, a more ample use should be made of the Church's musical heritage both ancient and modern, always ensuring that this does not impede the active participation of the faithful.
>
> —*Paschalis Solemnitatis* 42

The pervasiveness throughout history of musical creativity couched in fidelity to tradition offers an overarching criterion for choosing and composing entrance songs today. In its origins, the introit was an adaptation to imperial Roman ceremony and the basilica setting. Popular enthusiasm for the psalms also influenced the shape of the Roman Rite, including the proper chants of the Mass. Harmonic embellishment of the introit antiphon and psalm verses was common throughout history, beginning with improvised parallel harmonies and eventually resulting in polyphonic settings. Textual embellishment through introit tropes in the Middle Ages is another example of local creativity. After the decline of such creativity—which was itself a form of cultural adaptation—it makes sense that over time other types of music more accessible to the liturgical assembly have in practice come to replace the proper chants. But is it possible to utilize, adapt, or derive from the proper chant tradition music that is both accessible *and* faithful to tradition?

The criterion of creative fidelity can act as a guide to the adaptation of the entrance song tradition to our present-day context. It also implies that the entrance song can be an outlet for the musical creativity and genius of our own age. The treasures of the church's musical heritage (chant, polyphony) should be employed when pos-

---

138. See K. Irwin, *Context and Text*, 54, 229, 251 on contextualization. One must ask, for example, how this particular culture views and interprets this particular type of music. As Judith Kubicki explains, "The meaning mediated by music can be discovered when, like all symbols, it is interpreted in relationship with the whole of which it is a part. Hence the importance of accounting for context, cultural codes and the experience-domain of the community, as individuals, and as a social group." Judith Kubicki, *Liturgical Music as Ritual Symbol: A Case Study of Jacques Berthier's Taizé Music* (Louvain: Peeters, 1999), 192.

sible and useful,[139] but it is important to emphasize again that it is not useful or possible to return to an exclusive use of the introit in the present-day celebration of the Mass. The introit's original context is no longer our context, and other song traditions have since flowered that have by now also become customary and traditional.

Nevertheless, the present-day entrance song is a way to recover and trans-late the musically and theologically rich ancient introit tradition for the twenty-first-century church. It is especially useful to do so because this ancient tradition offers an example of effective entrance song practice, which might help the church today through its confusion regarding the entrance song in the Roman Rite. Its musical form might be duplicated in new musical settings; its melodies might be adapted to vernacular translations; its proper texts—with their rich theological insights and festal particularity—might and should serve as the basis or inspiration for newly composed entrance song texts. All of these characteristics of the introit not only offer a model for effective enactment but also enable the official proper texts and melodies to function as a means of maintaining communion in the Roman Rite through a common textual and musical tradition. As Peter Jeffery and Margot Fassler advise: "Just as theology today cannot ignore the historical development of doctrine from the early church to the present, so our musical life will not be healthy if it is expected to operate in a historical vacuum cut off from the past. The continued study and performance of this treasury of sacred music are therefore not optional but essential, and would have the beneficial side-effect of dramatically improving the standards of quality expected of all the other kinds of music performed in modern worship."[140] It is worthwhile, therefore, to plumb the depths of the entrance song tradition—the official introit texts and melodies as well as past forms of creative fidelity.[141]

---

139. See *Paschalis Solemnitatis* 42. The Consilium cautioned that "we cannot ask the people to learn a set of songs which, no matter how short and simple, is completely new each Sunday and feast day. The important thing, therefore, is that the chants maintain and underscore the concepts that inspire a season or feast rather than that the congregation be bound to a text proper to a particular melodic form with which it is closely connected." Consilium, 6 November 1966, as quoted in Bugnini, *Reform of the Liturgy*, 895.

140. Fassler and Jeffery, "Christian Liturgical Music," 116.

141. Other long-standing entrance song traditions, such as the hymn, also offer insights into a solution to the problem. See Anthony Ruff, *Sacred Music*

**Choosing an Entrance Song for the Holy Thursday Evening Mass
of the Lord's Supper**

To be sure, no one song or type of song can meet all the above
criteria. The choice of a song, furthermore, must always take into consideration the particular context in which it will be sung. Nevertheless, a few suggestions in the abstract can help to clarify the purpose
of the functional, aesthetic, pastoral, and traditional characteristics
of an entrance song.

"Come, Let Us Glory" (2002; see example 7) meets all the necessary criteria to some degree. Its particular musical form—a metrical
refrain with verses—suits the function of an entrance song in that its
length can vary with the length of the entrance procession. Pastorally,
the song facilitates active participation; it is in the vernacular and
can be sung entirely by the assembly. The hymn tune, Wareham, is a
melody from the eighteenth century that has stood the test of time.
The text is a fairly successful poetic translation, though the adaptation of the antiphon is more successful than that of the psalm verses.
This song uses the traditional text of the introit antiphon and psalm
and thus passes on the ancient textual tradition of the Roman Rite.

In *By Flowing Waters* (1999), Paul Ford provides an English-
language adaptation of both the text and melody of the *Nos autem
gloriari* chant from the *Graduale Simplex* (see example 5). Thus, it
transmits not only the textual tradition but also the melodic tradition of the Roman Rite. Like "Come, Let Us Glory," it mirrors the
variable-length musical form of the Latin chant. The setting affords
ample opportunity for active participation in that the antiphon is to
be sung by the assembly and the verses by a cantor or *schola*. The
psalm verses are taken from the NRSV translation of the Bible and
thus are of high quality, though one could argue that a more poetic
translation of the psalms would be better for singing.

Another setting of a vernacular translation of the traditional antiphon and psalm verses has been composed by the Collegeville Composers Group (2008; see example 10).[142] Like Ford's setting, it has a
variable-length musical form and utilizes the traditional text. This

---

and Liturgical Reform: Treasures and Transformations (Chicago: Liturgy Training
Publications, 2007), 508–611.

142. Recalling the fact that the antiphon text of the *Graduale Simplex* is a
truncated version of the full antiphon text found in the *Graduale Romanum*, new
vernacular settings that incorporate the entire antiphon text might prove even
more effective.

setting provides harmonization in its setting of the psalm verses—an embellishment that harkens to the ancient tradition of chant harmonization discussed in chapter one. It does not, however, adapt the *Graduale Simplex* melody, providing instead a metrical setting. In many contexts this metrical setting might be more pastorally appropriate because assemblies are often more familiar with metrical music than with chant. The psalm verses are taken from the Grail translation, which when compared to the NRSV translation in Ford's setting seem much more aesthetically pleasing and singable.

In many contexts, a metrical hymn might be the best choice for the entrance song. On the one hand, their musical form is closed and thus less useful for a procession. On the other hand, good hymns mean great texts and tunes. New texts are in order—texts inspired by the broad context and tradition of the Holy Thursday entrance antiphon. One usable hymn currently available is "Lift High the Cross" (see example 11). This hymn is well known, and its text and tune are memorable and singable. Even though its text will be too triumphalistic for some, it does effectively communicate the mystery of the cross ("sign," "seal," life through death). Because it is a refrain hymn, its form is more adaptable in terms of length. "In the Cross of Christ I Glory" (see example 12) is another possible choice. The hymn tune is less familiar, but its text achieves a successful contrast between the themes of despair and glory. Its first line hearkens to Galatians 6:14—the primary source text for the Holy Thursday entrance antiphon.

Finally, in some contexts the entrance song on Holy Thursday evening might be sung by the choir alone. In this case, the repertoire is extremely limited. Here, one must look mainly to the past to find musical settings and to a future in which choral composers will again turn their attention to the proper texts of the Mass. One option would be for the choir to sing the entirety of the introit as found in the *Graduale Romanum* (see example 3), which is too complex for congregational singing. Leo Nestor, in his *Plainsong New* (see example 19), provides a chant setting of a translation of the *Graduale* antiphon and verses, which is intended for choral singing. Alternatively, the choir could sing a polyphonic setting (see appendix A).[143] Annibale Stabile's (1525–95) eight-voice setting of *Nos autem gloriari* (pub. 1607;

---

143. Given its antiquity, the setting found in the Trent Codex might be too foreign for most assemblies (see example 13). The Isaac setting is difficult (see example 14), but some assemblies would be familiar with the sixteenth-century choral style.

see example 17), while excellent, would require a choir comprised of highly skilled singers. The setting also utilizes *basso continuo*, so it would require one or more instrumentalists. Giovanni Pierluigi da Palestrina (1524–94), a contemporary of Stabile, composed an unaccompanied setting of the proper text for four voices (see example 15). This setting would be accessible to choirs of at least intermediate skill. The Iberian composer Manuel Cardoso (1566–1650) also composed an unaccompanied setting of *Nos autem gloriari* for five voices of similar difficulty to Palestrina's setting (see example 16). Grayston Ives is one of the few present-day composers to have set *Nos autem gloriari* (1997; see example 18). His choral motet is finely crafted and its length appropriate for a long processional route. This setting and Nestor's are unique examples of the great composers of our day turning their attention to the proper texts of the Mass. In each of these settings for choir, great care has been taken to ensure the comprehensibility of the text. Because most assemblies today do not understand Latin, however, a vernacular translation would need to be made available for the settings other than Nestor's. In addition, the length of the polyphonic settings is not variable, except in cases where the entrance procession is extremely long, allowing for the singing of psalm verses in between repetitions of the polyphony.

The task ahead is not a matter of prescribing or proscribing particular liturgical musical forms and texts for the entrance song. Such a task would be immense, given the thousands of songs available, both ancient and contemporary, not to mention the fact that it would inevitably cause conflict between advocates of particular musical styles. Not only this, but the task would need to be repeated for every particular culture, making it daunting if not impossible. Rather, the task must be rooted in the functional, aesthetic, pastoral, and traditional criteria above. In order to effectively apply these criteria, it is crucial to immerse oneself in the wealth of the liturgical-musical tradition that has come down to us so far. Then, with a close familiarity with this wealth in hand, pastors, liturgists, and music directors must discern what within the tradition meets the criteria within their context, and liturgical composers must consider the tradition and criteria when creating new texts and musical settings.

CHAPTER FIVE

Conclusion—A Way Forward

Do we now know what to sing at the beginning of Mass? The answer is complex and multifaceted, to say the least. This book, grounded in the methodological principles articulated in its introduction, has proceeded in two stages in an attempt to answer this question. First, the context of the entrance song was explored through a consideration of its history and its place in ecclesiastical documents. Chapter one began by discussing the foundational contexts and origins of Christian music and early Christian singing. The precise origins of the introit are lost to history, even if certain historical *terminus post quem* and *terminus ante quem* for the development of a proper chant tradition in the West can be gleaned from the historical record. Evidence of a fully developed introit are found in the *Ordines Romani* and in later liturgical manuscripts. From these manuscripts it is clear that by the eighth century the introit tradition had developed into a stable and fixed corpus of liturgical chants. The chant texts make use of Scripture and other textual traditions of the church in a variety of ways. From at least the ninth century, it is clear that introit texts and melodies were embellished through harmonization and the addition of text, leading eventually to polyphonic settings of the introit texts.

Chapter one spoke of the "dis-integration" of the entrance song's form, function, and theology in the Middle Ages. It also spoke of the entrance song in terms of the liturgical reforms of the Council of Trent and the liturgical developments of the nineteenth and early twentieth centuries. Chapter two made clear the fact that—at least in terms of the principles put forth by the postconciliar ecclesiastical documents—the form, function, and theology of the entrance song have now been restored or "re-integrated." This conclusion was reached, first, through a consideration of the nature, implementation, and sources of liturgical norms after the Second Vatican Council. These norms were then considered insofar as they apply to the entrance song. And from this consideration the chapter arrived at several foundational norms for the postconciliar entrance song: the importance of singing in the liturgy, the active participation of the faithful, the fact that certain texts by their very nature should be sung, the translation of Latin liturgical texts to the vernacular, and the composition of new texts.

The second section of the book shifted from context to practical application. Chapter three delineated five models of the entrance song for use in present-day celebrations of the Mass. Indeed, given the insights and conclusions of chapters one and two, it is clear that the "re-integrated" postconciliar entrance song can be effectively enacted in a variety of ways. Chapter four articulated a theology of the entrance song organized around three characteristics fundamental to any liturgical-ritual unit: function, text, and facilitation. In terms of *function*, the chapter explored what the entrance song does (or should do) within the celebration of the Eucharist. Through a consideration of the introit *Nos autem gloriari* from the Holy Thursday Evening Mass of the Lord's Supper, conclusions were drawn as to the function of a particular entrance song *text*. This inquiry necessitated a study of the origins and history of the Holy Thursday feast and the Paschal Triduum, as well as the way in which *Nos autem gloriari* made use of Scripture and the particular theological themes expressed in the chant. Finally, in terms of *facilitation*, the chapter explored how to choose an entrance song for use in a particular context and then provided some suggestions for the Holy Thursday Evening Mass of the Lord's Supper. Here, criteria fell into four categories: functionality, aesthetic quality, pastoral effectiveness, and creative fidelity to the tradition of the Roman Rite.

As this book draws to a close, it is important to recall that conciliar liturgical reforms often take some time to come to fruition. The musical-liturgical directives of the Council of Trent, for example, initially met with resistance but eventually found advocates among the great composers of the day.[1] After periods of fervent creativity

---

1. The parallel between the musical reforms of Trent and Vatican II are rough, but real, in terms of the move toward a renewed appreciation and reappropriation of earlier musical forms after a period of intense creativity. Philip Cavanaugh states, "Perhaps the perseverance in setting Proper items in a period in which more affective texts seemed to be preferred can be attributed to a devel-

and exploration, it is not unusual if there comes, as Philip Cavanaugh states, "a development in sensitivity toward propriety in liturgical music."[2] The renewed interest of late in the proper chants of the Mass, evidenced by the number of vernacular collections published recently, and the fact that the U.S. Bishops' document Sing to the Lord seeks a middle ground through its even-handed treatment of both ancient and modern forms of liturgical music reflect this propriety to a degree. And the translation principles of *Liturgiam Authenticam* certainly reflect this trend.[3]

Almost immediately after the implementation of the Vatican II liturgical reform began, two directions for the future of liturgical music were set in motion. One—the congregational singing of Gregorian chant—is rooted firmly in the late nineteenth- and early twentieth-century liturgical movement. The movement saw in the liturgical chant tradition (itself renewed and reformed at that time through the study of early manuscripts) as an effective means of promoting the spiritual development and active participation of the assembly. The other—what Fassler and Jeffery call an "openness to the worldwide spectrum"[4] of music—sought to make the postconciliar rites more accessible to local

---

opment in sensitivity toward propriety in liturgical music. It is not unreasonable to assume that the Council of Trent, by insisting upon the implementation of the earlier reforms . . . succeeded in encouraging composers to respond to liturgical needs in the latter half of the century. Indeed, some composers—Vincenzo Ruffo and Constanzo Porta, for example—began to advertise their compositions as complying with the spirit of the Council. It is evident that the many settings utilizing plainsong melodies went far in meeting the requirements for liturgical music suggested by the Council. Such settings admirably renewed the centuries-old spirit of the Church regarding propriety in liturgical music which traditionally had given first place to Sacred Chant. Allowing for the development of polyphony, the Church saw these chant settings as an unfolding of the original basic plan. Finally, composers undoubtedly were influenced by the spirit of the humanists who saw in the texts of the Proprium a return to 'the clean, the unadulterated form' of the liturgy as practiced in Rome up to the eleventh century." Cavanaugh, "Early Sixteenth-Century Cycles of Polyphonic Mass Propers," 161.

2. Ibid.

3. On *Liturgiam Authenticam*, see Peter Jeffery, *Translating Tradition: A Chant Historian Reads* Liturgiam Authenticam (Collegeville, MN: Liturgical Press, 2006). To be sure, *Liturgiam Authenticam* has many flaws (content, method, motivation, etc.), but its overarching idea—passing on the liturgical tradition with integrity to new generations—is sound.

4. Margot Fassler and Peter Jeffery, "Christian Liturgical Music from the Bible to the Renaissance," in *Sacred Sound and Social Change: Liturgical Music in*

congregations, more reflective of local cultural traditions, and more open to culture-specific musical forms and texts. Now, more than a century removed from the beginning of the liturgical movement and nearly fifty years after the Second Vatican Council, these two directions have evolved into long-standing customs.

What we need is a "new synthesis"[5] of the two directions in the postconciliar development of liturgical music.[6] Such a synthesis is impossible as long as the either-or dichotomy prevails between the

---

Jewish and Christian Experience (Notre Dame, IN: University of Notre Dame Press, 1992), 115.

5. Fassler and Jeffery recount that "for the first half of the twentieth century, the promotion of congregational singing of Gregorian chant was a major goal of the liturgical movement. After Vatican II, however, the disappearance of Latin and the new openness to the worldwide spectrum of folk and popular music led to a general abandonment of Gregorian chant and to a polarization between those church musicians who wished to preserve chant, polyphony, and classical music and those who thought it more important to promote popular music in the renewed liturgy. After a quarter-century standoff, however, it is time to move to a new synthesis." Ibid., 115.

6. In the midst of the healthy yet sometimes overwhelming postconciliar musical diversity, the forthcoming "directory or repertory of texts intended for liturgical singing" (*Liturgiam Authenticam* 108) from the USCCB will be useful. The directory indicates that the USCCB will eventually formulate a "core repertoire" of about sixty to one hundred songs. J. Michael McMahon notes that "it is not intended as an exclusive list of songs . . . but rather as a core set of selections that would appear in any published hymnal, service book, or periodical worship aid." J. Michael McMahon, "Establishing Criteria for Liturgical Songs: The Directory for Music and Liturgy," *Pastoral Music* 31:6 (August–September 2007): 18–19. The directory will be helpful, especially because it seeks to guide, rather than restrict, musical creativity. It could serve as a wide and low-banked channel through which to direct the continuing renewal and future development of liturgical music in the Roman Rite in the U.S. The Holy See has called for such a collection since 1964. See Jo Hermans, "The Directory of Liturgical Songs in the Vernacular: Background and Liturgical Criteria," *Antiphon* 11:1 (2007): 55–61; Consilium, Epistle (25 March 1964); Congregation for Divine Worship, Instruction *Constitutione Apostolica* (20 October 1969) 12; Congregation for Divine Worship, Instruction *Liturgicae Instaurationes* (5 September 1970) 3; Congregation for Bishops, Directory *Ecclesiae Imago* (22 February 1973) 90; and the current General Instruction of the Roman Missal 48. The Directory for Music and the Liturgy for use in the Dioceses of the United States of America was approved by the USCCB in November 2006 and then submitted to the Holy See for *recognitio*, which has not yet been granted. The document notes that liturgical songs "should be consonant with Catholic teaching and free from doctrinal error" and that, taken together, the songs of a local repertoire "should reflect the

two directions, but it is crucial if the Church in the U.S. is to move beyond the "liturgy wars" and toward the requisite love and charity that is fundamental to our communion. Those committed to the first direction must remember that Gregorian chant is itself a result of cultural adaptation and a synthesis of at least two older chant traditions (Frankish and Old Roman) and that Renaissance choral polyphony is the creative response of sixteenth- and seventeenth-century composers to the proper chant tradition. Thus neither chant nor polyphony is inherently unchangeable, superior, universally appropriate, or sacred—it is their liturgical context and tradition of use that give them pride of place. Those committed to the second direction are sometimes so fervently opposed to anything that hints of liturgical traditionalism that they instinctively reject the use of Gregorian chant and polyphony, forgetting that even the most contemporary liturgical music is based upon centuries-old formal and tonal systems. To be sure, a complete separation from the musical traditions of the past is in reality impossible. Unflinching advocacy of the principles of the Vatican II liturgical reform is crucial today, to be sure, but disregard for the church's musical heritage—in this case the proper chants of the Mass—is to disregard these principles as well as the official texts of the Roman Rite, and thus to diminish the pastoral effectiveness of the celebration of the liturgy, which is this second direction's most fundamental aim.

The synthesis is crucial to an integral implementation of the principles of the postconciliar liturgy, which demand *both* the preservation of our musical and textual tradition *and* active participation and cultural adaptation (see SC 14, 37–40). Thus, the liturgical reform requires that these two postconciliar customs be put into conversation. The criteria put forth in chapter four can serve as a foundation for this synthesis. And Christian charity, along with quality musical formation, can be the tools to instigate and guide the necessary conversation.

In this dialectic of customs, one must recognize the inherently multivalent nature of liturgical symbols, rites, and texts. Indeed, as Margaret Mary Kelleher notes, it is this "ambiguity of symbols which allows them to be multivocal."[7] The entrance song at the celebration of the Eucharist is among these multivocal ritual elements and is thus able to mediate "meaning within and among such diverse collective

---

full spectrum of the Catholic faith." J. M. McMahon, "Establishing Criteria for Liturgical Songs," 17–18.

7. Kelleher, "Liturgy: An Ecclesial Act of Meaning," 496.

subjects."[8] The implications of this are at least fourfold. First, *ortho-praxis*—which involves such things as quality performance and active participation—and *orthodoxy*—which requires theologically sound and high-quality texts—are both crucial. The message communicated must not be foreign to the (admittedly broad) Catholic theological tradition, and the song must be successfully sung if it is to put forward its multivalent message.[9] Second, cultural adaptation and musical formation are essential. If a song is foreign to a particular context or has not been made familiar through formation, it cannot achieve its purpose. Third, if liturgical symbols, rites, and texts are truly multivocal and multivalent, no entrance song is inherently incompatible with a particular culture. This fact can temper any trend toward cultural hyperspecificity in the choice of liturgical music. Fourth and finally, this dialectic of customs needs to be operative in the choice and creation of musical settings and texts. It is a complex task, continually to be worked out in practice, but it promises to bear fruit in more effective celebrations of the liturgy.

The liturgical reform of the Second Vatican Council is still a work in progress. Indeed, such a penetrating reform can *only* be worked out through the repeated experience of the enacted liturgy over time. For while the principles of the council and the directives of postconciliar liturgical books and ecclesiastical documents can and must serve to guide the reform, their application is necessarily left to the celebration of the liturgy in particular parish communities. The Eucharist, which is celebrated again and again following Jesus' command to "do this in memory of me," provides ample opportunity for finding the way forward. A new synthesis in the reform of the music of the Roman Rite is underway, from which we can grasp the opportunity to develop ever-more effective means of enacting the entrance song. This book has sought to point us in the right direction.

8. Ibid.

9. The meaning of text and music "may be altered or repressed in the performance." Kelleher, "Liturgy and the Christian Imagination," 135.

APPENDIX A

Settings of *Nos autem gloriari* for Choir

Example 13. Polyphonic setting of the introit *Nos autem gloriari* in Trent Codex 1375.[1]

1. Rebecca L. Gerber, ed. and introd., *Sacred Music from the Cathedral at Trent: Trent, Museo Provinciale D'arte, Codex 1375 (OLIM 88)* (Chicago and London: University of Chicago Press, 2007). Used by permission.

Glo - ri - a pa-tri et fi - li - o et spi - ri - tu - i san - cto.

Si - cut e -

Si - cut e -

Si - cut e -

- rat in prin - ci - pi - o   et____ nunc____ et sem - - per

- rat in prin - ci - pi - o   et____ nunc____ et sem - - per

- rat in prin - ci - pi - o   et____ nunc____ et sem - - per

et in se - cu - la se - cu - lo - rum____   a - - - - men.

et in se - cu - la se - cu - lo - rum____   a - - - men.

et in se - cu - la se - cu - lo - rum____   a - - - - men.

Example 14. Polyphonic setting of the introit *Nos autem gloriari* in the *Choralis Constantinus* (Heinrich Isaac) *In Festo Inventionis S. Crucis.*[2]

2. Heinrich Isaac, *Choralis Constantinus III*, transcr. from Formschneider First Edition (Nürnberg, 1555) by Louise Elvira Cuyler (Ann Arbor: University of Michigan Press, 1950) © Estate of Louise Elvira Cuyler, 1978.

et re- sur- re-cti-o   no-
vi-   ta et   re-   sur- re-   cti-
est sa-   lus vi-   ta   et re- sur- re-   cti-o
quo est   sa-   lus vi-   ta   et re-   sur-re-   cti-

stra   per quem sal-   va- ti et li-be- ra- ti
o   no-stra per   quem   sal- va- ti
                no-   stra   per quem sal-va-   ti et li- be- ra-
o no-   stra   per   quem   sal- va- ti et

su-   mus   [su-   mus
et   li- be-ra- ti   su-
ti   su-   mus   [su-
li-   be- ra-   ti su-

VERSUS

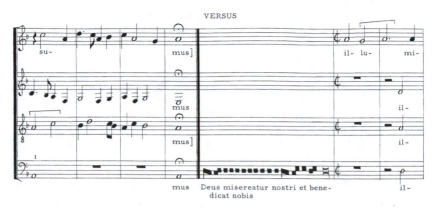

ALLELUIA

Example 15. Polyphonic setting of *Nos autem gloriari* from Giovanni Pierluigi da Palestrina's *Motecta festorum totius anni cum Communi sanctorum quarternis vocibus liber primus* (1563).[3]

3. Anthony Monata, ed. Choral Public Domain Library, www.cpdl.org.

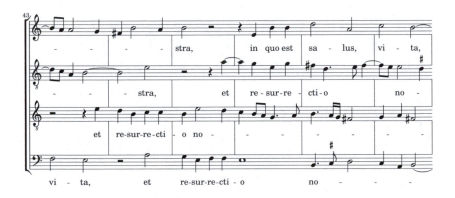

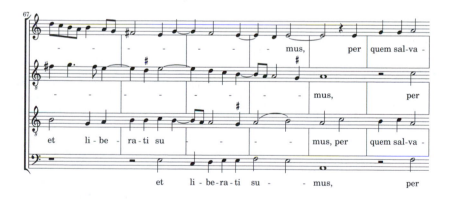

Example 16. Polyphonic setting of *Nos autem gloriari* from Manuel Cardoso's *Libro de varios motetes* (1648).[4]

4. Ivan Moody, ed. and transcriber, Series A: Spanish and Portuguese Church Music 82. Lochs, Scotland: Vanderbeek & Imrie Ltd, 1993. © Vanderbeek & Imrie Ltd. Used by permission.

Example 17. Polyphonic setting of *Nos autem gloriari* by Annibale Stabile (pub. 1607).[5]

5. Annibale Stabile, *Nos autem gloriari*, Urtext edition by Salvatore Villani (Italy: Ut Orpheus Edizioni, 1999). Used by permission.

Example 18. Polyphonic setting (excerpt) of *Nos autem gloriari* by Grayston Ives (1997).[6]

6. Used by permission. For reasons of copyright, only the first fifteen measures appear here.

Example 19. Chant setting of *Nos autem gloriari* for Schola from *Plainsong New* by Leo Nestor (b. 1948).[7]

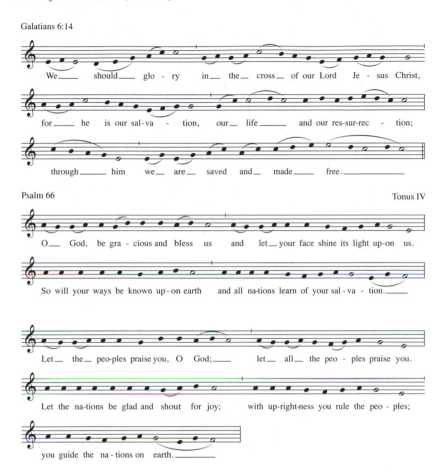

Galatians 6:14

We should glo - ry in the cross of our Lord Je - sus Christ,
for he is our sal-va - tion, our life and our res-sur-rec - tion;
through him we are saved and made free.

Psalm 66   Tonus IV

O God, be gra - cious and bless us and let your face shine its light up-on us.
So will your ways be known up - on earth and all na-tions learn of your sal - va - tion.

Let the peo-ples praise you, O God; let all the peo - ples praise you.
Let the na-tions be glad and shout for joy; with up-right-ness you rule the peo - ples;
you guide the na - tions on earth.

7. *Plainsong New* © 1982–2011 by Leo Nestor. All rights reserved. English translation of the Antiphon from *The Roman Missal* © 1973, International Commission on English in the Liturgy Corporation. All rights reserved. Psalm translation from *The Revised Grail Psalms: A Liturgical Psalter* © 2010 by Conception Abbey/The Grail, administered by GIA Publications, Inc. All rights reserved.

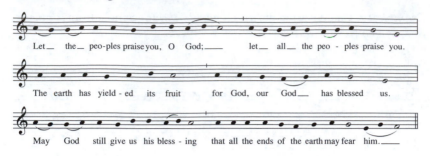

Let__ the__ peo-ples praise you, O God;___ let__ all__ the peo - ples praise you.

The earth has yield - ed its fruit for God, our God__ has blessed us.

May God still give us his bless - ing that all the ends of the earth may fear him.___

11 September 1997
Revised 5 September 2011
Washington, District of Columbia

APPENDIX B

Instrumental Introits

Example 20. Organ Mass introit versets from the *Buxheimer Orgelbuch* (ca. 1470).[1]

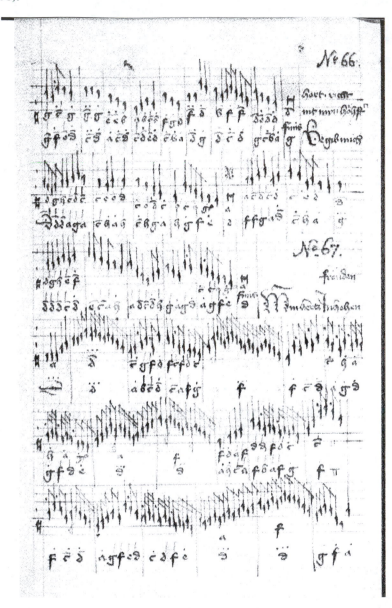

1. Mus. ms. 3725, fol. 169r. Image is in the public domain. See also E. Southern, *The Buxheim Organ Book* (Brooklyn, NY, 1963); and H. R. Zöbeley, *Die Musik des Buxheimer Orgelbuchs: Spielvorgang, Niederschrift, Herkunft, Faktur* (Tutzing: Schneider, 1964).

Example 21. Organ Mass introit versets from Girolamo Frescobaldi's *Fiori Musicali* (1635).[2]

2. Girolamo Frescobaldi, *Orgel und Klavierwerke Gesamtausg. Nach dem Urtext hrsg. von Pierre Pidoux*, vol. 5 (Kassel: Barenreiter-Verlag, 1957). Used by permission.

Example 22. Improvisatory organ introit (excerpt) from Olivier Messiaen's *Messe de la Pentecôte* (1949–50).[3]

3. Olivier Messiaen, *Messe de la Pentecôte* (Paris: Alphonse Leduc, 1951). For reasons of copyright, only the first page of this piece is included here.

Bibliography

Achtemeier, Paul. "*Omne Verbum Sonat*: The New Testament and the Oral Environment of Late Western Antiquity." *Journal of Biblical Literature* 109:1 (1990): 3–27.

Adam, Adolf. *The Eucharistic Celebration: The Source and Summit of Faith.* Translated by Robert C. Schultz. Collegeville, MN: Liturgical Press, 1994.

———. *Foundations of Liturgy.* Translated by Matthew O'Connell. Collegeville, MN: Liturgical Press, 1992.

———. *The Liturgical Year: Its History and Meaning After the Reform of the Liturgy.* Translated by Matthew J. O'Connell. New York: Pueblo, 1981.

Ainslie, John, ed. *The Simple Gradual for Sundays and Holy Days: Full Music Edition for Cantor, Choir and Organist.* Texts of antiphons and refrains by The International Committee on English in the Liturgy. London: Geoffrey Chapman, 1969.

Alberigo, Giuseppe, ed. *The History of Vatican II.* 5 vols. Translated by Matthew J. O'Connell. English version edited by Joseph A. Komonchak. Louvain: Peeters, 1995–2006.

Alesandro, John A. "General Introduction." In *The Code of Canon Law: A Text and Commentary.* Edited by James A. Coriden, Thomas J. Green, and Donald E. Heintschel. New York and Mahwah, NJ: Paulist Press, 1985.

Alexander, J. Neil, ed. *Time and Community.* Washington, DC: Pastoral Press, 1990.

———. *With Ever Joyful Hearts: Essays on Liturgy and Music Honoring Marion J. Hatchett.* New York: Church, 1999.

Alföldy, Géza. *The Social History of Rome.* Translated by David Braund and Frank Polluck. Baltimore: Johns Hopkins University Press, 1989.

Amalorpavadass, D. S. "Theological Reflections on Inculturation." *Studia Liturgica* 20 (1990): 36–54, 116–36.

Anderson, E. Byron. *Worship and Christian Identity: Practicing Ourselves.* Collegeville, MN: Liturgical Press, 2003.

Anderson, Roberta, and Dominic Aidan Bellenger, eds. *Medieval Worlds: A Sourcebook.* New York: Routledge, 2003.

Andrieu, Michel, ed. *Le pontifical romain au moyen-âge.* 4 vols. Studi e Testi 86–88, 99. Vatican City, 1938–40, 1941.

———. *Les "Ordines Romani" du haut moyen âge.* 5 vols. Spicilegium Sacrum Lovaniense 11, 23–24, 28–29. Louvain, 1931, 1948–51, 1956–61.

Anglès, Higini. "The Various Forms of Chant Sung by the Faithful in the Ancient Roman Liturgy." In *Scripta Musicologica,* 1:57–75. 3 vols. Edited by José López-Calo. Rome: Edizioni Storia e Letteratura, 1975.

Apel, Willi. *Gregorian Chant.* Bloomington: Indiana University Press, 1958. Reprint, 1990.

Apostolos-Cappadona, Diane, ed. *Art, Creativity, and the Sacred.* New York: Crossroad, 1984.

Arbuckle, Gerald A. *Earthing the Gospel: An Inculturation Handbook for Pastoral Workers.* Maryknoll, NY: Orbis; London: Geoffrey Chapman, 1990. Reprint, Eugene, OR: Wipf and Stock, 2002.

Archdiocese of Milwaukee. *The Milwaukee Symposia for Church Composers: A Ten-Year Report.* Washington, DC: Pastoral Press; Chicago: Liturgy Training Publications, 1992.

Arlt, W., and G. Björkvall, eds. *Recherches nouvelles sur les tropes liturgiques.* Studia Latina Stockholmiensia 36. Stockholm: Almquist & Wiksell, 1993.

Atkinson, Charles M. "Glosses on Music and Grammar and the Advent of Music Writing in the West." In *Western Plainchant in the First Millennium: Studies in the Medieval Liturgy and Its Music,* 199–216. Edited by Sean Gallagher et al. Burlington, VT: Ashgate, 2003.

Augustine [Bachofen], Charles. *Liturgical Law: A Handbook of the Roman Liturgy.* St. Louis, MO: B. Herder, 1931.

Austin, Gerard. "The Church as Worshipping Community." In *The Gift of the Church: A Textbook on Ecclesiology,* 177–92. Edited by Peter C. Phan. Collegeville, MN: Liturgical Press, 2000.

———, ed. *Fountain of Life.* In memory of Niels K. Rasmussen. Washington, DC: Pastoral Press, 1991.

Austin, Gerard, et al. *Eucharist: Toward the Third Millennium.* Chicago: Liturgy Training Publications, 1997.

Bailey, Terence. *The Processions of Sarum and the Western Church.* Toronto: Pontifical Institute of Mediaeval Studies, 1971.

Baldovin, John F. "The Body of Christ in Celebration: On Eucharistic Liturgy, Theology, and Pastoral Practice." In *Source and Summit: Commemorating Josef A. Jungmann, S.J.*, 49–61. Edited by Joanne M. Pierce and Michael Downey. Collegeville, MN: Liturgical Press, 1999.

————. "Kyrie Eleison and the Entrance Rite of the Roman Eucharist." *Worship* 60 (July 1986): 334–47.

————. *Liturgy in Ancient Jerusalem.* Alcuin/GROW Liturgical Study 9. Grove Liturgical Study 57. Bramcote, UK: Grove Books Limited, 1989.

————. "The Urban Character of Christian Worship in Jerusalem, Rome, and Constantinople from the Fourth to the Tenth Centuries: The Origins, Development, and Meaning of Stational Liturgy." PhD diss., Yale University, 1982.

————. *The Urban Character of Christian Worship: The Origins, Development, and Meaning of Stational Liturgy.* Orientalia Christiana Analecta 228. Rome: Pontifical Institute of Oriental Studies, 1987.

————. "The Uses of Liturgical History." *Worship* 82:1 (January 2008): 2–18.

————. *Worship: City, Church and Renewal.* Washington, DC: Pastoral Press, 1991.

Bangert, Mark P. "Liturgical Music, Culturally Tuned." In *Liturgy and Music: Lifetime Learning*, 360–83. Edited by Robin A. Leaver and Joyce Ann Zimmerman. Collegeville, MN: Liturgical Press, 1998.

Barba, Maurizio. *La riforma Conciliare dell' "Ordo Missae": Il percorso storico-redazionale dei riti d'ingresso, di offertorio e di communione.* Bibliotheca Ephemerides Liturgicae, Subsidia 120. Rome: CLV Edizioni Liturgiche, 2002.

Barnes, Andrew E. "Religious Reform and the War against Ritual." *Journal of Ritual Studies* 4 (1990): 127–33.

Barrett, Sam. "Music and Writing: On the Compilation of Paris Bibliothèque National Lat 1154." *Early Music History* 16 (1997): 55–96.

Baumstark, Anton. *Comparative Liturgy.* Revised by Bernard Botte. Edited and translated by F. L. Cross. Westminster, MD: Newman Press, 1958.

Bayer, Oswald. "Theology in the Conflict of Interpretations—Before the Text." Translated by Gwen Griffith-Dickson. *Modern Theology* 16:4 (October 2000): 495–502.

Beal, John P., James A. Coriden, and Thomas J. Green, eds. *New Commentary on the Code of Canon Law: An Entirely New and Comprehensive Commentary by Canonists from North America and Europe, with a Revised English Translation of the Code*. Commissioned by the Canon Law Society of America. New York and Mahwah, NJ: Paulist Press, 2000.

Beardslee, William A. "Poststructuralist Criticism." In *To Each Its Own Meaning: An Introduction to Biblical Criticisms and Their Application*, 253–67. Edited by Stephen L. McKenzie and Stephen R. Haynes. Louisville, KY: Westminster / John Knox Press, 1993.

Beckwith, R. T. "The Jewish Background to Christian Worship." In *The Study of Liturgy*, 68–79. Rev. ed. Edited by Cheslyn Jones, Geoffrey Wainwright, and Edward Yarnold. New York: Oxford University Press; London: SPCK, 1992.

Begbie, Jeremy. *Resounding Truth: Christian Wisdom in the World of Music*. Grand Rapids, MI: Baker Academic, 2007.

———. *Theology, Music, and Time*. Cambridge Studies in Christian Doctrine 4. Cambridge, UK: Cambridge University Press, 2000.

Béhague, Gerard, ed. *Performance Practice: Ethnomusicological Perspectives*. Westport, CT: Greenwood Press, 1984.

Békés, G., and G. Farnedi, eds. *Lex Orandi. Lex Credendi: Miscellannea in onore di P. Cipriano Vagaggini*. Studia Anselmiania 79. Sacramentum 6. Rome: Editrice Anselmiana, 1980.

Bell, Catherine. *Ritual: Perspectives and Dimensions*. New York: Oxford University Press, 1997.

———. *Ritual Theory, Ritual Practice*. New York: Oxford University Press, 1992.

Bell, John L. *The Singing Thing: A Case for Congregational Song*. Chicago: GIA Publications, 2000.

Berger, Teresa. "The Challenge of Gender for Liturgical Tradition." *Worship* 82:3 (May 2008): 243–61.

———. " 'Doxology,' 'Jubilate,' 'Liturgical Theology': Zum Verhältnis von Liturgie und Theologie: Publikationen aus dem englishesprachinget Raum." *Archiv für Liturgiewissenschaft* 28 (1986): 247–55.

———. "Lex orandi, lex credendi, lex agendi. Auf dem Weg zu einer ökumenisch konesensfahigen, Verhaltniesbestimmung von Liturgie, Theologie und Ethik." *Archiv für Liturgiewissenschaft* 27 (1985): 425–32.

———. "Liturgy—a Forgotten Subject Matter of Theology?" *Studia Liturgica* 17 (1987): 10–18.

————. "Liturgy and Theology—An Ongoing Dialogue." *Studia Liturgica* 19 (1989): 14–16.

————. *Theology in Hymns: A Study of the Relationship of Doxology and Theology According to a Collection of Hymns for the Use of People Called Methodists (1780).* Translated by Timothy E. Kimbrough. Nashville, TN: Abingdon Press, 1995.

Bernard, P. "L'origine des chants de la messe selon la tradition musicale du chant romain ancien improprement dit «chant vieux-romain»." In *L'Eucharistie: célébrations, rites, piétés*, 19–97. Edited by A. M. Triacca and A. Pistoia. Bibliotheca Ephemerides Liturgicae, Subsidia 79. Rome: CLV Edizioni Liturgiche, 1995.

Berry, Mary. *Cantors: A Collection of Gregorian Chants.* New York: Cambridge University Press, 1979.

Bevans, Stephen B. *Models of Contextual Theology.* Faith and Cultures Series. Maryknoll, NY: Orbis Books, 1992.

Bevil, Jack. "Centonization and Concordance in the American Southern Uplands Folksong Melody: A Study of the Musical Generative and Transmititive Processes of an Oral Tradition." PhD diss., North Texas State University, 1984.

Binford-Walsh, Hilde Marga. "The Melodic Grammar of Aquitanian Tropes." PhD diss., Stanford University, 1992.

Bischoff, Bernard. *Latin Paleography: Antiquity and the Middle Ages.* Translated by Dáibhí Cróinin and David Ganz. Cambridge, UK: Cambridge University Press, 1989.

Björkvall, G., Gunilla Iversen, and Ritva Jonsson, eds. *Tropes du propre de la messe 2. Cycle de Pâques.* Edition critique des textes. Corpus Troporum 3. Studia Latina Stockholmiensia 25. Stockholm: Almquist & Wiksell, 1982.

Blacking, John. "The Biology of Music-Making." In *Ethnomusicology: An Introduction.* Edited by Helen Myers. New York: W. W. Norton and Co., 1992.

Blackwell, Albert. *The Sacred in Music.* Louisville, KY: Westminster / John Knox Press, 1999.

Blijlevens, Ad. "Zeitgemäße Liturgie und klassische Polyphonie." In *Omnes Circumadstantes: Contributions Towards a History of the Role of the People in the Liturgy*, 279–89. Edited by Charles Caspers and Marc Schneiders. Kampen, The Netherlands: J. H. Kok, 1990.

Bobertz, Charles A. "Prolegomena to a Ritual/Liturgical Reading of the Gospel of Mark." In *Reading in Christian Communities: Essays on Interpretation in the Early Church*, 174–87. Edited by Charles A. Bobertz and David Brakke. Christianity and Judaism in Antiquity Series 14. Notre Dame, IN: University of Notre Dame Press, 2002.

Boccardi, Donald. *The History of Catholic Hymnals since Vatican II*. Chicago: GIA Publications, 2001.

Boe, John. "Old Roman Votive-Mass Chants in Florence, Biblioteca Riccardiana, MSS 299 and 300 and Vatican City, Biblioteca Apostolica Vaticana, Archivio San Pietro F 11: A Source Study." In *Western Plainchant in the First Millennium: Studies in the Medieval Liturgy and Its Music*, 261–318. Edited by Sean Gallagher et al. Burlington, VT: Ashgate Publishing, 2003.

Bolinger, Dwight. *Intonation and Its Uses: Melody in Grammar and Discourse*. Stanford, CA: Stanford University Press, 1989.

Bornet, Roger. "Pour une interprétation comparative de la reforme liturgique." *Questions Liturgiques* 67 (1986): 1–32.

Bouma-Prediger, Steven. *The Greening of Theology: The Ecological Models of Rosemary Radford Ruether, Joseph Stiller, and Jürgen Moltmann*. American Academy of Religion Academy Series 91. New York: Oxford University Press, 1995.

Bradshaw, Paul F. "Ancient Church Orders: A Continuing Enigma." In *Fountain of Life*, 3–22. Edited by Gerard Austin. In memory of Niels K. Rasmussen. Washington, DC: Pastoral Press, 1991.

———. "The Changing Face of Early Liturgy." *Music and Liturgy* 33:1–2 (2007): 23–26, 7–9.

———. "Difficulties in Doing Liturgical Theology." *Pacifica* 11 (June 1998): 181–94.

———. *Eucharistic Origins*. New York: Oxford University Press, 2004.

———. "The Homogenization of Christian Liturgy—Ancient and Modern: Presidential Address." *Studia Liturgica* 26:1 (1996): 1–15.

———, ed. "Liturgical Space." *Studia Liturgica* 24:1 (1994): 1–126.

———, ed. "Liturgical Theology." *Studia Liturgica* 30:1 (2000): 1–128.

———. *The Search for the Origins of Christian Worship: Sources and Methods for the Study of Early Liturgy*. 2nd ed. New York: Oxford University Press, 2002.

———. "The Use of the Bible in Liturgy: Some Historical Perspectives." *Studia Liturgica* 22:1 (1992): 35–52.

Bradshaw, Paul F., Maxwell E. Johnson, and L. Edward Phillips. *The Apostolic Tradition: A Commentary*. Edited by Harold W. Attridge. Minneapolis: Fortress Press, 2002.

Brans, Eugene. "The Liturgical Function of Music: Music in Its Relationship to the Texts of the Liturgy." PhD diss., University of Hidelbert, 1959.

Brightman, F. E. "Apostolic Constitutions 8." In *Liturgies: Eastern and Western*. Vol. 1. *Eastern Liturgies*, 4–13. Oxford: Clarendon Press, 1896.

Brocato, Francis William. "The Vernacular Chant of St. Meinrad Archabbey." PhD diss., University of Minnesota, 1986.

Brown, Frank Burch. *Religious Aesthetics: A Theological Study of Making and Meaning*. Princeton, NJ: Princeton University Press, 1989.

Brown, Howard Mayer, and Stanley Sadie, eds. *Performance Practice: Music before 1600*. Norton/Grove Handbooks in Music. New York: W. W. Norton, 1990.

Brundage, James A. *Medieval Canon Law*. London: Longman Publishing Group, 1995.

Bugnini, Annibale, ed. *Documenta Pontificia ad Instaurationem Liturgicam Spectantia*. 2 vols. Rome: Edizioni Liturgiche, 1953, 1959.

———. *The Reform of the Liturgy (1948–1975)*. Translated by Matthew J. O'Connell. Collegeville, MN: Liturgical Press, 1990.

Bugnini, Annibale, and Carlo Braga, eds. *The Commentary on the Constitution and on the Instruction on the Sacred Liturgy*. New York: Benzinger, 1964.

Bullough, D. A., and Alice L. H. Corréa. "Texts, Chants and the Chapel of Louis the Pious." In *Charlemagne's Heir: New Perspectives on the Reign of Louis the Pious (814–840)*, 489–508. Oxford: Clarendon Press, 1990.

Burdon, Adrian. "'Till in Heaven'—Wesleyan Models for Liturgical Theology." *Worship* 71 (July 1997): 309–17.

Caccamo, James F. "The Listener as Musician: The Importance of Audience in the Moral Power of Music." In *God's Grandeur: The Arts and Imagination in Theology*, 59–79. Edited by David C. Robinson. Maryknoll, NY: Orbis Books, 2007.

Caglio, Ernest Moneta. "Sacred Music." In *The Commentary on the Constitution and the Instruction on the Sacred Liturgy*. Edited by Annibale Bugnini and Carlo Braga. New York: Benzinger Bros., 1965.

Cain, Elizabeth Ann. "English Chant Tradition in the Late Middle Ages: The Introits and Graduals of the Temporale in the Sarum Gradual." PhD diss., Harvard University, 1982.

Caldwell, John. *English Keyboard Music before the Nineteenth Century*. Oxford, 1973.

Call, Jerry, comp. *Census-catalogue of Manuscript Sources of Polyphonic Music 1450–1550*. 5 vols. Edited by Herbert Kellman and Charles

Hamm. University of Illinois Renaissance Manuscript Studies 1. Neuhausen and Stuttgart: Hänssler-Verlag, 1979–88.

Campbell, Stanislaus. *From Breviary to Liturgy of the Hours: The Structural Reform of the Roman Office, 1964–1971*. Collegeville, MN: Liturgical Press, 1995.

Capelle, Bernard. "Regnavit a ligno." In *Travaux liturgiques de doctrine et d'histoire*, vol. 3, 211–14. Louvain: Abbaye du Mont César, 1967.

Cardine, Eugène. "De l'édition critique du Graduel: nécessité, avantages, méthode." *Revue grégorienne* 29 (1950): 202–8.

———. "La psalmodie des introïts." *Revue grégorienne* 26 (1947): 172–77, 229–36; 27 (1948): 16–25.

Carlin, Patrick I. "An Analysis of the Liturgical Music of the St. Louis Jesuits." PhD diss., New York University, 1982.

Carminati, Giancarlo. "Una teoria semiologica del linguaggio liturgico: una verifica sul 'Ordo Missae.'" *Ephemerides Liturgicae* 102 (1988): 184–233.

Carr, Ephrem. "Liturgical Families in the East." In *Handbook for Liturgical Studies*, 1:11–24. Edited by Anscar J. Chupungco. Collegeville, MN: Liturgical Press, 1997.

Carroll, Catherine A. *A History of the Pius X School of Liturgical Music: 1916–1969*. St. Louis, MO: Society of the Sacred Heart, 1989.

Carroll, Thomas K., and Thomas Halton, eds. *Liturgical Practice in the Fathers*. Message of the Fathers of the Church 21. Wilmington, DE: Michael Glazier, 1988.

Casey, Sara Gibbs. "Songs for the Peregrini: Proper Chants for Irish Saints as Found in Continental Manuscripts of the Middle Ages." PhD diss., University of Pittsburgh, 2003.

Casson, Lionel. *Everyday Life in Ancient Rome*. Rev. exp. ed. Baltimore: Johns Hopkins University Press, 1999.

Catella, Alceste. "Theology of the Liturgy." In *Handbook for Liturgical Studies*, 3:3–28. Edited by Anscar J. Chupungco. Collegeville, MN: Liturgical Press, 1998.

Catella, Alceste, Ferdinandus Dell'Oro, and Aldus Martini, eds. *Liber Sacramentorum Paduensis (Padova, Biblioteca Capitolare, Cod. D 47)*. Biblioteca Ephemerides Liturgicae, Subsidia. Monumenta Italiae Liturgica III. Rome: CLV Edizioni Liturgiche, 2005.

Cavanaugh, Philip. "Early Sixteenth-Century Cycles of Polyphonic Mass Propers, an Evolutionary Process or the Result of Liturgical Reforms?" *Acta Musicologica* 48:2 (July–December 1976): 151–65.

Chandler, Michael. *An Introduction to the Oxford Movement.* New York: Church Publishing, 2003.

Chapman, Raymond. "Linguistics and Liturgy." *Theology* 76 (November 1973): 594–99.

Chase, Steven. *The Tree of Life: Models of Christian Prayer.* Ada, MI: Baker Academic, 2005.

Chavasse, Antoine. *Les ancêtres du Missale Romanum (1570).* Analecta Liturgica 20. Studia Anselmiana 118. Rome: Centro Studi S. Anselmo, 1995.

———. "Cantatorium et antiphonale missarum: quelques procédés de confection, dimanches après la Pentecôte graduels du sanctoral." *Ecclesia Orans* 1 (1984): 15–55.

———. "Evangélaire, épistolier, antiphonaire et sacramentaire: les livres romains de la messe aux VIIe au VIIIe siècle." *Ecclesia Orans* 6 (1989): 177–255.

———. "La formation de l'*Antiphonale missarum.*" *Bulletin du Comité des Etudes de Saint-Sulpice* 32 (1961): 29–41.

———. "Les plus anciens types du lectionnaire et de l'antiphonaire romains de la messe." *Revue bénédictine* 62 (1952): 3–94.

———. "La Préparation de la Pâque, à Rome, avant le Ve siècle, jeûne et organisation liturgique." In *Memorial J. Chaine*, 5:61–80. Lyon: Facultés Catholiques, 1950.

———. *Le Sacramentaire Gelasian.* Tournai, 1958.

Chupungco, Anscar J. *The Cosmic Elements of Christian Passover.* Studia Anselmiana 72. Analecta Liturgica 3. Rome: Editrice Anselmiana, 1977.

———. *Cultural Adaptation of the Liturgy.* New York: Paulist Press, 1982.

———. "Greco-Roman Culture and Liturgical Adaptation." *Notitiae* 15 (1979): 202–18.

———, ed. *Handbook for Liturgical Studies.* 5 vols. Collegeville, MN: Liturgical Press, 1997–2001.

———. "History of the Liturgy until the Fourth Century." In *Handbook for Liturgical Studies*, 1:95–114. Edited by Anscar J. Chupungco. Collegeville, MN: Liturgical Press, 1997.

———. "History of the Roman Liturgy until the Fifteenth Century." In *Handbook for Liturgical Studies*, 1:131–52. Edited by Anscar J. Chupungco. Collegeville, MN: Liturgical Press, 1997.

———. *Liturgical Inculturation: Sacramentals, Religiosity, and Catechesis.* Collegeville, MN: Liturgical Press, 1992.

————. *Liturgies of the Future: The Process and Method of Inculturation.* New York: Paulist Press, 1989.

————. *Shaping the Easter Feast.* Washington, DC: Pastoral Press, 1992.

————. "The Translation of Liturgical Texts." In *Handbook for Liturgical Studies*, 1:381–98. Edited by Anscar J. Chupungco. Collegeville, MN: Liturgical Press, 1997.

Clarke, Eric F. "Generative Principles in Music Performance." In *Generative Processes in Music: The Psychology of Performance, Improvisation and Composition*, 1–26. Edited by John A. Sloboda. Oxford: Clarendon Press, 1988.

Clauss, Manfred. *The Roman Cult of Mithras: The God and His Mysteries.* New York: Routledge, 2001.

Claussen, M. A. *The Reform of the Frankish Church: Chrodegang of Metz and the* Regula canonicorum *in the Eighth Century.* Cambridge Studies in Medieval Life and Thought, Fourth Series 60. New York: Cambridge University Press, 2005.

Clooney, Francis X. "Liturgical Theology in a Comparative Context: Some Hindu Perspectives on *Lex Orandi / Lex Credendi.*" *Worship* 63 (July 1989): 341–50.

Clothey, Fred W. "Toward a Comprehensive Interpretation of Ritual." *Journal of Ritual Studies* 2:2 (1988): 147–61.

Cobb, Peter G. "The Liturgy of the Word in the Early Church." In *The Study of Liturgy*, 219–29. Rev. ed. Edited by Cheslyn Jones et al. London: SPCK; New York: Oxford, 1992.

Coelho, Ivo. *Hermeneutics and Method: The "Universal Viewpoint" in Bernard Lonergan.* Toronto: University of Toronto Press, 2000.

Collegeville Composers Group. *Psallite: Sacred Song for Liturgy and Life.* Collegeville, MN: Liturgical Press, 2008.

Collins, Mary. "An Adventuresome Hypothesis: Women as Authors of Liturgical Change." In *Proceedings of the North American Academy of Liturgy* (1993).

————. *Contemplative Participation: Sacrosanctum Concilium Twenty-Five Years Later.* Collegeville, MN: Liturgical Press, 1990.

————. "Critical Questions for Liturgical Theology." *Worship* 53 (July 1979): 302–17.

————. "Eucharist and Christology Revisited: The Body of Christ." *Theological Digest* 39:4 (1992): 321–25.

———. "Liturgical Methodology and the Cultural Evolution of Worship in the United States." *Worship* 49 (February 1975): 85–102.

———. "The Public Language of Ministry." In *Official Ministry in a New Age*, 7–40. Edited by James H. Provost. Permanent Seminar Studies 3. Washington, DC: Canon Law Society of America, 1981.

———. *Worship: Renewal to Practice*. Washington, DC: Pastoral Press, 1987.

Collins, Mary, and David N. Power, eds. *Liturgy: A Creative Tradition. Concilium* 162. New York: Seabury, 1983.

Collins, Mary, David N. Power, and Mellonee Burnim, eds. *Music and the Experience of God. Concilium* 202. Edinburgh: T. & T. Clark, 1989.

Collins, Raymond F. *Models of Theological Reflection*. Lanham, MD: University Press of America, 1984.

Colloton, Paul H. "The Meaning of Our Signs: The Pastoral Theology of the *General Instruction*." *Pastoral Music*. 27:5 (June–July 2003): 28–33, 36.

Colombari, Bari, and Michael R. Prendergast, eds. *The Song of the Assembly: Pastoral Music in Practice; Essays in Honor of Father Virgil C. Funk*. Studies in Church Music and Liturgy. Portland, OR: Pastoral Press, 2007.

Combe, Pierre. *Histoire de la restauration of chant grégorienne d'après des documents inédits*. Solesmes: Abbaye de Solesmes, 1969.

———. *Justine Ward and Solesmes*. Washington, DC: Catholic University of America Press, 1987.

Comotti, Giovanni. *Music in Greek and Roman Culture*. Translated by Rosaria V. Munson. Baltimore: Johns Hopkins University Press, 1991.

Congar, Yves. "L'Ecclesia ou communauté chrétienne, sujet intégral de l'action liturgique." In *La Liturgie après Vatican II*, 246–82. Edited by J. P. Jossua and Y. Congar. Paris: Les Editions du Cerf, 1967.

Connell, Martin F. "On the U.S. Aversion to Ritual Behavior and the Vocation of the Liturgical Theologian." *Worship* 78:5 (September 2004): 386–403.

Connolly, Thomas H. "Introits and Archetypes: Some Archaisms of the Old Roman Chant." *Journal of the American Musicological Society* 25 (1972): 157–74.

Coquin, R. G. "Une reforme liturgique du concile de Nicea." *Comptes-rendus des séances de l'Académie des Inscriptions et Belles-Lettres*. 111:2 (1967): 178–92.

Coriden, James A., et al., eds. *The Code of Canon Law: A Text and Commentary*. New York: Paulist Press, 1985.

Cortese, Ennio. *Il diritto nella storia medievale*. 2 vols. Rome, 1995.

Costa, Eugenio, Jr. "Tropes et séquences dans le cadre de la vie liturgique au moyen âge." DTS diss., Institut Catholique de Paris, 1975.

Crainshaw, Jill Y. *Wise and Discerning Hearts: An Introduction to Wisdom Liturgical Theology*. Collegeville, MN: Liturgical Press, 2000.

Crichton, J. D. *The Liturgy of Holy Week*. Dublin: Veritas Publications, 1983. Reprint, 1987.

Crocker, Richard L. "Gregorian Studies in the Twenty-First Century." *Plainsong and Medieval Music* 4 (1995): 33–86.

———. *An Introduction to Gregorian Chant*. Guildford and Kings Lynn, UK: Biddles Ltd., 2000.

Cuming, Geoffrey J. "The Early Eucharistic Liturgies in Recent Research." In *The Sacrifice of Praise: Studies on the Themes of Thanksgiving and Redemption in the Central Prayers of the Eucharistic and Baptismal Liturgies*, 65–69. Edited by Bryan D. Spinks. Bibliotheca Ephemerides Liturgicae, Subsidia 19. Rome: CLV Edizioni Liturgiche, 1981.

———. *Hippolytus: A Text for Students, with Introduction, Translation, Commentary and Notes*. Bramcote, UK: Grove Books Ltd., 1987. Reprint, 1991.

Cuneo, Michael W. *The Smoke of Satan: Conservative and Traditionalist Dissent in Contemporary American Catholicism*. Baltimore: Johns Hopkins University Press, 1999.

Curran, John R. *Pagan City and Christian Capital: Rome in the Fourth Century*. Oxford: Clarendon Press, 2000.

Cutter. Paul F. *Musical Sources of the Old-Roman Mass*. Musicological Studies and Documents 36. Stuttgart: American Institute of Musicology, 1979.

Dalmais, I. H. *Introduction to the Liturgy*. Translated by Roger Capel. Baltimore: Helicon, 1961.

———. "La liturgie comme lieu théologique." *La Maison-Dieu* 78 (1964): 97–106.

———. "Le Mysterion, contribution a une théologie de la liturgie." *La Maison-Dieu* 158 (1984): 14–50.

———. "Note sure la sociologie des processions." *La Maison-Dieu* 43 (1955): 37–43.

———. "Symbolique liturgique et theologique de l'art romain." *La Maison-Dieu* 123 (1975): 135–48.

———. "Theology of Liturgical Celebration." In *Principles of the Liturgy*, 229–80. *The Church at Prayer*, vol. 1. Translated by Matthew J. O'Connell. Collegeville, MN: Liturgical Press, 1987.

Damian, Ronald. "A Historical Study of the Caecilian Movement in the United States." DMA diss., The Catholic University of America, 1984.

Davies, John Gordon. *The Early Christian Church*. History of Religions Series. New York: Holt, Rinehart and Winston, 1965.

———. *Holy Week: A Short History*. Ecumenical Studies in Worship 11. London: Lutterworth Press, 1963.

Davis, Raymond, ed. and trans. *The Book of Pontiffs (Liber Pontificalis): The Ancient Biographies of the First Ninety Roman Pontiffs to AD 715*. Translated Texts for Historians, Latin Series 5. Liverpool, 1989.

Davison, Nigel. "So Which Way Round Did They Go? The Palm Sunday Procession at Salisbury." *Music and Letters* 61:1 (January 1980): 1–14.

De Benedictis, Elaine. "The 'Schola Cantorum' in Rome during the High Middle Ages." PhD diss., Bryn Mawr College, 1983.

De Blaauw, Sible. "Architecture and Liturgy in the Late Antique and the Middle Ages: Traditions and Trends in Modern Scholarship." *Archiv für Liturgiewissenschaft* 33 (1991): 1–34.

———. "The Solitary Celebration of the Supreme Pontiff: The Lateran Basilica as the New Temple in the Medieval Liturgy of Maundy Thursday." In *Omnes Circumadstantes: Contributions towards a History of the Role of the People in the Liturgy*, 120–43. Edited by Charles Caspers and Marc Schneiders. Kampen, The Netherlands: J. H. Kok, 1990.

De Clerck, Paul. "Improvisation et livre liturgique, leçons d'une histoire." *Communautés et liturgie* 60 (1978): 109–26.

———. "'Lex orandi lex credendi,' sens originel et avatars historiques d'un adage équivoque." *Questions Liturgiques* 59 (1978): 193–212.

———. "L'«Ordo Missae» de Vatican II: ses innovations et sa réception." In *L'Eucharistie: célébrations, rites, piétés*, 183–201. Edited by A. M. Triacca and A. Pistoia. Bibliotheca Ephemerides Liturgicae, Subsidia 79. Rome: CLV Edizioni Liturgiche, 1995.

Deiss, Lucien. *Spirit and Song of the New Liturgy*. New rev. ed. Translated by Lyla L. Haggard and Michael L. Mazzarese. Cincinnati: World Library Publications, 1976.

———. *Springtime of the Liturgy: Liturgical Texts of the First Four Centuries*. Translated by Matthew J. O'Connell. Classics in Liturgy. Collegeville, MN: Liturgical Press, 1979.

————. *Visions of Liturgy and Music for a New Century.* Translated by Jan M.-A. Burton. English text edited by Donald Molloy. Collegeville, MN: Liturgical Press, 1996.

Dekkers, Eloi. "Créativité et orthodoxie dans la 'lex orandi.'" *La Maison-Dieu* 111 (1972): 23–30.

Delattre, Roland A. "Ritual Resourcefulness and Cultural Pluralism." *Soundings* 61 (1978): 281–301.

Delling, Gerhard. *Worship in the New Testament.* Translated by Percy Scott. Philadelphia: Westminster Press, 1962.

Demacopoulos, George E. *Models of Spiritual Direction in the Early Church.* Notre Dame, IN: University of Notre Dame Press, 2006.

Deshusses, J. "Chronologie des grands sacramentaires de Saint-Amand." *Revue bénédictine* 87 (1977): 230–37.

————, ed. *Le sacramentaire grégorien: Ses principales formes d'après les plus anciens manuscrits.* 3 vols. Spicilegium friburgense 16, 24, 28. Fribourg, 1971, 1979, 1982.

de Simone, Oronzo, de. 'De nozione et officio liturgici iuris." *Monitor Ecclesiasticus* 85 (1960): 151–59.

The Didache: A Commentary. Edited by Kurt Niedermeyer. 2nd ed. Translated by Linda M. Maloney. Edited by Harold W. Attridge. Minneapolis: Fortress Press, 1998.

The Didache: Its Jewish Sources and Its Place in Early Judaism and Christianity. Huub Van de Sandt and David Flusser, eds. Compendia Rerum Iudaicarum ad Novum Testamentum, Section III, Jewish Traditions in Early Christian Literature 5. Minneapolis: Fortress Press; Assen: Royal Van Gorcum, 2002.

The Didache: Text, Translation, Analysis, and Commentary. Edited by Aaron Milavec. Collegeville, MN: Liturgical Press, 2003.

Didascalia Apostolorum: The Syriac Version Translated and Accompanied by the Verona Latin Fragments. Edited and translated by R. Hugh Connolly. Oxford: Clarendon Press, 1929.

Dobszay, László. "Concerning a Chronology for Chant." In *Western Plainchant in the First Millennium: Studies in the Medieval Liturgy and Its Music,* 217–30. Edited by Sean Gallagher et al. Burlington, VT: Ashgate Publishing, 2003.

————. "Experiences in the Musical Classification of Antiphons." In *Cantus planus: Papers Read at the Third Meeting, Tihany, Hungary, 19–24 Sep-*

tember 1988, 143–56. Edited by L. Dobszay et al. Budapest: Hungarian Academy of Sciences Institute for Musicology, 1990.

———. "The Types of Antiphons in Ambrosian and Gregorian Chant." In *Chant and Its Peripheries: Essays in Honour of Terence Bailey*, 50–61. Edited by Bryan Gillingham and Paul Merkley. Musicological Studies 72. Ottawa: Institute of Medieval Music, 1998.

Dobszay, László, with Guy Nicholls, Martin Baker, Bill East, and Laurence Hemming, eds. London: T. & T. Clark (Continuum), 2011.

Doran, Carol, and Thomas H. Troeger. "Recognizing an Ancient Unity: Music and Liturgy as Complemental Disciplines." *Worship* 60:5 (September 1986): 386–98.

Dourthe, Pierre. "How Liturgical Space Was Organized in a Rural Paleo-Christian Basilica." *Studia Liturgica* 24 (1994): 66–70.

Downey, Michael, and Richard Fraggomeni, eds. *A Promise of Presence: Studies in Honor of David N. Power, O.M.I.* Washington, DC: Pastoral Press, 1992.

Duchesneau, C. "Musique Sacreé, Musique d'Église, Musique Liturgique: changement de mentalité?" *Notitiae* 23 (1987): 1189–99.

Duchesne, Louis. *Christian Worship, Its Origins and Evolution. A Study of the Latin Liturgy up to the Time of Charlemagne.* 5th ed. Translated by M. L. McClure. London: Society for Promoting Christian Knowledge / New York: Macmillan, 1949.

———, ed. *Le Liber Pontificalis texte, introduction et commentaire.* Vols 1 and 2. Paris, 1886, 1892. Vol. 3. Edited by C. Vogel. Paris, 1957.

Dulles, Avery. *Models of the Church.* New York: Doubleday, 1974.

———. *Models of Revelation.* New York: Doubleday, 1983.

Dyer, Joseph. "The Desert, the City and Psalmody in the Late Fourth Century." In *Western Plainchant in the First Millennium: Studies in the Medieval Liturgy and Its Music*, 11–44. Edited by Sean Gallagher et al. Burlington, VT: Ashgate Publishing, 2003.

———. "The Introit and Communion Psalmody of Old Roman Chant." In *Chant and Its Peripheries: Essays in Honour of Terence Bailey*, 110–42. Edited by Bryan Gillingham and Paul Merkley. Musicological Studies 72. Ottawa: Institute of Medieval Music, 1998.

Egeria: Diary of a Pilgrimage. Translated and annotated by George E. Gingras. Ancient Christian Writers: The Works of the Fathers in Translation 38. New York: Newman Press, 1970.

Egeria's Travels to the Holy Land: Newly Translated with Supporting Documents and Notes. 3rd ed. Edited by John Wilkinson. Warminster, UK: Aris & Phillips, 1999.

Eisenhofer, Ludwig, and Joseph Lechner. *The Liturgy of the Roman Rite.* New York: Herder & Herder, 1961.

Ekenberg, A. *Cur Cantatur? Die Funktionen des liturgischen Gesanges nach den Autoren der Karolingerzeit.* Bibliotheca Theologiae Practicae. Kyrkovetenskapliga studier 41. Stockholm: Almquist & Wiksell, 1987.

Elich, Tom. "Using Liturgical Texts in the Middle Ages." In *Fountain of Life*, 69–83. Edited by Gerard Austin. In memory of Niels K. Rasmussen. Washington, DC: Pastoral Press, 1991.

Empereur, James. *Models of Liturgical Theology.* Bramcote: Grove Books, 1987.

———. *Worship: Exploring the Sacred.* Washington, DC: Pastoral Press, 1987.

Encyclopedia of Early Christianity. 2nd ed. 2 vols. Edited by Everett Ferguson. New York: Garland Publishing, 1997.

Erdö, Péter. *Storia della scienza del diritto canonico: Una introduzione.* Rome: Editrice Pontificia Università Gregoriana, 2000.

Erian, Nabila Meleka. "Coptic Music—An Egyptian Tradition." PhD diss., University of Maryland, 1986.

Escudier, Denis. "Les manuscrits musicaux du moyen âge (du IXe au XIIe siècles): essai de typologie." *Codicologica* 3 (1980): 34–35.

Fagerberg, David W. "Traditional Liturgy and Liturgical Tradition." *Worship* 72 (November 1998): 482–501.

———. *What Is Liturgical Theology? A Study in Methodology.* Collegeville, MN: Liturgical Press, 1992.

Falconer, Keith. "The Modes before the Modes: Antiphon and Differentia in Western Chant." In *The Study of Medieval Chant: Paths and Bridges, East and West*, 131–46. Edited by Peter Jeffery. Rochester, NY: Boydell Press, 2001.

Farr, David. "Newly-composed Eucharistic Entrance Antiphons, with Commentary." PhD diss., Graduate Theological Union, Berkeley, 1986.

Fassler, Margot, and Peter Jeffery. "Christian Liturgical Music from the Bible to the Renaissance." In *Sacred Sound and Social Change: Liturgical Music in Jewish and Christian Experience*, 84–123. Edited by Lawrence A. Hoffman and Janet Walton. Two Liturgical Traditions 3. Notre Dame, IN: University of Notre Dame Press, 1992.

Faulkner, Quentin. *Wiser Than Despair: The Evolution of Ideas in the Relationship of Music and the Christian Church*. Contributions to the Study of Music and Dance 40. Westport, CT: Greenwood Press, 1996.

Fellerer, K. G. "Church Music and the Council of Trent." *Musical Quarterly* 39:4 (October 1953): 576–94.

———. *The History of Catholic Church Music*. Translated by F. A. Brunner. Baltimore, Helicon Press, 1961.

Ferguson, Everett. "Psalm-Singing at the Eucharist: A Liturgical Controversy in the Fourth Century." *Austin Seminary Bulletin* 98 (1983): 52–77.

Ferme, Brian Edwin. *Introduzione alla storia del diritto canonico*. Vol. 1. *Il diritto antico fino al decretum di Graziano*. Quaderni di Apollinaris 1. Vatican City: Pontificia Università Lateranense, 1998.

Fernandez, Pedro. "Liturgia y teologia. Historia de un problema metodologico." *Ecclesia Orans* 6 (1989): 261–83.

Ferreira, Manuel Pedro. "Music at Cluny: The Tradition of Gregorian Chant for the Proper of the Mass. Melodic Variants and Microtonal Nuances." 2 vols. PhD diss., Princeton University, 1997.

Fink, Peter E. "Three Languages of Christian Sacraments." *Worship* 52 (November 1978): 561–75.

———. "Towards a Liturgical Theology." *Worship* 47 (December 1973): 601–9.

Finn, Peter, and ICEL. "Translation of the *Missale Romanum, editio tertia*: Questions and Issues Related to the Translation of the Antiphons." Unpublished study. Washington, DC, 2004.

Finney, Paul Corby. "Early Christian Architecture: The Beginnings (A Review Article)." *Harvard Theological Review* 81:3 (1988): 319–39.

Fisch, Thomas, ed. *Primary Readings on the Eucharist*. Collegeville, MN: Liturgical Press, 2004.

Fish, Stanley. *Is There a Text in This Class? The Authority of Interpretive Communities*. Cambridge, MA: Harvard University Press, 1980.

Flanagan, Kieran. "Liturgy, Ambiguity, and Silence: The Ritual Management of Real Absence." *British Journal of Sociology* 36:2 (June 1985): 193–223.

———. "Liturgy as Play: A Hermeneutics of Ritual Re-Presentation." *Modern Theology* 4 (July 1988): 345–72.

Flanigan, C. Clifford, Kathleen Ashley, and Pamela Sheingorn. "Liturgy as Social Performance: Expanding the Definitions." In *The Liturgy of the*

Medieval Church, 695–714. Edited by Thomas J. Heffernan and E. Ann Matter. Kalamazoo, MI: Medieval Institute Publications, 2001.

Flynn, William T. "Paris, Bibliotheque de L'Arsenal, MS 1169: The Hermeneutics of Eleventh-Century Burgundian Tropes, and Their Implications for Liturgical Theology." PhD diss., Duke University, 1992.

Foley, Edward. *Foundations of Christian Music: The Music of Pre-Constantinian Christianity*. American Essays in Liturgy. Collegeville, MN: Liturgical Press, 1996.

———. "Liturgical Music: A Bibliographic Essay." In *Liturgy and Music: Lifetime Learning*, 411–52. Edited by Robin A. Leaver and Joyce Ann Zimmerman. Collegeville, MN: Liturgical Press, 1998.

———. "Music in Catholic Worship: A Critical Reappraisal." *Liturgy 90* (February–March 1991): 8–12.

———. "Review of James W. McKinnon, *The Advent Project*." *Theological Studies* 63:1 (March 2002): 97–98.

———. *Ritual Music: Studies in Liturgical Musicology*. Beltsville, MD: Pastoral Press, 1995.

———. "The Structure of the Mass, Its Elements and Its Parts." In *A Commentary on the General Instruction of the Roman Missal: Developed under the Auspices of the Catholic Academy of Liturgy and Cosponsored by the Federation of Diocesan Liturgical Commissions*. Edited by Edward Foley, Nathan D. Mitchell, and Joanne M. Pierce. Collegeville, MN: Liturgical Press, 2007.

———, ed. *Worship Music: A Concise Dictionary*. Collegeville, MN: Liturgical Press, 2000.

Foley, Edward, and Mary McGann. *Music and the Eucharistic Prayer*. American Essays in Liturgy. Collegeville, MN: Liturgical Press, 1988.

Foley, Edward, Nathan D. Mitchell, and Joanne M. Pierce, eds. *A Commentary on the General Instruction of the Roman Missal: Developed under the Auspices of the Catholic Academy of Liturgy and Cosponsored by the Federation of Diocesan Liturgical Commissions*. Collegeville, MN: Liturgical Press, 2007.

Folsom, Cassian. "Liturgical Books of the Roman Rite." In *Handbook for Liturgical Studies*, 1:245–314. Edited by Anscar J. Chupungco. Collegeville, MN: Liturgical Press, 1997.

Ford, Paul. F. *By Flowing Waters: Chant for the Liturgy; A Collection of Unaccompanied Song for Assemblies, Cantors, and Choirs*. Collegeville, MN: Liturgical Press, 1999.

Ford, Terence. "Index to the Facsimiles of Polyphonic Music before 1600 Published in *Die Musik in Geschichte und Gegenwart.*" *Notes* 39 (1983): 283–315.

Fortescue, Adrian. *The Ceremonies of the Roman Rite Described.* 10 editions. 3rd and following with J. B. O'Connell. London, 1917–58.

———. *The Holy Week Book: Compiled By Authority from the Roman Missal and Breviary as Reformed by Order of Pope Pius X.* London: Burns & Oates Ltd., 1916.

———. *The Mass: A Study of the Roman Liturgy.* London: Longmans, Green & Co., 1937.

Francis, Mark. *Liturgy in a Multicultural Community.* American Essays in Liturgy. Collegeville, MN: Liturgical Press, 1991.

———. *Shaping a Circle Ever Wider: Liturgical Inculturation in the United States.* Chicago: Liturgy Training Publications, 2000.

———. "Uncluttering the Eucharistic Vestibule: The Entrance Rites through Time." *Liturgical Ministry* 3 (1994): 1–12.

———. "Well Begun Is Half Done: The New Introductory Rites in the Revised Sacramentary." In *Liturgy for the New Millennium: A Commentary on the Revised Sacramentary,* 65–76. Edited by Mark R. Francis and Keith F. Pecklers. Collegeville, MN: Liturgical Press, 2000.

Francis, Mark R., and Keith F. Pecklers, eds. *Liturgy for the New Millennium: A Commentary on the Revised Sacramentary; Essays in Honor of Anscar J. Chupungco, O.S.B.* Collegeville, MN: Liturgical Press, 2000.

Franquesa, A. "Antifonas del Introito y de la Comunion en las Misas sin Canto." *Notitiae* (1970): 213–21.

Frend, William H. C. *Archaeology and History in the Study of Early Christianity.* London: Variorum Reprints, 1988.

———. *The Archaeology of Early Christianity: A History.* Minneapolis: Fortress Press, 1996.

———. *The Early Church from the Beginning to 461.* 3rd edition. London, 1991.

Frere, Walter. *Graduale Sarisburiense: A Reproduction in Facsimile of a Manuscript of the Thirteenth Century, with a Dissertation and Historical Index Illustrating Its Development from the Gregorian Antiphonale Missarum.* London: Quartich, 1894.

———. *The Winchester Troper, from Mss. of the Xth and XIth Centuries, with Other Documents Illustrating the History of Tropes in England and France.* Henry Bradshaw Society 8. London: Harrison, 1984.

Frescobaldi, Girolamo. *Fiori musicali 1635*. Vol. 5. *Organ and Keyboard Works*. Complete edition edited from the original by Pierre Pidoux. Kassel, Germany: Bärenreiter, 1954.

Froger, J. "Le chant de l'introït." *Ephemerides Liturgicae* 21 (1948): 248–55.

———. "Les chants de la messe aux VIIIe et IXe siècles." *Revue grégorienne* 26 (1947): 165–72.

———. "The Critical Edition of the Roman Gradual by the Monks of Solesmes." *Journal of the Plainsong and Mediaeval Music Society* 10 (1987): 1–14.

Fryxell, Regina. *Introits and Graduals for the Church Year Set to Music*. Philadelphia: Fortress Press, 1966–69.

Funk, Virgil C., ed. *Music in Catholic Worship (Bishops' Committee on the Liturgy): The NPM Commentary; A Collection of Articles First Published in* Pastoral Music Magazine. Washington, DC: Pastoral Press, 1983.

Gallagher, Clarence. *Church Law and Church Order in Rome and Byzantium: A Comparative Study*. Birmingham Byzantine and Ottoman Monographs 8. Aldershot, England: Ashgate, 2002.

Gallagher, Sean, et al., eds. *Western Plainchant in the First Millennium: Studies in the Medieval Liturgy and Its Music*. Burlington, VT: Ashgate Publishing, 2003.

Galliardetz, Richard T. "North American Culture and the Liturgical Life of the Church: The Separation of the Quests for Transcendence and Community." *Worship* 68 (September 1994): 403–16.

Gamber, Klaus. *Codices liturgici latini antiquiores*. Spicilegii friburgensis Subsidia 1. Universitätsverlag Freiburg Schweiz, 1963, 1964. *Supplementum, Ergänzungs- und Registerband*. Spicilegii friburgensis Subsidia 1A. Freiburg, 1988.

Gaudemet, Jean. *Les sources du droit canonique, VIIIe–XXe siècle: Repères canoniques, sources occidentales*. Paris: Éditions du Cerf, 1993.

———. *Les sources du droit de l'Église en Occident du IIe au VIIe siècle*. Paris: Éditions du Cerf / Éditions du CNRS, 1985.

Gaudemet, Jean, with Gabriel Le Bras, eds. *Histoire du droit et des institutions de l'Église en Occident*. Several volumes. Paris: Cujas, 1955–.

Gauthier, Albert. *Roman Law and Its Contribution to the Development of Canon Law*. Ottawa: Saint Paul University, 1996.

Geertz, Clifford. *The Interpretation of Cultures*. New York: Basic Books, 1973.

————. "Thick Description: Toward an Interpretive Theory of Culture." In *The Interpretation of Cultures: Selected Essays*. New York: Basic Books, 1973.

Gelineau, Joseph. *The Grail Gelineau Psalter: 150 Psalms and 18 Canticles*. Chicago: GIA Publications, 1972.

————. *Liturgical Assembly, Liturgical Song*. Translated by Paul Inwood and Bernadette Gasslein. Studies in Church Music and Liturgy. Portland, OR: Pastoral Press, 2002.

————. "Music and Singing in the Liturgy." In *The Study of Liturgy*, 493–507. Rev. ed. Edited by Cheslyn Jones et al. New York: Oxford University Press, 1992.

————. "The Path of Music." In *Music and the Experience of God*, 135–47. Edited by Mary Collins, David N. Power, and Mellonee Burnim. *Concilium* 202. Edinburgh: T. & T. Clark, 1989.

————. "Les psaumes à l'époque patristique." *La Maison-Dieu* 135 (1978): 99–116.

————. *Voices and Instruments in Christian Worship: Principles, Laws, Applications*. Translated by Clifford Howell. Collegeville, MN: Liturgical Press, 1964.

Gerber, Rebecca L., ed. and introd. *Sacred Music from the Cathedral at Trent: Trent, Museo Provinciale D'arte, Codex 1375 (OLIM 88)*. Monuments of Renaissance Music 12. Chicago: University of Chicago Press, 2007.

Gerbert, Martin. *Monumenta veteris Liturgiae Alemannicae*. St. Blaise, 1779.

Gilbert, Harold W. *Introits and Graduals for the Church Year Set to Music and Pointed for Speech Rhythm Singing*. Philadelphia: Fortress Press, 1964.

Gillingham, Bryan, and Paul Merkley, eds. *Chant and Its Peripheries: Essays in Honour of Terence Bailey*. Musicological Studies 72. Ottawa: Institute of Medieval Music, 1998.

Glen, Genevieve. "Mediator Dei (1947)." In *The Song of the Assembly: Pastoral Music in Practice; Essays in Honor of Father Virgil C. Funk*, 9–11. Edited by Bari Colombari and Michael R. Prendergast. Studies in Church Music and Liturgy. Portland, OR: Pastoral Press, 2007.

Godlovitch, Stan. "Performance Authenticity: Possible, Practical, Virtuous." In *Performance and Authenticity in the Arts*, 154–74. Edited by Salim Kemal and Ivan Gaskell. Cambridge Studies in Philosophy and the Arts. New York: Cambridge University Press, 1999.

Gold, Barbara K., and John F. Donahue, eds. *Roman Dining*. *American Journal of Philology*, special edition (2005).

Gómez, Raúl R. "Beyond Serapes and Maracas: Liturgical Theology in a Hispanic/Latino Context." *Journal of Hispanic/Latino Theology* 8:2 (November 2000): 55–72.

Gordon, Ignatius. "Constitutio de Sacra Liturgia et Canones 1256–1257." *Periodica* 54 (1965): 89–140, 352–405, 517–82.

The Grail. *The Psalms: A New Translation*. Chicago: GIA Publications, 1963.

Grant, Robert M. *Augustus to Constantine: The Rise and Triumph of Christianity in the Roman World*. Rev. ed. Foreword by Margaret M. Mitchell. Louisville, KY: Westminster / John Knox Press, 2004.

Grimes, Ronald. "Emerging Ritual." In *Proceedings of the North American Academy of Liturgy*. Valparaiso, IN: North American Academy of Liturgy, 1990.

———. "Liturgical Supinity, Liturgical Erectitude: On the Embodiment of Ritual Authority." *Studia Liturgica* 23:1 (1993): 51–69.

———. *Reading, Writing and Ritualizing: Ritual in Fictive, Liturgical, and Public Places*. Washington, DC: Pastoral Press, 1993.

———. "Victor Turner's Definition, Theory and Sense of Ritual." In *Victor Turner and the Construction of Cultural Criticism: Between Literature and Anthropology*, 141–46. Edited by Kathleen M. Ashley. Bloomington: Indiana University Press, 1990.

Grisbrooke, W. Jardine. "An Orthodox Approach to Liturgical Theology: The Work of Alexander Schmemann." *Studia Liturgica* 23:2 (1993): 140–57.

Guéranger, Prosper. *Institutions liturgiques*. 3 vols. Paris: Le Mans, 1940–51.

———. *Institutions liturgiques. Extraits*. Montréal: Éditions de Chiré, 1977.

———. *The Liturgical Year: Passiontide and Holy Week*. Translated by Laurence Shepherd. Westminster, MD: Newman Press, 1949.

Gushee, Marion. "The Polyphonic Music of the Medieval Monastery, Cathedral and University." In *Antiquity and the Middle Ages: From Ancient Greece to the 15th Century*, 143–69. Edited by James W. McKinnon. Music and Society Series. Englewood Cliffs, NJ: Prentice Hall, 1991.

Gy, Pierre-Marie. "The Different Forms of Liturgical 'Libelli.'" In *Fountain of Life*, 22–34. Edited by Gerard Austin. In memory of Niels K. Rasmussen. Washington, DC: Pastoral Press, 1991.

———. "La géographie des tropes dans la géographie liturgique du moyen âge carolingien et postcarolingien." In *Tradizione dei tropi liturgici*, 13–24. Edited by Claudio Leonardi and Enrico Menestò. Spoleto: Centro italiano di studi sull'alto medioevo, 1990.

————. "Les tropes dans l'histoire de la liturgie et de la théologie." In *Research on Tropes*, 7–16. Edited by Gunilla Iversen. Konferenser 8. Stockholm: Almquist & Wiksell, 1983.

Haar, James. "Monophony and the Unwritten Tradition." In *Performance Practice: Music before 1600.* Edited by Howard Mayer Brown and Stanley Sadie. The Norton/Grove Handbooks in Music. New York: W. W. Norton, 1990.

Habinek, Thomas. *The World of Roman Song: From Ritualized Speech to Social Order.* Baltimore: Johns Hopkins University Press, 2005.

Hall, D. J. *Thinking the Faith: Christian Theology in a North American Context.* Minneapolis: Augsburg Press, 1989.

Haller, Robert B. "Early Dominican Mass Chants: A Witness to Thirteenth Century Chant Style." PhD diss., The Catholic University of America, 1986.

Halmo, Joan. *Antiphons for Paschal Triduum—Easter in the Medieval Office.* Musicological Studies 64. Ottawa: Institute of Medieval Music, 1995.

————. "Hymns for the Paschal Triduum." *Worship* 25 (March 1981): 137–59.

Halmo, Joan, and Todd Ridder. "Liturgical Musicology." *Worship* 64 (1990): 460–62.

Hambye, Edouard R. "An Antiphon of the East Syrian Liturgy and Some Patristic Sources." In *Studia Patristica*, 10:345–50. Berlin: Akademie Verlag, 1970.

Hameline, J.-Y. "Eléments d'anthropologie, de sociologie historique et de musicologie du culte chrétien." *Recherches de Sciences religieuses* 78 (1990): 297–424.

Hamman, A. "Valeur et signification des renseignements liturgiques de Justin." *Studia Patristica* 13 (1975): 364–74.

Hansen, James. "Divini Cultus (1928)." In *The Song of the Assembly: Pastoral Music in Practice; Essays in Honor of Father Virgil C. Funk*, 5–7. Edited by Bari Colombari and Michael R. Prendergast. Studies in Church Music and Liturgy. Portland, OR: Pastoral Press, 2007.

Hanssens, J. M., ed. *Liber officialis*. In Amalarii Episcopii Opera Liturgica Omnia. 3 vols. Studi e testi 138–40. Vatican City, 1948–50.

Happel, Stephen. "Prayer and Sacrament: A Role in Foundational Theology." *The Thomist* 45 (1981): 243–61.

————. "The Structure of Our Utopian *Mitsein* (Life-Together)." In *Heaven*. Edited by Edward Schillebeeckx and Bas Van Iersel. *Concilium* 123. New York: Seabury, 1979.

———. "Worship as a Grammar of Social Transformation." In *The Linguistic Turn and Contemporary Theology: Essays on a Theme.* Edited by George Kilcourse. Current Issues in Theology 2. The Catholic Theological Society of America, 1987.

Harmon, Kathleen Anne. "Liturgical Singing as Ritual Enactment of the Paschal Mystery." PhD diss., Drew University, 2001.

———. *The Mystery We Celebrate, the Song We Sing: A Theology of Liturgical Music.* Collegeville, MN: Liturgical Press, 2008.

Harper, John. *The Forms and Orders of Western Liturgy from the Tenth to the Eighteenth Century: A Historical Introduction and Guide for Students and Musicians.* Oxford: Clarendon Press; New York: Oxford University Press, 1991. Reprints, 1993, 1994.

Harting-Correa, Alice, ed. and trans. *Walahfried Strabo's Libellus de exordiis et incrementis quarundam in observationibus ecclesiasticis rerum: A Translation and Liturgical Commentary.* Mittellateinische Studien und Texte 19. Leiden, 1996.

Hastings, Thomas J. *Practical Theology and the One Body of Christ: Toward a Missional-Ecumenical Model.* Studies in Practical Theology. Grand Rapids, MI: William B. Eerdmans, 2007.

Hausreither, J. *Semiotik des liturgischen Gesanges: Ein Beitrag zur Entwicklung einer integralen Untersuchungsmethode de Liturgiewissenschaft.* Liturgia Condenda 16. Louvain: Peeters, 2004.

Häussling, Angelus. "Die kritische Funktion der Liturgiewissenschaft." In *Liturgie und Gesellschaft,* 103–30. Edited by Hans Meyer. Innsbruck: Tyrolia Verlag, 1970.

Hawkins, Judith Adele. "Formal Implications of Music and the Revised Rite of the Roman Catholic Eucharistic Celebration." DMA diss., New York University, 1994.

Hayburn, Robert F. *Papal Legislation on Sacred Music 95 A.D. to 1977 A.D.* Collegeville, MN: Liturgical Press, 1979.

Hebert, Thomas J., and E. Ann Matter, eds. *The Liturgy of the Medieval Church.* Kalamazoo, MI: Medieval Institute Publications, 2001.

Hellreigel, Martin B. "Holy Week in the Parish." *Worship* 30:4 (1956): 234–57.

Hen, Yitzhak, and Rob Meens. *The Bobbio Missal: Liturgy and Religious Culture in Merovingian Gaul.* New York: Cambridge University Press, 2004.

Hermans, Jo. "The Directory of Liturgical Songs in the Vernacular: Background and Liturgical Criteria." *Antiphon* 11:1 (2007): 46–64.

Herzo, Anthony Marie. "Five Aquitanian Graduals: Their Mass Propers and Alleluia Cycles." PhD diss., University of Southern California, 1967.

Hesbert, R. J. *Antiphonale Missarum Sextuplex, d'après les Graduel de Monza et les Antiphonaires de Rheinau, du Mont-Blandin, de Compiègne, de Corbie, et de Senlis.* Brussels: Vromant, 1935. Reprint, Rome: Herder, 1967.

Hesselgrave, David J., and Edward Rommen. *Contextualization: Meanings, Methods, and Models.* Grand Rapids, MI: Baker Book House, 1989. Reprint, Pasadena, CA: William Cary Library, 2003.

Higginbottom, Edward. "Organ Music and the Liturgy." In *The Cambridge Companion to the Organ,* 130–47. Edited by G. Webber and N. Thistlewaite. New York: Cambridge University Press, 1999.

Hiley, David. "Cluny, Sequences and Tropes." In *Tradizione dei tropi liturgici,* 125–38. Edited by Claudio Leonardi and Enrico Menestò. Spoleto: Centro Italiano di studi sull'alto medioevo, 1990.

———. "Plainchant Transfigured: Innovation and Reformation through the Ages." In *Antiquity and the Middle Ages: From Ancient Greece to the 15th Century,* 120–42. Edited by James W. McKinnon. Music and Society Series. Englewood Cliffs, NJ: Prentice Hall, 1991.

———. *Western Plainchant: A Handbook.* Oxford: Clarendon Press, 1993.

Hiscock, Nigel, ed. *The White Mantle of Churches: Architecture, Liturgy, and Art around the Millennium.* International Medieval Research 10. Art History Subseries 2. Turnhout, Belgium: Brepols, 2003.

Hoffman, Lawrence A. *Beyond the Text: A Holistic Approach to Liturgy.* Bloomington: Indiana University Press, 1987.

———. "Does God Remember? A Liturgical Theology of Memory." In *Memory and History in Christianity and Judaism,* 41–72. Notre Dame, IN: University of Notre Dame Press, 2001.

———. "Liturgy, Drama, and Readership Strategies: Avoiding Alienation from Our Rites." *Liturgical Ministry* 2 (Spring 1993): 49–55.

Hoffman, Lawrence A., and Janet R. Walton, eds. *Sacred Sound and Social Change: Liturgical Music in Jewish and Christian Experience.* Two Liturgical Traditions 3. Notre Dame, IN: University of Notre Dame Press, 1992.

Holleman, A. W. J. "Early Christian Liturgical Music." *Studia Liturgica* 8 (1992): 185–92.

———. "The Oxyrhynchus Papyrus 1786 and the Relationship between Ancient Greek and Early Christian Music." *Vigiliae Christianae* 26 (1972): 1–17.

Houssiau, Albert. "La liturgie." In *Initiation à la pratique de la théologie*, 5:155–201. Paris: Éditions du Cerf, 1983.

———. "La liturgie, lieu privilégié de la théologie sacramentaire." *Questions Liturgiques* 54 (1973): 7–12.

———. "The Rediscovery of the Liturgy by Sacramental Theology." *Studia Liturgica* 15 (1982–83): 158–77.

Howell, Clifford. "From Trent to Vatican II." In *The Study of Liturgy*, 285–93. Rev. ed. Edited by Cheslyn Jones et al. New York: Oxford University Press, 1992.

Howell, Peter, Ian Cross, Robert West, eds. *Musical Structure and Cognition*. London: Academic Press, 1985.

Hsia, R. Po-chia. *The World of Catholic Renewal 1540–1770*. 2nd ed. New Approaches to European History 30. New York: Cambridge University Press, 2005.

Hucke, Helmut. "Die Entwicklung des christlichen Kultgesangs zum Gregorianischen Gesang." *Römische Quartalschrift* 48 (1953): 147–94.

———. "Musical Requirements of Liturgical Reform." *The Church and the Liturgy*, 45–74. *Concilium* 1. New York: Paulist Press, 1966.

———. "Toward a New Historical View of Gregorian Chant." *Journal of the American Musicological Society* 33:3 (Autumn 1980): 437–67.

Huels, John M. "Canonical Observations on *Redemptionis Sacramentum*." *Worship* 78:5 (September 2004): 404–20.

———. "The Interpretation of Liturgical Law." *Worship* 55 (May 1981): 218–37.

———. *Liturgical Law: An Introduction*. American Essays in Liturgy 4. Washington, DC: Pastoral Press, 1987.

———. *Liturgy and Law: Liturgical Law in the System of Roman Catholic Canon Law*. Montreal: Wilson & Lafleur, 2006.

———. *One Table, Many Laws: Essays in Catholic Eucharistic Practice*. Collegeville, MN: Liturgical Press, 1986.

Hughes, Andrew. *Medieval Manuscripts for Mass and Office: A Guide to Their Organization and Terminology*. Toronto: University of Toronto Press, 1982. Reprints, 1986, 1995.

Hughes, David G. "From the Advent Project to the Late Middle Ages: Some Issues of Transmission." In *Western Plainchant in the First Millennium: Studies in the Medieval Liturgy and Its Music*, 181–98. Edited by Sean Gallagher et al. Burlington, VT: Ashgate Publishing, 2003.

Hughes, Graham. *Worship as Meaning: A Liturgical Theology for Late Modernity.* Cambridge Studies in Christian Doctrine 10. New York: Cambridge University Press, 2003.

Huglo, Michel. "L'antiphonaire: archétype ou répertoire originel?" In *Grégoire le Grand,* 661–69. Colloques internationaux du Centre national de recherche scientifique. Paris: Éditions du CNRS, 1986.

———. "Centres de composition des tropes et cercles de diffusion." In *Tradizione dei tropi liturgici,* 139–44. Edited by Claudio Leonardi and Enrico Menestò. Spoleto: Centro italiano di studi sull'alto medioevo, 1990.

———. "L'édition critique de l'antiphonaire grégorien." *Scriptorium* 39 (1985): 130–38.

———. "Les *libelli* de tropes et les premiers tropaires-prosaires." In *Pax et Sapientia: Studies in Text and Music of Liturgical Tropes and Sequences,* 13–22. Studia Latina Stockholmiensia 29. Stockholm: Almquist & Wiksell, 1986.

———. *Les livres de chant liturgique.* Typologie des sources du Moyen Âge occidental 52. Turnhout, Belgium: Brepols, 1988.

———. *Les tonaires: Inventaire, analyse, comparaison.* Paris: Société Française de Musicologie, 1971.

Huijbers, Bernard. *The Performing Audience: Six and a Half Essays on Music and Song in the Liturgy.* 2nd ed. Cincinnati: North American Liturgy Resources, 1974.

Hunt, E. D. *Holy Land Pilgrimage in the Later Roman Empire A.D. 312–460.* Oxford: Clarendon Press, 1984.

Hunt, Emily J. *Christianity in the Second Century: The Case of Tatian.* New York: Routledge, 2003.

Hurd, Robert. "Liturgiam Authenticam (2001)." In *The Song of the Assembly: Pastoral Music in Practice; Essays in Honor of Father Virgil C. Funk,* 75–77. Edited by Bari Colombari and Michael R. Prendergast. Studies in Church Music and Liturgy. Portland, OR: Pastoral Press, 2007.

———. "A More Organic Opening: Ritual Music and the New Gathering Rite." *Worship* 72 (1998): 290–315.

Husmann, H. *Die Tropen- und Sequenzhandschriften.* International Inventory of Musical Sources (RISM) 5. Munich, 1964.

Hutchings, Arthur. *Church Music in the Nineteenth Century.* London: Herbert Henkins, 1967.

Ilnitchi, Gabriela. "The Music of the Liturgy." In *The Liturgy of the Medieval Church*, 645–72. Edited by Thomas J. Heffernan and E. Ann Matter. Kalamazoo, MI: Medieval Institute Publications, 2001.

International Commission on English in the Liturgy. *Documents on the Liturgy 1963–1979: Conciliar, Papal, and Curial Texts*. Collegeville, MN: Liturgical Press, 1982.

———. *The Simple Gradual: An English Translation of the Antiphons and Responsories of the* Graduale Simplex *for Use in English-Speaking Countries*. Washington, DC, 1968.

Irwin, Joyce, ed. "Sacred Sound: Music in Religious Thought and Practice." *Journal of the American Academy of Religion Thematic Studies* 50:1 (1983): 1–172.

Irwin, Kevin W. *Context and Text: Method in Liturgical Theology*. Collegeville, MN: Liturgical Press, 1994.

———. "The Critical Task of Liturgical Theology: Prospects and Proposals." In *Eucharist: Toward the Third Millennium*, 65–80. Chicago: Liturgy Training Publications, 1997.

———. "Critiquing Recent Liturgical Critics." *Worship* 74 (January 2000): 2–19.

———. *Easter: A Guide to the Eucharist and Hours*. Collegeville, MN: Liturgical Press, 1991.

———. "Liturgical Method: Issues for the Third Millennium." *Theology Digest* 44 (Spring 1997): 43–54.

———. *Liturgical Theology: A Primer*. American Essays in Liturgy. Collegeville, MN: Liturgical Press, 1990.

———. "Liturgical Theology: What Do the East and West Have to Say to Each Other?" *Studia Liturgica* 30:1 (2000): 94–111.

———. "Method in Liturgical Theology: Context Is Text." *Église et Théologie* 20:3 (1989): 407–24.

———. *Models of the Eucharist*. Mahwah, NJ: Paulist Press, 2005.

———. Review of *La riforma Conciliare dell "ordo Missae": Il percorso storico-redazionale dei riti d'ingresso, di offertorio e di communione*, by Maurizio Barba. *Worship* 77:5 (September 2004): 473–76.

———. "A Sacramental World—Sacramentality as the Primary Language of Sacraments." *Worship* 76:3 (May 2002): 197–210.

Isaac, Heinrich. *Choralis Constantinus I*. Edited by Emil Bezecny and Walter Rabl. Denkmäler der Tonkunst in Österreich. Graz: Akademische Druck-U. Verlagsanstalt, 1959.

————. *Choralis Constantinus II*. Edited by Anton von Webern. Denkmäler der Tonkunst in Österreich. Graz: Akademische Druck-U. Verlagsanstalt, 1959.

————. *Choralis Constantinus III*. Transcribed from the Formschneider First Edition (Nürnberg, 1555) by Louise Cuyler. Ann Arbor: University of Michigan Press, 1950.

Iverson, Gunilla. "*Cantans—orans—exultans*: Interpretations of Chants of the Introit Liturgy." In *Labore fratres in unum: Festschrift László Dobszay zum 60 Geburtstag*, 125–50. Edited by Janka Szendrei and David Hiley. Hildesheim: Georg Olms Verlag, 1995.

————. "*Pax et Sapientia*; A Thematic Study on Tropes from Different Traditions." In *Pax et Sapientia: Studies in Text and Music of Liturgical Tropes and Sequences*, 23–58. Studia Latina Stockholmiensia 29. Stockholm: Almquist & Wiksell, 1986.

————, ed. *Research on Tropes*. Konferenser 8. Stockholm: Almquist & Wiksell, 1983.

Ivey, Paul Eli. Review of *Theology in Stone: Church Architecture from Byzantium to Berkeley* by Richard Kieckhefer. *Journal of the American Academy of Religion* 73:2 (June 2005): 47–50.

Jacobsson, Ritva, ed. *Pax et Sapientia: Studies in Text and Music of Liturgical Tropes and Sequences*. Studia Latina Stockholmiensia 29. Stockholm: Almquist & Wiksell, 1986.

Jacobsson, Ritva, and Leo Treitler. "Tropes and the Concept of Genre." In *Pax et Sapientia: Studies in Text and Music of Liturgical Tropes and Sequences*, 59–90. Studia Latina Stockholmiensia 29. Stockholm: Almquist & Wiksell, 1986.

Jattiez, Jean-Jacques. *Music and Discourse: Toward a Semiology of Music*. Translated by Carolyn Abbate. Princeton, NJ: Princeton University Press, 1990.

Jeanrond, Werner G. *Text and Interpretation as Categories of Theological Thinking*. Translated by Thomas J. Wilson. New York: Crossroad, 1988.

————. *Theological Hermeneutics: Development and Significance*. New York: Crossroad, 1991.

————. "Theology in the Context of Pluralism and Postmodernity: David Tracy's Theological Method." In *Postmodernism, Literature and the Future of Theology*, 143–63. New York: St. Martin's Press; London: Macmillan, 1993.

Jeffery, Peter. "Chant East and West: Toward a Renewal of the Tradition." In *Music and the Experience of God*, 20–29. Edited by Mary Collins,

David N. Power, and Mellonee Burnim. *Concilium* 202. Edinburgh: T. & T. Clark, 1989.

————. "The Earliest Christian Chant Repertory Recovered: The Georgian Witnesses to Jerusalem Chant." *Journal of the American Musicological Society* 47:1 (Spring 1994): 1–38.

————. "The Earliest Oktoechoi: The Role of Jerusalem and Palestine in the Beginnings of Modal Ordering." In *The Study of Medieval Chant: Paths and Bridges, East and West*, 147–210. Edited by Peter Jeffery. Rochester, NY: Boydell Press, 2001.

————. "The Introduction of Psalmody into the Roman Mass by Pope Celestine I (422–432): Reinterpreting a Passage in the *Liber Pontificalis*." *Archiv für Liturgiewissenschaft* 26:2 (1984): 147–65.

————. "The Lost Chant Tradition of Early Christian Jerusalem: Some Possible Melodic Survivals in the Byzantine and Latin Chant Repertories." *Early Music History* 11 (1992): 151–90.

————. "The Meanings and Functions of *Kyrie Eleison*." In *The Place of Christ in Liturgical Prayer: Trinity, Christology, and Liturgical Theology*, 127–94. Edited by Bryan D. Spinks. Collegeville, MN: Liturgical Press, 2008.

————. "Monastic Reading and the Emerging Roman Chant Repertory." In *Western Plainchant in the First Millennium: Studies in the Medieval Liturgy and Its Music*, 45–104. Edited by Sean Gallagher et al. Burlington, VT: Ashgate Publishing, 2003.

————. "The Musical Heritage of Two Great Cities in the Formation of the Medieval Chant Traditions." In *Cantus Planus*, 163–74. Edited by L. Dobszay et al. Budapest, 1992.

————. "The Oldest Sources of the Graduale: A Preliminary Checklist of MSS Copied before about 900 A.D." *The Journal of Musicology* 2:3 (Summer 1983): 316–21.

————. *Re-Envisioning Past Musical Cultures: Ethnomusicology in the Study of Gregorian Chant*. Chicago: University of Chicago Press, 1992.

————. "Review of James W. McKinnon, *The Advent Project*." *Journal of the American Musicological Society* 56:1 (Spring 2003): 169–79.

————. "Rome and Jerusalem: From Oral to Written Repertory in Two Ancient Liturgical Centers." In *From Rome to the Passing of the Gothic: Western Chant Repertories and the Influence on Early Polyphony*. Edited by G. Boone. Isham Library Papers 4. Cambridge, MA: Harvard University Department of Music, 1995.

————, ed. *The Study of Medieval Chant: Paths and Bridges, East and West*. Rochester, NY: Boydell Press, 2001.

————. *Translating Tradition: A Chant Historian Reads* Liturgiam Authenticam. Collegeville, MN: Liturgical Press, 2006.

Jennings, Theodore W. "Ritual Studies and Liturgical Theology: An Invitation to Dialogue." *Journal of Ritual Studies* 1 (1987): 35–56.

Johnson, Cuthbert. *Prosper Guéranger (1805–1875): A Liturgical Theologian.* Analecta Liturgica 9. Rome: Studia Anselmiana, 1984.

————. *Sources of the Roman Missal (1975). Notitiae* 32 (1996): 105.

Johnson, Maxwell E. "Can We Avoid Relativism in Worship? Liturgical Norms in the Light of Contemporary Liturgical Scholarship." *Worship* 74:2 (March 2000): 135–55.

————. *Images of Baptism.* Forum Essays 6. Chicago: Liturgy Training Publications, 2001.

Joncas, Jan Michael. *"Ex Aetate Mediali Lux?* On the Use of Tropes for the *Cantus ad introitum." Pray Tell Blog* (www.praytellblog.com), 3 January 2011.

————. *From Sacred Song to Ritual Music: Twentieth-Century Understandings of Roman Catholic Worship Music.* Collegeville, MN: Liturgical Press, 1997.

————. "Giorgio Bonaccorso's Semiotic Approach to Liturgical Studies: A Review of *Introduzione allo Studio della Liturgia." Questions Liturgiques* 73 (1992): 161–69.

————. "Hymnum Tuae Gloriae Canimus. Toward an Analysis of the Vocal Expression of the Eucharistic Prayer in the Roman Rite: Tradition, Principles, Method." Thesis ad Lauream 168. SLD diss., Pontifical Liturgical Institute, San Anselmo, 1991.

————. "The *Institutio Generalis Missalis Romani* 2002: An Overview." *Worship* 77:1 (January 2003): 42–51.

————. "Joyce Ann Zimmerman's 'Text Hermeneutics' Approach to Liturgical Studies: A Review and Some Methodological Reflections." *Questions Liturgiques* 74 (1993): 208–20.

————. "Lawrence A. Hoffman's 'Holistic' Approach to Liturgical Studies." *Questions Liturgiques* 72 (1991): 89–107.

————. "Liturgical Music as Music: The Contribution of the Human Sciences." In *Liturgy and Music: Lifetime Learning,* 220–30. Edited by Robin A. Leaver and Joyce Ann Zimmerman. Collegeville, MN: Liturgical Press, 1998.

————. "Liturgical Musicology and Musical Semiotics: Theoretical Foundations and Analytic Techniques." *Ecclesia Orans* 8 (1991): 181–206.

————. "Liturgy and Music." In *Handbook for Liturgical Studies*, 2:281–322. Edited by Anscar J. Chupungco. Collegeville, MN: Liturgical Press, 1998.

————. "Musical Elements in the *Ordo Missae* of Paul VI." In *Handbook for Liturgical Studies*, 3: 209–44. Edited by Anscar J. Chupungco. Collegeville, MN: Liturgical Press, 1999.

————. "Musical Semiotics and Liturgical Musicology: Theoretical Foundations and Analytic Techniques." *Ecclesia Orans* 8 (1991): 181–206.

————. "Reforming and Renewing the Music of the Roman Rite." *Pastoral Music* 18 (August–September 1994): 29–36.

————. "Re-reading *Musicam Sacram*: Twenty-Five Years of Development in Roman Rite Liturgical Music." *Worship* 66 (May 1992): 212–31.

————. "Semiotics and the Analysis of Liturgical Music." *Liturgical Ministry* 3 (Fall 1994): 144–54.

————. "A Tale of Two Acclamations: The Priestly Function of Liturgical Music." *Pastoral Music* 28:6 (August–September 2004): 13–20.

Jones, Cheslyn, Geoffrey Wainwright, Edward Yarnold, and Paul Bradshaw, eds. *The Study of Liturgy*. Rev. ed. London: SPCK; New York: Oxford University Press, 1992.

Jonsson, Ritva. "The Liturgical Function of the Tropes." In *Research on Tropes*, 99–123. Edited by Gunilla Iversen. Konferenser 8. Stockholm: Almquist & Wiksell, 1983.

Jonsson, Ritva, and Leo Treitler. "Medieval Music and Language: A Reconsideration of the Relationship." In *Music and Language*. Studies in the History of Music 1. New York: Broude, 1983.

Jörns, Klaus-Peter. "Proklamation und Akklamation: Die antiphonische Grundordnung des frühchristlichen Gottesdienstes nach der Johannesoffenbarun." In *Liturgie und Dichtung*. Vol. 1. EOS Verlag Erzabtei St. Ottilien, 1983.

Jungmann, Josef A. *The Early Liturgy to the Time of Gregory the Great*. Translated by Francis A. Brunner. University of Notre Dame Liturgical Studies VI. Notre Dame, IN: University of Notre Dame Press, 1959.

————. *The Mass of the Roman Rite: Its Origins and Development*. 2 vols. Translated by F. A. Brunner. New York: Benzinger Bros., 1951. Reprint, Allen, TX: Christian Classics, 1986.

————. *The Place of Christ in Liturgical Prayer*. Translated by A. Peeler. Collegeville, MN: Liturgical Press, 1989.

Karp, Theodore. *Aspects of Orality and Formularity in Gregorian Chant.* Evanston, IL: Northwestern University Press, 1998.

Kartsovnik, Viatcheslav. "Proper Tropes in the Old Roman Gradual of Santa Cecilia in Trastevere (A.D. 1071)." In *Chant and Its Peripheries*, 62–109. Edited by Bryan Gillingham and Paul Merkley. Musicological Studies 72. Ottawa: Institute of Medieval Music, 1998.

Kavanagh, Aidan. *Elements of Rite: A Handbook of Liturgical Style.* New York: Pueblo, 1982.

———. *On Liturgical Theology.* New York: Pueblo, 1984. Reprint, Collegeville, MN: Liturgical Press, 1992.

———. "Primary Theology and Liturgical Act." *Worship* 57 (July 1983): 323–24.

Keifer, Ralph A. "Liturgical Text as Primary Source for Eucharistic Theology." *Worship* 51 (May 1977): 186–96.

———. "Our Cluttered Vestibule: The Unreformed Entrance Rite." *Worship* 48:5 (1974): 270–77.

———. "Translating Theology into Pastoral Music: A View from the Pew." *Pastoral Music* 10 (October–November 1985): 34–40.

Kelleher, Margaret Mary. "The Communion Rite: A Study of Roman Catholic Liturgical Performance." *Journal of Ritual Studies* 5:2 (1991): 99–122.

———. "Hermeneutics in the Study of Liturgical Performance." *Worship* 67 (July 1993): 292–318.

———. "Liturgical Theology: A Task and a Method." *Worship* 62:1 (1988): 2–25.

———. "Liturgy and the Christian Imagination." *Worship* 66:2 (March 1992): 148.

———. "Liturgy as an Ecclesial Act of Meaning." *Worship* 59 (1985): 482–97.

———. "Liturgy as an Ecclesial Act of Meaning: Foundations and Methodological Consequences for a Liturgical Spirituality." PhD diss., Catholic University of America, 1983.

———. "Liturgy as Source for Sacramental Theology." *Questions Liturgiques* 72 (1991): 25–42.

———. "Ritual Studies and the Eucharist: Paying Attention to Performance." In *Eucharist: Toward the Third Millennium*, 51–64. Chicago: Liturgy Training Publications, 1997.

———. "Sacraments and the Ecclesial Mediation of Grace." *Louvain Studies* 23 (1998): 180–97.

Kelly, Columba. "De Musica Sacra et Sacra Liturgia (1958)." In *The Song of the Assembly: Pastoral Music in Practice; Essays in Honor of Father Virgil C. Funk*, 13–15. Edited by Bari Colombari and Michael R. Prendergast. Studies in Church Music and Liturgy. Portland, OR: Pastoral Press, 2007.

———. *Entrance and Communion Antiphons for Sundays and Feasts*. Oregon Catholic Press, 2008.

Kelly, Joseph F. *The World of the Early Christians*. Message of the Fathers of the Church. Collegeville, MN: Liturgical Press, 1997.

Kelly, Walter J. "The Authority of Liturgical Laws." *The Jurist* 28 (1968): 397–424.

Kieckhefer, Richard. *Theology in Stone: Church Architecture from Byzantium to Berkeley*. New York: Oxford University Press, 2004.

Kilmartin, Edward J. *Christian Liturgy: Theology and Practice*. Vol. 1. *Systematic Theology of Liturgy*. Kansas City, MO: Sheed and Ward, 1988.

———. *The Eucharist in the West: History and Theology*. Edited by Robert J. Daly. Collegeville, MN: Liturgical Press, 1998.

———. "Liturgical Theology." *Worship* 50 (July 1976): 312–15.

———. *The Particular Liturgy of the Individual Church: The Theological Basis and Practical Consequences*. Placid Lecture Series 7. Bangalore: Dharmaram Publications, 1987.

———. "Sacraments as Liturgy of the Church." *Systematic Theology*. Edited by Walter J. Burghardt. *Theological Studies* 50 (September 1989): 419–570.

Kirby, Marc-Daniel. "The Proper Chants of the Paschal Triduum: A Study in Liturgical Theology." STL thesis, Catholic University of America, 1996.

———. "Sung Theology: The Liturgical Chant of the Church." In *Beyond the Prosaic: Renewing the Liturgical Movement*, 127–48. Edinburgh: T. & T. Clark, 1998.

Klauser, Theodor. *Die konstantinschen Altäre der Lateranbasilika. RQ* 43 (1935): 179–86.

———. *A Short History of the Western Liturgy*. 2nd ed. London, 1979.

Klemm, David E., and William Schweiker, eds. *Meanings in Texts and Actions: Questioning Paul Ricoeur*. Charlottesville: University Press of Virginia, 1993.

Kloppers, Elizabeth Catharina. "Liturgical Music as Communicative Act in a Postmodern Age." DTh diss., University of South Africa, 1998.

Kockelmans, Joseph J. "Why Is It Impossible in Language to Articulate the Meaning of a Work of Music?" In *Performance and Authenticity in the Arts*, 175–94. Edited by Salim Kemal and Ivan Gaskell. New York: Cambridge University Press, 1999.

Kodály, Zoltan. *Missa Brevis*. New York: Boosey & Hawkes, 1956.

Kodell, Jerome. *The Eucharist in the New Testament*. Collegeville, MN: Liturgical Press, 1991.

Komonchak, Joseph A. "The Church in the United States Today." In *The Spirit Moving in the Church in the United States*, 1–31. Edited by Francis A. Eigo. Villanova, PA: Villanova University Press, 1989.

———. "The Local Realization of the Church." In *The Reception of Vatican II*. Edited by Giuseppi Albergo, Jean-Pierre Jossua, and Joseph Komonchak. Washington, DC: Catholic University of America Press, 1987.

———. "The Theology of the Local Church: State of the Question." In *The Multicultural Church: A New Landscape in U.S. Theologies*, 35–49. Edited by William Cenkner. New York: Paulist Press, 1996.

Krautheimer, Richard. *Early Christian and Byzantine Architecture*. 4th ed. Rev. by R. Krautheimer and Slobodan Curcic. Pelican History of Art. New Haven, CT: Yale University Press, 1986.

———. "Introduction to an 'Iconography of Medieval Architecture.'" *JWCI* 5. 1942, 1–33. Also in *Studies* (as no. 25).

———. *Rome: Profile of a City, 312–1308*. Rev. ed. Princeton, NJ: Princeton University Press, 2000.

Krautheimer, Richard, et al. *Corpus basilicarum Christianarum Romae: The Early Christian Basilicas of Rome (IV–IX Centuries)*. 5 vols. Vatican City: Pontificio istituto di archeologia cristiana, 1937–77.

Krochalis, Jeanne E., and E. Ann Matter. "Manuscripts of the Liturgy." In *The Liturgy of the Medieval Church*, 433–72. Edited by Thomas J. Heffernan and E. Ann Matter. Kalamazoo, MI: Medieval Institute Publications, 2001.

Kroesen, J. E. A., and R. Steensma. *The Interior of the Medieval Village Church*. Louvain: Peeters, 2004.

Kubicki, Judith Marie. "How Does Music Evangelize in the Liturgy?" *Pastoral Music* 28:5 (June–July 2004): 20–22.

———. "Jacques Berthier's Taizé Music: A Case Study of Liturgical Music as Ritual Symbol." PhD diss., Catholic University of America, 1997.

———. *Liturgical Music as Ritual Symbol: A Case Study of Jacques Berthier's Taizé Music*. Liturgia codenda 9. Louvain: Peeters, 1999.

————. "Tra le Sollecitudini (1903)." In *The Song of the Assembly: Pastoral Music in Practice; Essays in Honor of Father Virgil C. Funk*, 1–3. Edited by Bari Colombari and Michael R. Prendergast. Studies in Church Music and Liturgy. Portland, OR: Pastoral Press, 2007.

Kunnie, Julian. *Models of Black Theology: Issues in Class, Culture, and Gender*. Philadelphia: Trinity Press International, 1994.

La Croix, Richard R., ed. *Augustine on Music*. Studies in the History and Interpretation of Music 6. Lewiston, NY: Edwin Mellen Press, 1988.

LaCugna, Catherine Mowry. "Can Liturgy Ever Again Be a Source for Theology?" *Studia Liturgica* 19 (1989): 1–16.

Ladrière, Jean. "The Performativity of Liturgical Language." Translated by John Griffiths. *Concilium* 9/1 (1973): 50–62.

Lamb, J. A. *The Psalms in Christian Worship*. London: Faith Press, 1962.

Lamberts, J. "Active Participation as the Gateway towards an Ecclesial Liturgy." In *Omnes Circumadstantes: Contributions towards a History of the Role of the People in the Liturgy*, 234–61. Edited by Charles Caspers and Marc Schneiders. Kampen: Uitgeversmaatschappij J. H. Kok, 1990.

————, ed. *La Participation Active: 100 ans après Pie X et 40 ans après Vatican II*. Louvain: Peeters, 2004.

Lampe, Peter. *From Paul to Valentinus: Christians at Rome in the First Two Centuries*. Minneapolis: Fortress Press; London: Continuum, 2003.

Landwehr-Melnicki, Margaret, transcrib. *Die Gesänge des altrömischen Gradual Vat Lat. 5319*. Introduced and edited by Bruno Stäblein. Monumenta monodica Medii Aevi 2. Kassel: Bärenreiter, 1970.

Lardner, Gerald V. "Communication Theory and Liturgical Research." *Worship* 51 (July 1977): 299–307.

Larrainzar, Carlos. *Introduccion al derecho canonico*. 2nd ed. Instituto de Derecho Europeo Clasico, Serie B: Monografías. Santa Cruz de Tenerife, Canary Islands: Idecsa, 1991.

Lathrop, Gordon W. *Holy People: A Liturgical Ecclesiology*. Minneapolis: Fortress Press, 1999.

————. *Holy Things: A Liturgical Theology*. Minneapolis: Fortress Press, 1993.

LaVerdiere, Eugene. *The Eucharist in the New Testament and the Early Church*. Collegeville, MN: Liturgical Press, 1996.

Lawrence, Frederick. "Method and Theology as Hermeneutical." In *Creativity and Method: Essays in Honor of Bernard Lonergan*, 79–104. Edited by M. Lamb. Milwaukee, WI: Marquette University Press, 1981.

Leaver, Robin A. "Christian Liturgical Music in the Wake of the Protestant Reformation." In *Sacred Sound and Social Change: Liturgical Music in Jewish and Christian Experience*, 124–46. Edited by Lawrence A. Hoffman and Janet Walton. Two Liturgical Traditions 3. Notre Dame, IN, and London: University of Notre Dame Press, 1992.

Leaver, Robin A., and Joyce Ann Zimmerman, eds. *Liturgy and Music: Lifetime Learning*. Collegeville, MN: Liturgical Press, 1998.

Leeb, Helmut. *Die Gesänge im Gemeinegottesdienst von Jerusalem vom 5. bis 8. Jahrhundert*. Vienna: Herder, 1970.

Leech-Wilkinson, Daniel. "Ars Antiqua—Ars Nova—Ars Subtilior." In *Antiquity and the Middle Ages: From Ancient Greece to the 15th Century*, 218–40. Edited by James W. McKinnon. Music and Society Series. Englewood Cliffs, NJ: Prentice Hall, 1991.

Leichtentritt, H. "The Reform of Trent and Its Effect on Music." *Musical Quarterly* 30:3 (July 1944): 319–28.

Leonard, John K. "Liturgical Singing: A Case for *Theologia Prima*." In *Source and Summit*, 225–41. Edited by Joanne M. Pierce and Michael Downey. Collegeville, MN: Liturgical Press, 1999.

Levy, Kenneth. "Charlemagne's Archetype of Gregorian Chant." *Journal of the American Musicological Society* 40:1 (Spring 1987): 1–30.

———. *Gregorian Chant and the Carolingians*. Princeton, NJ: Princeton University Press, 1998.

———. "On Gregorian Orality." *Journal of the American Musicological Society* 43:2 (Summer 1990): 185–227.

Lewars, Ralph. *Musical Settings for the Introits and Graduals of the Church Year*. Philadelphia: Muhlenberg College, 1948.

Liderbach, Daniel. *Christ in the Early Christian Hymns*. Mahwah, NJ: Paulist Press, 1998.

Lindsey, Mack Clay, III. "Klosterneuburg, Augustinechorherrenstift, Codices 69 and 70: Two Sixteenth-Century Choirbooks, Their Music, and Its Liturgical Use." PhD diss., Indiana University, 1981.

Liszt, Franz. "Introitus." In *Orgelkompositionem Franz Liszt*. Vol. 1. Edited by Karl Straube. New York: Peters, 1910.

———. *Requiem für Männerstimmen. Messen und Requiem mit Orgel. Kirchliche und Geistliche Gesangswerke Band III. Franz Liszts Musikalische Werke V*. Leipzig: Breitkopf & Härtel, 1966.

The Liturgy Documents: A Parish Resource. 3rd and 4th eds. Chicago: Liturgy Training Publications, 1991, 2004.

Loewe, William P. *The College Student's Introduction to Christology.* College-ville, MN: Liturgical Press, 1996.

Logan, F. Donald. *A History of the Church in the Middle Ages.* London and New York: Routledge, 2002. Reprint, 2003.

Löhr, Aemiliana. *The Great Week: An Explanation of the Liturgy of Holy Week.* Translated by D. T. H. Bridgehouse. London: Longmans; Westminster, MD: Newman Press, 1958.

Lonergan, Bernard. *Method in Theology.* London: Darton, Longman & Todd Ltd., 1973. Reprint, Toronto: University of Toronto Press, 1996.

———. "Revolution in Catholic Theology." In *A Second Collection*, 231–38. Philadelphia: Westminster Press, 1975.

Lossky, N. "Principes théologiques de la musique liturgique." In *L'Eucharistie: célébrations, rites, piétés*, 259–65. Edited by A. M. Triacca and A. Pistoia. Bibliotheca Ephemerides Liturgicae, Subsidia 79. Rome: CLV Edizioni Liturgiche, 1995.

Lotrecchiano, Gaetano R. "Ethnomusicology and the Study of Musical Change: An Introduction and Departure for Ethnoliturgiology." *Liturgical Ministry* 6 (Summer 1997): 108–19.

Lukken, Gerard M. "Die architektonischen Dimensionen des Rituals." *LI* 39 (1989): 19–36.

———. "La liturgie comme lieu theologique irremplaçable." *Questions liturgiques* 56 (1975): 97–112.

———. "Liturgy and Language: An Approach from Semiotics." *Questions liturgiques* 73 (1992): 36–52.

———. *Per Visibilia ad Invisibilia: Anthropological, Theological and Semiotic Studies on the Liturgy and the Sacraments.* Edited by Louis van Tongerer and Charles Caspers. Kampen: Pharos, 1994.

———. "Plaidoyer pour une approche intégrale de la liturgie comme lieu théologique: un défi à toute la théologie." *Questions liturgiques* 68 (1987): 242–55.

———. *Rituals in Abundance: Critical Reflections on the Place, Form and Identity of Christian Ritual in Our Culture.* Liturgia Condenda 17. Louvain: Peeters, 2004.

———. "Les transformations du rôle liturgique du people: la contribution de la sémiotique à l'histoire de la liturgie." In *Omnes Circumadstantes: Contributions towards a History of the Role of the People in the Liturgy*, 15–30. Edited by Charles Caspers and Marc Schneiders. Kampen: Uitgeversmaatschappij J. H. Kok, 1990.

————. "The Unique Expression of Faith in the Liturgy." In *Liturgical Experience of Faith*, 11–21. *Concilium* 82. Edited by Herman Schmidt and David N. Power. New York: Herder & Herder, 1973.

Lukken, Gerard M., and Mark Searle. *Semiotics and Church Architecture: Applying the Semiotics of A. J. Greimas and the Paris School to the Analysis of Church Buildings*. Liturgia Codenda 1. Kampen: Kok Pharos, 1993.

Lütolf, Max, ed. *Das Graduale von Santa Cecilia in Trastevere (1071): (Cod. Bodmer 74)*. 2 vols. Cologny-Geneva: Fondation Martin Bodmer, 1987.

MacMullen, Ramsey. *Christianizing the Roman Empire (A.D. 100–400)*. New Haven, CT: Yale University Press, 1984.

Maggiani, Silvano. "Liturgy and Aesthetics." In *Handbook for Liturgical Studies*, 2:263–80. Edited by Anscar J. Chupungco. Collegeville, MN: Liturgical Press, 1998.

Maiani, Bradford Charles. "The Responsory-Communions: Toward a Chronology of Selected Proper Chants." PhD diss., University of North Carolina at Chapel Hill, 1996.

Maldonado, Luis, and David N. Power, eds. *Liturgy and Human Passage*. *Concilium* 112. New York: Seabury Press, 1978.

Mannion, M. Francis. "The Need for an Adequate Liturgical Musicology." *Worship* 64 (1990): 78–81.

Marini, Piero. *A Challenging Reform: Realizing the Vision of the Liturgical Renewal 1963–1975*. Edited by Mark R. Francis, John R. Page, and Keith F. Pecklers. Collegeville, MN: Liturgical Press, 2007.

————. "Elenco degli 'Schemata' del 'Consilium' et della Congregazione per il Culto Divino (Marzo 1964–Luglio 1975)." *Notitiae* 195–96 (1982): 455–772.

Marshall, Paul V. "Reconsidering 'Liturgical Theology': Is There a *Lex Orandi* for All Christians? *Studia Liturgica* 25:2 (1995): 129–50.

Marsili, Salvatore. "Dalle origini Liturgia cristiana alla caratterizzazione rituale." In *Anamnesis*, 2:11–54. Edited by S. Marsili et al. Turin: Marietti, 1978.

————. *I Segni del Mistero di Cristo*. Rome: Edizione Liturgiche, 1987.

————. "La Liturgia: Momento storico della Salvezza." In *Anamnesis*, 1:33–156. Edited by B. Neunheuser et al. Turin: Marietti, 1974.

————. *Mistero di Cristo e Liturgia nello Spirito*. Edited by Maria Anselma Abignente. Vatican City: Libreria Editrice Vaticana, 1986.

————. "Teologia della celebrazione dell' eucaristia." In *Anamnesis*, 3/2:11–186. Edited by S. Marsili et al. Turin: Marietti, 1983.

Martimort, Aimé-Georges. *Les "Ordines," les ordinaires et les cérémoniaux.* Typologie des sources du Moyen Âge occidental 56. Turnhout, Belgium: Brepols, 1991.

Mason, Paul. "The Pastoral Implications of John Paul II's Chirograph for the Centenary of the *Motu Proprio* 'Tra Le Sollecitudini' on Sacred Music." *Worship* 82:5 (September 2008): 386–413.

Matthews, E. "The Use of Hymns in the Churches: Roman Catholic Tradition." In *Singing the Faith: Essays by Members of the Joint Liturgical Group on the Use of Hymns in Liturgy.* Edited by Charles Robertson. Norwich, UK: Canterbury Press, 1990.

———. "Sing Hymns or Sing Liturgy." In *Singing the Faith: Essays by Members of the Joint Liturgical Group on the Use of Hymns in Liturgy.* Edited by Charles Robertson. Norwich, UK: Canterbury Press, 1990.

Matthews, Thomas F. *The Early Churches of Constantinople: Architecture and Liturgy.* University Park: Pennsylvania State University Press, 1971.

———. "An Early Roman Chancel Arrangement and Its Liturgical Function." *Rivista di archeologia cristiana* 38 (1962): 71–95.

Mauriac, François. *Holy Thursday: An Intimate Remembrance.* Manchester, NH: Sophia Institute Press, 1991. First English edition titled *The Eucharist.* New York: Longmans, Green Publishing Company, 1944.

Mazza, Enrico. *The Celebration of the Eucharist: The Origin of the Rite and the Development of Its Interpretation.* Translated by Matthew J. O'Connell. Collegeville, MN: Liturgical Press, 1999.

———. "The Eucharist in the First Four Centuries." In *Handbook for Liturgical Studies*, 3:9–60. Edited by Anscar J. Chupungco. Collegeville, MN: Liturgical Press, 1999.

McLeod, Norma, and Marcia Herndon, eds. *The Ethnography of Musical Performance.* Norwood, PA: Norwood Editions, 1980.

McFague, Sally. *Metaphoric Theology: Models of God in Religious Language.* Philadelphia: Fortress Press, 1982.

———. *Models of God: Theology for an Ecological, Nuclear Age.* Minneapolis: Augsburg Fortress, 1987.

McGann, Mary E. *Exploring Music as Worship and Theology.* American Essays in Liturgy. Collegeville, MN: Liturgical Press, 2002.

———. "Interpreting the Ritual Role of Music in Christian Liturgical Practice." PhD diss., Graduate Theological Union, Berkeley, CA, 1996.

———. *A Precious Fountain: Music in the Worship of an African American Catholic Community.* Collegeville, MN: Liturgical Press, 2004.

McKay, Heather A. *Sabbath and Synagogue: The Question of Sabbath Worship in Ancient Judaism.* Leiden: E. J. Brill, 1994.

McKenna, Edward J. "Chronicle: Use of Music in the Roman Sacramentary." *Worship* 65 (January 1991): 65–68.

McKinnon, James. *The Advent Project: The Later-Seventh-Century Creation of the Roman Mass Proper.* Berkeley: University of California Press, 2000.

————, ed. *Antiquity and the Middle Ages: From Ancient Greece to the 15th Century.* Music and Society Series. Englewood Cliffs, NJ: Prentice Hall, 1991.

————. "Antoine Chavasse and the Dating of Early Chant." *PMM* 1 (1992): 123–47.

————. "The Book of Psalms, Monasticism, and the Western Liturgy." In *The Place of the Psalms in the Intellectual Culture of the Middle Ages*, 43–58. Edited by Nancey Van Deusen. Albany: State University of New York Press, 1999.

————. "Christian Antiquity." In *Antiquity and the Middle Ages: From Ancient Greece to the 15th Century*, 68–87. Edited by James W. McKinnon. Music and Society Series. Englewood Cliffs, NJ: Prentice Hall, 1991.

————. "Compositional Planning in the Roman Mass Proper." *Studia Musicologica Academiae Scientiarum Hungaricae* 39: 2/4 (1998): 241–45.

————. "Desert Monasticism and the Later Fourth-Century Psalmodic Movement." *Music & Letters* 75:4 (November 1994): 505–21.

————. "Early Western Civilisation." In *Antiquity and the Middle Ages: From Ancient Greece to the 15th Century*, 1–44. Edited by James W. McKinnon. Music and Society. Englewood Cliffs, NJ: Prentice Hall, 1991.

————. "The Emergence of Gregorian Chant in the Carolingian Era." In *Antiquity and the Middle Ages: From Ancient Greece to the 15th Century*, 88–119. Edited by James W. McKinnon. Music and Society Series. Englewood Cliffs, NJ: Prentice Hall, 1991.

————. "The Exclusion of Musical Instruments from the Ancient Synagogue." *Proceedings of the Royal Musical Association* 106 (1979–80): 77–87.

————. "Festival, Text and Melody: Chronological Stages in the Life of Chant?" In *Chant and Its Peripheries*, 1–11. Edited by Bryan Gillingham and Paul Merkley. Musicological Studies 72. Ottawa: Institute of Medieval Music, 1998.

————. "The Fourth-Century Origin of the Gradual." *Early Music History* 7 (1987): 91–106.

———. "Gregorius presul composuit hunc libellum musicae artis." In *The Liturgy of the Medieval Church*, 673–94. Edited by Thomas J. Heffernan and E. Ann Matter. Kalamazoo, MI: Medieval Institute Publications, 2001.

———. "Lector Chant vs. Schola Chant: A Question of Historical Plausibility." In *Labore fratres in unum: Festschrift László Dobszay zum 60 Geburtstag*, 201–11. Edited by Janka Szendrei and David Hiley. Hildesheim: Georg Olms Verlag, 1995.

———. "Liturgical Psalmody in the Sermons of St. Augustine: An Introduction." In *The Study of Medieval Chant: Paths and Bridges, East and West*, 7–24. Edited by Peter Jeffery. Rochester, NY: Boydell Press, 2001.

———. "The Meaning of the Patristic Polemic against Musical Instruments." *Current Musicology* 1 (1985): 69–82.

———. *Music in Early Christian Literature*. Cambridge, UK: Cambridge University Press, 1987.

———. "On the Question of Psalmody in the Ancient Synagogue." *Early Music History* 6 (1986): 159–91.

———. "Properization: The Roman Mass." In *Cantus planus*, 15–22. Edited by László Dobszay. Budapest, 1993.

———. *The Temple, the Church Fathers, and Early Western Chant*. Brookfield, VT: Ashgate, 1998.

McMahon, J. Michael. "Establishing Criteria for Liturgical Songs: The Directory for Music and Liturgy." *Pastoral Music* 31:6 (August–September 2007): 18–19.

———. "General Instruction of the Roman Missal (2003)." In *The Song of the Assembly: Pastoral Music in Practice; Essays in Honor of Father Virgil C. Funk*, 87–90. Edited by Bari Colombari and Michael R. Prendergast. Studies in Church Music and Liturgy. Portland, OR: Pastoral Press, 2007.

McManus, Frederick R. "The Church at Prayer: Going beyond Rubrics to the Heart of the Church's Worship." *The Jurist* 53:2 (1993): 263–83.

———. "Gregorian Chant in Official Documents." In *Gregorian Chant in Pastoral Ministry Today*, 13–33. Washington, DC: Center for Ward Method Studies, 1986.

———. "Liturgical Law." In *Handbook for Liturgical Studies*, 1:399–420. Edited by Anscar J. Chupungco. Collegeville, MN: Liturgical Press, 1997.

———. "Liturgical Law and Difficult Cases." *Worship* 48 (1974): 347–66.

———. *Liturgical Participation: An Ongoing Assessment.* American Essays in Liturgy 10. Washington, DC: Pastoral Press, 1988.

———. *The Rites of Holy Week: Ceremonies, Preparations, Music, Commentary.* Paterson, NJ: St. Anthony Guild Press, 1956.

McMichael, Ralph N. "The Redemption of Creation: A Liturgical Theology. In *Creation and Liturgy*, 145–60. Washington, DC: Pastoral Press, 1993.

McNapsy, Clement J. "The Sacral in Liturgical Music." In *Revival of the Liturgy*, 163–90. Edited by Frederick R. McManus. New York: Herder & Herder, 1963.

Meeks, Wayne A. *The First Urban Christians: The Social World of the Apostle Paul.* New Haven, CT: Yale University Pres, 1983.

Megivern, James J., ed. *Official Catholic Teachings: Worship and Liturgy.* Wilmington, NC: Consortium Books, 1978.

Messenger, Ruth Ellis. "Processional Hymnody in the Later Middle Ages." *Transactions and Proceedings of the American Philological Association* 81 (1950): 185–99.

Messiaen, Olivier. *Messe de la Pentecôte.* Paris: Alphonse Leduc, 1951.

Metzger, Marcel. "The History of the Eucharistic Liturgy in Rome." In *Handbook for Liturgical Studies*, 3:103–32. Edited by Anscar J. Chupungco. Collegeville, MN: Liturgical Press, 1999.

Metzinger, Joseph P. "The Liturgical Function of the Entrance Song: An Examination of the Introits and Introit Tropes of the Manuscript Piacenza, Archivio Capitolare, 65." DMA diss., Catholic University of America, 1993.

Meyer, Ben F. "The Primacy of the Intended Sense of Texts." In *Lonergan's Hermeneutics*, 81–119. Washington, DC: Catholic University of America Press, 1989.

Migne, Jacques Paul, ed. *Patrologia Græca.* Paris: Migne, 1857–66.

———. *Patrologia Latina.* Rome: Typis Vaticanis, 1906–8.

Milner, Anthony. "The Instruction on Sacred Music." *Worship* 41 (1967): 322–33.

Missale Romanum. Editio princeps (1570). Monumenta liturgica Concilii Tridentini 2. Vatican City: Libreria Editrice Vaticana, 1998.

Mitchell, Leonel L. "The Liturgical Roots of Theology." In *Time and Community*, 243–54. Edited by J. Neil Alexander. Washington, DC: Pastoral Press, 1990.

Mitchell, Nathan D. "Celebrating the *Constitution on the Sacred Liturgy*." *Pastoral Music* 28:1 (October–November 2003): 19–27.

———. *Liturgy and the Social Sciences*. American Essays in Liturgy. Collegeville, MN: Liturgical Press, 1999.

———. "Ritual as Reading." In *Source and Summit*, 161–81. Edited by Joanne M. Pierce and Michael Downey. Collegeville, MN: Liturgical Press, 1999.

———. "Sacrosanctum Concilium (1963)." In *The Song of the Assembly: Pastoral Music in Practice; Essays in Honor of Father Virgil C. Funk*, 17–20. Edited by Bari Colombari and Michael R. Prendergast. Studies in Church Music and Liturgy. Portland, OR: Pastoral Press, 2007.

———. "Silent Music." *Worship* 67 (May 1993): 261–68.

Mitchell, Nathan D., and John F. Baldovin, eds. *Rule of Prayer, Rule of Faith*. Collegeville, MN: Liturgical Press, 1996.

Mohlberg, Leo Cunibert, ed. *Liber Sacramentorum Romanae Aeclesiae Ordinis Anni Circuli (Cod. Vat. Reg. lat. 316 / Paris Bibl. Nat. 7193, 41/56) (Sacramentarium Gelasianum)*. Rome: Herder, 1960.

Mohrmann, Christine. "Les origines de la latinité chrétienne à Rome." *Vigiliae Christianae* 3:3 (July 1949): 163–83.

Möller, H. "Research on the Antiphonar: Problems and Perspectives." *Journal of the Plainsong and Mediaeval Music Society* 10 (1987): 1–14.

Mooney, Christopher F. *Theology and Scientific Knowledge: Changing Models of God's Presence in the World*. Notre Dame, IN: University of Notre Dame Press, 1996.

Morin, G. "Le plus ancien lectionnaire ou Comes de l'Eglise romaine." *Revue bénédictine* 27 (1910): 41–74.

Morozowich, Mark. "Holy Thursday in the Jerusalem and Constantinopolitan Traditions: The Liturgical Celebrations from the Fourth to the Fourteenth Centuries." SEOD diss., Pontifical Oriental Institute, 2002.

Morrill, Bruce T., and Andrea Goodrich. "Liturgical Music: Bodies Proclaiming and Responding to the Word of God." In *Bodies of Worship*, 157–72. Collegeville, MN: Liturgical Press, 1999.

Mullett, Michael A. *The Catholic Reformation*. New York: Routledge, 1999.

Murphy, Roland E. "Reflections on Contextual Interpretation of the Psalms." In *The Shape and Shaping of the Psalter*, 21–28. Sheffield: JSOT Press, 1993.

Murrett, John C. *The Message of the Mass Melodies*. Collegeville, MN: Liturgical Press, 1960.

Music, D. W. *Hymnology: A Collection of Source Readings*. Lanham, MD: Scarecrow Press, 1996.

Myers, Helen, ed. *Ethnomusicology: An Introduction*. New York: W. W. Norton and Co., 1992.

Neunheuser, Burkhard. "Roman Genius Revisited." In *Liturgy for the New Millennium: A Commentary on the Revised Sacramentary*, 35–48. Edited by Mark R. Francis and Keith F. Pecklers. Collegeville, MN: Liturgical Press, 2000.

New Catholic Encyclopedia. 2nd ed. Edited at The Catholic University of America. Farmington Hills, MI: Gale, 2002.

New Dictionary of Sacramental Worship. Ed. Peter E. Fink. Collegeville, MN: Liturgical Press, 1990.

New Grove Dictionary of Music and Musicians. Edited by Stanley Sadie. London: Macmillan, 1980. 2nd ed. edited by Stanley Sadie and John Tyrrell. London: Macmillan, 2001.

Newman, David R. "Observations on Method in Liturgical Theology." *Worship* 57 (July 1983): 377–84.

New Oxford Dictionary of Music: Early Medieval up to 1300. Ed. Anselm Hughes. London: Oxford, 1954.

Nichols, Bridget. "The Bible in the Liturgy: A Hermeneutical Discussion of Faith and Language." *Studia Liturgica* 27:2 (1997): 200–16.

———. *Liturgical Hermeneutics: Interpreting Liturgical Rites in Performance*. Frankfurt am Main: Peter Lang, 1996.

Nketia, J. H. Kwabena. "Musical Interaction in Ritual Events." In *Music and the Experience of God*, 111–24. Edited by Mary Collins, David Power, and Mellonee Burnim. *Concilium* 202. Edinburgh: T. & T. Clark, 1989.

Nock, A. D. *Conversion: The Old and New in Religion from Alexander the Great to Augustine of Hippo*. Baltimore: Johns Hopkins University Press, 1998.

Noirot, Marcel. "La 'rationabilitas' des usages contraires aux lois liturgiques dequis la promulgation du Code de droit canonique." *L'Année Canonique* 1 (1952): 129–40.

———. "Réflexions canoniques sur des lois liturgiques depuis la promulgation du Code de droit canonique." *Maison-Dieu* 46 (1956): 137–53.

Nowacki, Edward. "Reading the Melodies of the Old Roman Mass Proper: A Hypothesis Defended." In *Western Plainchant in the First Millennium: Studies in the Medieval Liturgy and Its Music*, 319–30. Edited by Sean Gallagher et al. Burlington, VT: Ashgate Publishing, 2003.

O'Connell, J. B. *The Celebration of Mass: A Study of the Rubrics of the Roman Missal*. 3 vols. Milwaukee, MI: Bruce, 1940–41.

O'Grady, John F. *Models of Jesus*. Garden City, NY: Doubleday, 1981.

———. *Models of Jesus Revisited*. Mahwah, NJ: Paulist Press, 1994.

O'Keefe, John J., and R. R. Reno. *Sanctified Vision: An Introduction to Early Christian Interpretation of the Bible*. Baltimore: Johns Hopkins University Press, 2005.

Örsy, Ladislas. "Ecclesiastical Laws." In *The Code of Canon Law: A Text and Commentary*. Edited by James A. Coriden, Thomas J. Green, and Donald E. Heintschel. New York: Paulist Press, 1985.

———. "The Interpretation of Laws: New Variations on an Old Theme." *Studia Canonica* 17 (1983): 107–11.

———. "The Interpreter and His Art." *The Jurist* 40 (1980): 27–56.

———. *Theology and Canon Law: New Horizons for Legislation and Interpretation*. Collegeville, MN: Liturgical Press, 1990.

Ostdiek, Gilbert, ed. *Finding a Voice to Give God Praise: Essays in the Many Languages of Liturgy*. Introduction by Kathleen Hughes. Collegeville, MN: Liturgical Press, 2002.

———. "Ritual and Transformation: Reflections on Liturgy and the Social Sciences." *Liturgical Ministry* 2 (1993): 38–48.

Palazzo, Eric. "Confrontation du répertoire des tropes et du cycle iconographique du tropaire d'Autun." In *Tradizione dei trope*, 95–123.

———. *A History of Liturgical Books from the Beginning to the Thirteenth Century*. Translated by Madeleine Beaumont. Collegeville, MN: Liturgical Press, 1998.

———. "Le rôle des *libelli* dans la pratique liturgique du haut Moyen Age: Histoire et typologie." *Revue Mabbillon* 62 (1990): 9–36.

Parker, Elizabeth C. "Architecture as Liturgical Setting." In *The Liturgy of the Medieval Church*, 273–326. Edited by Thomas J. Heffernan and E. Ann Matter. Kalamazoo, MI: Medieval Institute Publications, 2001.

Parsons, Mark David. "Text, Tone, and Context: A Methodological Prolegomenon for a Theology of Liturgical Song." *Worship* 79:1 (January 2005): 54–69.

———. "'With Sighs Too Deep for Words': Liturgical Song as Metaphor." PhD diss., Graduate Theological Union, 2003.

Pass, David B. *Music and the Church: A Theology of Church Music.* Nashville, TN: Broadman Press, 1989.

Pecklers, Keith F. *Dynamic Equivalence: The Living Language of Christian Worship.* Collegeville, MN: Liturgical Press, 2003.

———. "History of the Roman Liturgy from the Sixteenth until the Twentieth Centuries." In *Handbook for Liturgical Studies*, 1:153–78. Edited by Anscar J. Chupungco. Collegeville, MN: Liturgical Press, 1997.

———. *The Unread Vision: The Liturgical Movement in the United States of America 1926–1955.* Collegeville, MN: Liturgical Press, 1998.

Pennington, Kenneth. "A Short History of Canon Law." http://faculty.cua.edu/pennington/Canon%20Law/ShortHistoryCanonLaw.htm.

Perrot, Charles. "Music in the Primitive Church." In *Liturgy: A Creative Tradition*, 3–9. *Concilium* 162. Mary Collins and David N. Power, eds. New York: Seabury, 1983.

Phan, Peter C. "Contemporary Theology and Inculturation in the United States." In *The Multicultural Church: A New Landscape in U. S. Theologies*, 109–30. Edited by William Cenkner. New York: Paulist Press, 1996.

———. "How Much Uniformity Can We Stand? How Much Unity Do We Want? Church and Worship in the Next Millennium." *Worship* 72 (May 1998): 194–210.

———. "The Liturgy of Life as the 'Summit and Source' of the Eucharistic Liturgy: Church Worship as Symbolization of the Liturgy of Life?" In *Incongruities: Who We Are and How We Pray*, 5–33. Edited by Timothy Fitzgerald and David Lysik. Collegeville, MN: Liturgical Press, 2000.

Pierce, Joanne M., and Michael Downey, eds. *Source and Summit: Commemorating Josef A. Jungmann, S.J.* Foreword by Balthasar Fischer. Collegeville, MN: Liturgical Press, 1999.

Pietri, Charles. "Liturgy, Culture and Society: The Example of Rome at the End of the Ancient World (Fourth–Fifth Centuries)." In *Liturgy: A Creative Tradition*, 38–45. *Concilium* 162. Mary Collins and David N. Power, eds. New York: Seabury, 1983.

Piil, Mary Alice. "The Local Church as the Subject of the Action of the Eucharist." In *Shaping English Liturgy*, 173–96. Washington, DC: Pastoral Press, 1990.

Pinell i Pons, Jordi. "History of the Liturgies of the Non-Roman West." In *Handbook for Liturgical Studies*, 1:179–98. Edited by Anscar J. Chupungco. Collegeville, MN: Liturgical Press, 1997.

Pirrotta, Nino. *Music and Culture in Italy from the Middle Ages to the Baroque: A Collection of Essays*. Cambridge, MA: Harvard University Press, 1984.

———. "The Oral and Written Traditions of Music." In *Music and Culture in Italy from the Middle Ages to the Baroque: A Collection of Essays*, 72–79. Cambridge, MA: Harvard University Press, 1984.

Planchart, Alejandro Enrique. "On the Nature of Transmission and Change in Trope Repertories." *Journal of the American Musicological Society* 41 (Summer 1988): 214–15, 220.

———. *The Repertory of Tropes at Winchester*. 2 vols. Princeton, NJ: Princeton University Press, 1977.

Pond, Edward Wiatt. "A Select Study of the Liturgical Music of Bernard Huijbers: The Theological Principles Which Are Fundamental to His Music, and the Means by Which He Translated These Principles into Music for the Assembly." DMA diss., Catholic University of America, 1991.

Pontifical Biblical Commission. *The Interpretation of the Bible in the Church*. Boston: Pauline Books and Media, 1993.

Pottie, Charles. *A More Profound Alleluia: Gelineau and Routley on Music in Christian Worship*. Washington, DC: Pastoral Press, 1984.

Power, Brian Edward. "The Polyphonic Introits of 'Trento, archivio capitolare, MS 93': A Stylistic Analysis." PhD diss., University of Toronto, 1999.

Power, David N. "Cult to Culture: The Liturgical Foundation of Theology." *Worship* 54 (November 1980): 482–95.

———. *The Eucharistic Mystery: Revitalizing the Tradition*. New York: Seabury, 1992. Reprint, New York: Crossroad, 1997.

———. "Liturgical Praxis: A New Consciousness at the Eye of Worship." *Worship* 61:4 (July 1987): 290–304.

———. "Liturgy as an Act of Communication and Communion: Cultural and Practical Implications in an Age Becoming Digital." *Mission* 3:1 (1996): 43–62.

———. "People at Liturgy." In *Twenty Years of Concilium—Retrospect and Prospect*, 8–14. *Concilium* 170. Edited by P. Brand, E. Schillebeeckx, and A. Weiler. Edinburgh: T. and T. Clark, 1983.

———. *Sacrament: The Language of God's Giving*. A Herder & Herder Book. New York: Crossroad, 1999.

————. *The Sacrifice We Offer: The Tridentine Dogma and Its Reinterpretation.* Edinburgh: T. and T. Clark, 1987.

————. "Theology of Eucharistic Celebration." In *Handbook for Liturgical Studies*, 3:321–66. Edited by Anscar J. Chupungco. Collegeville, MN: Liturgical Press, 1999.

————, ed. *The Times of Celebration. Concilium* 142. New York: Seabury, 1981.

————. "Two Expressions of Faith: Worship and Theology." *Liturgical Experience of Faith*, 95–103. *Concilium* 82. Edited by H. Schmidt and David Power. New York: Herder & Herder, 1973.

————. "Unripe Grapes: The Critical Function of Liturgical Theology." *Worship* 52 (September 1978): 386–99.

————. *Unsearchable Riches: The Symbolic Nature of Liturgy.* New York: Pueblo Publishing Company, 1984.

————. *"The Word of the Lord": Liturgy's Use of Scripture.* Maryknoll: Orbis, 2001.

————. *Worship, Culture and Theology.* Washington, DC: Pastoral Press, 1990.

————. "Worship in a New World: Some Theological Considerations." In *The Changing Face of Jewish and Christian Worship in North America*, 161–83. Edited by Paul F. Bradshaw and Lawrence A. Hoffman. Notre Dame, IN: University of Notre Dame Press, 1991.

Power, David N., and Herman Schmidt, eds. *Liturgical Experience of Faith. Concilium* 82. New York: Herder & Herder, 1973.

————. *Politics and Liturgy. Concilium* 92. New York: Herder & Herder, 1974.

Quasten, J. *Music and Worship in Pagan and Christian Antiquity.* Translated by Boniface Ramsey. NPM Studies in Church Music and Liturgy. Washington, DC: National Association of Pastoral Musicians, 1983.

Quinn, Franck C. "Ministers, Music, and the New Sacramentary." *Pastoral Music* 18 (February–March 1994): 17–22.

————. "Music in Catholic Worship: The Effect of Ritual on Music and Music on Ritual." *Proceedings of the Annual Meeting of the North American Academy of Liturgy* (1989): 161–76.

Qureshi, Regula Burckhardt. "Musical Sound and Contextual Input: A Performance Model for Musical Analysis." *Ethnomusicology* 31:1 (1987): 56–86.

Rahner, Karl. "Towards a Fundamental Theological Interpretation of Vatican II." *Theological Studies* 40 (1979): 716–27.

Ramis, Gabriel. "The Eucharistic Celebration in the Non-Roman West." In *Handbook for Liturgical Studies*, 3:245–62. Edited by Anscar J. Chupungco. Collegeville, MN: Liturgical Press, 1999.

———. "Liturgical Books of the Non-Roman West." In *Handbook for Liturgical Studies*, 1:315–30. Edited by Anscar J. Chupungco. Collegeville, MN: Liturgical Press, 1997.

———. "Liturgical Families in the West." In *Handbook for Liturgical Studies*, 1:25–32. Edited by Anscar J. Chupungco. Collegeville, MN: Liturgical Press, 1997.

Rasmussen, Niels K. *Les Pontificaux du haut Moyen Âge: Genèse du livre liturgique de l'évêque.* Spiciligium sacrum lovaniense. Lovain, 1998.

———. "Quelques réflexions sur la théologie des tropes." In *Research on Tropes*, 77–88. Edited by Gunilla Iversen. Konferenser 8. Stockholm: Almquist & Wiksell, 1983.

Ray, Walter. "Toward a Narrative-Critical Approach to Early Liturgy." In *Studia Liturgica Diversa*. Edited by Maxwell E. Johnson and L. Edward Philipps. Portland, OR: Pastoral Press, 2004.

Regan, Patrick. "The Three Days and the Forty Days." *Worship* 54:1 (1980): 2–18.

Reid, Duncan. *Energies of the Spirit: Trinitarian Models in Eastern Orthodox and Western Theology.* New York: Oxford University Press, 1997.

Reier, Ellen Jane. "The Introit Trope Repertory at Nevers: MSS Paris B.N. Lat. 9449 and Paris B.N. N.A. Lat. 1235." 3 vols. PhD diss., University of California, Berkeley, 1981.

Rendler-McQueeny, Elaine. "Music in Catholic Worship (1972): and Liturgical Music Today (1982)." In *The Song of the Assembly: Pastoral Music in Practice; Essays in Honor of Father Virgil C. Funk*, 25–27. Edited by Bari Colombari and Michael R. Prendergast. Studies in Church Music and Liturgy. Portland, OR: Pastoral Press, 2007.

Renoux, Athanase. *Le Codex arménien Jérusalem 121.* Vol. 2. *Édition comparée du texte et de deux autres manuscrits.* Patrologia Orientalis 36.2:168. Turnhout, 1969.

Reynolds, Roger. "The Organisation, Law and Liturgy of the Western Church, 700–900." In *The New Cambridge Medieval History*, 2:587–621. Edited by Rosamond McKitterick. Cambridge, UK: Cambridge University Press, 1991.

Rice, Timothy. "Toward the Remodeling of Ethnomusicology." *Ethnomusicology* 31:3 (1987): 469–88.

Richstatter, Thomas. "Changing Style of Liturgical Law." *The Jurist* 38 (1978): 415–25.

———. *Liturgical Law Today: New Style, New Spirit.* Chicago: Franciscan Herald Press, 1977.

———. "Obedience to Liturgical Law: A Historical Study of the Theological Context of Roman Catholic Liturgical Law before and after the Second Vatican Council." DST diss., Institut Catholique de Paris, 1976.

Ricoeur, Paul. *Interpretation Theory: Discourse and the Surplus of Meaning.* Fort Worth: Texas Christian University Press, 1976.

———. "The Model of the Text: Meaningful Action Considered as a Text." In *Hermeneutics and the Human Sciences: Essays on Language, Action and Interpretation,* 197–221. Edited and translated by John B. Thompson. Cambridge, UK: Cambridge University Press, 1981.

Ridder, R. Todd. "Antiphons for Paschal Triduum-Easter in the Medieval Office." *Worship* 70 (March 1996): 187–89.

———. "Musical and Theological Patterns Involved in the Transmission of Mass Chants for the Five Oldest Marian Feasts: An Examination of Proper Chants and Tropes in a Select Group of Medieval Manuscripts." 2 vols. PhD diss., Catholic University of America, 1993.

Righetti, Mario. *Manuale di Storia Liturgica.* 4 vols. Milan: Editrice Àncora, 1950–56.

Roederer, Charlotte Dianne. "Eleventh-Century Aquitanian Chant: Studies Relating to a Local Repertory of Processional Antiphons." PhD diss., Yale University, 1971.

Romita, Fiorenzo. *Codex Juris Musicae Sacrae.* Rome: Desclée, 1952.

———. *Ius musicae liturgicae.* Turin: Marietti, 1936.

Routley, Erik. *Christian Hymns Observed.* London: A. R. Mowbray, 1983.

———. *Church Music and Theology.* Philadelphia: Muhlenberg Press, 1960.

———. *Words, Music and the Church.* Nashville, TN: Abingdon Press, 1968.

Rouwhorst, Gerard. "La célébration de l'eucharistie selon les Actes de Thomas." In *Omnes Circumadstantes: Contributions towards a History of the Role of the People in the Liturgy.* Edited by Charles Caspers and Marc Schneiders. Kampen: Uitgeversmaatschappij J. H. Kok, 1990.

Rowley, H.H. *Worship in Ancient Israel: Its Forms and Meaning.* Philadelphia: Fortress Press; London: SPCK, 1967.

Ruff, Anthony. "The Music 'Specially Suited to the Roman Liturgy': On the One Hand . . ." *Pastoral Music* 32:5 (June–July 2008): 15–16.

———. *Sacred Music and Liturgical Reform: Treasures and Transformations.* Chicago: Liturgy Training Publications, 2007.

Saliers, Don E. "The Integrity of Sung Prayer." *Worship* 55 (July 1981): 290–303.

———. *Music and Theology.* Horizons in Theology. Nashville, TN: Abingdon Press, 2007.

———. *Worship as Theology: Foretaste of Glory Divine.* Nashville, TN: Abingdon Press, 1994.

———. *Worship Come to Its Senses.* Nashville, TN: Abingdon Press, 1996.

Saxer, Victor. "L'utilisation pour la liturgie de l'espace urbain et suburbain, l'exemple de Rome dans l'Antiquité et le haut Moyen Age." *Actes du XIᵉ Congrès international d'Archéologie Chrétienne.* Rome, 1989.

Schaefer, Edward. *Catholic Music through the Ages: Balancing the Needs of a Worshipping Church.* Chicago: Liturgy Training Publications, 2008.

Schaefer, Mary M. "Latin Mass Commentaries from the Ninth through the Twelfth Centuries: Chronology and Theology." In *Fountain of Life.* Edited by Gerard Austin. In memory of Niels K. Rasmussen. Washington, DC: Pastoral Press, 1991.

Schillebeeckx, Edward. "Liturgy and Theology." In *Revelation and Theology.* Vol. 1. New York: Sheed and Ward, 1967.

Schmemann, Alexander. *The Eucharist: The Sacrament of the Kingdom.* Crestwood, NY: St. Vladimir's Seminary Press, 1988.

———. *Introduction to Liturgical Theology.* London: Faith Press, 1966.

———. "Liturgical Theology: Its Task and Method." *St. Vladimir's Seminary Quarterly* 1: 4 (October 1957): 16–27.

———. "Liturgy and Theology." *The Greek Orthodox Theological Review* 17 (Spring 1972): 86–100.

———. *Liturgy and Tradition: Theological Reflections of Alexander Schmemann.* Edited by Thomas Fisch. Crestwood, NY: St. Vladimir's Seminary Press, 1990.

———. "Theology and Liturgical Tradition." In *Worship in Scripture and Tradition,* 165–78. Edited by Massey Shepherd. New York: Oxford University Press, 1963.

Schmidt, Hermanus A. P. *Hebdomada Sancta.* 2 vols. Rome: Herder, 1956–57.

Schmitz, Walter J. "The New Holy Week Ordo." STD diss. abstract. The Catholic University of America Studies in Sacred Theology (Second Series) 96. Washington, DC: The Catholic University of America Press, 1956.

Schubart, Wilhelm, and Carl Schmidt, eds. *Acts of Paul*. Hamburg: J. J. Augustin, 1936.

Schueller, Herbert M. *The Idea of Music: An Introduction to Musical Aesthetics in Antiquity and the Middle Ages*. Early Drama, Art, and Music Monograph Series 9. Kalamazoo, MI: Medieval Institute Publications, 1988.

Schutz, Alfred. "Making Music Together: A Study in Social Relationship." *Social Research* 18:1 (1951): 76–97.

Schweibert, Jonathan. "Evading Rituals in New Testament Studies." *CSSR Bulletin* 33:1 (February 2004): 10–13.

Scicolone, Ildebrando. "La Memoria dell'Istituzione dell'Eucaristia." In *La Celebrazione del Triduo Pasquale: Anamnesis e Mimesis*, 55–69. Studia Anselmiana 102. Analecta Liturgica 14. Edited by Ildebrando Scicolone. Rome: Pontificio Ateneo S. Anselmo, 1990.

Searle, Mark. "*Fons vitae*: A Case Study in the Use of Liturgy as a Theological Source." In *Fountain of Life*. Edited by Gerard Austin. In memory of Niels K. Rasmussen. Washington, DC: Pastoral Press, 1991.

———. "Introduction to the Semiotics of Liturgy." Presented to Ritual-Language-Action: Social Sciences Study Group of the North American Academy of Liturgy. Nashville, TN. 2–5 January, 1990.

———. "New Tasks, New Methods: The Emergence of Pastoral Liturgical Studies." *Worship* 57:4 (1983): 291–308.

———. "Ritual and Music: A Theory of Liturgy and Implications for Music." *Assembly 12* (1986): 314–17.

———. "Semper Reformanda: The Opening and Closing Rites of the Mass." In *Shaping English Liturgy*, 53–92. Edited by Peter C. Finn and James M. Schellman. Washington, DC: Pastoral Press, 1990.

Searle, Mark, and Gerard Lukken. *Semiotics and Church Architecture*. Kampen: Kok Pharos, 1993.

Seasoltz, R. Kevin. "Anthropology and Liturgical Theology: Search for a Compatible Methodology." In *Liturgy and Human Passage*, 3–13. *Concilium* 112. Edited by David N. Power and Luis Maldonado. New York: Seabury, 1979.

———. *New Liturgy, New Laws*. Collegeville, MN: Liturgical Press, 1980.

Seeger, Anthony. "Ethnography of Music." In *Ethnomusicology: An Introduction*. Edited by Helen Myers. New York: W. W. Norton and Co., Inc., 1992.

Senn, Frank C. *Christian Worship and Its Cultural Setting*. Philadelphia: Fortress Press, 1983.

―――. *The People's Work: A Social History of the Liturgy*. Minneapolis: Fortress Press, 2006.

―――. "Worship, Doctrine, and Life: Liturgical Theology, Theologies of Worship, and Doxological Theology." *Currents in Theology and Mission* 9 (February 1982): 11–21.

Shepherd, Massey H. "The Liturgical Reform of Damasus I." In *Kyriakon: Festschrift Johannes Quasten*, 2:847–63. Vol. 2. Edited by Patrick Granfield and Josef A. Jungmann. Aschendorff: Münster Westfalen, 1970.

Sherman, Anthony F. "A New Resource: The *Pastoral Introduction to the Order of Mass*." *Pastoral Music*. 27:5 (June–July 2003): 40–42.

Silagi, G. *Liturgische Tropen*. Münchener Beiträge zur Mediävistik und Renaissance-Forschung 36. Munich, 1986.

Silbiger, Alexander. "The Roman Frescobaldi Tradition, c. 1640–1670." *Journal of the American Musicological Society*. 33:1 (Spring 1980): 42–87.

Silverberg, Ann Louise. "Caecilian Reform in Baltimore, 1868–1903." PhD diss., University of Illinois at Urbana-Champaign, 1992.

Sirota, Victoria. "An Exploration of Music as Theology." *The Arts in Religious and Theological Studies* 5:3 (Summer 1993): 24–28.

Skelley, Michael. *The Liturgy of the World: Karl Rahner's Theology of Worship*. Collegeville, MN: Liturgical Press, 1991.

Slaa, Willibrod. "Liturgical Law: Existence, Exigency and Pastoral Dimension of Conciliar and Post Conciliar Liturgical Legislation." JCD diss., Pontifical Urban University, 1983.

Sloboda, John A., ed. *Generative Processes in Music: The Psychology of Performance, Improvisation, and Composition*. Oxford: Clarendon, 1988.

Slough, Rebecca Jo. "'Let Every Tongue, by Art Refined, Mingle Its Softest Notes with Mine': An Exploration of Hymn-Singing Events and Dimensions of Knowing." In *Religious and Social Ritual: Interdisciplinary Exploration*, 175–208. Edited by Michael B. Aune and Valerie De Martinis. Albany: State University of New York Press, 1996.

―――. "A Method for Describing the Practice and Theology of Worship: A Study of Prayer in Three Free Church Congregations." PhD diss., Graduate Theological Union, Berkeley, CA, 1989.

Sloyan, Gerard. "The Lectionary as a Context for Interpretation." *Interpretation* 31 (1977): 131–38.

Small, Christopher. *Musicking: The Meanings of Performing and Listening.* Hanover, NH: University Press of New England, 1988.

Smith, Dennis E. *From Symposium to Eucharist: The Banquet in the Early Christian World.* Minneapolis: Fortress Press, 2003.

Smith, J. A. "The Ancient Synagogue, the Early Church, and Singing." *Music and Letters* 65:1 (January 1984): 1–16.

———. "First-Century Christian Singing and Its Relationship to Contemporary Jewish Religious Song." *Music and Letters* 75 (February 1994): 1–15.

Smith, William Sheppard. *Musical Aspects of the New Testament.* Amsterdam: Uitgeverij w. Ten Have N. V., 1962.

Smolarski, Dennis C. *The General Instruction of the Roman Missal, 1969–2002: A Commentary.* Collegeville, MN: Liturgical Press, 2003.

Smulders, Piet. "Sacramenta et Ecclesia, Ius Canonicum—Cultus—Pneuma." *Periodica* 48 (1959): 3–53.

The Snowbird Statement on Catholic Liturgical Music. Salt Lake City, UT: Madeleine Institute, 1995.

Snyder, Gradon F. *Ante-Pacem: Archaeological Evidence of Church Life before Constantine.* Rev. ed. Macon, GA: Mercer University Press, 2003.

Sodi, Manlio, and Achille Maria Triacca, eds. *Missale Romanum Editio Princeps (1570).* Vatican City: Libreria Editrice Vaticana, 1998.

Sodi, Manlio, and Alessandro Toniolo. *Concordantia et indices Missalis Romani. Editio typica tertia.* Vatican City: Libreria Editrice Vaticana, 2002.

Söhngen, Oskar. "Music and Theology: A Systematic Approach." *Journal of the American Academy of Religion Thematic Studies* 50:1 (1983): 1–19.

Southern, E. *The Buxheim Organ Book.* Brooklyn, NY, 1963.

Sparksman, Brian Joseph. "The Minister of Music in the Western Church: A Canonical-Historical Study." JCD diss., Catholic University of America, 1981.

Speelman, Willem Marie. *The Generation of Meaning in Liturgical Songs: A Semiotic Analysis of Five Liturgical Songs as Syncretic Discourses.* Kampen, The Netherlands: Kok Pharos, 1995.

Spencer, Jon Michael. *Theological Music: Introduction to Theo-Musicology.* New York: Greenwood Press, 1991.

Sperry-White, Grant, ed. *Testamentum Domini*. Cambridge, UK: Grove Books Ltd., 1991.

Spinks, Bryan D., ed. *The Place of Christ in Liturgical Prayer: Trinity, Christology, and Liturgical Theology*, 127–94. Collegeville, MN: Liturgical Press, 2008.

Springer, Carl P. E. "Ambrose's *Veni redemptor gentium*: The Aesthetics of Antiphony." *Jahrbuch für Antike und Christentum* 34 (1991): 76–87.

Stäblein, Bruno, ed. *Monumenta monodica medii aevi*. Kassel: Bärenreiter, 1956–.

Stansbury-O'Donnell, Mark Douglas. "The Shape of the Church: The Relationship of Architecture, Art, and Liturgy at the Cathedral of Trier." 2 vols. PhD diss., Yale University, 1990.

Stark, Rodney. *The Rise of Christianity: How the Obscure, Marginal Jesus Movement Became the Dominant Religious Force in the Western World in a Few Centuries*. Princeton, NJ: Princeton University Press, 1996.

Staufer, Anita, ed. *Worship and Culture in Dialogue*. Geneva: Lutheran World Federation, 1994.

Stefani, Gino. "L'espressione vocale nella liturgia primitiva." *Ephemerides Liturgicae* 84 (1970): 97–112.

Steiner, Ruth. "Epulari autem et gaudere oportebat." In *Western Plainchant in the First Millennium: Studies in the Medieval Liturgy and Its Music*, 331–50. Edited by Sean Gallagher et al. Burlington, VT: Ashgate Publishing, 2003.

———. *Studies in Gregorian Chant*. Aldershot, UK: Ashgate, 1999.

Stevenson, Kenneth. *The First Rites: Worship in the Early Church*. Collegeville, MN: Liturgical Press, 1989.

———. *Jerusalem Revisited: The Liturgical Meaning of Holy Week*. Washington, DC: Pastoral Press, 1988.

———. "Lex Orandi and Lex Credendi—Strange Bedfellows? Some Reflections on Worship and Doctrine." *Scottish Journal of Theology* 39 (1986): 225–41.

———. "A Liturgist's Response." In *The Interpretation of the Bible in the Church*, 156–63. London: SCM Press, 1995.

———. "On Keeping Holy Week." *Theology* 89 (January 1986): 32–38.

Stewart-Sykes, Alistair, ed. *The Didascalia Apostolorum: An English Version with Introduction and Annotation*. Turnhout, Belgium: Brepols, 2009.

———. *Hippolytus: On the Apostolic Tradition*. Crestwood, NY: St. Vladimir's Seminary Press, 2001.

Stoltzfus, Philip. *Theology as Performance: Music, Aesthetics, and God in Western Thought*. New York: T. & T. Clark, 2006.

Strange, James Riley. *The Emergence of the Christian Basilica in the Fourth Century*. International Studies in Formative Christianity and Judaism. Binghamton, NY: Global Publications, 2000.

Strickland, Amy Jill. "In Essentials, Unity: Liturgical Law and the *General Instruction*." *Pastoral Music*. 27:5 (June–July 2003): 37–39.

Stringer, Martin D. "Liturgy and Anthropology: The History of a Relationship." *Worship* 63 (1989): 503–21.

———. "Text, Context and Performance: Hermeneutics and the Study of Worship." *Scottish Journal of Theology* 53:3 (2000): 365–79.

Stroik, Christopher V. *Path, Portal, Path: Architecture for the Rites*. Meeting House Essays 10. Chicago: Liturgy Training Publications, 1999.

Studer, Basil. "Liturgical Documents of the First Four Centuries." In *Handbook for Liturgical Studies*, 1:199–224. Edited by Anscar J. Chupungco. Collegeville, MN: Liturgical Press, 1997.

———. "Liturgy and the Fathers." In *Handbook for Liturgical Studies*, 1:53–80. Edited by Anscar J. Chupungco. Collegeville, MN: Liturgical Press, 1997.

Swain, Joseph. "An Apology for the Hymn." *America* 156:19 (23 May 1987): 421–23.

Tabor, Jerry, ed. *Otto Laske: Navigating New Musical Horizons*. Contributions to the Study of Music and Dance 53. Westport, CT: Greenwood Press, 1999.

Taft, Robert F. *Beyond East and West: Problems in Liturgical Understanding*. 2nd rev. enlarged ed. Rome: Edizioni Orientalia Christiana, 1997.

———. *The Byzantine Rite: A Short History*. American Essays in Liturgy. Collegeville, MN: Liturgical Press, 1992.

———. "Liturgy as Theology." *Worship* 56 (March 1982): 113–17.

———. *The Liturgy of the Hours in East and West*. 2nd rev. ed. Collegeville, MN: Liturgical Press, 1986.

———. "What Does Liturgy Do? Toward a Soteriology of Liturgical Celebration: Some Theses." *Worship* 66:3 (1992): 194–211.

Taft, Robert F., and Gabrielle Winkler, eds. *Comparative Liturgy Fifty Years after Anton Baumstark (1872–1948)*. Orientalia Christiana Analecta 265. Rome: Pontifical Oriental Institute, 2001.

Talley, Thomas J. "Afterthoughts on *The Origins of the Liturgical Year*." In *Western Plainchant in the First Millennium: Studies in the Medieval Liturgy and Its Music*, 1–10. Edited by Sean Gallagher et al. Burlington, VT: Ashgate Publishing, 2003.

———. "The Future of the Past." In *Worship: Reforming Tradition*, 143–55. Washington, DC: Pastoral Press, 1990.

———. "History and Eschatology in the Primitive Pascha." In *Worship: Reforming Tradition*, 75–86. Washington, DC: Pastoral Press, 1990.

———. "Liturgical Time in the Ancient Church: The State of Research." In *Liturgical Time*, 34–51. Edited by Wiebe Vos and Geoffrey Wainwright. Rotterdam: Liturgical Ecumenical Center Trust, 1982. *Studia Liturgica* 14:2–4 (1982).

———. "The Liturgical Year: Pattern and Proclamation." In *Worship: Reforming Tradition*, 125–42. Washington, DC: Pastoral Press, 1990.

———. *The Origins of the Liturgical Year*. 2nd emended ed. Collegeville, MN: Liturgical Press, 1991.

Tanner, Norman P. *The Councils of the Church: A Short History*. New York: Crossroad, 2001.

———, ed. *Decrees of the Ecumenical Councils*. London: Sheed & Ward; Washington, DC: Georgetown University Press, 1990.

Tarchnischvili, Michel, ed. *Le grand lectionnaire de l'Église de Jérusalem (Ve– VIIIe siècle)*. Louvain : Secréteriat du Corpus SCO, 1959–60.

Taylor, Joan E. *Christians and the Holy Places: The Myth of Jewish-Christian Origins*. Oxford: Clarendon Press, 1993.

Taylor, Richard. *How to Read a Church: A Guide to Symbols, Images, and Rituals in Churches and Cathedrals*. Mahwah, NJ: Paulist Press, 2005.

Terrien, Samuel. *The Psalms: Strophic Structure and Theological Commentary*. Grand Rapids, MI: William B. Eerdmans, 2003.

Thompson, Bard. *Liturgies of the Western Church*. Philadelphia: Fortress Press, 1980.

Tietze, Christoph. "Graduale or Missale: The Confusion Resolved." *Sacred Music*: 133:4 (Winter 2006): 4–13.

———. *Hymn Introits for the Liturgical Year: The Origin and Early Development of the Latin Texts*. Chicago: Liturgy Training Publications, 2005.

Treitler, Leo. *With Voice and Pen: Coming to Know Medieval Song and How It Was Made.* New York: Oxford University Press, 2003.

Troelsgård, Christian. "Methodological Problems in Comparative Studies of Liturgical Chant." In *Comparative Liturgy Fifty Years after Anton Baumstark (1872–1948).* Edited by Robert F. Taft and Gabriele Winkler. Orientalia Christiana Analecta 265. Rome: Pontifical Oriental Institute, 2001.

Truitt, Gordon E. "Musicam Sacram (1967)." In *The Song of the Assembly: Pastoral Music in Practice; Essays in Honor of Father Virgil C. Funk,* 21–24. Edited by Bari Colombari and Michael R. Prendergast. Studies in Church Music and Liturgy. Portland, OR: Pastoral Press, 2007.

Turner, Paul. *Confirmation: The Baby in Solomon's Court.* Rev. and updated ed. Chicago: Liturgy Training Publications, 2006.

Turner, Victor. "Liminality and Communitas." In *Readings in Ritual Studies,* 511–19. Edited by Ronald Grimes. Englewood Cliffs, NJ: Prentice Hall, 1995.

———. *The Ritual Process: Structure and Anti-Structure.* London: Routledge, 1969.

———. "Ritual, Tribal and Catholic." *Worship* 50 (1976): 504–26.

Vagaggini, Cypriano. "Fede a dimensione pastorale della teologia." *Seminarium* 22 (1970): 908–23.

———. "Riflesioni in prospettiva teologica sui dieci anni di riforma liturgica e sulla aporia del problema liturgico in questo momento." *Rivista Liturgica* 41 (1974): 35–72.

———. *Theological Dimensions of the Liturgy: A General Treatise on the Theology of the Liturgy.* Translated by Leonard J. Doyle and W. A. Jurgens. Collegeville, MN: Liturgical Press, 1976.

Valenziano, Crispino. "Liturgy and Anthropology: The Meaning of the Question and the Method for Answering It." In *Handbook for Liturgical Studies,* 2:189–226. Edited by Anscar J. Chupungco. Collegeville, MN: Liturgical Press, 1998.

———. "'Mimesis Anamnesis' spazio-temporale per il triduo pasquale." In *La Celebrazione del Triduo Pasquale: Anamnesis e Mimesis,* 13–54. Studia Anselmiana 102. Analecta Liturgica 14. Edited by Ildebrando Scicolone. Rome: Pontificio Ateneo S. Anselmo, 1990.

Vallée, Gérard. *The Shaping of Christianity: The History and Literature of the Formative Centuries (100–800).* Mahwah, NJ: Paulist Press, 1999.

Van der Werf, H. *The Emergence of Gregorian Chant: A Comparative Study of Ambrosian, Roman, and Gregorian Chant*. Rochester, NY: H. van der Werf, 1983.

Van Deusen, Nancy, ed. *The Place of the Psalms in the Intellectual Culture of the Middle Ages*. Albany: State University of New York Press, 1999.

Van de Wiel, Constant. *History of Canon Law*. Louvain Theological and Pastoral Monographs 5. Louvain: Peeters, 1991.

Van Dijk, S. J. P. "The Old-Roman Rite." In *Studia Patristica*, 5:185–205. Edited by F. L. Cross. Berlin: Akademie-Verlag, 1962.

———, ed. *Sources of the Modern Roman Liturgy: The Ordinals by Haymo of Faversham and Related Documents (1243–1307)*. 2 vols. Leiden: E. J. Brill, 1963.

———. "The Urban and Papal Rites in Seventh- and Eighth-Century Rome." *Sacris erudiri: Jaarboek voor Godsdienstwetenschappe* 12 (1961): 411–87.

Van Dijk, S. J. P., and J. Hazelden Walker. *The Ordinal of the Papal Court from Innocent III to Boniface VIII and Related Documents*. Spicilegium Friburgense 22. Fribourg: University Press, 1975.

———. *The Origins of the Modern Roman Liturgy: The Liturgy of the Papal Court and the Franciscan Order in the Thirteenth Century*. Westminster, MD: Newman Press; London: Darton, Longman & Todd, 1960.

Van Wye, Benjamin. "Ritual Use of the Organ in France." *Journal of the American Musicological Society* 33:2 (Summer 1980): 287–325.

Vellian, Jacob, ed. *The Romanization Tendency*. The Syrian Churches Series 8. Kottayam, India: K. P. Press, 1975.

Verheul, Ambrosius. *Introduction to the Liturgy: Towards a Theology of Worship*. Collegeville, MN: Liturgical Press, 1968.

Vermes, G. *The Dead Sea Scrolls in English*. Revised complete edition. London: Penguin Books, 2004.

Vidal, Theodore M. *Liturgy Wars: Ritual Theory and Protestant Reform in Nineteenth-Century Zurich*. New York: Routledge, 2003.

Viladesau, Richard R. "Melody and Meaning: Music in Worship." *Church* 6 (Spring 1990): 19–23.

———. *Theology and the Arts: Encountering God through Music, Art and Rhetoric*. New York: Paulist Press, 2000.

Vincie, Catherine. *Celebrating the Divine Mystery: A Primer in Liturgical Theology*. Collegeville, MN: Liturgical Press, 2008.

Vogel, Cyrille. *Medieval Liturgy: An Introduction to the Sources.* Translated and revised by William. G. Storey and Niels. K. Rasmussen, with the assistance of John K. Brooks-Leonard. NPM Studies in Church Music and Liturgy. Washington, DC: Pastoral Press, 1986.

Vogel, Cyrille, and R. Elze. *Le Pontifical romano-germanique du Xe siècle.* Studi e Testi 226, 227, 269. Vatican City, 1963–1972.

Vogel, Dwight W., ed. *Primary Sources of Liturgical Theology: A Reader.* Collegeville, MN: Liturgical Press, 2000.

Volp, Rainer. "Space as Text: The Problem of Hermeneutics in Church Architecture." *Studia Liturgica* 24 (1994): 168–77.

Wagner, Peter J. *Einführung in die gregorianischen Melodien: ein Handbuch der Choralwissenschaft.* I: *Ursprung und Entwicklung der liturgischen Gesangformen bis zum Ausgang des Mittelalters.* Leipzig, 1901.

———. "Introduction to the Gregorian Melodies." *Caecelia* 84 (1957), 85 (1958).

Wainwright, Geoffrey. "The Church as Worshipping Community." *Pro Ecclesia* 3:1 (1993): 56–67.

———. *Doxology: The Praise of God in Worship, Doctrine and Life; A Systematic Theology.* New York: Oxford University Press, 1980.

———. "Der Gottesdienst als 'Locus Theologicus,' oder: Der Gottesdienst als Quelle und Thema der Theologie." *Kerygma und Dogma* 28 (1982): 248–58.

———. "Tradition as a Liturgical Act." In *The Quadrilog: Tradition and the Future of Ecumenism*, 129–46. Collegeville, MN: Liturgical Press, 1994.

Walsh, P. G., trans. *Pliny: Complete Letters.* New York: Oxford University Press, 2009.

Ward, Anthony. "Euchology for the Mass 'In Cena Domini' of the 2000 *Missale Romanum.*" *Notitiae* 45:11–12 (2008): 611–34.

Ward, Daniel J. " Liturgy and Law." *Proceedings of the Canon Law Society of America* 44 (1982): 184–97.

Warren, F. E. *The Liturgy and Ritual of the Ante-Nicene Church.* London: Society for Promoting Christian Knowledge; New York: E. & J. B. Young & Co., 1897.

Watson, J. R. "The Language of Hymns: Some Contemporary Problems." In *Language and the Worship of the Church*, 174–95. New York: St. Martin's Press, 1990.

Weakland, Rembert G. "The Song of the Church." *Origins* 23 (May 20, 1993): 12–16.

———. *Themes of Renewal*. Beltsville, MD: Pastoral Press, 1995.

Wegman, Herman. *Christian Worship in East and West: A Study Guide to Liturgical History*. Translated by Gordon W. Lathrop. Collegeville, MN: Liturgical Press, 1990.

———. "Procedere und Prozession: eine Typologie." *Liturgisches Jahrbuch* 27 (1977): 28–39.

Weller, Philip. "Frames and Images: Locating Music in Cultural Histories of the Middle Ages." *Journal of the American Musicological Society* 50:1 (Spring 1997): 7–54.

Werner, Eric. *The Sacred Bridge: The Interdependence of Liturgy and Music in Synagogue and Church during the First Millennium*. London: Dobson; New York: Columbia University Press, 1959.

Westerfield Tucker, Karen B. "Music as a Language of Faith." *Ecclesia Orans* 23 (2006): 81–98.

Westermeyer, Paul. *Te Deum: The Church and Music*. Minneapolis: Fortress Press, 1998.

Wheelock, Wade T. "The Problem of Ritual Language: From Information to Situation." *Journal of the American Academy of Religion* 50 (1982): 49–71.

White, James F. *Christian Worship in North America: A Retrospective; 1955–1995*. Collegeville, MN: Liturgical Press, 1997.

———. *Documents of Christian Worship: Descriptive and Interpretive Sources*. Louisville, KY: Westminster / John Knox Press, 1992.

———. *Roman Catholic Worship: Trent to Today*. New York: Paulist Press, 1995.

White, L. Michael. *The Social Origins of Christian Architecture*. 2 vols. Harvard Theological Studies 42. Valley Forge, PA: Trinity Press International, 1990, 1997.

Williams, Peter. *A New History of the Organ: From the Greeks to the Present Day*. Bloomington: Indiana University Press, 1980.

Willis, G. G. *A History of Early Roman Liturgy to the Death of Pope Gregory the Great*. London: Henry Bradshaw Society, 1994.

Wilmart, A. "Le Comes de Murbach." *Revue bénédictine* 30 (1913): 25–69.

———. "Le lectionnaire d'Alcuin." *Ephemerides Liturgicae* 51 (1937): 136–97.

Wilson-Dickson, Andrew. *The Story of Christian Music: From Gregorian Chant to Black Gospel.* Minneapolis: Fortress Press, 1992.

Winter, Miriam Therese. "Catholic Prophetic Sound after Vatican II." In *Sacred Sound and Social Change: Liturgical Music in Jewish and Christian Experience,* 150–73. Edited by Lawrence A. Hoffman and Janet Walton. Two Liturgical Traditions 3. Notre Dame, IN: University of Notre Dame Press, 1992.

———. "Vatican II in the Development of Criteria for the Use of Music in the Liturgy of the Roman Catholic Church in the United States and Their Theological Bases." PhD diss., Princeton Theological Seminary, 1983.

———. *Why Sing? Toward a Theology of Catholic Church Music.* Washington, DC: Pastoral Press, 1984.

Witczak, Michael G. "The Introductory Rites: Threshold of the Sacred, Entry into Community, or Pastoral Problem?" *Liturgical Ministry* 3 (Winter 1994): 22–27.

———. "The Sacramentary of Paul VI." In *Handbook for Liturgical Studies,* 3:133–76. Edited by Anscar J. Chupungco. Collegeville, MN: Liturgical Press, 1999.

Wren, Brian. *Praying Twice: The Music and Words of Congregational Song.* Louisville, KY: Westminster / John Knox Press, 2000.

Wright, Stephen K. "Scribal Errors and Textual Integrity: The Case of Innsbruck Universitätsbibliothek Cod. 960." *Studies in Bibliography* 39 (1986): 79–92.

Wyndham, Thomas, ed. *Composition, Performance, Reception: Studies in the Creative Process in Music.* Preface by Jonathan Harvey. Brookfield, VT: Ashgate, 1998.

———. *The Temple, the Church Fathers, and Early Western Chant.* Brookfield, VT: Ashgate, 1998.

Zan, Renato De. "Criticism and Interpretation of Liturgical Texts." In *Handbook for Liturgical Studies,* 1:331–66. Edited by Anscar J. Chupungco. Collegeville, MN: Liturgical Press, 1997.

———. "Liturgical Textual Criticism." In *Handbook for Liturgical Studies,* 1:367–80. Edited by Anscar J. Chupungco. Collegeville, MN: Liturgical Press, 1997.

Zetterholm, Magnus. *The Formation of Christianity in Antioch: A Social-Scientific Approach to the Separation between Judaism and Christianity.* New York: Routledge, 2003.

Zimmerman, Joyce Anne. "Liturgical Assembly: Who Is the Subject of the Liturgy?" In *Liturgy and Music: Lifetime Learning*, 38–59. Edited by Robin A. Leaver and Joyce Ann Zimmerman. Collegeville, MN: Liturgical Press, 1998.

———. "Liturgical Notes." *Liturgical Ministry* 3 (Winter 1994): 35–36.

———. *Liturgy and Hermeneutics*. American Essays in Liturgy. Collegeville, MN: Liturgical Press, 1999.

———. *Liturgy as Language of Faith: A Liturgical Methodology in the Mode of Paul Ricouer's Textual Hermeneutics*. Lanham, NY: University Press of America, 1988.

Zöbeley, H. R. *Die Musik des Buxheimer Orgelbuchs: Spielvorgang, Niederschrift, Herkunft, Faktur*. Tutzing: Schneider, 1964.

Index

acclamations, 106
acoustical environment, 16
active participation, xxxii, 70, 76, 89, 93, 96, 98, 106, 110, 130, 133, 143, 192, 194, 203
adaptation, cultural. *See* inculturation.
addresses (legislation), 102
Admonitio generalis, 44
Advent Project, 23
alleluia (chant), 37, 42, 54
Amalar of Metz, 5, 121
Ambrose of Milan, 21, 104
Anglican Church, 69
ante-evangelio chants, 17
Antioch, 18
antiphon: christological lens, as, 45, 47, 128; definition of, 45; function of, 45; genre of, 167; interpretive relationships, 167; modal relationship to its psalm, 34; nonpsalmic, 47; normatively sung, as, 106; recitation of, 153, 154; relationship to psalm verses, its, 54, 150; relative antiquity of, 47; repetition of, 33, 34, 86, 87; revision of in *Missale Romanum, editio typica tertia*, 101; textual sources of, 45; translation of, 129; source texts, use of, 47–50; verses, number of, 87

antiphona ad prelegendum, xxv
Antiphonale Missarum, 37, 41, 42, 44: earliest notated, 40; Old Roman, 40
Antiphonale Missarum Sextuplex, 37, 173, 177
Antiphonarius, 42
apostolic constitution, 82, 101
apostolic letter *motu proprio*, 82, 101
ars nova, 60
Augustine of Hippo, 5, 12
Augustinians, 56

baroque style (in music), 67, 68
basilica, xxv, 14, 196
Bevans, Stephan, 124
Bible: allusions to in liturgical texts, 166; Greek, 20; Latin, 21; Old Latin, 51; translation of, 21; Vulgate, 51
bishop, diocesan, 72, 82, 146: legislator, as, 103
Bishops' Committee on Divine Worship (formerly Bishops' Committee on the Liturgy), 102, 103
books, liturgical, 73, 77, 78, 80
Browning, John, 144
Built of Living Stones, 163, 164
Burchard, John, 59